What people are saying about …

What's It Like to Be Married to Me?

"*What's It Like to Be Married to Me?* by Linda Dillow is a phenomenal book; in fact, it may well be the *best* book on marriage I have ever read. It is bursting with wisdom, practical advice, and heart-wrenching stories that will melt the hardest heart. Even better, it is based on biblical truth and the call to grow in love. If you want to honor God in your marriage, if you want deeper intimacy with your spouse, if you want to become more like Christ, please read this book. It is a rare and signature achievement that combines a penetrating look at marriage with practical spiritual formation. If all this sounds overstated, let me assure you that it is actually the opposite: Words fail me to describe just how marvelous this book really is. It is *that* good!"

Gary Thomas, writer in residence at Second Baptist
Church in Houston and author of *Sacred Marriage*

"Every wife needs to read this book! Linda Dillow, as usual, is practical, insightful, and grounded. Not only will you understand yourself better with each page, but the journey will take you deep into the heart of the marriage you've always wanted. Don't miss out on this message."

Drs. Les and Leslie Parrott, founders of
RealRelationships.com and authors of *Love Talk*

"Over the thirty-five years I have known Linda, she has exhibited great integrity, bringing grace, beauty, and dignity to her home and marriage. From her vast biblical wisdom and experience, she has crafted a masterpiece that calls us to regard marriage as one of God's highest callings. Whatever the season of your marriage, you will be inspired, instructed, and encouraged by Linda's powerful and timely message."

Sally Clarkson, speaker, director of Mom
Heart Ministry, and author of six books
including *The Mission of Motherhood*

"Linda Dillow knows marriage. Through her extensive ministry to women, she has 'heard it all.' And through her years of study, she understands God's way. Most impressive, she has lived the message with her husband, Jody. Thanks, Linda, for this labor of love for all of us who want to see 'Well Done' on the marriage line of our final report card."

Roc Bottomly, pastor, senior fellow for Marriage
Studies at Focus on the Family Institute,
and author of *The Promised Power*

"As someone who travels, speaks, and writes with Linda Dillow, I've witnessed the gut-wrenching secret choices she's made in her own marriage as she's died to her own selfishness and lived to please God. This book and the stories within are so honest they will make your teeth hurt. Only read it if you're willing to be changed from the inside out."

Lorraine Pintus, speaker, writing coach, and
author of *Jump Off the Hormone Swing*

"Is it okay to say there were times I wanted to throw this book across the room? Sometimes the truth hurts—but how vital that we hear it. Linda Dillow delicately weaves her words among the tough questions and the truths of Scripture, speaking with gentle thunder to today's wives. Being willing to listen to a mentor like Linda and then putting these truths into practice will change your perspective, your marriage, and your life."

Kathy Cordell, life coach, speaker, and
founding president of Women of Worship

"With tenderness, depth, humor, and spiritual understanding, Linda Dillow has carefully chosen topics that will impact any marriage. Linda's wisdom has come from over forty years of marriage plus countless interactions with other women. The book is brimming with practical ways to implement change. No one can read this book and remain the same."

Mimi Wilson, coauthor of *Once-A-Month Cooking,*
Holy Habits, and *Trusting in His Goodness*

"Compelling, provocative, authentic, and practical! With wisdom and wit, Linda invites the reader to focus the mirror on her own soul so that she might gain a transparent view of how she is perceived in her marriage. Whether you've been married five years or fifty, this book will challenge you to honestly consider the question *What's it like to be married to me?*"

Becky Harling, speaker and author of *Finding*
Calm in Life's Chaos, Rewriting Your Emotional
Script, and *Freedom from Performing*

"Linda's book is an absolute inspiration to stop the destructive pattern of blaming and criticizing our husbands and look at ourselves, challenging us to be honest about our attitudes and choices. After reading Linda's book, I wanted to love my husband in a more God-honoring way."

Cyndy Sherwood, author of *Road Map to Healing*
and director of His Healing Light Ministries

"*What's It Like to Be Married to Me?* impacted me profoundly and brought my own marriage into focus more clearly as the joyous and holy calling it is, rather than as a duty or obligation. As a dear friend and personal example, Linda has lived these truths out beautifully in her own life, and now she is passing them along to us. Rich with Scripture, poignant examples, and practical exercises, this book clearly identifies and forges a path to a more satisfying marriage by simply revealing the loving and healing choices a wife can make on behalf of the man she loves."

Shannon Wexelberg, worship leader, songwriter, and artist

"Whether you are contemplating marriage, are a newlywed, or have been married for decades, this book will have a profound impact on your heart. Be brave and ask these dangerous questions in your women's Bible studies or small groups, and watch God transform lives and marriages."

Judy Dunagan, director of women's ministries at Woodmen Valley Chapel in Colorado Springs, Colorado

"Please, please, please give this book to every young married woman you know! We have so few positive role models on what it means to be a godly wife, and this book gives us a roadmap on how to live by design not default. I truly believe this book has radically changed the trajectory of my life and marriage. Linda has taught me how to define my goals as a wife, empowered me with practical steps to make those goals a reality, and encouraged me to humbly cry, 'Change *me*, Lord!'"

Eva Daniel, married seven months

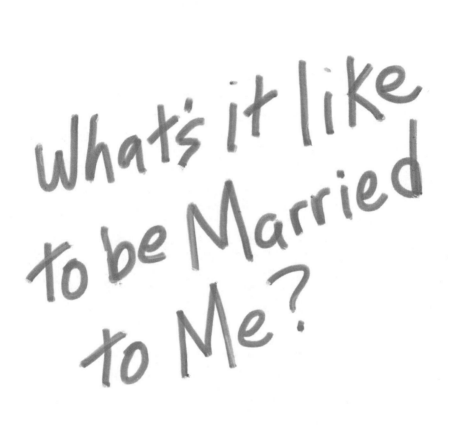

What's it like to be Married to Me?

And Other Dangerous Questions

LINDA DILLOW

David C Cook®

transforming lives together

To every wife who is brave enough to ask,
What's It Like to Be Married to Me?

WHAT'S IT LIKE TO BE MARRIED TO ME?
Published by David C Cook
4050 Lee Vance View
Colorado Springs, CO 80918 U.S.A.

David C Cook Distribution Canada
55 Woodslee Avenue, Paris, Ontario, Canada N3L 3E5

David C Cook U.K., Kingsway Communications
Eastbourne, East Sussex BN23 6NT, England

David C Cook and the graphic circle C logo
are registered trademarks of Cook Communications Ministries.

Personal accounts throughout, including survey responses and written accounts,
are used with permission, and some names have been changed for privacy purposes.

The Web site addresses recommended throughout this book are offered as a resource
to you. These Web sites are not intended in any way to be or imply an endorsement
on the part of David C Cook, nor do we vouch for their content.

All Scripture quotations, unless otherwise noted, are taken from the *New American Standard Bible,*
© Copyright 1960, 1995 by The Lockman Foundation. Used by permission. Scripture quotations
marked AB are taken from *The Amplified Bible.* Copyright © 1954, 1958, 1962, 1964, 1965, 1987
by The Lockman Foundation. Used by permission. Scripture quotations marked ASV are from The
American Standard Version. (Public Domain.) Scripture quotations marked KJV are taken from
the King James Version of the Bible. (Public Domain.) Scripture quotations marked MSG are taken
from *THE MESSAGE.* Copyright © by Eugene H. Peterson 1993, 1994, 1995, 1996, 2000, 2001,
2002. Used by permission of NavPress Publishing Group. Scripture quotations marked NIV are
taken from the Holy Bible, New International Version®, NIV®. Copyright © 1973, 1978, 1984 by
Biblica, Inc™. Used by permission of Zondervan. All rights reserved worldwide. www.zondervan.
com. Scripture quotations marked NLT are taken from the New Living Translation of the Holy
Bible. New Living Translation copyright © 1996, 2004 by Tyndale Charitable Trust. Used by
permission of Tyndale House Publishers. Scripture quotations marked PH are taken from *The New
Testament in Modern English,* revised editions © J. B. Phillips, 1958, 1960, 1972, permission of
Macmillan Publishing Co. and Collins Publishers. Scripture quotations marked TLB are taken from
The Living Bible, © 1971, Tyndale House Publishers, Wheaton, IL 60189. Used by permission.
The author has removed italics from quotations for emphasis.

LCCN 2010940550
ISBN 978-1-4347-0056-8
eISBN 978-0-7814-0609-3

© 2011 Linda Dillow

The Team: Terry Behimer, Liz Heaney, Amy Kiechlin, Caitlyn York, Karen Athen
Cover Design: JWH Graphic Arts, James Hall
Cover Image: Rights-managed, Getty Images, Sophie Broadbridge

Printed in the United States of America
First Edition 2011

1 2 3 4 5 6 7 8 9 10

112910

Contents

Acknowledgments

I am thankful to God for:

My husband, Jody, who believes in me and pushes and encourages me to be all God wants me to be.

My coauthor and soul sister, Lorraine Pintus, who prayed for this book, read every word, and showed me how to make the words sing.

My editor, Liz Heaney, who worked so hard to make up for my "brain weakness." This book flows because Liz is the "Super Editor." She is also my friend.

The Cook Team: Dan Rich. I said I wouldn't follow you, but here I am. It is a joy to team with you! Terry Behimer: Your counsel moved this book to a new level. Your friendship made it fun! Amy Kiechlin, Caitlyn York, Karen Athen: Your work made this book better!

Every wife who gave permission to use her story in this book. All your names are changed, but I think you are brave, and your stories will pour hope and healing into every wife who reads these pages. God is grateful to you, and I am too.

To the special women in the pilot Bible study: Chee-Hwa Tan, Judy Dunagan, Valerie Cox, Darlene Kordic, Jodi Nunn, Penny Semmelbeck, Nanci McAlister, Deb Leach, Debbie Wood, Debbie Eng, Colleen Flora. You helped so much to shape this book and study!

To the special women who did the Bible study by email: Bev DeSalvo, Kathy Cordell, Sandi Funkhauser. Your comments were such a help!

By Design, Not Default

I played the roving reporter and asked women why they got married. Here are some of their answers:

The truth? Well, all my friends were getting married and the whole dream dress, dream day thing—I just wanted to be the Princess Bride too.

Obviously, it was because I was in love—I had found "the man of my dreams."

It was time—the clock was ticking, and it was time to move on to marriage and kids.

Kevin was my knight in shining armor who rescued me from a bipolar mom and alcoholic father.

I couldn't seem to make enough money to live the way I wanted to live. Trevor offered me security and the lifestyle I'd always wanted.

Women are a bit complicated. We want security, companionship, a lover, a soul mate, a fixer-of-things. Men are more simple. Consider the following newspaper ad:

> *Single black female seeks male companionship, ethnicity unimportant. I'm a very good-looking girl who LOVES to play. I love long walks in the woods, riding in your pickup truck, hunting, camping and fishing trips, cozy winter nights lying by the fire. Candlelight dinners will have me eating out of your hand. I'll be at the front door when you get home from work, wearing only what nature gave me.*
>   *Call (404) 875–6420 and ask for Daisy. I'll be waiting.*[1]

Fifteen thousand men responded to this ad, wanting to talk with Daisy. Guess who answered the phone? The Atlanta Humane society. Daisy was an eight-week-old black Labrador retriever.

People marry for different reasons, but one man definitely takes the prize for the most unique reason. How I laughed when I read the following advertisement, which was said to appear in the want ads of a New York newspaper:

> *Farmer with 160 irrigated acres wants marriage-minded woman with tractor. When replying, please show picture of tractor.*[2]

I certainly didn't marry to gain a piece of farm equipment—or equipment of any kind! I married Jody because I wanted to be his lover and best friend, forever. One of the most beautiful verses of Scripture shows us the heart of a young bride as she describes her feelings for her husband. She has set forth the physical attributes of her beloved and ends with this statement:

"His mouth is full of sweetness
And he is wholly desirable.
This is my beloved and this is my friend." (Song 5:16)

A perfect combination: a lover and best friend, all wrapped up in one package called a husband. My neighbor Val showed me this note her husband had hidden under her pillow before he left on a business trip.

Dearest Val,

By now you are missing me. I want you to know that I love you and I am thinking of you even now. I miss every minute that I have to be away from you. I would much rather be holding you in my arms, pressing my lips against yours.

What I miss most of all is having a good walk and talking with you. I cherish having you to talk to and share with—someone who really wants to understand me and love me. I will be back soon. I love you a LOT.

Your lover,
Marc

This note graphically illustrates this perfect combo: a lover whose arms and lips you long for; a best friend whose deep communication and companionship you miss. This is what we dreamed of when we walked down the aisle and said, "I do."

I hope this is your everyday reality with your husband.

For many, though, the dream fades, and real life takes over. Children, jobs, house payments, and an economic downswing cause your lover/best-friend intimacy with your husband to slide down in your priorities. One day you wake up and say, "Where did the intimacy go? And how do I get it back?"

As I've spoken around the world, thousands of women have shared with me their questions, their hopes, and their dreams for their marriages. What I see happening in marriages today prompted me to write this book.

I'm angry.

I remember as a new bride in 1964 hearing Dr. Bill Bright, founder of Campus Crusade for Christ, quote a Harvard sociologist who said that one out of every two marriages ended in divorce. But in Christian marriages, it was very different. Only 1 out of every 1,015 marriages ended in divorce.[3] I felt proud. Being a Christian made a difference. That is no longer the case. Today, one out of every two marriages ends in divorce—and it is the same for those who know Christ and those who don't. What happened?

I'm sad.

Of the 50 percent of couples who stay married, many are angry and resentful. Others are simply resigned. They're living by default, not design. They're hanging on in marriage because it is the right thing to do. They stay because of the kids. They've given up and settled for ho hum, status quo. It shouldn't be this way.

I'm filled with hope.

I refuse to settle for mediocrity. I refuse to live out scripts handed to me by the media, by mothers, by anyone other than God. He is the Creator of marriage, and He has a design for you and for me. I'm filled with hope that you can be different, that your marriage can be different.

I wrote this book for all wives: those in good marriages and those in not-so-good. I wrote this book to encourage you as a wife, to help you change the things you can because I strongly believe that Christian marriages should—and can—be different. As part of my research, I surveyed five hundred Christian wives about the best and worst things they did in their marriages. I've seen the hurt in their eyes, and I've cried with them. I've prayed for them. I've asked God, "What will help Your precious women be all You desire them to be as wives?" I believe His answer to my question is this: *Ask them Dangerous Questions about themselves.* So, my friend, I will ask you the same Dangerous Questions I ask myself.

The title of this book, *What Is It Like to Be Married to Me?*, asks the overarching question. Too often we focus on all the things about our husbands that we don't like and wish we could change. You know what it is like to be married to your mate, but how often do you think about what it is like for him to be married to you? If you woke up tomorrow and discovered you were married to you, would you be delighted? Or would you be devastated? I believe that if you are willing to ask yourself this question and let me guide you to the Designer's personal answers for you and your marriage, you will find what Janee discovered doing the pilot Bible study: "This marriage study is life- and heart-changing."

To guide you in discovering what it is like to be married to you, this book will discuss seven Dangerous Questions:

1. What is really important to me?
2. What does it feel like to be my husband?
3. Am I willing to change my attitude?
4. What will it take for me to get close to you?
5. What is it like to make love to me?
6. Why do I want to stay mad at you?
7. Is it possible to grow together when things fall apart?

You'll see that each Dangerous Question contains several short insights meant to help you answer the Dangerous Question. You can read each Dangerous Question in one sitting, or you can read each one over a period of days or weeks. Do what works best for you.

I want this book to be practical, and so I've included exercises and ideas to help you put the concepts and insights into action. Don't read on until you have done these exercises. You'll need a separate journal or notebook. These exercises are really important. And to get the most for *you,* find a friend (or a group) and do the Bible study at the back of the book. (See page 209.) God's Word brings transformation.

It isn't fun to ask ourselves Dangerous Questions like these. It can be difficult and even threatening. But I believe that by honestly reflecting on these questions and by seeking God's help and wisdom, a wife can move to a place where she can say, "Being married to me is really pretty good." And maybe she'll even be able to affirm, "Being married to me is *better* than pretty good."

But even if we can say that, none of us is where we want to be.

When I was thirty-four, I wrote, "I want to work as hard at my marriage as if I were striving to be the president of a company." Thirty-four more years have passed since I made that statement. Looking back over these years, how did I do?

Did I work hard at creating a home that pleased him? Yes.

Did I seek to honor him before our children? I tried very hard.

Did I always make my intimate oneness with Jody my priority? No, but I worked hard at it. Still, I have a lot to learn.

So, as you ponder these Dangerous Questions, know that I'm pondering along with you. Yes, it might get a little uncomfortable as we look deeply within, but I promise you, you will also laugh and even have fun. My desire is to help you see how to live out your marriage, not by default, but by design.

So let's get started!

What Is Really Important to Me?

Insight 1: WHAT DO MY CHOICES SAY?

Some couples have low-maintenance marriages, some medium-, and others high-maintenance marriages. Mine has been of the high variety. My wonderful husband, Jody, and I are not just different—we are wildly different. Jody is an introvert, I'm an extrovert. Jody is a thinker, I am a feeler.

Jody, Mr. Flow with It, dislikes plans. Plans give me a sense of security, and I love structure.

I remember a road trip from Vienna, Austria, to Katawice, Poland. When I plan a trip, I have maps, contact numbers, and backup contact numbers. When Jody plans a trip, he does "whatever." As we were driving toward Poland, I asked the "whatever" man where he put the map. He had no map. To clarify, this trip was taken when Poland was still under Communist rule, and road signs were either nonexistent or incomprehensible. A map was a necessity. But we had no map.

I started to fume inside.

We made it to Poland, and I asked Jody where he had put the directions to the hotel. No directions … and he wasn't sure which hotel it was … but he could find it. Now my insides were tangled inside out, and I wanted very much to say everything I was thinking, but I was sure that when he couldn't find the hotel, he would see that planning was the best way to travel. Jody found the hotel in half an hour. Sometimes, life just isn't fair.

Over the years, my "whatever" husband has graciously learned to bring maps and other information to help me feel more comfortable.

Jody is an entrepreneur and lives in the future. I live for today and think practically how to make today work. I followed this man I'm married to from the United States to Europe, where we lived for fourteen years. From Europe we moved to Asia for three years and then back to the States. Jody has a new plan every day, and with each new idea, I feel sick to my stomach. Which country is next on his world tour?

Because Jody and I are from different planets, growing in intimate oneness has not been easy. It has taken lots of adapting, lots of accepting, and lots of forgiving. It has also meant paying attention to the choices I make.

When we had three children and the oldest was just three, we lived in Dallas, Texas. There were days I was so tired, I couldn't think. Our youngest had asthma, and many nights I slept on a thin mattress next to his bed.

When he woke unable to breathe at 3:00 a.m. it was a rush into the bathroom turned into a steam cave or a rush to the emergency room.

One day I realized that my choices said something about what was important to me. I started asking myself what message my choices said to Jody about how important he was to me. What message did Jody get from me? Did I walk away from him and say, "Don't even think about sex or a good meal. Can't you see I'm wiped out?" Or did I walk toward him, put my arms around him, and whisper, "I can't wait until life is easier and I can spend a day loving you"? What attitude did I project? What atmosphere did I create? What did my choices say was really most important to me? Sometimes what is most important to us is not obvious and can be seen only by how we respond to our husbands in everyday life.

When four teens roamed our home, we lived in Vienna, Austria. Life was filled with soccer, track, volleyball, ski team, musicals, boyfriends, girlfriends, and so much more. Jody traveled on long trips to Communist Eastern Europe. When he was gone, the boys and I were on coal-furnace duty. That thing hated me—no matter what I did, it went out. I can't count the times I cried over the coal furnace. What message did I give Jody when he arrived home after a long and dangerous trip? Did I run into his arms and indicate I couldn't wait until later, or did I gripe and complain about the coal furnace and every little thing that had gone wrong with the house, kids, and life during the month he was traveling? What did my behavior say was most important to me?

Now we live in Monument, Colorado, and the house is quiet. Only Bailey, our big golden retriever, is here to make noise and create a mess. So ... now it is easy to make Jody a priority, right? Wrong. Exciting ministry, precious women's problems, and just plain-old life get in the way. If it isn't little children, teens, a friend in need, or a demanding job, it is illness, a broken-down car, or a bear break-in. The list goes on.... One thing is clear:

My choices must say that Jody is my first priority of all the people on earth.

I remember a time I did this right. Jody and I were leaving for a five-day celebration of our thirteenth anniversary in the Arkansas mountains. Visions of deep communication and romantic walks by the river filled my head. It was going to be wonderful. The children were parceled out to friends' houses. While I had gone to the store to get a few last-minute things for the trip, Jody tried to fix the leak in the bathroom. And the drip, instead of diminishing, turned into a gush that became a flood.

Returning home from the store, I walked into a world of water-soaked carpets, neighbors madly mopping and scooping water. It was a water-logged nightmare. I vacuumed carpets with a water vacuum, pulled carpets up and hung them over the fence. Jody emptied our water bed of water so we could get the water-soaked carpet out from under the bed and over the fence to drip-dry. The final blow came while moving furniture in the bedroom. My wedding ring, which had been on the dresser, was lost. This was my anniversary, and I didn't even have a wedding ring. Instead of taking a romantic walk by the river, I walked around the house with a flashlight, tears streaming down my face, looking in every nook and cranny for my ring, but no ring was to be found.

Early the next morning, I was ready for action. First the ring, then the soggy carpets. Before I could put my planning into gear, Jody made an incredible statement, the kind of statement that only a man can make. "Honey, let's just forget all this mess, bring the carpets in off the fence, pile them in the living room, and head for the mountains. We still have four days left of our vacation trip." I looked at the waterlogged house and then in amazement at my man. He really meant it! How could I just leave the mess and forget it?

At this point, the last thing I wanted was a romantic walk by the river. I wanted to find my wedding ring and salvage my carpets. My feelings screamed, "No, I can't go," so I took my feelings and my will to the bathroom, locked the door, sat on the closed potty, and prayed.

Lord, You know how I feel; I don't want to be alone with my husband. All I can think about is my stale, smelling house and my wrinkled carpets. But, Lord, my husband has said "let's go," and I know he's right. There will always be a reason why it's not a good time to escape. This time the reason just seems very big, but I choose in my will to go with my husband. I choose to forget the mess. I trust You to change my feelings.

The five-hour ride to the Arkansas mountains remains clear in my memory, because it was a five-hour battle between my feelings and my will. Every ten minutes, I started to think about my lost ring, the soggy carpets, and the mess. Each time I had to choose to reject the thoughts and concentrate on my husband. Gradually, and I do mean gradually, my feelings went along with the choices in my will.

By the time we arrived at our hideaway, we had three days left. How do I describe those thirty-six hours? There truly are no words to relate the beautiful, deep intimacy that we experienced. The depth of our communication amazed me. We sensed a more profound oneness between us, and we even had a romantic walk by the river.

I have always believed that God rewarded me with those beautiful hours because I made a secret choice to let Jody know he was important to me when my feelings were screaming, "I can't walk away from this muggy mess!"

Often I ask myself, *Will I be happy with my choice five years from now or twenty years in the future?* My choice to leave the waterlogged disaster and *go* with my husband was thirty-four years ago. Yes, I am happy—oh, so thankful—that I chose to make my husband my priority and to put my marriage first. That is what is really important.

P.S. Seven years after the notorious Dillow Flood, the couple renting our house found my lost ring. Jody saved it and gave it to me on our twentieth wedding anniversary.

Insight 2: MARRIAGE MATTERS

Think back for a moment to your marriage, the day you entered into a sacred covenant with your husband before God. When you floated down the aisle wearing white, ready to have that ring on your finger and that man as yours alone, you likely weren't thinking about marriage as a sacred covenant. I sure wasn't! My mind was centered more on thoughts of being "naked with no guilty feelings"! But God was thinking about this special union at your wedding and mine. To Him, marriage is the most sacred commitment between two people.

In modern language, a covenant signifies that two people have become one. Look with me at how God defines marriage in the book of Genesis:

> *For this reason a man will leave his father and mother and be united to his wife, and they will become one flesh. (2:24 NIV)*

Moses wrote down this scripture as part of the Torah, the Hebrew Scriptures long before it was called Genesis. The Israelites, like you and me, had less-than-perfect marriages, so God sent His prophets to remind them about the covenant they had made before God with their marriage partner. In this next passage, the Jewish people were weeping and wailing because God no longer paid attention to their offerings. They asked God, "Why don't you hear us?" God answered in Malachi 2:14–15:

> *It is because the LORD is acting as the witness between you and the wife of your youth, because you have broken faith with her, though she is your partner, the wife of your marriage covenant.*
>
> *Has not the LORD made them one? In flesh and spirit they are his…. So guard yourself in your spirit, and do not break faith with the wife of your youth. (NIV)*

My friend, if you were married by a minister of the gospel, you were saying, "There is a divine dimension to marriage, and we are making a covenant before God."

Marriage as a sacred covenant has two parts: something you do and something God does.

Your part: You agreed to exchange vows, pledges, that you will honor before God and others. God was also a witness as you made your solemn covenant commitment to each other.

God's part: After you declare your covenant promises, God then does something to you and your husband. He takes the two very different people, and in a beautiful and holy way, makes them one, one in flesh and one in spirit.

Jody and I recently attended a wedding where the bride and groom, Bethany and Chris, read the following vows, which they had each written:

> *I, Bethany, take you, Chris, to be my husband, to have and to hold, to respect and admire, to comfort and encourage. God has blessed me with a greater gift than I ever could have asked for or imagined, and that gift is you. I will strive throughout the good times and the bad times, to be your greatest cheerleader, to consistently affirm you and support you. I will prioritize and grow in my relationship with you and with the Lord. I promise to trust you. Where you go I will go, and where you stay I will stay. Your people will be my people, and your God will be my God. I commit to love and to cherish you from this day forward until death do us part.*

> *I, Chris, take you, Bethany, to be my wife. To have and to hold, to support, encourage, and protect as God's precious gift to me. You are—and always will be—my best friend, and I am so happy that from this day forward we will face all of life's joys and trials together. I will do my best to approach our marriage with gentleness, compassion, humility, openness, and grace. I will always*

pursue God first and you second above all else. I promise to strive to lead according to God's will and lean on His grace and love as a perfect example of how I am to love you. You will always be honored, appreciated, and safe in our marriage. I commit to love and cherish you from now until death do us part.

As I listened to these beautiful covenant promises to each other, I thought, *And now God does His part and begins to make them one.*

There is a holy reverence about the marriage covenant. Your marriage matters to God, and I believe it matters to you. My friend, you willingly vowed to bind yourself to this man you loved, and God supernaturally began to make you one. It is a glorious thing. I bow and worship and thank my God. He is an amazing Creator!

As you read Bethany and Chris's wedding vows, what were your thoughts? Did you think, *I remember being that young and in love, but it is gone … gone … gone. We are soooo far from that kind of love relationship at this point in our marriage. I wish I had the chance to do things over, to make different choices.*

If so, there is hope!

Insight 3: THE TREADMILL WON'T STOP!

When a friend's husband dies, you look with new eyes at your husband. Listen to these words from some friends of a grieving wife.… They speak volumes:

> *The little things that used to be so big have all but faded away. It's a lot easier to see and live in the broader picture, appreciating and savoring the moments we have. My life will never be the same … and neither will my thankfulness that my husband is here living it with me. I have such a longing to make sure I say what's important—to communicate my heart of gratefulness to my husband and children.*

Watching my friend in such pain has brought an urgency about today—to not let things that have gone untended in our marriage go any longer. To take hard steps to fight for something better and even dream about having something wonderful again.

God has confirmed to me that my priorities are seriously out of whack, and how badly I need Him to help me truly make my marriage a priority.

When a husband dies, when divorce strikes someone close and children are weeping because Daddy's gone, when your friend can't stop crying because of her husband's affair, pain pushes you to remember that your husband is important. But the question is: *How do I keep my husband a priority in the chaos of everyday life? How do I get God's perspective in my brain and heart?*

Jesus didn't mince words about keeping first things first. He said, love God first and love your neighbor as yourself (Matt. 22:37–39). Simple and clear. So who is your closest neighbor? The one who shares your bed and daily bread: your husband.

Do I see you shaking your head and saying, "Linda, what planet do you live on? That might look good on paper, but it just doesn't fly in reality." If so, know you have lots of company. Many of the wives I've talked with feel stuck on the treadmill:

I work a stressful job and come home to kids, cooking, laundry, and a husband with needs. Everyone at home and work wants a piece of me.

I homeschool four children, my husband works from home, and I'm his accountant. If I step off the treadmill … oh, it's not possible.

If I'm really honest, the real truth is, I don't want to get off the treadmill. If life slows down, I'll have to look in the mirror—and Dangerous Questions? Not me!

Believe me, I understand. I had three children in three years, adopted a fourth when he was a teen, and had teenagers ages thirteen, fourteen, fifteen, and seventeen. I can still feel that overwhelming scatteredness that made my head spin. Children do that to you.

When life hammers us, priorities are smashed. While the notations on our calendars are unique to each of us, in one way we are all alike: We each must make a daily choice about what we will prioritize and about what must be demoted to a "do later" status. While it's easy to put our husbands on the back burner, it can be devastating to a marriage. In fact, when I asked women to tell me the worst thing they had done in their marriage, many of them said that it was not making their husband a priority. Here is a sampling of their responses:

I focus on other things in life; I don't take time for my marriage. I put more thought, energy, and effort into my relationship with our kids and grandkids than in my own husband and our relationship. (Married twenty-eight years)

I got too busy and had no time for my husband. I allowed my kids to take priority over my hubby. (Married seven years)

I have put my children first before my husband. (Married seventeen years)

I never think about my marriage. My life is a treadmill, and I can't stop running and think. I just move from one area of need to another. My children and job scream louder than my husband, so he gets left out. (Married fourteen years)

Is it just me, or do you also see a pattern in these answers? One woman said it well: "I don't always get it straight. I get caught up in the thick of thin things. What matters most—my walk with God and love affair with my husband—gets buried under layers of pressing problems and immediate concerns."

Are you on a treadmill? When was the last time you stopped long enough to think deeply about your marriage? I want to ask you to do something for me. STOP! Step off your treadmill, and find a quiet place to read the next few pages. I know, you're laughing because there isn't a quiet place. Then go in the bathroom, lock the door, put the lid down, and sit there.

When life is hectic, we don't stop and think about our priorities. We don't think about what is really important. We avoid looking within and reflecting. We neglect looking at God's Word and praying, *Search my heart, O God.* We mistakenly think that it is easier to stay busy. And truth be told, we like the way others see us when we're balancing five things at once. Friends say, "Cara is amazing. I just don't see how she does it all." That feels good—better than stepping off the treadmill and asking heart-wrenching Dangerous Questions.

Perhaps you're braver than that. Are you willing to look in the mirror and honestly ask, *What is* really *important to me?*

How can you gain perspective on your marriage relationship when life just won't stop? You must live with the end in view. Read on to find out more.

Insight 4: LIVE WITH THE END IN VIEW

I've been privileged, thus far, to have had forty-six years, five months, and twenty-six days with my lover and best friend. Living with the end in view means that I am aware of how I spend these hours, conscious that they are a gift, that there are only so many hours I have left, and that only God knows the number. It may be five years or fifty years. No matter how many years we have to grow in our intimate oneness, the time is short. When we realize this, *really realize it,* it can change the way we look at time, at love, and at our lover. Sadly, many wives discover too late the gift they possessed.

One such wife is seen in the Pulitzer Prize-winning drama *Our Town*. Emily, the young wife in the drama, had died at age twenty-six but was allowed the privilege of returning to an ordinary day from her earthly life. But with the opportunity, she was warned: "At least, choose an unimportant day. Choose the least important day in your life. It will be important enough."[1]

She chooses to relive her twelfth birthday, but soon she cries, "I can't. I can't go on. It goes so fast. We don't have time to look at one another. I didn't realize. So all that was going on and we never noticed."[2]

Another character comments from the grave.

> *Yes.... That's what it was to be alive. To move about in a cloud of ignorance; to go up and down trampling on the feelings of those ... about you. To spend and waste time as though you had a million years. To be always at the mercy of one self-centered passion, or another.*[3]

But it is Emily's question that pierces the heart: "Do any human beings ever realize life while they live it?"[4] The answer given is no.

We're encouraged in the Scriptures not to move about in ignorance, not to waste time as if we had a million years, but to realize life is short.

> *Teach us to number our days and recognize how few they are; help us to spend them as we should. (Ps. 90:12 TLB).*

> *Live life then, with a due sense of responsibility, not as [women] who do not know the meaning and purpose of life but as those who do. Make the best use of your time, despite all the evils of these days. Don't be vague but firmly grasp what you know to be the will of the Lord. (Eph. 5:15–16 PH)*

I've often thought that if we knew exactly how many hours, days, years we had together, we might be more aware of how important each choice we make is. But God has not chosen to let us know. At the end of his life, the apostle Paul was able to say, "I have fought the good fight, I have finished the race…. Now there is in store for me the crown of righteousness" (2 Tim. 4:7–8 NIV). Too often a woman approaches the end of life and inwardly laments, *I've fought a mediocre fight as a wife. I didn't run well in my race.*

I want to be a woman of focus. I don't want to live by default, but by design. So, how do I begin to live by design? I go to the Designer and pray:

> *Lord, You created me, You created my husband. You gave us our personalities, our strengths and weaknesses. You know us both intimately. You see exactly how we can mesh together, glorify You, and enjoy each other. So, God, it feels scary, but I'm going to be brave; I'm willing to think about me as a wife. I'll even reflect on this Dangerous Question: What is it like to be married to me?*

I want to take you on a journey with me, a journey through your life as a wife; I want to help you live your marriage backwards.

To help you live with the end in view, I want to take you to a funeral. Now don't put down the book. I assure you that I have not lost my mind and that I know what I'm doing.

In your mind's eye, visualize yourself going to the funeral of a loved one.[5] Picture yourself driving to the church, parking the car, and getting out. As you enter the sanctuary, you hear your favorite worship song being played, you see the faces of friends and family and feel the sorrow of loss and the joy of having known that is so evident on their faces. As you walk to the front of the church and look inside the casket, you come face-to-face with yourself. With disbelief, you realize that this is your funeral, thirty years from today. The people gathered together are here to express their love and appreciation for your life. Numb with shock, you are led to a seat and handed a program.

You look at the program in your hand and see that there is to be a speaker, your husband. Now think long and hard.

- What would you like your husband to say about you after many years of marriage?
- What character qualities would you like him to have seen in you?
- What kind of love relationship would you want him to describe?
- What kind of love would you have wanted him to have received from you during all those years?

As you think deeply about these questions, write down your thoughts and feelings. This exercise will reveal to you what your deepest values are, who you want to become as a wife. To live your life with the end in view is to align your daily and secret choices with this picture. It is to examine each part of your life—what you do today, tomorrow, next week, next year; how you chose to spend the time with your lover—in the context of the whole, of what really matters most to you.

When you are at the beginning of something, it is very difficult to think about its end. I'm headed toward the home stretch of my marriage, and it's still difficult to have this perspective. We are "daily" people, not lifetime people, but God wants us to be eternal people. How I wish someone had asked me to visualize my funeral at the beginning of my marriage. This thought process helps put all we hope and desire into perspective. Don't move on until you have completed this exercise, and be sure to keep what you write so that you can refer to it later.

Insight 5: AIM FOR THE GOAL

Kathy is a woman of focus, purposeful about her role as a mom, in her job, in her ministry. She has goals for every area of her life—except her marriage. I sent her this Dangerous Question to critique as I was writing the book. She responded by email.

Hey Coach Linda,

I'm sitting here in tears. This was waaaaay tougher than I thought it would be. I mean, I'm a life coach, "coaching" women about their purpose in life. And you know that I have goals for every area of my own life—but I've never thought about a marriage goal. Hello???

This assignment really made me focus on Scott ... and on my marriage. Marriage really is an "our" thing, isn't it? Hearing what he may say about me as a wife when I'm "gone" was a gut-wrenching exercise. Thanks, once again, for making me think.

Your mentee,
Kathy

Have you ever thought about your goals as a wife? If you want to spend your days with the end in view, you need to take what you wrote about what you want your husband to say at your funeral and change those thoughts into goals. Keep in mind that there is a difference between a goal and a desire. That alone will have a tremendous effect on your level of contentedness in marriage.

Sarah learned this the hard way. She had a goal for her marriage: to have an intimate oneness, a close, wonderful relationship with her husband, Sam. Being a young woman of purpose and commitment to Christ, she read every book on sex, on communication in marriage, attended seminars on being a wife, and worked hard to create intimacy with her husband.

But after five years of marriage, Sarah was angry, frustrated, and disillusioned. She felt that her marriage was a farce. She'd tried so hard to communicate, but Sam, the strong, silent type, simply grew more silent. The more she talked about closeness, the more he retreated. Without realizing what she was doing, Sarah gradually spent her hours and days devising plans to change "silent Sam" into "sharing Sam." The more she demanded an intimate oneness, the more she and Sam grew into two separate people with a chasm between them.

My heart ached for Sarah. She desperately desired intimate closeness with Sam, and God desired it as well. After all, He is the One who said, "The two shall become one." Sarah's motives were right, but her goal was wrong, and this was the cause of her anger and disillusionment.

Are you saying, "Wait a minute, Linda—Sarah's goal was in alignment with God's purpose for marriage, so how can it be wrong?" If so, I understand. It's easy to confuse our goals and our desires. I once had my goals and desires mixed up too.

So, what is a goal?

A *goal* is a purpose to which a woman is unalterably committed.[6] She assumes unconditional responsibility for a goal, and it can be achieved if she is willing to work at it.

A *desire* is something wanted that cannot be obtained without the cooperation of another person. It is an objective for which a person can assume no responsibility because it is beyond her control. Reaching a desire must never become the motivating purpose behind behavior, because then a person is assuming responsibility for something she cannot fulfill on her own.

A goal is something I want that I can also control.

A desire is something I want that I cannot control.

If I desire to lose weight, I can make it my goal, because I am responsible for what I eat and whether I exercise. But if I desire my husband to lose weight, it does no good to put a tiny chicken breast and three stalks of broccoli on his plate. I can't make his weight my goal because I can't control another person's eating or exercise. Women who try to get their husbands to lose weight by programming their eating only end up angering their husbands and feeling frustrated and unhappy when their "goal" is not achieved. I polled several wives, asking, "What is your goal for your marriage?" The responses were similar to Sarah's:

To have an exciting, romantic relationship.

To have a wonderful marriage.

To have my marriage be a picture of Christ's love.

To develop a deep intimacy in all areas of our marriages.

Each of these goals sounds positive, even lofty. They are good goals to have, right? Sorry, wrong. Go back to the definition of a goal. My goal for my marriage has to be something I can control, something I can work toward. One of the most important things to learn in life and love is that I can be responsible only for what I can control. While I can't control my husband (or anyone else), I can control me.

Sarah's anger and frustration came because she couldn't control her husband, Sam. He wouldn't do *his* part to bring about a wonderful openness and intimacy in their marriage. Sarah's goal—to have an intimate oneness, a close, wonderful relationship with her husband—could only be a desire, not a goal. To be achievable, our goals for our marriage must be things we are responsible for and can control. So, a legitimate goal for Sarah would be for her to do her part to bring about intimacy in her marriage.

I know you join me in saying that every husband should do his part to have a lover and best-friend relationship with his spouse, to be everything that God has commanded him to be as a husband. But that is a choice a husband makes before God. We can't force our husbands to do these things, nor should we try to nag or manipulate. We cannot control them into doing these. God must motivate your husband. A wife can do things to invite her husband into deeper intimacy, but ultimately she must entrust her man to Him.

Recently, I found some notes, written years ago. At that time I was trying to discover why I was frustrated when I'd worked so hard at being a loving wife. Here is what I wrote in the wee hours of the morning:

> *My goal can only be to be a godly wife. My desire and earnest prayer—to have a wonderful marriage. I am responsible for me. I am not responsible for Jody. I can't be responsible for what I can't control, and I certainly cannot control my husband. BUT I can control me, or better stated, I can learn to control me. I can learn, with God's power and motivation, to daily make the choices that will lead me toward my goal of being a godly wife.*

So, my friend, you and I can make it a goal to be a godly wife. We can make it a goal to be as open and intimate with our husband as possible. Let's work toward our goals, and pray for the things we desire for our marriages.

Insight 6: GET A VISION FOR YOUR MARRIAGE

It's time to get practical. You've visualized your funeral and thought deeply about who you want to become as a wife. We've discussed the difference between a desire and a goal. Now, I want to help you write a personal Marriage Purpose Statement. A Marriage Purpose Statement is your conscious creation of who you want to become. It outlines your goals as a wife—the things you can do to become the wife you want to be. Like a rudder on a ship, it steers your marriage boat, so that you know where you are heading. Your personal Marriage Purpose Statement can be a letter you write to yourself, a prayer, a poem, a verse, or a passage of Scripture. It can be anything that declares your goals for your marriage. It is a statement about what is *really* important to you as a wife.

I asked the women in my pilot Bible studies to read these pages and to visualize their own funerals. Once they had identified what they wanted their husbands to say about them, I had them articulate the kind of wife they wanted to be and become by writing their own personal Marriage Purpose Statement.

Kathy wrote the following poem as her Marriage Purpose Statement.

Echoes

The gap so wide, the canyon so deep
I can barely see the other side
From the wife I am to who I desire to be
What bridges this great divide?

The sound of His voice on that distant day
Makes me stop and rethink my steps
Will he be a better man for the choices I've made?
Will he rejoice in the vows I've kept?

How can he see you in the home we make
Living from day to day
As this wife looks ahead to the end of our time
What would I want my husband to say?

"She was patient and kind
Mindful of our time
She was faithful, trustworthy and honest
She forgave and sought my heart

Was attentive to my needs
She encouraged me to lead

"She was playful and fun
Her smile like the sun
She was my comforter, lover, and friend
She persevered, believed the truth
Saw dreams I couldn't see
She found the best in me

"Lord, I thank You for this woman
Who fought for this man
She prayed and never stopped
She cherished me body, mind, and soul
Deeper than I ever knew
Her love led me to You."

Words echo in the canyon, tears pool in my eyes
Can I ever become this wife?
Can my actions speak without a word
To tell of everlasting life?

I desire to become the wife of his dreams
While uniquely walking this course
Your Word spans the distance across this divide
Your truth is my constant source.[7]

Jossie, a young mom with four little ones, used her husband's name, Aaron, as the basis for her Marriage Purpose Statement. She said that she uses her husband's name a lot and that having his name in her statement would help her think about it often. She wrote:

I will be:

Attentive to Aaron, our friendship, romance, partnership in
parenting, and to the state of our marriage.

I will:

Admire and appreciate who he is, all he contributes, and
ways he is growing/being challenged in life.

I will take:

Responsibility for my attitudes and approach to life in
submission to the Lord and partnership with Aaron.

I will remain:

Open to growing, learning, and investing and to the Holy
Spirit as He leads us.

I will draw:

Near to God and Aaron as we navigate each day and every
season.

Alice wrote her Marriage Purpose Statement as a prayer based on
Philippians 4:8–9:

*Lord, I want to fix my eyes on everything about Gary that is true
and honorable and right because Gary IS an honorable man. I want
to think and act admirably, pure, and lovely and make a peaceful
home for him. I want to be a woman who is excellent and worthy
of praise because he deserves no less. I want to put these things into
practice—wrapped up with love and infused with a generous supply
of humor, adventure, and fun. I want to keep learning and working
and trying to be God's best so that God's peace will be a hedge of
protection around our home, our lives, and our hearts.*

Let me close by sharing with you my personal Marriage Purpose Statement.
It is an acrostic of the word *faithful,* followed by declarative statements.

My marriage matters to God and to me, so I choose to be:

F	A	I	T	H	F	U	L
o	t	n	h	e	o	n	a
c	t	t	a	l	r	w	s
u	i	i	n	p	g	a	t
s	t	m	k	e	i	v	i
	u	a	f	r	v	e	n
	d	c	u		i	r	g
	e	y	l		n	i	
					g	n	
						g	

I choose to   **F**ocus.

I choose a positive   **A**ttitude.

I choose deep   **I**ntimacy.

I choose to be   **T**hankful.

I choose to be a   **H**elper.

I choose to be   **F**orgiving.

I choose to be   **U**nwavering.

I choose a   **L**asting marriage.

As I write, it is so evident to me that I still have a long way to go in becoming the wife God desires me to be and that I long to be, but I realize also that because I have made these commitments before the Lord, I am much farther down the path of becoming that wife.

It is time for you to reflect, think, pray, and write your own Marriage Purpose Statement. Find a quiet place (this will be the hardest step). Get out the notes you took when you thought about what you would want your husband to say about you at your funeral. These words describe who you hope to become. It's time to turn them into goals.

Your personal Marriage Purpose Statement can be a:

- Resolution or declaration
- Prayer
- Scripture
- Poem or song
- Letter you write to yourself
- Acrostic
- List or paragraph

Your Marriage Purpose Statement doesn't have to sound beautiful or be perfect in any way. This is a personal commitment between you and God, something for you to keep in the forefront of your mind, to pray about often, to use as a thermometer when you are taking your "wife temperature." It is something to go back to and reflect on each anniversary when you thank God for your husband and for the growth in your life and relationship during the preceding year.

Now that you have reflected on what is really important to you and written down who you want to become, you are on your way to being a wife, not by default but by design.

Dangerous Prayer!

Lord, You are showing me what is really important to me. Please help me stop being a wife by default. I want to become a wife by design!

What Does It Feel Like to Be My Husband?

A new Perfect Husband Shopping Center opened where a woman could go to choose from among many men to find the perfect husband. It was laid out on five floors, with the men increasing in positive attributes as you ascended the floors. The only rule was that once you open the door to any floor, you must choose a man from that floor, and if you go up a floor, you can't go back down except to leave the store. So, two girlfriends go to the store to find a man to marry.

> The first-floor sign reads: "These men have high-paying jobs and love kids."
>
> The women read the sign and say, "Well, that's wonderful! ... But I wonder what's on the next floor."
>
> The second-floor sign reads: "These men have high-paying jobs, love kids, and are extremely good looking."
>
> "Hmmm," say the girls. "What's further up?"
>
> The third-floor sign reads: "These men have high-paying jobs, love kids, are extremely good looking, and will help with the housework."
>
> "Wow!" say the women. "Very tempting, but there's more further up!"

The fourth-floor sign reads: "These men have high-paying jobs, love kids, are extremely good looking, will help with house-work, and are great in bed!"

"Oh, mercy me. But just think! What must be awaiting us further up?!" say the women.

So, up to the fifth floor they go.

The fifth-floor sign reads: "This floor is just to prove that women are impossible to please."[1]

Insight 1: SOPHISTICATED VENTING

When Dr. Laura Schlessinger surveyed husbands for her book *The Proper Care and Feeding of Husbands*, she learned that the universal complaint of men was that their wives criticize, complain, nag, rarely compliment or express appreciation, are difficult to satisfy, and basically are not as nice to them as they'd be to a stranger ringing their doorbell at 3:00 a.m.

Listen to what one husband said about how his wife made him feel:

> *At work I have always had superlative evaluations on my per-*
> *formance. AT HOME I CAN'T DO ANYTHING RIGHT! I*
> *sometimes spend several minutes in thought on a task at hand,*
> *trying to decide exactly what to do. After weighing the pros and*
> *cons, I make a decision and act. Almost invariably I get, "What*
> *did you do that for? Now I can't ...," or I hear, "Who put the ???*
> *here," or sometimes I get a straight-out "That's stupid." ... It is*
> *something that wears you down like erosion.*[2]

I personally talked to a sad husband who said this about his wife:

> *My wife is always depressed and negative, and her complaining*
> *gets to me. One day I found myself following a lovely, laughing*

woman around Walmart—I was embarrassed, but it just felt good
to be around a happy, positive woman.

Lest you think, *I'm not that bad,* I wonder what would your husband say?

A few years ago, Jody and I were involved in a project surveying five hundred Christian couples. The husbands were asked, "What is the one thing you would most like to have in a wife?" Surprisingly, the majority answered, "A positive attitude about life." So, these five hundred men wanted just what the men in Dr. Laura's survey wanted—wives who encouraged them.

Some wives are unaware that they are gold-medal gripers. This was true of Reba. She went to her pastor with pages of complaints against her husband. After hours of uninterrupted listening, he couldn't help but ask, "If your husband is that bad, why did you marry him?" Immediately the wife replied, "He wasn't like this at first." The pastor had to ask, "So are you saying that he is like this because he's been married to you?"[3]

I know, not funny. But the pastor has a point. How did Reba change from a dreamy-eyed bride to a nagging wife with pages of complaints against her husband? Did she make choices that turned her into a griping wife?

The book of Proverbs says, "A wise woman builds her home, but a foolish woman tears it down with her own hands" (14:1 NLT). How does a wife tear down and destroy her man? Oh, there are overt ways, but some of us are really good at what I call *sophisticated venting.*

Listen to one woman's comments about how some women act when they get together.

> *The women's group was not the help I'd been hoping for.… [T]he*
> *group was a gripe session for women to vent about their husbands'*
> *idiosyncrasies, bad attitudes, and failures in general and in spe-*
> *cific. I was becoming trained to complain and whine about real*

*or imagined behavior and look for sympathy from other women. I
discontinued participation.*[4]

A young friend relayed the following story to me: "I was waiting at the
elementary school for my kids to get out and saw two women I knew, so I
walked up to them. I could hear them venting about their husbands long
before I reached them. Knowing that I had heard their caustic gripes, one
laughingly said, 'Oh, this is just what we do!'"

Two Christian women think it is a joke to rag on their husbands. That's
just not funny.

The hundreds of women involved in my survey believed that attitude
is a Big Deal. In fact, many felt that the worst thing they did for their marriages was to have a crummy attitude. Listen to their comments.

> *I took my husband for granted. He gets the worst part of me on my
> bad days and what's left of me most days. (Married thirty-four years)*

> *Nagging. Trying to make my husband who I want him to be.
> (Married ten years)*

> *My glass is always half-empty. I have been the wet blanket that
> has held him back from some of his dreams. (Married forty years)*

> *I criticize my husband on a daily basis. (Married seventeen years)*

> *I always complain about where we live. My husband has a won-
> derful job, and I know my grumbling and ingratitude has hurt
> him. (Married seventeen years)*

> *Just being an old nag about his smoking, and you know what, I might
> as well shut up as it is killing me to be a nag. (Married a long time)*

Thinking about what I don't have in a husband instead of working on being the best wife. (Married eleven years)

How do you respond when you read about grumbling, griping, nagging, venting, complaining wives?

Do you think:

I'm not like that! I'm a positive person.

Or do you think:

If you were married to my husband, you'd gripe too!

Many of the wives I talk with believe that adultery, drinking too much, abusing prescription drugs, using four-letter words—even gossip—is wrong. But griping? "Linda, life is hard; complaining is just part of life."

I often hear statements like these:

My attitude just happens. I have no control over it.

I deserve to be able to gripe.

Griping isn't so bad.

I find that most Christian women think it is okay to whine and complain, now and then. Problem is, now and then turns into daily routine.

Let me balance this picture by saying that I know many incredible wives whose husbands feel loved and appreciated. You may be like them and bring delight to your unique man. Or you may fall somewhere in between.

No matter where you fall on the griping spectrum, I feel certain you don't want your husband to think, *I can't do anything right.* None of us wants our husband following strange women around Walmart just because they want to be in the presence of a positive woman. God will help you honestly answer the Dangerous Question: *What does it feel like to be my husband?*

All of us can benefit from understanding why we are so prone to griping, so let's explore that next.

Insight 2: WHERE DID I CATCH THE GRIPING DISEASE?

Barbara Johnson, author of many books, could make anything funny. I think you'll agree with me that lots of wives would vent about Bill's idea of what qualifies as a creative gift.

> *In most marriages, husbands and wives eventually adapt to each other's differences, no matter how eccentric they are. One of the things I've had to adapt to is that Bill is very frugal (TIGHT is the word!). For instance, sometime back when my publisher notified us that sales of my books had reached the one million mark, Bill said we ought to celebrate. He got in the car and disappeared for a while, and I imagined him arranging some quiet little dinner party at a fancy restaurant or even shopping for some special gift for me. Jewelry would be nice, I thought.*
>
> *Instead he came home, smiling broadly, with two bunches of fresh asparagus! "I know how much you love it," he said as he dropped his gift into the kitchen sink. Hardly my way of celebrating!*[5]

Perhaps you think, *Getting asparagus as a gift—that's nothing to gripe about. That's a piece of cake compared to my life.* You may be right. No one knows what happens inside your marriage but you. Even so, your husband is not the cause of your griping. You didn't catch the griping disease from him.

Joyce Meyer believes that your thinking patterns gave you the disease. She writes:

> *Thinking about what you're thinking about is very valuable because Satan usually deceives [women] into thinking that the source of their misery or trouble is something other than what it*

really is. He wants them to think they are unhappy due to what is going on around them (their [husbands]), but the misery is actually due to what is going on inside them (their thoughts).[6]

God's Word validates Joyce Meyer's words. The message of Proverbs 23:7 is: You are going to become what you dwell on. We become what we think. Yikes! That's scary!

It's much like GIGO. If you are a computer whiz, you know this acronym. For those who are not, let me explain. GIGO means "garbage in, garbage out." Computer programmers know that whatever they feed into a computer will inevitably show up in the printouts. So if garbage goes in, garbage will come out.

Your brain is a fabulous computer, capable of recording eight hundred memories per second for seventy-five years without ever getting tired.[7] Amazing! God's Word says that what you feed into your mind will come out in your life (Prov. 23:7). So, if you go to a Sophisticated Venting Club and train your mind to think negative thoughts about your husband, if you meditate on all you don't like about him, if you fill your mind and heart with garbage about your man, garbage will be printed out—gripe, grumble, murmur, and vent will fill the pages of your life.

The often-quoted verse Philippians 4:8 commands us to think and mediate, not on garbage, but on all the positive, commendable, excellent, and praiseworthy qualities in others—and "others" includes husbands:

> *Finally, brethren, whatever is true, whatever is honorable, whatever is right, whatever is pure, whatever is lovely, whatever is of good repute, if there is any excellence and if anything worthy of praise, dwell on these things.*

The tragedy is that oh, so many wives have retranslated this precious verse, and their revised translation goes like this:

> *Finally, my sisters, concerning your husband, if there is anything that is untrue or dishonorable, if you can find an action that is not right, a thought that is impure, if you see anything unlovely (a receding hairline or potbelly), if anything about his work or habits is not commendable, if you can think of one thing about him that is not excellent or praiseworthy, dwell on these things. Reflect on them, chew them over, and mediate on them. Stir the pot of negative thinking about your man, and the god of griping and discontent will be with you.*

That was Jean's mantra, until a comment from one of her kids brought her up short and showed just how negative her attitude toward her husband had become. According to Jean, their married life was blissful until their fourth child was born and her husband, Jack, began a business. They had no automatic appliances or air-conditioning. Cooking really meant cooking, and most of the family responsibilities fell to Jean. Jack's schedule was nonexistent. He had to be at the store six days a week, all day long. One evening, he came home even later than normal, and as usual Jean started into her whining and griping. "Why are you so late *again?* Why can't you ever be on time for dinner?" You name it, Jean said it. Then one of her kids looked at her and said, "Mommy, why are you always mad at Daddy?"

God worked in her heart when she heard those words. Almost immediately the Holy Spirit spoke to her: *When you stand before your heavenly Father, He will not ask you about Jack's weaknesses, but He will ask you about your attitude of acceptance.*

She prayed, *God, do You mean that even though he interrupts my schedule and upsets our family, I'm supposed to be loving and kind and supportive?*

She said, "The Holy Spirit answered me sweetly, 'Yes, Jean.' … I had received a rebuke from the Lord and [knew] it was my responsibility to make things right."[8]

Jean's child's guileless words and the Holy Spirit's YES pushed her to begin to change. Jean wrote about this encounter when she had been married sixty years, which was long after it had happened. But she never forgot the lesson. God helped her learn to stop thinking of herself and her rights, and to be more sensitive to how her husband felt—and to how she could encourage rather than discourage him. She realized that only God can change the behavior of another, and when we point our finger at our husbands' shortcomings, three fingers are pointing back at us.

But Jean is unique among Christian wives. As I've said, most seem to think it is okay to whine and complain, at least now and then. So, we need to ask, what does God think about our "sometimes griping is okay" mentality?

Insight 3: GOD—ON GRIPING

God is the One we look to for wisdom about everything in our lives. What does He say about griping and what it does to us? I think you'll find His answer as we look at the two kinds of wives described in the book of Proverbs:

The Nag

A quarrelsome wife is as annoying
*   as constant dripping on a rainy day.*
Stopping her complaints is like trying to stop the wind
*   or trying to hold something with greased hands. (Prov.*
*   27:15–16 NLT)*

It's better to live alone in the corner of an attic
*   than with a quarrelsome wife in a lovely home. (Prov. 25:24*
*   NLT)*

The Crown

An excellent wife is the crown of her husband,
But she who shames him is like rottenness in his bones.
(Prov. 12:4)

Her husband can trust her,
and she will greatly enrich his life.
She brings him good, not harm,
all the days of her life. (Prov. 31:11–12 NLT)

My friend Lorraine read these labels and said, "Some of us think we are nags with a crown on our heads!" Sadly, God mentions no crowned nags in Proverbs.

One thing about our Lord God—He is descriptive. And in these passages, He's black and white. No room for gray here! Either you're so impossible to live with that your husband camps out in a corner of the cold, dreary attic just to find a little peace, or you do him only good and enrich his life.

I have studied the book of Proverbs, and I see in its pages what I call "gender sins." A gender sin is a wrongful action or attitude commonly displayed by one gender as opposed to the other. *Gender sin* may not be in the dictionary, but Proverbs attributes "anger sin" to men and "nag sin" to women. Of course, wives get angry and husbands gripe, but every time Proverbs mentions a nagging, grumbling, contentious person, it is a married woman, a wife.

Clearly, God thinks it is bad to grumble—to gripe, bellyache, and complain. In fact, Scripture often points to people who failed God. Here's an example: In his first letter to the Corinthian believers, Paul reminds them about all the wonderful ways God demonstrated His power and faithfulness to the Israelites in the wilderness. They were guided by a cloud and by fire. God parted the Red Sea so the waves stood up like towers, and they walked across the Red Sea on dry ground. Amazing! Miraculous provisions! Yet Scripture says God was not pleased with the Israelites. Why? Three reasons: They were idolaters, they tested God, and they grumbled (1 Cor. 10:1–13).

This last reason caused me to have a little talk with God. Our discussion went something like this:

Linda: Wait a minute, God. Are You putting grumbling alongside immorality? Saying griping is as bad as adultery? Surely not!

God: Yes, Linda, that is exactly what I am saying.

Linda: That is really hard.

God: Yes, it is. Linda, do you love Me?

Linda: Lord, You know I love You.

God: Do you remember what I said in 1 John 5:3? Loving Me means keeping My commandments.

Linda: I get it, God. To You, griping is sin.

God: You got it.

God is against griping. He was not pleased when the Israelites complained in the wilderness. The apostle Paul tells us that what happened to them is a warning to us: "And do not grumble, as some of them did—and were killed by the destroying angel. These things happened to them as examples and were written down as warnings for us" (1 Cor. 10:10–11 NIV).

The Israelites' journey seemed unending; it was hot, and no one knew how many years this tedious desert walk would last. They became impatient and depressed because of the fierce trials along the way. And what did they do? They grumbled, griped, and complained to Moses—and also to God. Listen to their whining: "Why have you [God] brought us up out of Egypt to die in the desert? There is no bread! There is no water! And we detest this miserable food!" (Num. 21:5 NIV). (Yes, this was the miracle manna that they had earlier thanked God for sending from heaven.)

God is serious about grumbling. He says, "Do everything without complaining and arguing, so that no one can criticize you" (Phil. 2:14–15 NLT).

So, what prompts us to grumble and gripe? What prompts you? Is it because of the loss of income or a job? An overwhelming house payment? Having too many children? Not having any children? Or do your gripes center on your husband?

I've never met a woman who got married to be miserable. I married because I couldn't live without Jody Dillow, and I suspect you married because you couldn't imagine life without your husband either. But as the years pass, there are days when "the man I couldn't live without" becomes impossible to live with. The weaknesses that paled beside his glorious strengths now blare so loudly that his strengths are silenced.

When we vent, we often tell ourselves, *I am directing my complaints at this man who is so hard to live with,* but we are really griping to God. Our complaints say to God, "I know, Lord, that I asked You for this man, but I didn't know! I didn't know what it would be like to be married to him year after year after year. Yes, I thanked You for bringing us together. It seemed like a miracle then, but now, this husband You gave me is _____." (You fill in the blank.)

When we spend year after year dwelling on our husband's negative qualities and complaining about him to God (and to him and others), we can end up like this woman, who wrote:

I haven't made him happy at all. He never achieved his marvelous potential, even though he was an air force pilot, rose to a high rank, and earned a PhD. He has potential for greatness, but I stifled it. (Married fifty years)

When I read this comment on my survey, I felt like crying.

My friend, how is your attitude? Are you a "nag" like this woman or a "crown" like my friend Ruth?

I asked Ruth, who has been married for fifty years to Dr. Earl Radmacher, to take my survey. She went to her husband and asked him to describe the worst thing she had done for their marriage. His answer? "I can't think of any worst thing you've done." This made me smile. Ruth is her husband's crown.

You can be too.

Insight 4: GRIPES BE GONE!

You may be married to a man who is consistently thoughtful and kind, tenderly attentive to your needs. Yours is the model husband, amazingly unselfish and purposely helpful. If so, I hope you don't take him for granted. I hope you thank God—and your husband—daily.

But most of us live with an imperfect husband. What do we do with our complaints? Let's look at some spiritual and practical ways that have helped me make gripes be gone. My prayer is that they will help you, too.

Give your gripes to God. When David wrote Psalm 142, he was hiding in a dark, damp cave, fleeing from Saul and his bloodhounds. He was in deep soul trouble, burdened with complaints. David gives us a valuable lesson in how to pray when a complaining spirit quivers on the tip of our tongue.

I cry out to the LORD;
  I plead for the LORD's mercy.
I pour out my complaints before him
  and tell him all my troubles.

When I am overwhelmed,
  you alone know the way I should turn. (vv. 1–3 NLT)

First, we see that David spilled it all out—not whispering but crying, begging, pouring out his gripes *to God alone.* Did you get that? He complained only to God.

Where do we go when we are irritated beyond belief with the man God gave us? Too often we play our complaints over and over in our mind until we feel crazy. Or tired of carrying them inside, we spill them out to a friend. While there are certainly times when we need to share our disappointments and frustrations with a trusted mentor, counselor, or close friend, they should not be where we go first. Yet that is not the case. I've been a woman for a lot of years, and in my experience, most of us go more quickly to a friend than to our Father.

David bundled up his gripes and took them to the only One who could bring relief. I love how C. H. Spurgeon says it: "We do not show our trouble to the Lord that He may see it, but that we may see Him. It is for our relief, and not for His information, that we make plain statements concerning our troubles. It does us much good to list our sorrows."[9]

Have you ever listed your complaints before the Lord? I have, and it helps. Find a place where you can be alone, take a pen and paper, and let your mind go wild. Record every complaint you have about your circumstances, about your husband. Don't skimp. Record it all, and then tear up your list. Fall on your face before God, and lay your complaints at His feet. David did this, and his griping turned to gratitude. Look at the next verses in Psalm 142:

Griping

I look for someone to come and help me,
  but no one gives me a passing thought!

No one will help me;
   no one cares a bit what happens to me.
   (Ps. 142:4 NLT)

Gratitude

Then I pray to you, O LORD.
   I say, "You are my place of refuge.
   You are all I really want in life." (Ps. 142:5 NLT)

Pour out your complaints to God alone. This is the first thing you do. Next:

Accept your husband. If I asked you if you desired to bring praise to God with your choices and with your life as a wife, I think you'd answer, "Of course."

In Romans 15:5–7, we are specifically instructed in one way we can praise God:

> *May the God who gives endurance and encouragement give you a spirit of unity among yourselves as you follow Christ Jesus, so that with one heart and mouth you may glorify the God and Father of our Lord Jesus Christ.*
>
>   *Accept one another, then, just as Christ accepted you, in order to bring praise to God. (NIV)*

God commands us—men, women, young and old, husbands and wives—to accept one another. He says that our acceptance of others produces a spirit of unity and brings glory to Him. What a great combination: praise and glory to God, and a spirit of unity. All as a result of our following God's command to accept one another.

Here's how I've personalized Romans 15:5–7 …

Linda: I can accept my husband because Christ first accepted me. I can extend to my man the same grace and understanding that Christ poured on me. Jesus forms the foundation of my acceptance and gives me the example to follow.

Now go back and read the above paragraph, putting *your* name in place of mine. Then, declare the following paragraph out loud to your Father God.

Christ accepted me unconditionally. Therefore, I can accept my husband, which promotes unity between us and brings praise and glory to God.

God makes it clear: Wives are to accept their husbands.

When a wife chooses not to accept her husband, she is sending him this message: "I don't like you as you are." A lack of acceptance will result in two things: (1) She will try to change her husband; (2) she will become a nag. Both have a devastating effect on the wife and on the marriage.

So ask God to help you accept your unique husband. When we have truly accepted our husbands, it makes this next step easier (notice, I did *not* say it was easy).

Move *from* Change HIM, Lord, *to* Change ME, Lord. Stormie Omartian in her excellent book *The Power of a Praying Wife* says God convicted her of heart issues and asked her to change her three-word favorite prayer, *Change HIM, Lord,* into God's favorite three-word prayer, *Change ME, Lord.*[10] I like Stormie. She is an honest woman. If we are as honest, we'll admit her favorite three-word prayer flows off our lips with greater ease than God's favorite three-word prayer.

One day I asked myself, *Why do you make continual suggestions to Jody, ask him continual questions, both of which Jody calls "sophisticated nagging"?* Taking a good, hard look within at my inner motives, I saw ugliness that was not pleasant to see: pride and selfishness lurked in my heart.

I am full of pride when I think my way of doing things is superior to my husband's way.

I am full of selfishness when I insist that he change and do things my way so that my life will be easier.

The Lord says to me as a wife, "Linda, why are you concentrating about the speck in Jody's eye, when you have a log in your eye? Get rid of the log in your own eye first" (my paraphrase of Matthew 7:3–5).

For most of my married life, I have used a simple chart to help get the log out of my eye. My natural response is to only see what Jody is doing wrong (somehow his weaknesses shout so much louder than mine!). I call this my Log Removal Chart. To help you grow toward accepting your husband, get out a sheet of paper or use a page on your computer. Make two columns. At the top of the left-hand column, write, *His Faults*. At the top of the right-hand column, write, *My Wrong Responses*. Your Log Removal Chart should look like this:

His Faults	My Wrong Responses

Now you get to fill it in!

Write down all your husband's faults. (This is the easy part.)

Go before the Lord and ask Him to reveal your wrong responses to your husband's faults. (This is the hard part.)

Will you be brave enough to pray God's favorite three-word prayer? *God, change me!*

One of the best things I did for my marriage was to ask God to change me; and to make a secret choice to accept Jody, who is so different from me; and to ask God to bring unity to our team and praise and glory to Him.

When I asked other wives to tell me about the best thing they did for their marriages, they said:

> *I placed my marriage in the Lord's hands and pray every day for it. Sometimes several times during the day. (Married twenty-four years)*

> *The best thing I did for my marriage was to quit pecking at my husband. I put these things in their proper place—in the quiet corner of my mind. Then I was able to see the good in this man I fell in love with. (Married fifteen years)*

> *My best thing was to be willing to change without my having to change him first. I made a choice to begin using more kind words, showing appreciation for things he did (even if not done my way), initiating sex, greeting him with a kiss every time we met (even if I was busy). Amazingly, in the last two years since my decision, my husband has changed to be more like the man I wanted. (Married fourteen years)*

> *I released my husband to a sovereign God who loves him more than I ever could. I have watched God build a godly man with gold, silver, and precious gems. I was trying to build a godly man out of LEGOs. (Married twenty-three years)*

I hope these comments convict and motivate you to put these ideas into practice. I can't promise that your husband will change if you do these things, but I can promise that *you* will change in a way that glorifies God and frees you from trying to take control of your husband.

I have one more idea to share with you. It is the topic of the next insight. Get ready for an amazing yet simple and practical project that I promise will push gripes out the door.

Insight 5: PUT ON A BRACELET

Will Bowen, a Lutheran pastor, wanted to help the people in his church improve their lives. He was convinced that thoughts held in mind produce after their kind. He knew that if we talk about what's wrong, it affects what we focus on, and we start seeing other things we don't like. Our negativity expands. His hope was to help the people in his church eradicate complaining from their lives, and, being a clever pastor, he devised a creative way to help them accomplish this.

He gave his church a 21-Day No-Complaint Challenge, complete with a purple bracelet that said A Complaint Free World.[11] He encouraged his congregation to put on the bracelet, and instructed them to move it from one wrist to the other every time a gripe escaped their lips. According to Pastor Bowen, wearing the bracelet makes you aware of when you complain, which can help you catch yourself before you do it the next time. The movement of switching the purple bracelet from wrist to wrist ingrains "Do not gripe!" in the brain.

When I read about the 21-Day No-Complaint Challenge, I told God I was willing to take the challenge and asked Him to help me become more aware of what tempts me to gripe and to help me stop my complaining.

Do you think you can live twenty-one days with no complaining, griping, murmuring, or nagging? If you think this is no big deal, let me give you the truth. The average person who takes the No-Complaint Challenge needs four to eight months to string together twenty-one gripe-free days. Are you surprised? Think it just can't be that hard? Pastor Bowen thought the same, but switching the bracelet from wrist to wrist convinced him that he complained all the time. A news reporter asked him how he was doing with this challenge. The pastor replied, "Well, after two weeks of really trying, I've made it almost six hours straight with no complaints."[12]

I put on the bracelet and watched and prayed, and within two hours, God showed me two things that bring out the whine in me. The first is technological gadgets. My iPhone, even my cute little pink notebook computer, drive me to gripe. This week while talking to a friend on my cell phone, voice messages started playing in the middle of the conversation. When I cut and pasted a paragraph in this manuscript, the text was also randomly pasted into an email. Jody, Mr. Computer Nerd, just shakes his head and says, "How do you do these things? They don't happen to anyone else."

The second thing that brings out griping is driving with Jody. My husband doesn't plan the best way to get someplace, and when he chooses the slowest route, my mouth opens automatically and says, "This way takes ten minutes longer." Wearing the bracelet has made me more aware of my critical, nagging attitude and is helping me to keep my mouth shut.

I challenged the women in my Bible study to put on a bracelet too. Read this comment from Sandy, a mom of four, during her first days of wearing the bracelet:

> *Well, the bracelet challenge is good. I'm discovering very specifically when I complain—when I think Chad isn't doing his part to cooperate with my plans to deal with a situation, and when we're under pressure (i.e., getting to church on time, etc.). I'm making myself apologize to Chad each time I complain, just to drive it home. Getting tired of that already! I think I've had to apologize to him three times today!*

My funny friend Nanci sent me this email as she prepared for the bracelet challenge.

> *Before starting the No-Complaint Challenge, I wanted to understand exactly what I was to be sensitive to. Not that I had any lack of understanding about the word* complain, *but I wanted to be sure about* gripe. *I wondered, Is it* griping *to make a statement of fact, such as: Wow, it still smells like broccoli in this kitchen.*

I got up the next morning after reading the definition of gripe, walked into the kitchen, and said, "It stinks in here! I can't believe that broccoli smell is still here!" Now that falls under the definition of gripe: to complain naggingly or constantly grumble. It was the grumble that got me. Of course, I looked that up too. Grumble: to murmur or mutter in discontent. Yup, busted. I definitely grumbled/griped in the morning.

When I shared Nanci's email with the Bible study, everyone chuckled. But when I read what Valerie had written in her journal about what God had been showing her about griping, it brought all of us to a place of stunned silence.

Monday—I'm home from the hospital. I hugged my children and cried for joy to be in my home with those I love. I slept and rested. What a joy to be with Landon, to sit at the dinner table—even if I can't yet eat what they eat. I am in heaven on earth compared to my last three weeks....

Tuesday—Last night I slept in my own bed—what luxury! I was inches from Landon, and I had the privilege of listening to him breathe. It is a beautiful thing!

Thursday—Last night I slept five hours without waking. Hospital time is finally fading, and real time is coming back. It is wonderful! My wounds are healing, and I didn't have to come home with a wound vacuum. That was a huge blessing. My scars have multiplied, but so has my joy in the Lord. God is good. I have been living in heaven this past week. I have not changed my bracelet over once. Nothing like another prolonged stay in the hospital and a sixth major abdominal surgery in the last fifteen months to give

*me a large dose of perspective. I am here. I am alive. All is well
with my soul. Praise God!*

Do you remember me asking, "What will it take for us to make our marriage a priority, to concentrate on our blessings?" Valerie's spirit of gratitude caused each of us in the Bible study to be embarrassed at our complaints. Put on a bracelet and take the 21-Day No-Complaint Challenge. You will learn a lot about yourself. You can use any expandable bracelet or order your own "Gripes Be Gone" bracelets from www.LindaDillow.org.

If you had asked me four years ago, "Linda, do you gripe?" I would have said, "I've worked hard to train my mind to think before I speak, to stop words of griping." I think my husband and those who know me well would have said that I am not a complainer. Then my life was turned upside down, and I mean that literally. I fell down a staircase in an airport and landed on my head. Several hours later, I woke up in a trauma hospital and began the journey of healing from a traumatic brain injury. God is gracious; I can walk and talk and even speak at conferences, but I am not who I was before my accident. And one huge area of change is that my brain has forgotten all the years I worked with it to *not* let a complaining spirit be my spirit.

So, my friend, if you feel you're starting from ground zero, I'm right there with you. I'm having to relearn many things, especially "no griping." Jody would tell you that I almost daily ask him to forgive me for nagging, griping, sighing, complaining, and displaying an air of discontent with him. Today I feel like a first-class failure. I set aside the day to worship, wait, and write—a day of quiet with the Lord. But when Jody came home, thankfulness and praise to God was not what met him at the door. So I go back to God's Word, fall to my knees, and do what I've encouraged you to do:

First: I go to God alone and pour out my complaints.

Second: I make a secret choice to accept my husband.

Third: I move from, *Change HIM, Lord,* to *Change ME, Lord.*

Fourth: I wear my "Gripes Be Gone" bracelet.

I want to conquer griping for many reasons, but the most important is because of what the Lord says:

Linda,

In everything you do, stay away from complaining and arguing, so that no one can speak a word of blame against you. You are to live a clean, innocent life as a child of God in a dark world full of people who are crooked and stubborn. Shine out among them like a beacon light, holding out to them the Word of Life. (Phil. 2:14–16, author's paraphrase)

Have you ever seen a wife who overflows, not with gratitude but with griping? She is alive but her spirit is dead—years of grumbling, complaining, venting, griping, and nagging have killed the light in her eyes and the smile on her lips. The liar fed her lie upon lie about her husband, and she believed him. She grumbled and crumbled. The liar watches her and laughs, "A lighthouse? Ha! I won!"

I refuse to let the liar win.

I will trust in the One who gives me power through the Spirit.

I will retrain my brain to kick out gripes.

I will shine like a lighthouse on a fog-filled night to lead God's women away from griping to gratitude. Will you join me?

Dangerous Prayer!

Lord, I give You permission to search my heart and mind.
Please show me every day what it feels like to be my husband.

Am I Willing to Change My Attitude?

The man who has forgotten to be
thankful has fallen asleep in life.
Robert Louis Stevenson

The most important prayer in the world
is just two words long: Thank you.
Meister Eckhart

If you treat a man as he is, he will stay as he is. If you
treat him as if he were what he ought to be and could
be, he will become that bigger and better man.
Johann Wolfgang von Goethe

Thanksgiving is our dialect.
Ephesians 5:4 (MSG)

Insight 1: BUILDING A HOUSE OF GRATITUDE

Kaye turned on the car radio and heard Dr. Laura firmly tell a wife who
had called in on her radio talk, "Stop whining! You have forgotten to be

grateful." WHAMO! The exhortation hit home. Kaye says, "It was as though God took me by the shoulders and said, 'Hello! This is you, idiot!' Right at that moment in the car, I began to thank God for my husband and for every excellent quality he has."

Since then, Kaye says she has made a conscious effort to do the following:

- Every day she thanks God for her man, being sure to mention several specific qualities for which she is grateful.
- Every day she looks for ways to be a blessing to her husband (like trying to understand what pleases him, trying to anticipate his needs).
- She is committed to stay away from books, magazines, and TV shows that paint a false picture of what marriage and husbands ought to be like, and she makes an effort to be grateful for things as they are instead of trying to change the people around her.[1]

Kaye impresses me. What a woman! She heard truth—"You have forgotten to be grateful"—and immediately went into attack mode. She realized that griping was her native language and said, "I'm making a conscious choice to change me and learn to be thankful!"

Are you ready to do the same? I am!

Since I've put on the bracelet and taken the 21-Day No-Complaint Challenge, I've been more aware of the nagging, complaining, and murmuring words that come out of my mouth. It is not pleasant to see what fills my mind and mouth. I'm sure it hasn't been enjoyable for you to take this challenge either—but we had to see, to understand. Now it is time to replace the negative with the positive. Are you ready to replace the wrong with the right, to move gratitude into the house where griping has lived? God wants you to build a house of gratitude.

Did you know God says a wife is a builder? "A wise woman builds her home, but a foolish woman tears it down with her own hands" (Prov. 14:1 NLT).

I have thought a lot about how I build my marriage and how I tear it down. To me it has become fairly simple:

Griping tears down and destroys my sweetness with my husband.

Gratitude builds the sweetness in our relationship.

If you are wearing your "Gripes Be Gone" bracelet (and I hope, hope, hope you are), you are also becoming aware of whether you are demolishing or building your relationship with your husband. Are you building a house of gratitude? Is the word *gratitude* written on a plaque on your front porch? Each secret choice you make to have an attitude of gratitude is like an extra piece of wood that strengthens and reinforces your marriage house. You build either with quality materials and high craftsmanship or with just enough to get by. And you daily live with what your secret choices build.

Each time we say, "I will choose gratitude" or "I won't choose gratitude," we make a choice, a secret choice. I say "secret" because the choices that determine our faithfulness are made first on the inside, known only to us and God. Later, the results are seen by all.

Who watches, who observes what we build?

Single women watch. During the fourteen years my husband and I ministered in Communist Eastern Europe, we worked with many couples and a few singles. Something one of the single women said is engraved on my mind: "I've been watching the forty wives on our team and have decided that only two or three of them are really glad they are married." Only a few out of forty? This is sobering. I wonder what those watching me think. Do my words reflect delight in Jody or disapproval? Do my actions communicate that marriage is a wonderful union or an agonizing relationship to endure?

In her excellent book *Choosing Gratitude,* another godly single woman, Nancy Leigh DeMoss, says that many years ago she began giving a thirty-day encouragement challenge to wives: "I encouraged them to confront ingratitude and cultivate a thankful spirit in their marriage with two simple steps:

1. For the next thirty days, purpose not to say anything negative about your husband—not to him, and not to anyone else about him.

2. Every day for the next thirty days, express at least one thing you admire or appreciate about your husband. Say it to him and to someone else about him."[2]

Do you see what I see? Nancy didn't give this challenge to single women. She gave it to wives because she saw the same thing the single woman on our staff saw. My friend, single women are watching us.

Even more sobering, our children are watching. What would your son or daughter say about how you treat your husband? Would it be, "My mom loves being the wife of my dad," or "Mommy really doesn't like being married to Daddy." Women have told me, "My mother modeled a complaining spirit. I saw it every day." God forbid that when your daughter grows up, she says, "I learned to gripe from my mom."

I'm very aware that at least one more important Person is watching. My Father God is watching *me*. He is very serious about Linda embracing an attitude of gratitude. According to the commentaries, the word *thankful* is used over three hundred times in Scripture, but as I read my Bible I see thankfulness *everywhere*. Psalm 136 has twenty-six verses devoted solely to thanking God.

Here are a few of my favorite "thankful verses":

Praise the LORD!
    Oh give thanks to the LORD, for He is good;
    For His lovingkindness is everlasting. (Ps. 106:1)

I will give You thanks with all my heart. (Ps. 138:1)

Overflowing with gratitude. (Col. 2:7)

I want to overflow with thanksgiving. I want gratitude to pour out of my mind, my words, and my life! How grateful I am that God delights in turning my griping into gratitude. This paraphrase of Psalm 30:11–12 from *Psalms Now* by Leslie Brandt says it all:

> *And You turned my griping into gratitude,*
> *My screams of despair into proclamations of joy.*
> *Now I can explode with praises,*
> *And I will spend eternity in thanksgiving to You.*[3]

Oh, I long to live in a house of gratitude and explode with praises—to spend all eternity thanking God. I know God will do His part to turn my griping into gratitude, but it will also take work on my part. My problem is that griping is my mother tongue. Gratitude is my second language.

If you've ever tried to learn a second language, you know it takes practice. You must go over and over vocabulary words, repeating common phrases like a first grader. I remember my first project in German, the language I struggled to learn during our years in Europe. I picked up a chicken at the grocery store and was unpleasantly surprised to discover I'd purchased the *whole* bird—complete with head, dangling feet, and gooey innards. Chicken is sold this way in many parts of the world but not in the U.S., and I'd never had to prepare a whole chicken before. I learned what a ridiculously squeamish woman I was. The only way I could cut off that disgusting chicken head was to cover it with newspaper, close my eyes, and whack away! This experience motivated me to create my first German paragraph. With dictionary in hand, I wrote the following words, and then memorized them in preparation for my next chicken purchase.

So my German sounded something like this: *Ich möchte ein Huhn bitte. Können Sie bitte den Kopf und die Füsse abschneiden, die Innereien herausmachen und es in kleine Stücke schneiden?*

I was trying to express: "I would like a chicken. Would you please cut off the head and feet and clean out the insides? Then please cut it into small pieces."

The butcher laughed at my stumbling German, but he did what I asked.

How are you doing with the language of gratitude? Are you taking time to learn it? How does gratitude become a language we speak naturally?

First, remove the negative—thus the No-Complaint Bracelet project.

Second, impart the positive.

Earlier I shared with you that my brain injury somehow put griping back in me. Before my fall, thanking God and my husband came naturally to me. I had worked on having an attitude of gratitude. Then, overnight, it disappeared. So I went before my God and asked Him to show me how to relearn gratitude. I needed to find new ways to practice being thankful. Whether you need to relearn like me or are learning an attitude of gratitude for the first time, I believe my "growing in gratitude" projects will help you learn the language of gratitude. During the rest of this section, I'll outline some of these projects....

Insight 2: GROWING IN GOD GRATITUDE

Last July I read Psalm 92:1–2 in my morning quiet time: "It is good to give thanks to the LORD and to sing praises to Your name, O Most High; to declare Your lovingkindness in the morning and Your faithfulness by night." I have read these verses many times before and always thought, *What a perfect thing to do; give thanks to God every morning for His lovingkindness and every night for His faithfulness.* That morning I decided to take the next four weeks to study these two words *faithfulness* and *lovingkindness* and to ask my Father to teach me how to thank Him. I wanted to be caught up in His lovingkindness before I leave my bed each morning and to delight in His faithfulness as I go to sleep each night.

For twenty-eight days I used Psalm 92:1–2 as my pattern of morning and evening worship to give thanks to God, and I recorded all I was learning in my journal. As I studied, I prayed, *My Lord, reveal, teach, and take me deeper in all You are as a God who loves me with lovingkindness. Take me deeper in all You are as a faithful God to me.*

What follows are my journal entries.

July 21

I learned today that the word "lovingkindness" is translated from the Hebrew word "hesed," which is used often in the Old Testament to signify God's covenant, steadfast love for me. In the Psalms (and this is true in Psalm 92) hesed is associated with the call to worship. I see that my morning and evening times of reflective thankfulness are all about worshipping the One who loves me, not just with a love like I love, but with a deep unfailing love.

Hesed is the unmerited and generous favor of God. Hesed love is gentle and always reaches out to the object of that love—which means me. Old Testament scholar Daniel Block describes hesed as "that quality that moves a person to act for the benefit of another without respect to the advantage that it might bring to the one who expresses it.... [T]his quality is expressed fundamentally in action rather than word or emotion."[4]

Father, thank You for leading me to learn about thanking You and Your precious lovingkindness to me. I see clearly that what I'm learning isn't just to encourage me; it's also meant to teach me how to love my husband. I'm to do things that are best for Jody—not for me. To love him with my actions, not just my words.

July 30

I love it, my Father, that not one English word can hold all the meaning of hesed, so we string words together. It is never just love but "steadfast, covenant-love," "unfailing love," and "lovingkindness." It is like when I talk to one of our grandchildren. Just saying "I love you" isn't enough, so it is, "I love you more than all the ice cream in the whole world!" Thank You that You needed more than one word to express Your everlasting love for me ... that touches me in a deep place.

August 4

Time to move on from lovingkindness to faithfulness. In Psalm 92, the Hebrew word for faithfulness is "aman," or its derivative "emunah." These two words carry the ideas of firmness, steadiness, sureness, steadfastness, faithfulness, trust, honesty, safety, and certainty. When faithfulness is applied to God, it is talking about His believability. Beth Moore says, "Faithfulness is resting in His certainty, being persuaded by His honesty, trusting in His reality, being won over by His veracity.... [B]eing sure that He's sure and believing He's worth believing."[5]

So when I meditate on God's faithfulness in the evening, I am thanking Him that He is always true and always the same, that He is good, even when I can't understand Him, and that He loves me, even when I don't feel His love. Beth Moore says that the degree of our faithfulness to others is the direct result of our regard for God's faithfulness to us.[6] That is some statement, and in my spirit, I know it is true.

August 9

Lord, it just hit me that love and faithfulness are fruit of the Spirit. They are what I need to love this complicated man You gave me. My personal Marriage Purpose Statement is the word faithful, and forever faithful is what I long to be. So thank You, my Father, for leading me to thank You for just what I need. I see that my faithfulness and love is the direct result of how big and wide and deep Your love and faithfulness is to me. Teach me, please.

August 15

Oh, I am excited about what I learned today! Psalm 59:10 says that God in His lovingkindness will meet me. I see my Father coming to sit with me and *share a cup of tea. How precious that He meets me in His lovingkindness. I feel embraced by His love. I've been walking around all day thanking the Holy One for personally meeting with me in His unfailing love.*

August 21

Lord, I thank You today for showing me in Psalm 36 that Your lovingkindness is as vast as the heavens and that Your faithfulness reaches beyond the clouds. As I sit by this beautiful lake, drinking in your serene presence, I thank You that You declare that Your lovingkindness is precious (Ps. 36:7) and that You pour out Your lovingkindness on those who love You (Ps. 36:10). Because You declare this to me today, I proclaim the preciousness of Your unfailing love to me. Thank You for this quiet day to bask in Your presence and literally feel the delight of Your lovingkindness poured out on me. Oh, how I love You!

Six months have passed, and I am still thanking God and praising Him every morning for His lovingkindness and every evening for His faithfulness. I have felt my gratitude growing. I've been focusing on God gratitude, but it is overflowing and turning into gratitude for my husband.

How about you? It is really very simple to imitate my God-Gratitude Project. Why don't you get out your Bible and memorize Psalm 92:1–2? It is easy to remember—even my injured brain learned it quickly. Then begin to journal and see your gratitude grow!

Insight 3: GROWING IN HUSBAND GRATITUDE

I've been asking myself more hard questions: How often do I take Jody for granted? Do I let him know how much his encouragement means to me? Do I thank him for little things, like filling my car with gas? Or do I assume he knows I appreciate that he does these things, and so say nothing?

My wise editor and friend, Liz, told me that her husband, Casey, wakes up every day and asks, "How can I make Liz happy today?" When she told me this, I said, "Wow! That's amazing." I asked Liz if she knew how rare her husband is. "Yeah, I know," Liz replied. "I'm so blessed, and I know it is easy to take my great husband for granted."

When my heart is full of gratitude, it encourages me not to take Jody for granted. My Psalm 92 Project took me deeper in God gratitude, so I asked my Lord to show me how to go deeper in husband gratitude. He encouraged me to do two things:

1. Begin a Thankful Journal. Bridal showers are filled with an atmosphere of anticipation. I was invited to a shower for the daughter of a dear friend, and my gift bag was filled with practical encouragements for her first year of marriage. One gift captured the interest of the bride-to-be—a Thankful Journal. It was a simple journal labeled, "Kelly's Thankful Journal." These instructions were included:

1. Choose one day each week to be your time to write in this journal—Sunday is a good time.

2. Reflect over the last week with your new husband and record your "I am thankful" for James because_____, or I am thankful for our marriage because _____.

3. Write a prayer of thanks to God.

If Kelly writes in her Thankful Journal for fifty-two weeks, even if she records her gratitude for only twenty-five weeks of her first year of marriage, think what a treasure she will have! How I wish someone had given me a Thankful Journal and encouraged me to write my thank-yous about my new husband when Jody and I married in 1964. How special it would be to be able to read the thoughts, thank-yous, and prayers I wrote when I was a twenty-one-year-old bride!

Whether you are newly married, an older married woman like me, or somewhere in between, I encourage you to keep a Thankful Journal this year. This project isn't just for the first year of marriage; it's a good idea for every year.

I've written thank-yous to God in journals over the years, but now I have a special journal just for gratitude. I have been writing in it for three months now. Today has not been a good marriage day. When I was on my knees in prayer, the Lord whispered to me to get out my Thankful Journal and read it. Guess what happened in my heart? As I read twelve weeks of gratitude, I remembered how much I have to be grateful for. I even remembered why I love this man!

My second project took me still deeper in husband gratitude.

2. Dwell on the positive. You have probably read Philippians 4:8 several times, or even memorized it, but have you ever directly applied it to your husband?

> *Finally, brethren, whatever is true, whatever is honorable, whatever is right, whatever is pure, whatever is lovely, whatever is of good repute, if there is any excellence and if anything worthy of praise, dwell on these things.*

I began my project by looking through many translations of this verse and making my own paraphrase.

> *Linda, fix your thoughts on what is true and worthy of respect. Dwell on what is right and pure and lovely about Jody. Think about things that are excellent and worthy of praise in this man you married.*

Next, I made a list of these words:

- True

- Worthy of respect
- Right
- Pure
- Lovely
- Excellent
- Worthy of praise

Each day of the week, I thought about one of the above attributes and asked God to reveal how Jody displayed that quality, and then I wrote it all in my Thankful Journal. For example:

Sunday—True

　　Jody is committed to truth, and he lives what is true. This man doesn't lie. I can trust him.

Monday—Worthy of Respect

　　Jody has saved for our retirement, even when, in our thirties, I argued with him about it and said, "We don't have the money for this." He has started a college fund for each of our grandchildren. Few husbands and fathers have done what Jody has done. As I write this, I hear God whisper: Linda, have you told Jody how you respect him for his financial faithfulness?

Tuesday—Just

　　Jody fights for what is right and just. Whether it is evolution and creation or a political issue, he is on the side of right (or what he is convinced is right).

I did this exercise for several weeks and was amazed that God brought different things to my mind each time. Every week I thanked Jody for who he is and for all the positive attributes I see in him.

Maybe you're thinking, *If I did this project, all I would think of is negative qualities.* Go back to Philippians 4:8 and read it again. It doesn't say, "If *everything* is excellent and worthy of praise"; it says, "If there is anything excellent and worthy of praise." If you commit to dwelling on the positive, I believe God will show you something excellent in your husband's character, something worthy of praise.

Don't delay! Today is the day to express your thanks to your husband. My friend Peggy is so grateful she didn't delay.

> *Life can be so busy that we forget to be thankful. I am so thankful for the years of loving Don. Now I watch as the brain tumors slowly take him away from me. I knew this would be our last Valentine's Day, and I wanted it to be special. Unexpectedly, I found three love letters I'd written to Don over the years. I decided sharing them with him would be the best Valentine's card I could give him.*
>
> *1985: Thank you for loving me for twenty-nine years. I still get excited just to be with you and hold your hand.*
>
> *1988: After thirty-two years, I am overwhelmed at the privilege of being your wife.*
>
> *1995: Thank you for loving me unconditionally and unselfishly and continually looking for ways to make me happy. Thank you for giving me the freedom to develop my gifts. I am so grateful for you!*
>
> *2010. Three months after I gave Don his special Valentine, he went to be with the Lord. I am alone. I'm so thankful I expressed my gratitude to him.*

Don't delay! Tell your husband you are thankful for him today!

To help you on your journey to being thankful, I have one more project for you.

3. *Get a Thankful Bookmark.* You can keep the bookmark in your Bible or this book to help you grow in gratitude. My prayer is that the Thankful Bookmark will prompt you to look up and thank God, to look across the table at your husband, open your mouth, and thank him. It will encourage you to journal what you learn about yourself as you grow in gratitude. You can order the Thankful Bookmark for yourself or your Bible study from: www.LindaDillow.org.

Let's not wait until something happens that pushes us to think about our blessings. May we work to grow deeper in husband gratitude *now.* May we grow deeper in husband gratitude, may we open our mouths and express the positive we see in our husband, not only to him, but to others.

Practical Gratitude

Here are some additional Gratitude Projects from women in my survey:

Every night before my husband and I go to sleep we say our "I appreciates." We take the time to mention three things we appreciated about each other that day. They have to be different every day—and it is a wonderful time of connection and communication. (Married three years)

I have just begun to reach out to my husband with thanksgiving. It was harder at first, but now I find the words rolling off my lips. I now thank him for all of his many acts of kindness towards me. This simple act pleases him so much. (Married forty years)

I made a decision to do at least one kind act every day for my husband. (Married thirteen years)

Every night I write down five things that I am thankful for about my husband. I write about big things, little things, good things. First thing in the morning, I read what I wrote the night before and start my day with positive thoughts about my husband. (Married seventeen years)

Insight 4: OFFER A SACRIFICE OF THANKSGIVING

It's not hard to thank God when my husband is loving me sweetly and tenderly. I feel thankful. But thanking God when my husband is not loving me sweetly and tenderly? That is beyond hard. I definitely do not feel thankful. Instead, I must choose in my will to be thankful.

God rejoices when a wife makes that hard choice to give thanks (1 Thess. 5:18). Women have asked me, "Linda, isn't it fake to give thanks when you really want to punch your husband?" Good question. Dr. John Mitchell, cofounder of Multnomah University, answers it like this: "To give thanks when you don't feel like it is not hypocrisy; it's obedience."[7]

If you struggle with how to give thanks when you don't feel like it, I encourage you to read through psalms. You don't need to stuff your negative feelings or sweep them under an imaginary carpet. David poured out his heart to God (Ps. 62:8). If I say it like I see it, he sometimes spewed his questions, his grief and pain, all over His God. God was big enough to take David's doubts and questions and to bring him to a place of laying it all down as a sacrifice to the One he loved. God says He receives our anguished thanks as a sacrificial offering.

"He who offers a sacrifice of thanksgiving honors Me." (Ps. 50:23)

Through Him then, let us continually offer up a sacrifice of praise to God, that is, the fruit of lips that give thanks to His name. (Heb. 13:15)

Three words jump out at me from Hebrews 13:15 about a sacrifice of thanksgiving:

> 1. Continually. I am to offer God a sacrifice of praise over
> and over, whether I feel like it or not.
> 2. Sacrifice. My sacrifice of praise will burn; it will hurt.
> 3. Thanks. I am to give thanks to God over and over for
> things that hurt and are anything but good.

As I write this, I have an opportunity to offer a sacrifice of thanksgiving. I do not feel thankful that my house is a construction zone due to the water damage to all three floors. I do not feel thankful for the grimy dust everywhere. I do not feel thankful that the toilet is sitting in my wonderful big bathtub. My nightly bath is sacred to me. Nor do I feel thankful for the continual pounding and drilling. I want quiet, peace, and order. Instead, I have noise, confusion, and chaos. It is time to offer a sacrifice of thanksgiving.

So I go to the Lord and pray: *Lord, I don't understand Your timing, but I say, "My times are in Your hand" (Ps. 31:15). You know this book is due to my editor in twelve days. You know chaos is hard for my brain. You know everything. I don't feel thankful, but I choose in my will to offer a sacrifice of thanksgiving to You. I thank You that You are going to work everything together for good, even though I don't understand Your ways.*

In Hebrews 13:5, thanksgiving and praise are linked together as a sacrifice. I love what Merlin Carothers says:

> I have come to believe that the prayer of praise is the highest form of communion with God, and one that always releases a great deal of power into our lives. Praising Him is not something we do because we feel good; rather it is an act of obedience. Often the prayer of praise is done in sheer teeth-gritting willpower; yet when we persist in it, somehow the power of God is released into us and into the situation.[8]

I experienced God's power to bring peace in the midst of my house disaster, which is really a little thing. But God can—and does—release His power in us, even in horrific situations. I witnessed this power being released in Emma. Here is what she wrote in her journal one morning:

I don't know what I thought pornography would be like, but when I clicked on that site he left on the browser and saw what he had been looking at, it devastated my heart beyond words. Is this what he wants from me? Is this what he thinks I am? Is this who he is?

He betrayed our intimacy—there's nothing deeper to betray. And he did it when I was giving him myself with more and more abandon. I feel so inadequate—all of me isn't good enough for him. I feel so devalued—some naked woman doing vile things on a computer screen matters more than everything I am and everything we are together. How do I give myself to him again?

Lord, I have nowhere to go but to You. I have no answers, no ideas, no solutions. You say: "Offer to God a sacrifice of thanksgiving … Call upon Me in the day of trouble; I shall rescue you, and you will honor Me" (Ps. 50:14–15).

This is my day of trouble, Lord. I thank You because You will rescue me and I will honor You. Lord, thank You that throughout Your Word You show me You want to exchange all that You are for all of me—to exchange your liberty for my captivity, Your comfort for my grief, Your beauty for my ashes, Your oil of gladness for my mourning, Your mantle of praise for my spirit of fainting. You offer Your light for my darkness, Your strength for my weakness, Your hand for my stumbling, Your joy for my sorrow, Your truth for my chains, Your nearness for my broken heart.

You are my rock, my fortress, and my deliverer. Thank You that I can cling to You. Thank You that You are complete, never lacking, faithful, and secure. You are my beloved. I wait for You. I rest in You.

How could Emma choose an attitude of thankfulness in the aftermath of her husband's betrayal? If you have ever discovered your husband looking at pornography, you likely wanted to scream, kick (preferably him), run away, or just sit down and weep forever. You were filled with anger at your husband, and maybe even at God for not intervening and keeping this from happening. I'm sure Emma felt some of these things. I know, too, what she wrote for her Marriage Purpose Statement, and I share it with you here because it will help you see the deep commitment behind her sacrifice of thanksgiving.

Emma used the beautiful love passage in 1 Corinthians 13 as the basis for her Marriage Purpose Statement:

> *Lord, through Your love in me, I choose …*
>
> *To love Sam patiently, with a willingness to suffer long—when he doesn't understand, when I don't understand, and when neither of us does; when we face long-term struggles, battle sin, and when our weaknesses collide.*
>
> *To love Sam in kindness, when I'm angry, hurt, tired, and even premenstrual.*
>
> *To love Sam without jealousy—toward his role, his privileges, or toward other women for what they have in marriage. I will choose thankfulness for who he is and what we are together.*
>
> *To love Sam without bragging about what I know or think I know, but by choosing instead to build him up.*
>
> *To love Sam without pride and arrogance … when I'm wrong and when I'm right or when I think I'm right. I choose to have a humble heart that views him as more important than myself.*

To love Sam without being rude and critical when I see his weaknesses, when I'm hurt, angry, or frustrated. I choose to have a gentle and quiet spirit.

To love Sam without being self-seeking when I feel like my rights and feelings aren't seen or respected. I choose to have Your attitude, Jesus, to lay down every right I have and entrust myself and my needs to You.

To love Sam without being easily provoked when my feelings are hurt or his actions unjust. I choose to be quick to listen, slow to speak, and slow to become angry.

To love Sam without keeping a record of what he's done wrong. I choose to forgive unconditionally and continually, not holding wrongs I've suffered against him.

To love Sam by never delighting in evil … in our marriage or in either of us personally. I will rejoice when truth wins out.

To love Sam by having an attitude in our marriage that bears all things, believes all things, hopes all things, and endures all things.

Oh, Lord, give me Your love for Sam that will never fail.

Emma and her husband are doing well together. God used her sacrifice of thanksgiving to humble Sam, and he sought help for his addiction. He is accountable to a Christian counselor and is moving forward on the path to freedom.

God asks each of us to offer a sacrifice of thanksgiving. Sometimes our sacrificial offer is for a house in chaos, or for a brain injury, or for a marriage conflict. And like Emma, sometimes we offer to God a sacrifice of thanksgiving for very difficult things. I know that in the offering, God breathes into us power and peace, as He did for Emma. He is so pleased when we offer this deepest form of gratitude, a sacrifice of thanksgiving.

Insight 5: A DANGEROUS PRAYER

When Lynne was praying fervently for a friend's husband, God gave her the conviction that she was to pray for her own husband with the same passion and fervor. So Lynne prayed a dangerous prayer: *Lord, show me how to be devoted in prayer to my husband.* I'll let her tell you what happened next.

> *I prayed about the pain David was struggling through and asked God to intervene with power in his life. Then I called and told him what I saw in him, how God had gifted him and called him to leadership. I told him that I believed in him and that I was committed to pray for him.*
>
> *It was amazing to see his response—it had been a long time since I had breathed life into him with my words. We were both humbled by this experience. It was an unspoken softness we had for one another. I was humbled that I could pray so fervently for my friend's husband, who was missing, but miss my own husband simply by not praying for him.*

Many of us want to be devoted to prayer, but our requests are usually for a friend in need, someone in our church who has cancer, or the orphans with AIDS in Africa. Is it easier to pray for others than it is to pray for my husband? I think it is.

I know the book of Colossians has thankfulness flowing off of its pages, that each of its four chapters speaks of thankfulness. Since I am on a mission to grow in gratitude, I decided to get my Bible and study all Paul had to say. I discovered that, yes, gratitude is a major theme found in each chapter of Colossians (1:3, 12; 2:6–7; 3:15–17; 4:2). As I read through this precious love letter from God, I sensed He wanted me to paraphrase what it says to me about being a wife and then apply the message to my attitude toward my husband. Here is what I wrote:

As a wife, I give thanks to God the Father of our Lord Jesus Christ—praying always for you, my husband (Col. 1:3).

As a wife, I am always thanking the Father, who lets Jody and me walk in His light together (Col. 1:12).

As a wife, I am to walk by faith and build my life on Christ, and I am to overflow with gratitude for Jody (Col. 2:6–7).

As a wife, I am to be filled with God's peace. I am called to live in peace with Jody. AND always be thankful (Col. 3:15).

As a wife, I am to sing psalms and hymns and spiritual songs to God with a thankful heart (Col. 3:16).

As a wife, whatever I do, whatever I say, is to be as Jesus' representative, giving thanks through Him to God the Father (Col. 3:17).

As a wife, I am to devote myself to prayer for Jody with an alert mind and thankful heart (Col. 4:2).

Lots to think about, but the verse that pierced my heart is the last one. I am to devote myself to prayer for my husband. How am I to do this? With an alert mind and a thankful heart. It is the word *devote* that reaches deep into my spirit. *Devote* is such a strong word, implying a heavy commitment. What am I really devoted to? The dictionary says that "to devote" is to give of oneself, one's time, energy. God is asking me to sacrifice my time and my energy to pray for Jody. Only God will know if I make this deep secret choice.

When I sacrifice in this way, I'm not just to pray whatever comes to my mind, I am to be *alert* in my mind—attuned to Jody, attuned to his joys, attuned to his sorrows, attuned to his frustrations. I am to be *alert* to how I can help him, to how I can encourage him. Being alert is the opposite of being uninterested or passive. God is asking me to be keyed in to where Jody is physically, emotionally, and spiritually.

How easy it is to live in the same house, sleep in the same bed, and be oblivious to who our husband is at this moment and to who he is becoming! When we devote ourselves to pray for him, it is a sacrifice of time, of love, and of devotion. But when we devote ourselves to praying for him *with an alert mind and thankful heart,* we've given our husband the greatest gift we can give him.

My friend, I hope you can feel yourself growing in gratitude. Grab your Thankful Bookmark and *remember, reflect,* and *respond.* Open your mouth and express your thankfulness to God and to your husband. While you are at it, throw some thanks your children's way; they need it too! God is in the business of changing you! He is about changing your native language from griping to gratitude!

Dangerous Prayer!

Lord, please teach me to speak the language of gratitude.

What Will It Take for Me to Get Close to You?

Express appreciation for each other. Accepting each other makes a stable marriage. Appreciating each other, however, makes a sensational marriage.
Brett Selby

Married love is hard work, because it requires us to constantly think of our spouse instead of ourself, and our natural bent is to think of ourself first.
Bill and Nancie Carmichael

Insight 1: SURPRISE! MEN AND WOMEN ARE DIFFERENT

One of the most beautiful descriptions of emotional intimacy I've ever read was written by my friend Nanci. She and her husband waded through rough waters in their marriage and came out swimming strong on the other side. Here is what she says about emotional intimacy:

> *Emotional intimacy is being "naked and unashamed." To be fully known; my darkest thoughts, hateful words, biggest disappointments, and greatest fears—and yet be fully loved and accepted. To*

know that I have given my heart to my husband, that he takes seriously the role of protector; that he is careful with my heart. And I am careful with his heart. It is knowing him so well and having such a deep understanding of him that I can trust him beyond circumstances. It is being so entwined with one another, yet so different, that we are like one plant putting off two very different blooms.

Marriage is the adventure of discovering one another so you might deeply share:

> A soul intimacy
>
> A body intimacy
>
> A spirit intimacy

The three intimacies together are what yield oneness. Sex without soul intimacy is empty, satisfying only the body. Soul and body intimacy without spirit oneness is missing God's best. God made us three-dimensional people. Husband and wife are to meet body, soul, and spirit; the result will be a lover-best friend relationship.

God agrees.

Yet, many wives wonder, *Is it really possible to have emotional intimacy with my husband? We are just so different! Can I get close to him, and what will it take?*

I can only share with you how one right-brained-engineer-type man (Jody) and one left-brained-relational-type woman (me) created deep emotional oneness in our marriage. And in truth I can only share my part, because I can only make choices for me. What did I do to move closer to Jody?

The answer to that question starts on the first page of this book, because everything I've been writing about has been part of the process. I asked myself, *Who or what is really important to me? Is Jody first in my heart, or are the kids first?* I asked God to show me what it felt like to be my husband. When I saw that my pride and selfishness were sending Jody the message that "My way of living life is better than yours," and when I realized how I'm more prone to gripe and complain than to express gratitude, I asked God to change me. Truly, growing in gratitude transformed how I see my husband. When a wife asks these hard questions about herself, it sets the stage for emotional intimacy with her husband. Intimacy means "into me see." I can't see into Jody's heart if I'm fighting against our differentness or trying to change him.

That is the background. Jody's and my emotional intimacy didn't happen overnight. It happened over the many years of our marriage.

Moving closer to Jody also involved acknowledging that he is another species. This fact is often the subject of jokes like this humorous blurb I found on the Internet:

How to Treat a Woman

Wine her. Dine her. Call her. Hold her. Surprise her.
Compliment her. Smile at her. Listen to her. Laugh with her.
Cry with her. Romance her. Encourage her. Believe in her.
Pray with her. Pray for her. Cuddle with her. Shop with her.
Give her jewelry. Buy her flowers. Hold her hand.
Write love letters to her. Go to the ends of the earth and back again for her.

How to Treat a Man

Show up naked. Bring chicken wings. Don't block the TV.[1]

Indeed, men and women are different. It's one thing to read about these differences; it's something else altogether to live with such a foreign creature. That is no laughing matter! I realized that if I wanted emotional closeness with Jody, *I needed to stop fighting our differences and try to understand what makes him feel close to me.*

I'm going to tell you a closely kept secret about men. Men don't talk about it, so your husband may not even be aware of it. Closeness comes for him when you are body to body or shoulder to shoulder. Jody feels emotional intimacy with me in sexual intimacy. One husband said this about the connectedness he felt after making love with his wife: "I feel whole and complete. My life is at peace. I thank God for you and the special gift it is to love and be loved by you." Sounds like emotional intimacy to me! Another man said that after loving his wife sexually, he can go outside and smell the flowers. He can walk with his wife and have deep communication. *Sexual intimacy opens him to emotional connection.* Write that one down; it is important that you get this in your brain.

When women want to feel emotionally connected, they talk. Words are spoken, hearts connected, and secrets shared. Men, very different from us, can feel close without having any eye connection or heart contact. No secrets shared, very few words spoken. Being shoulder to shoulder is enough. Shoulder-to-shoulder connection is what happens when men watch football, basketball, or any kind of ball together. They eat yummy things and make comments about their favorite team. Their eyes are on the screen, not on each other. But in their male brains and hearts, they are connecting.

It took me a long time to understand this, and to act on my understanding. Jody feels close to me when we go to the Santa Fe Trail together. He takes off and runs four miles. I walk two miles listening to worship music and have a sweet time of prayer while waiting for him to finish his jog. We get back in the car, share about our respective exercise times, and drive home. To me, we are two people doing two different things. Jody loves it. I entered into his life and did an "activity" with him.

Jody studied engineering. His brain is analytical, focused—very unlike mine. I smile inside when I look back over the years and realize how this right-brained man of mine has learned to enter deeply into emotional intimacy with me.

Last month he took me out to dinner for my birthday and then said he had a surprise for me. This man who doesn't do details took me to our camper, where he had spent hours preparing it for my birthday. All of the little things he did spoke love to me. The cake even said, "I love Linda." (I asked him if the woman at the bakery laughed when he told her what to write. She did.) I had asked Jody that week what emotional intimacy meant to him. On a beautiful flowery card, Jody had written …

> *Emotional intimacy is sharing dreams and desires, plans and adventure. It is both encouragement and comfort. It is being best friends and lovers. Your love has made this real in my life.*

Not bad for a right-brained male.

It *is* possible for a husband and wife, two very different species who view life through different lens, to develop a lover/best-friend intimacy. Jody and I are proof that it can happen.

Insight 2: WE BOTH HAVE GAPS

If you haven't seen the original *Rocky*, rent it! The film is worth the rental price just to observe the love relationship between Rocky and Adrian. The big hunk and the wallflower from the pet shop were definitely an unexpected match. Adrian's brother, Paulie, an insensitive goon, could not figure out why Rocky would be attracted to his sister.

"What's the attraction?" Paulie asked.

"I don't know—she fills gaps."

"What's 'gaps'?"

"I don't know, she's got gaps, I got gaps, together we fill gaps."

In a simple but profound way, Rocky hit upon a truth. He was saying that without him, Adrian had empty places in her life, and without her, he had empty places in his. But when the two of them got together, they helped fill the gaps; they met the needs in the other.

God agrees with Rocky: All men and women have gaps. In Genesis 2, He clearly defines the deep-felt need of both man and woman—the need for an intimate companion.

In the garden of Eden, Adam had a perfect relationship with God, a perfect environment, something to occupy his time, and an infinity of things to explore. But he also had a gap. One thing was missing from his life: someone to walk through the garden with, to work with, to laugh with, to share with; someone to love. Adam had everything, but Adam was alone. Adam had gaps.

In the Chinese language, entire words are written with one symbol. Often two completely unlike symbols, when put together, have a meaning different from their two separate components. A beautiful example is the symbol of man and that of woman. When these symbols are combined, man plus woman equals good, and that is exactly what God said. In the creation account, we read seven times that "God saw that it was good." Then in Genesis 2:18, God says something is "not good"—"Then the LORD God said, 'It is not good for the man to be alone; I will make him a helper suitable for him.'"

When God brought the woman to Adam, his response was beyond good—he was ecstatic: "This is it!" (Gen. 2:23 TLB). Today he might say, "YES!" or "Wow, right on! She's the one!" Adam was definitely pleased with his "suitable helper." God had created for him a companion, someone to share the challenges of life with. Someone who would feel as he felt, exude joy at discovery, and problem solve with him in times of puzzlement. A companion who would discover what intimacy looked like with him. A wife to fill his gaps.

What an indescribably beautiful provision by God! Our needs for an intimate companion perfectly met in marriage. C. S. Lewis was an older bachelor when he married his beloved wife, Joy. In his powerful way with words, he describes their deep emotional intimacy:

> *[We] feasted on love, every mode of it—solemn and merry,*
> *romantic and realistic, sometimes as dramatic as a thunderstorm,*

sometimes comfortable and unemphatic as putting on your soft slippers…. She was … my pupil and my teacher, my subject and my sovereign; and always, holding all these in solution, my trusty comrade, friend, shipmate, fellow-soldier. My mistress, but at the same time all that any man friend … has ever been to me.[2]

C. S. Lewis discovered God's answer to man's gap was to give him a wife, someone who would come alongside him and be a vital part of his finding fulfillment.

Both husbands and wives carry within the need for an intimate companion. Both also have a driving need that is gender specific.

For the wife, her greatest need is for security. For the husband, his greatest need is for significance.

In a beautiful way, God set about filling the gaps of both husband and wife (Eph. 5:25–33). His command to the husband would fill the wife's *love gap.* His command to the wife would fill the husband's *respect gap.* God commanded:

The husband: Love your wife sacrificially (Eph. 5:25, 28).

The wife: Respect your husband unconditionally (Eph. 5:33).

I've gone on a hunt, searched this passage for an *if* that wrapped God's commands with conditions. It would read like this:

IF your husband is tender, understanding, compassionate, IF he loves you sacrificially every day, every hour, in every situation, THEN you respect him.

I can't find an *if* in this passage, and believe me, I've looked hard. It makes more sense to me to have conditions. *If* a wife is an evil shrew, why should a husband sacrifice to love her? *If* a husband is a slovenly couch potato, why should a wife respect him unconditionally? Get out your Bible and read Ephesians 5:21–33 carefully. Did you find an *if?* Nope. I didn't either. God clearly sums it all up to both partners; He believes this is so important that He repeats His commands again:

> *So again I say, each man must love his wife as he loves himself,*
> *and the wife must respect her husband. (Eph. 5:33 NLT)*

Did you notice the *must?*

An *if* means there are conditions. A *must* means no conditions. A *must* says, JUST DO IT.

In his excellent book *Love and Respect,* Dr. Emerson Eggerichs sums it up this way:

> *A wife has one driving need—to feel loved. When that need is met,*
> *she is happy. A husband has one driving need—to feel respected.*
> *When that need is met, he is happy.*[3]

May it be so in your marriage.

Your part in creating emotional intimacy with your husband not only involves admitting that you and your husband both have gaps. We'll talk more about how you can fill your husband's gaps, but first I want to talk with you about your divine calling as a wife.

Insight 3: A WIFE'S DIVINE CALLING

God has given each wife a divine calling. We need to go back to Genesis to see this call.

> *Then the LORD God said, "It is not good for the man to be alone;*
> *I will make him a helper suitable for him." (Gen. 2:18)*

Man's "suitable helper"[4] would provide the missing pieces from the puzzle of his life. She would complete him as a qualified, corresponding partner. This is good, but there is more: A mystery surrounds this one called helper. As the Creator declared His chosen name for her, I suspect the angels looked on in unbelief and exclaimed something like this: "This is unheard of! How can this be? She is set apart as special. The almighty God, Creator of heaven and earth honors her—He actually gives her one of His holy names! Oh, she is so blessed!"

Why were the angels so excited? What is this special name of God's that He shares with wives—with you? In Hebrew it is the name *Ezer.* In English it is translated as *helper.*

Helper? You may have mixed feelings about that name. It sounds drab, dreary, and depressing. Webster even defines a helper as "one that helps; especially a relatively unskilled worker who assists a skilled worker, usually by manual labor."[5] Sounds like a *hausfrau* from the 1940s, clothed in a housedress with a cutesy apron, down on her knees scrubbing a floor, right? But this is *not* what God has in mind here. Put those images—which are incorrect—aside and try to get your mind and heart around God's meaning of His name *Ezer.*

Ezer is used twenty-one times in the Old Testament and almost always refers to God. It is His name. The Lord God Almighty is called our helper:

> *"My father's God was my helper." (Ex. 18:4 NIV)*

> *You [God] are the helper of the fatherless. (Ps. 10:14 NIV)*

> *The LORD is with me; he is my helper. (Ps. 118:7 NIV)*

> *Our soul waits for the LORD;*
> *He is our help and our shield. (Ps. 33:20)*

Then in Genesis 2:18–25, God takes this strong name *Ezer* and in effect says, "Now you, the one called wife, have the same privilege and the responsibility that I have. I give you one of My names, Helper. Being a helper is godlike. As I come alongside you as your Helper, I ask you to come alongside your husband, and fill his respect gap as his personal, private, intimate helper. *Only you* will know what respect looks like for him. *Only you* can become his intimate ally, his closest companion. *Only you* will know how to design a personal program of helping for your unique man."

I am not talking about being your husband's secretary, seamstress, gardener, or accountant. As wives we are to help our husbands; it is part of the essence of who we are as women. It is within the fabric of our created being. However, the specific expression of what we do as a result of being helpers is unique for each marriage relationship. And it will vary over the course of our lifetimes.

While writing this chapter, I went to Jody and asked, "What practically can I do in this season of life to be a help to you?" His answer surprised me: "Come with me when I travel and speak." Groan. I already travel and don't want to travel more. But I had asked and told God, "I'll do what he suggests." So the next time Jody got ready to leave for a trip, I had my plane ticket in hand. However, I never got on the plane. The water damage to our house happened just at that time, and I needed to stay to talk to the insurance adjuster and supervise various workmen. But I tried, and my attitude of wanting to be there spoke love to my husband and blessed him. Next time, I might even make it on the plane.

My friend Tamra has thought deeply about being a helper to her husband, Barry, as is illustrated in her Marriage Purpose Statement, which I want to share with you:

> *Father, I thank You for forgiving me for all the years my marriage was dominated by my self-centeredness. I tossed Barry a bone of submission on the big decisions regarding career, church home,*

moving, etc., but in my daily life I was so much more contentious than gracious, so much more competing than completing, thinking so much more about my own interests rather than his. I was friendly to everyone else, but then I came home and was too often a grump.

Lord, I thank You for opening my eyes twelve years ago to see that Barry was not created for me, but I for him. That is part of the essence of who You have made me: I am to complement Barry in his person and in his work. Father, I pray that You would continue to reveal what that looks like in our marriage. I ask that I would have eyes to see and the wisdom to know how I can be a true helper and complement to this man to whom I have the privilege of being married. I pray that I will bring him good and not harm all the days of my life. I pray I will walk worthy of his heart safely trusting in me. I pray that all You have put within me will first serve my husband's abilities and life calling. I pray we will fulfill all of the will of God in our lifetime as we do the same work together, or complementary work that is different, and that all of our efforts will be in harmony toward the same goal.

Thank You, Father! I have had the joy and privilege of getting to know my husband more in the last twelve years than I did in the first fourteen. I was so blinded by my own ambitions that I wasn't interested in the finer points of who he is. You have shown me so much mercy! You have brought us together in emotional and spiritual intimacy that far outstrips the challenge of change that it took to get here. I thank You, Father, for the amazing privilege of marriage being the only picture in the earth of Jesus' relationship with the Church. I pray that in ever-increasing measure Barry and I will be a picture of that, as he exemplifies Christ's sacrificial love and leadership while, by Your grace, I am his adoring bride who responds to him with strength, beauty, wisdom, submission,

and respect, picturing the response of Your people to You. To Your
name be the glory! In Jesus' name, amen.

How does Tamra live out being a helper to Barry, who is both an entrepreneur businessman and a church-planting pastor? When he is working
through a business decision of any kind and chooses to talk it over with
her, she does two things:

>   1. She tries to ask good questions that can spur his think-
> ing on the matter.
>   2. She remembers that she doesn't have to have all the
> answers. She doesn't want to be a wife who overly chal-
> lenges or discourages her husband's initiatives in his world
> of work out of fear of the "what-ifs," so she keeps her con-
> fidence ultimately in God.

She comes alongside Barry by showing love and appreciation for his
employees, whether through a casual dinner for six, a big Christmas party,
or remembering to send a gift when a baby is born. She helps her pastor
husband by giving him space and quiet from Friday through Sunday every
week while he is preparing for his sermon. She practices the discipline of
"limited conversation topics." (She says she still has a long way to go in
really applying this one but is working on it!) She tries to be a keen and
attentive listener rather than an open fire hydrant, gushing chatter and
interrupting. She shares with him "what she sees" in ways that ultimately
build up their church and the work of the ministry.

I want to close this section with one more example of how a wife can
be a helper to her husband—keep in mind that this looks different for every
wife.

Recently Jody and I were invited to dinner at the home of his car-
diologist. We arrived at 5:00 p.m. with other friends. Chee-Hwa, the
doctor's wife, and their four children were there, but not Chris, the doctor.
I watched Chee-Hwa as the hours passed. I listened to her conversation

when Chris called to say he would be home "sometime." How was Chee-Hwa a helper to her husband? She didn't gripe and complain to him or to their guests. Instead, she cheerfully served dinner and had their children perform for us on the cello and violin. Chris arrived during the performance, three-and-a-half hours late.

Chee-Hwa is a professional pianist who taught music at a university. She says living the life of a single career woman was a breeze compared with being a helper and mother to four. Chee-Hwa is still a professional musician, but I love watching how she is also becoming a professional at her "second" career as a wife.

Tamra and Chee-Hwa are imperfect wives, just like you and me, but they have thought intentionally about how to fulfill their calling as a wife, which is one way a wife fills her husband's respect gap and invites emotional intimacy.

If you are feeling brave, ask your husband this question: *What one thing can I do today that would make me a better helper to you?*

In the next insights, we'll look at additional ways you can invite emotional intimacy with your husband.

Insight 4: FILL HIS GAPS WITH ENCOURAGEMENT AND RESPECT

A wife can do many things to her husband's gaps, but I want to look at two that speak loudly to me: *encouragement* and *respect*.

"Encourage one another and build up one another" (1 Thess. 5:11). The Hebrew word for encouragement means literally to "stir up," "to provoke," "to incite people in a given direction." One dictionary defines *encouragement* as "the act of inspiring others with renewed courage, renewed spirit, or renewed hope." I love that. As a wife, I encourage Jody on our journey together through the seasons of life by putting my arm around him, walking with him, and whispering words that spur him on to be more, to be all God desires him to be as a man, a husband, a father. When I encourage

Jody, I put courage into him to keep on keeping on when life is hard. And he does the same for me.

I see emotional intimacy as entering into each other's life and hearing not just the words but the heart. This last year, Jody entered into my emotional space and heard my heart. He saw my unshed tears. I'd had a very difficult brain day—that means nothing clicked, not thoughts or words, and I felt disoriented living my own life. I was discouraged and just plain sad. I walked in the door and saw a vase with pink roses and a card. My heart jumped. *Who sent the roses?* The card propped against the beautiful roses said, "Honey, I don't think I realized how hard the whole brain injury thing is for you. I know you work hard not to complain but I watch you—you're having to relearn life. I respect you so much for trusting God and wanting to honor Him in all this."

Jody lived Ephesians 4:29. God speaks in this verse in contrasts:

> *Let no unwholesome word proceed from your mouth, but only such a word as is good for edification according to the need of the moment, so that it will give grace to those who hear.*

Do not speak dirty, rotten garbage words, literally.

Do speak words that build up, meet the need of the moment, and give grace to the hearer.

Jody's words poured courage into me; they cradled my sad heart. *Jody respects me; he thinks I'm honoring God.* The tears of frustration I had held back all day now poured out as tears of hope.

I love the way *The Message* renders Ephesians 4:29: "Say only what helps, each word a gift." Can you imagine how your husband would feel if each word you spoke to him was a gift? You would certainly be inviting him into emotional intimacy with you! *Lord, pierce that thought into my heart and mind. Let me live today speaking only "gift words" to my husband.*

Jody loves to invite our ministry team couples over for dinner in the relaxed atmosphere of our home so that he can really get to know them. My introverted husband has commented over and over how much this little act of helping encourages him. When I pour encouragement into Jody by my words and actions, I am giving him a source of fresh energy.

Dr. Henry H. Goddary discovered that encouragement is actually an energy source, which can be measured in the laboratory. He pioneered studies using an instrument devised to measure fatigue. When an assistant would say to the tired child at the laboratory instrument, "You're doing fine, John," the boy's energy curve would soar. Discouragement and faultfinding were found to have an opposite effect, which could also be measured.[6] So when you encourage your husband, it pours courage and renewed strength in him, and when you criticize and complain, it drains him of courage and energy.

Respect will also have a powerful effect on your husband: "And let the wife see that she respects and reverences her husband" (Eph. 5:33 AB). Does your husband really need respect from you? Listen to wives' comments about the worst thing they did for their marriage:

> *I loved him the way I wanted to be loved. For many years he needed respect and so many other things from me, and I rarely met his needs. (Married twenty-six years)*

> *I took too long to figure out how important unconditional respect is to my husband. (Married thirty-one years)*

> *I did not respect and honor my husband—when I finally did after eighteen years of marriage, he became my God-given spiritual cover. (Married thirty-two years)*

> *I don't respect my husband in word and action. I talk negatively about him to others. (Married fourteen years)*

If those comments don't convince you, consider doing the following exercise.[7] Get out a piece of paper and pen and find a quiet place. Spend ten or fifteen minutes making a list of things you respect about your husband. Next, wait until your husband isn't busy or distracted, and say, "I was thinking about you today and several things about you that I respect, and I just want you to know that I respect you." After saying you respect him, do not wait for any response (this is very important!). Just smile and quietly start to leave the room. One woman said that after telling her husband she respected him, she turned to leave but she never made it out the door. He practically shouted, "What things?" Because this wife had made her list, she had things on the tip of her tongue to share with him. After she was finished, he said, "Wow! Hey, can I take the family out to dinner?"[8]

I have force-fed my favorite translation of Ephesians 5:33 into my brain because it makes the word *respect* come alive.

> And let the wife see that she respects and reverences her husband
> [that she notices him, regards him, honors him, prefers him, ven-
> erates, and esteems him; and that she defers to him, praises him,
> and loves and admires him exceedingly]. (AB)

Could the word *respect* really embody all of those words? These are strong words: *honor, prefer, esteem, praise, love,* and *admire exceedingly.* Is this really what God asks a wife to do? Yes, my friend, it is. I often pray, asking God to make this verse a reality in my relationship with Jody. My prayer sounds something like this:

> My Father, this verse says so much. Please show me how to notice
> Jody, to regard him. In what ways can I honor him, prefer him
> above others? Lord, what does it look like to venerate and esteem
> him? As I go through these words, I'm thinking, How does one

woman do all this? Only You can show me. I want to praise Jody in words that will speak to him—reveal to me what they are. I want to love and admire my man exceedingly. I want to express respect to him in all these ways today.

Writing out this prayer makes me sigh. It is so much, yet I am grateful that this one verse explains respect so well. Having these words in my heart and mind has encouraged me more than any other one thing in living out respect.

During a difficult time in her marriage, a wise wife wrote the following acrostic to help her remember how to show her husband respect:

Revere

Esteem

Submit

Prize

Enjoy

Comfort

Trust

My friend, learn how to respect your husband. This is important to him and to your marriage. Learning to respect your unique man is an art. Learning to meet his deep needs is a skill. It is a challenge that takes a lifetime. And when you pour encouragement and respect into your husband, you invite emotional intimacy.

Insight 5: WHO WILL FILL MY GAPS?

Maybe you are thinking, *Great, Linda—I'm supposed to be this super helper to my husband. I work hard to fill his respect gap, but isn't he supposed to do something for me?* Good question.

The commands to a husband are difficult; I believe those are more difficult to live out than the commands to a wife. When you read Ephesians 5:21–33, you know that God commands husbands to fill their wife's love gap. A husband is to love his wife as Christ loved the Church, which means laying down his life for her (v. 25). That is the ultimate love.

Husbands are also to love their wife's body as much as they love their own bodies (v. 28–29). That command confused me at first, and I thought, *Jody loves the curves of my body, not his body!* But then I remembered that many men get *very* concerned if they are sick. When a man is sick, sickness is serious. The verse means that Jody is to be as concerned about my head-ache as he is about his own headache, as caring about my sinus infection as about his stuffed-up head. This puts a different light on this verse.

But what do you do when your husband doesn't fill your love gap? What do you do with your unmet needs? What if you do all you know to do to get closer to him—you accept and act on God's call to you as your husband's helper and to pour encouragement and respect into him, but he doesn't care, doesn't try, and doesn't move toward you?

That is hard, very hard. If that is your situation, you may be thinking, *Easy for you to say, Linda. Your husband loves the Lord and loves you.* And you are right. I am blessed with a husband who loves the Lord and who loves me. But that doesn't mean our marriage has been easy.

When I said, "I do," I made an unconditional commitment to an imperfect person. I also made a commitment to God that I would seek to be Jody's helper—to meet his needs rather than to have my needs met. The world shouts, "It's all about you; get your needs met!" Jesus, the Christ, brings a different perspective: "I came not to be served but to serve" (Matt. 20:28, author's paraphrase). Jesus came to lay down His life that we might be free. Then He says to me, *Linda, will you follow in My steps and be Jody's helper? Will you seek to serve and not to be served?*

At a point in time, I said yes to this commitment, but I have to reaffirm my decision. Making this choice has freed me from expecting Jody to fill my love gap, and accept me, encourage me … the list goes on and on. When my dearly beloved understands me, shows me affection, or loves me sacrificially, it is a gift of God, given to me through my husband. It is not my right. Changing my perspective from *my right* to *God's gift* has enabled me more and more to seek to meet Jody's needs, and this is exactly what God wants me to do … what He wants every wife to do.

It took me years to get this perspective. Michelle is a young woman who learned much more quickly than I did. After she and her husband, Josh, had been married for a couple of years, Michelle began to feel depressed and unhappy. She married believing Josh would meet all her needs for love, acceptance, and security. She thought she would be married to someone who would always be on her side, adore and love her no matter what she did, and understand her completely, even when she didn't understand herself.

When this wasn't the case, Michelle became confused, frustrated, and angry. She thought, *Maybe I'm not trying hard enough,* so she worked hard to do all the things for Josh that communicated love to her, like writing little love notes and buying him surprises. She tried harder and harder at losing weight, cleaning house, and memorizing facts about current events, so she would be interesting. When trying harder didn't work, Michelle tried confronting Josh on how he wasn't loving her enough. She also tried appealing to his sympathy by crying and being pitiful. Nothing worked.

I believe that what God revealed to Michelle will encourage you, as it did me. She sent me the following in an email:

> *I vividly remember the afternoon when I concluded that Josh either would not or could not love me the way I needed to be loved. It just was not going to happen. I was furious at God. I told Him that I had prayed for my mate since I was in the ninth grade. I had prayed about my engagement to Josh. I had tried to follow God every step of the way. God, better than anyone, knew how I needed to be loved. How could He do this to me? I remember hitting my bed in anger and crying. As I sat there it became clear to me that somebody was going to have to give in this argument. It was going to be God or me, and chances were good it was going to be me.*

I knew that God was asking me to change. I needed to give those needs and desires to Him as a sacrifice and trust Him to meet them, however He chose. That is easy to say, but overwhelming to actually do. I felt as if God was literally asking me to cut my heart out and give it to Him. (On top of that, I had no anesthesia, and I had to do the surgery myself!) To be loved and cared for the way I had dreamed in marriage was what I had lived for all my life. To give up hope of having it seemed like giving up my life. It was like a death. I lay across my bed and cried and cried until I was exhausted both physically and emotionally.

Then it dawned on me that this is what it means in a practical way to deny myself and follow Christ. This is what it means to lose my life for His sake (Matt. 16:25). I decided to write out in my journal the specific things that I was giving to God that day. These are a few of the things that were on my list:

- *The belief that my marriage would make me secure.*
- *The belief that my marriage would completely fill my need for love.*
- *The idea that any human being can love me completely without ever wavering.*
- *The belief that my emotional maturity, my fulfillment and happiness was Josh's responsibility.*
- *The belief that Josh's emotional maturity, fulfillment, and happiness was my responsibility.*

After I wrote these things out in my journal I experienced peace and joy for the first time in weeks. I was even feeling humorous. I wrote in my journal, "Now, God, is there anything else You want, as long as I have the incision open here?"

As I look back over the years since that day, I see it as a real turning point. My mission in marriage was changed from getting my needs met to letting God teach me how to love Josh, just for the sake of obeying and pleasing God. This has been really hard. Many times the decision to love is very private. There is no one to applaud or to say, "Boy, Michelle, that was really an unselfish thing to do." There is no one there who knows how much it hurts in that moment to choose to love, except God.

I have learned and I am still learning how to tell God about my needs and trust Him to meet them. He does meet them in surprising ways. I am also learning that as I love Josh without pressuring him with expectations, God has been teaching him how to better love me and meet my needs.

Michelle expressed it well. God wants you to concentrate on how to please your husband. You have found him, your one unique man to love, an original unlike any other. You are on this marriage journey together, and you are the one close to his heart; you are the one who knows his deep needs. You don't have to fill the respect gap of any other man, only this one, but it can take a lifetime to intimately know, understand, and love your man.

> *Do nothing from selfishness or empty conceit, but with humility of mind let every wife regard her husband as more important than herself; do not merely look out for your own personal interests, but also for the interests of your husband.*

Philippians 2:3–4, my paraphrase

Insight 6: A WIFE CAN SET THE STAGE FOR INTIMACY

When I accept God's call on my life to be Jody's helper and apply "helping" specifically to him, I am creating an atmosphere of sweetness in our relationship. When sweetness reigns in our marriage, there is a deep emotional understanding, a flowing of tenderness and gentle touch. Soft words of love and silly smiles of connection abound. But when I put my rights over my husband's, I stifle that sweetness.

I shared my thoughts with Jody about the joy we had when emotional sweetness hovered. I asked him, "Honey, what do you think is the opposite of sweetness?"

His answer literally astounded me: "Loneliness."

Lord, is that how Jody feels on days when our love grates, when my voice has irritation to it because I am irritated?

The Lord's whisper of, *Yes, Linda, that is how he feels,* sent me once again to my Thankful Journal, and I wrote:

> *Today, Lord, how can my love be patient? I want to:*
> - *Give the grace I give to a friend to my lover/my friend.*
> - *Get behind his eyeballs and see the today of life as he sees it.*
> - *Be as understanding of his weaknesses as I was the first year of our marriage.*

It is a challenge for every wife to do her part to create emotional intimacy with her husband. It is especially difficult for American military wives. They are some of the most incredible women I know. Their husbands are away for a year or more at a time—in Iraq, Afghanistan, or another faraway country. These wives are alone a lot, and it is not easy.

Krista is such a wife. She made it her goal to fill her husband's gaps. Her loving plan poured encouragement, respect, and hope into her husband, Caleb. I'll let her tell you her story.

> *When I was ten years old, I was abducted on the way to school and sexually abused the whole day. In the evening I was able to get away. This day defined my life in many ways—I was told I wouldn't be able to have children.*

I met Caleb after he had finished medical school. He told me that he had had testicular cancer, and that even though he was declared healed, the doctors said he wouldn't be able to have children. It sounds crazy but on our second date we told each other that we couldn't have children. This was the medical story. God's story is that Caleb and I gave birth to three precious children.

Caleb became a brigade surgeon in the military and went to Iraq. After six months, he was coming home for two weeks—and I was excited. I listened to friends as their husbands came home for the two-week furlough, and it was, "Oh, this is my chance.... He'll watch the kids, and I'm going to the spa." God let me wrestle about this, and I cried out to Him and said, Lord, You orchestrate these two weeks.

To prepare spiritually, I prayed about my goal: Lord, I want to fill my husband up to full and overflowing—only You can show me how to fill him up, spirit, soul, and body. Only You can show me how to fill him up so he's ready to go back to war for six more months.

God speaks personally, and He is a very practical God. I asked Him to plan these special two weeks, and I did what He led me to do to prepare for our time together. To prepare practically:

- *I wrote Caleb and asked him everything he wanted to eat while home. I shopped and bought everything needed for the two weeks.*
- *I bought seven bedroom outfits in seven different colors.*
- *I arranged with a friend whose husband was also home to swap children so we would each have twenty-four hours alone with our husband.*
- *I bought a massage book and studied it.*

When the children and I picked Caleb up at the airport, we brought him fresh-smelling civilian clothes to put on. When soldiers come home from war, they reek of death and destruction. It is horrible beyond anything I can describe to you. After changing, Caleb threw his uniform into the back of the van. When we came out of the restaurant, the stench in the van was so foul we had to air it out before we could drive home.

We got the kids in bed and sat on the couch and made out— just because we could! Even then I am saying, Lord, show me how to love him. Caleb's love language is physical touch, and the Lord had whispered to me, "Give him a bath." So into the tub Caleb went. I straddled the tub with my big sponge and began to cleanse the smells of war. And as I washed the odor of war away, I prayed to cleanse his soul from the spirit of death and destruction. As I washed his head and hair, I prayed, Lord, let nothing he has thought harm him. As I wiped his eyes, I prayed, Lord, let nothing he has seen stay in his heart. As I washed his ears, I prayed, Lord, let nothing he has heard touch his spirit. I washed and prayed over every part of my husband, begging God that nothing would take root, that all evil would be washed away.

After this spiritual and physical cleansing, I got in the bath with him, and then I said, "Honey, pick a color." The poor man had no idea what was going on so I told him seven colors and said, "Just pick one … you'll be glad you did."

I put on the bedroom outfit in his choice of color, and we made love five times in the first twenty-four hours he was home— and one of those lovemaking sessions lasted two hours! We cracked up—was this even physically possible?

During our twenty-four hours alone we pulled down the shades and said, "We can walk around naked. We can do anything we want—such joy … such freedom … such delight!"

One day I put my new massage techniques into practice and gave Caleb a full-body massage. He was so relaxed he slept for two hours. His comment, "That was amazing. I never slept like that in Iraq."

I had asked God to reveal how to love my special man for two weeks. I love how God answers so tenderly and specifically when we cry out to Him.

- *I cooked Caleb's favorite meals.*
- *Paraded in seven outfits in seven colors.*
- *Gave him a physical and spiritual cleansing.*
- *Became his personal massage therapist.*

Our two weeks were a supernatural feast of intimacy with the Lord and with one another.

But the day came when my husband and the children's father had to get on a plane again and fly off to the death and destruction of war. Had I loved him, spirit, soul, and body, so he was ready to return to war? Three days after he got back, he emailed me and said, "Thank you for the best two weeks of my life."

Krista created a stage where emotional and sexual intimacy could flourish. Her story is one of the most beautiful I have ever heard. She asked God, "How can I be a helper to Caleb during these two weeks?" Her focus was giving to him, but I think she received joy, love, appreciation, and delight in return.

You are called to be your husband's helper, but to do that you need help—help that only the Divine Helper can give. For a husband to love his wife with a sacrificial love is impossible—impossible unless the Holy Spirit gives him the power. For a wife to respect her husband unconditionally is also impossible—impossible unless the Holy Spirit gives her power.

Cry out to God! Fall to your knees and ask Him to give you the creativity, the power, the knowledge to be the helper He created you to be to your unique man.

Dangerous Prayer!

Lord, change my selfish heart. Work in me so I can truly learn to be a helper to my husband. Show me what encouragement and respect look like to him. I want to do my part to create emotional intimacy with him.

What Is It Like to Make Love with Me?

*Certainly sex can be "I will do that for you if you will
do this for me," but what a lonely arrangement.
A caress should say "I love you," not pay off a debt. An
embrace should fill the heart as well as the arms.*
Hugh and Gayle Prather, *Notes to Each Other*

*Thrills come at the beginning and do not last....
Let the thrill go ... and you will find you are
living in a world of new thrills.*
C. S. Lewis, *Mere Christianity*

*Couples who frequently pray together are twice as likely as those who
pray less often to describe their marriages as being highly romantic....
But get this—married couples who pray together are ninety
percent more likely to report higher satisfaction with their
sex lives than couples who don't pray together....
Prayer, because of the vulnerability it
demands, also draws a couple closer.*
Les and Leslie Parrott, "Skimming the Surface?"
Marriage Partnership

The camaraderie of best friends who are also lovers
seems twice as exciting and doubly precious.
Ed Wheat, *Love Life for Every Married Couple*

Insight 1: HOW DID WE GET WHERE WE ARE?

Have you ever heard a story and wondered if it was true or the figment of a lively imagination? This story caused me to wonder, but I've been assured that it actually happened. The names have been changed to protect the innocent and guilty, and as you read the story you will see why.

Jacki and Jon were engaged. They promised themselves they would wait to have sex until they were married, but as the wedding got closer, restraining themselves seemed impossible. They wanted to obey God—they wanted His best—but this was beyond hard. People's comments didn't help. "You mean you're both virgins? That's awful. Your honeymoon won't be any fun. You should sleep together now so you can enjoy your honeymoon."

Motivated by this advice and weakened by their own strong desires, Jacki and Jon set aside their resolve and decided to take the plunge. Jacki lived with her parents, so she and Jon chose a time when the house would be empty. When they had progressed to the "sans clothing" stage, the phone rang. Jacki answered and rolled her eyes as she listened to her mother's voice. Yes, she would go downstairs and turn off the iron that her mother had left on. Feeling playful, Jon laughingly picked up his naked fiancèe and carried her down the stairs. Halfway down, he tripped, and she ended up at the bottom of the stairs with a broken leg. As Jon rushed to Jacki's side, relatives and friends burst through the door shouting, "Surprise! We're having a party for you! We called and asked you to turn off the iron to be sure you were home!"

You can guess who was surprised. How do you explain that you really haven't "done it" yet? That the only reason you are both naked is because you were afraid sex was going to be such a scary deal—that you had to perform just right—and you didn't want your honeymoon ruined? Who would believe that? Jacki hobbled down the aisle a few weeks later with a cast on her leg.

It makes me sad that this couple felt so pressured about sex. Has our society so indoctrinated us through the fantasy machines of movies and television that Christian young people are afraid to wait for marriage because they fear they won't be able to perform adequately? Don't the women of the twenty-first century understand that the wedding night is only the beginning of a lifetime of growing together in the intimacy of sexual love?

This story is just one of many I've heard that bear truth to this fact: God's women are confused about sexual intimacy in marriage. Since writing *Intimate Issues* in 1999 with my wonderful friend Lorraine Pintus, I have talked to thousands of women of all ages about their sexual intimacy in marriage. It's not just unmarried women who are confused; wives are as well. Many wives are:

- Afraid of sexual intimacy
- Disappointed in sexual intimacy
- Hindered by guilt over their wrong choices
- Confused over what a godly and sensuous wife looks like
- Ready to forget the whole thing

Where did these confused, disappointed, fearful, guilt-ridden mindsets originate? How did we get where we are?

I believe that our distorted ideas about sexual intimacy are due to three intimacy robbers: Satan, the media, and the Church. Let me explain.

Intimacy robber 1: Satan. If I had to name the top intimacy robber for women today, it would be the Enemy of your soul. *Devil* is a translation of the Greek word *diabolos,* which means "slanderer" or "accuser." The Devil is a murderer and a liar (John 8:44), an accuser (Rev. 12:10), and an adversary (1 Peter 5:8). He's also called the thief, and one of his targets is your sexuality. He tells you lies like, "You can't be godly if you are abandoned and intoxicated by delight in your husband's caresses," and "God just isn't pleased with you in the bedroom; you better be uptight, prim. Don't get carried away."

Lies, lies, lies. Straight from the mouth of the Liar.

Two of Satan's greatest lies are:

> 1. If you made mistakes in this area, forget it. There is no hope for you.
>
> 2. If evil was done to you by others, forget it. There is no hope for you.

The Liar sneers, "You blew it—look at all the sexual partners you've had. Remember that abortion? Sex can never be good for you. You're used goods, honey. Give up—your sexuality is beyond repair...."

But the Redeemer declares, "Yes, My child, you blew up, but it is for this that I died. I took all your sexual sin on Me. YOU ARE FORGIVEN! YOU ARE FREE! Now, My daughter, delight in your freedom—listen to My Word. It is truth."

The Liar shouts, "How can there be hope for you? Men used you—abused you. Do you think you can ever think differently about sex? About a man's body? Sex is messy, you are messy—scarred to your core. Give up—there is no hope...."

The Healer comes. He embraces you and tenderly whispers: "I can make *all* things new. Even your sexuality. I love you, precious one. Trust Me!"

Intimacy robber 2: the media. Running a close second to the Liar is the media and culture. Television, books, magazines, billboards, and hundreds of thousands of websites *overemphasize* sex and exploit the female body. Nothing is private. The message is this: sex anytime, anywhere, with anyone—hook up, hop into bed—it's just physical, and it feels soooooooo good!

Every time Viagra or Cialis ads come on during a football game, I think: *Twelve-year-old boys are snickering about four-hour erections. Young girls are trying to figure out what it all means.* It makes me sad; it makes me sick. If I feel this way, I can only imagine how God feels.

Make no mistake: The media is a fantasy machine. They project a larger-than-life view of sex in order to promote the fantasy. Remember, the goal of the media is to leave you breathless and wide-eyed, not better informed. The cops and robbers don't shoot real bullets in those movies, either. It's an elaborately staged setup.

Lindsey bought into the media's lies. She told me:

> *I see it now. I believed lies. The movies portrayed sex as always steamy, romantic, and fun—pleasure was always off the charts amazing. When it wasn't like this for us, I took a step back from intimacy in my mind and heart. After kids, sex was something I "put up with." I took more steps away. Without saying it out loud, inwardly I gave up and believed we'd never go to a place called "exciting sex."*

Lindsey felt sexual intimacy should always be as exciting as Hollywood's. Other Christian women go the opposite direction. They look at the degradation of sexuality portrayed by the media and, revolted, inwardly choose to believe that sex is something evil and not to be enjoyed. Meanwhile, the second robber—the media—gathers his stolen goods and thinks nothing of those who suffer the loss.

The truth is, your love life is the real thing and, pursued with elan, can provide infinitely better pleasure and intimacy than any manufactured fantasy.

Intimacy robber 3: the Church. The third thief is not so blatant in her actions. Her stealth is disguised with noble words and pious ideas. And in truth, the motivation behind her thefts is not dishonorable. Beginning with the early Church fathers and continuing through the centuries, the Church hoped to stifle immorality and inappropriate sex but instead stifled beautiful and appropriate sex in marriage. Listen to the voices cascading down through the centuries:

- Augustine allowed that sex is good, but that passion and desire are sin.[1]
- "The Holy Spirit leaves the room when a married couple has sex, even if they do it without passion"—Peter Lombard, theologian (circa 1100–1164).
- Martin Luther wrote: "Intercourse is never without sin; but God excuses it by his grace because the estate of marriage is his work."[2]
- In her book of encouragement to new brides, a pastor's wife in the late 1800s gave this sterling advice: "One cardinal rule of marriage should never be forgotten: give little, give seldom and above all give grudgingly. Otherwise what could have been a proper marriage could become an orgy of sexual lust."[3]

Oh, brother! What a positive, exciting, and uplifting picture of sexual intimacy!

The Church gave wrong advice. You probably never heard "Give little, give seldom and above all else, give grudgingly" from a godly pastor's wife, but many Christian wives have been influenced by distorted messages filtered down through the centuries. Sadly, they have adopted an incorrect sexual mind-set without even realizing where they got it.

We've looked at how we got where we are, but what we have to discern is: How do we get where we want to be?

Maybe your sexual intimacy with your husband is already where you want it to be. Your sexual relationship has been a dream—no past mistakes, no harm done to you. You came into marriage excited about sex, and the ride has been incredible. If this is your story, I shout "Hurrah" and rejoice with you! You are blessed. Thank God!

But many women have a different story, and they are nowhere close to where they want to be. With all the confusion and misinformation, what does it look like for you to become God's picture of an exciting lover? How do you exchange these harmful attitudes for God's attitude that you are to enjoy beautiful, free, abandoned delight—and exquisite pleasure—with your husband? The first thing you need to do is this: *Shut your eyes and open your ears.* Refuse to listen to the lies of the Enemy. Stop looking at the media. Refuse to listen to any source that feeds misinformation. Instead, start looking only at God and His viewpoint. And where is His perspective? In His Word. So open your Bible. Open wide your heart. Fling open your spiritual eyes and ears. God has some gifts that He longs for you to open. Each of these gifts will encourage you in answering the Dangerous Question: *What is it like to make love with me?* Keep reading to find out more.

Insight 2: OPEN THE GIFT OF SEXUAL PASSION

Picture in your mind a beautiful, big, shocking-pink gift bag with your name emblazoned across it in gold letters. Your Father God has this gift just for you, and He wants you to open it. What is the gift? Holy, pure, exciting, intoxicating sex.

Listen deeply to God's Word. He declares that He gave you the gift of sexual passion for *intimate oneness* and *pleasure.* Join me in imagining God at His creation. Adam and Eve are created in His image, and Adam has jumped up and down with excitement over the woman God has brought to him. Her skin, her hair, her smile … Adam is beside himself with joy, but God has one more surprise: "My children, I have designed your bodies so that they can literally become one. I've given you a tangible way to bridge the loneliness you will feel, and to enable you, whenever you choose, to lose yourselves in one another. And as amazing as it seems, this sexual oneness will picture for you the spiritual oneness I want to have with you—a holiness shrouds your sexual intimacy."

While the Genesis record does not mention God saying this to Adam and Eve, the words echo His intent. Does this seem "out there"? It's not. Look with me at Ephesians 5:31–32.

A man [shall] leave his father and mother, and shall cleave to his
wife; and the two shall become one flesh. This mystery is great: but
I speak in regard of Christ and of the church. (ASV)

In verse 31, Paul quotes from Genesis about leaving, cleaving, and becoming one flesh sexually. It is a reference to the act of sexual intercourse. Then Paul expounds on the great mystery of sexual oneness in verse 32. It's as if he says, "My children, revel in the intimacy, delight in the ecstasy, and when you experience this closest union on earth, lift your eyes and realize this is the degree of spiritual union God longs to have with you."

Do you understand? Do you see? God's gift to you contains a physical joy that speaks of a spiritual joy. His holiness infuses your intimate oneness with your husband. Close your eyes, bow to Him in worship, and thank Him for His gift.

God gave you the gift of passion so that you and your husband can experience intimate oneness. He also gave it to you so you could share exquisite pleasure.

God is for pleasure! He is very specific so that we know His heart and see what is good for our hearts. Let's look at two passages that declare God's perspective on sexual pleasure.

The first passage is from Proverbs 5. This is instruction from a father to his son, begging him to stay away from sexual pleasure outside of marriage (5:1–14). Then in the verses following, the father entices his son by saying there are unbelievable, amazing, exquisite sexual pleasures within marriage.

Drink water from your own cistern
  And fresh water from your own well....
Let your fountain be blessed,
  And rejoice in the wife of your youth.
As a loving hind and a graceful doe,

Let her breasts satisfy you at all times;
Be exhilarated always with her love. (vv. 15, 18–19)

What do you see in these verses?

I see pleasure.

I see delight.

I see fun.

I see freedom, abandonment, intoxication, ecstasy.

What do these words say to me as a wife?

I am to be a continual, flowing fountain of pleasure for my husband. I am to be a loving doe, a graceful deer; so cute, so soft that my husband wants to reach out and touch, to fondle and cuddle me. And there's more.

God's Word encourages my husband and yours to:

1. Let your wife's breasts satisfy you always.

2. Be captivated, exhilarated, intoxicated always with her sexual love.

This straightforward passage doesn't leave much to the imagination, does it? As a wife, I am to be a continual, delightful source of refreshing pleasure to this husband I love. I am to intoxicate him with my sexual love—always. That means every year of our marriage. Of course, all that I am to be and do goes for him, too. He is to intoxicate me as well. Amen and amen.

I see holiness in this passage. God delights in encouraging the husband and wife to rejoice in their sexual intimacy. He places His stamp of approval on it—making it holy—so I add holiness to the pleasure, delight, fun, freedom, abandonment, intoxication, and ecstasy I see in these verses. I bow and worship my God. He combines His holiness with sexual pleasure.

Now for the second passage that describes the pleasure a husband and wife are to experience in their sexual union. Put on your sunglasses—this will make your eyes pop. It is beautiful. It is sensuous. It is romantic. It is erotic. Okay, did I just apply words like *sensuous* and *erotic* to God's Word? Yep, I did. Those are the words that apply.

> *How beautiful are your sandaled feet,*
>   *O queenly maiden.*
> *Your rounded thighs are like jewels,*
>   *the work of a skilled craftsman.*
> *Your navel is perfectly formed*
>   *like a goblet filled with mixed wine.*
> *Between your thighs lies a mound of wheat*
>   *bordered with lilies.*
> *Your breasts are like two fawns,*
>   *twin fawns of a gazelle.*
> *Your neck is as beautiful as an ivory tower.*
> *Your eyes are like the sparkling pools in Heshbon*
>   *by the gate of Bath-rabbim.*
> *Your nose is as fine as the tower of Lebanon*
>   *overlooking Damascus.*
> *Your head is as majestic as Mount Carmel,*
>   *and the sheen of your hair radiates royalty.*
>   *The king is held captive by its tresses.*
> *Oh, how beautiful you are!*
>   *How pleasing, my love, how full of delights!*
> *You are slender like a palm tree,*
>   *and your breasts are like its clusters of fruit.*
> *I said, "I will climb the palm tree*
>   *and take hold of its fruit."*
> *May your breasts be like grape clusters,*
>   *and the fragrance of your breath like apples.*
> *May your kisses be as exciting as the best wine,*
>   *flowing gently over lips and teeth. (Song 7:1–9 NLT)*

In these verses Solomon describes his bride's dancing feet and progresses up her scantily clothed body. Either she is nude or in a shimmering, sheer garment, because Solomon can see every part of her body. He comments on her swaying thighs, saying they are like jewels, the perfect work of a skilled craftsman. Her "navel" is filled with mixed wine. (Sorry, but *navel* is a wrong translation. The translator could not bring himself to say the part of her body between her thighs and belly. Bet you can figure it out for yourself.) Her breasts are like twin fawns (once again, we see the imagery of a soft, touchable baby deer). The lover mentions his bride's breasts three times in verses 3, 7, and 8. He is delighted and intoxicated with the glory of his wife's curvy body as she passes before his eyes.

What do I see in these verses?

I see creativity.

I see seduction.

I see sexual adventure.

I see a wife who knows her man.

Solomon's bride knew God created her husband to be aroused through his eyes, so she entices, seduces, and delights him with her body. She knows her body is a gift for her husband.

I hope that as you read of the beauty and holiness in these biblical pictures, you grew excited about traveling with your husband to this place of joy, abandonment, and adventure. If so, you are feeling exactly what God wants you to feel.

If not, you may feel more like Claire, who was initially filled with fear and panic at the thought of journeying to deeper sexual intimacy. Let me share her story with you.

Claire doesn't know who her father is because her mother was with so many men. What's unimaginable to me is that this mother allowed her daughter to be photographed as part of the child pornography industry. Claire says, "I can still hear the photographer's words, 'Now smile, pretty honey … you're such a pretty little thing.' As I became a teenager, I felt viciously robbed of something that was mine to give away. I was ruined, scarred, and knew I could never get married."

When Claire's husband, Derek, first asked her to marry him, she told him no. But he wouldn't give up and asked until she finally said, "Yes, I'll marry you and just have to deal with the sex part." On their wedding day, Claire didn't experience the normal anticipation and excitement that a bride should feel. Instead she felt like "a vacant carcass dressed up in a pretty white dress."

Her incredible man didn't scare easily, and it was a good thing, because when they made love, Claire had panic attacks. She knew she wasn't being raped, but couldn't get over feeling used. She had a long list of places Derek couldn't touch, things she wouldn't do. This was their sex life for several years. She cried out to the Lord for help. *Do something, God. I'll do anything.*

Claire signed them up for a Family Life "Weekend to Remember," where they had to rate each other on passion. Derek rated her as a 2 on a scale of 10, but she knew in her heart she was a minus 2. At that conference Claire bought a copy of *Intimate Issues.* I asked her to tell you what happened next.

> *When I read the title of the first chapter, "What Does God Think About Sex?" my first thought was, God thinks about sex? Why would He do that? I read the chapter and said out loud to God, This can't be true. I determined to read it a second time and looked up all the Scripture references and wrote them down. God, IT IS TRUE! What have I done?*
>
> *I began meeting with a spiritual mentor and reading the Song of Solomon. I told my mentor, "Either every word of the Bible is true, or none of it is true. I can't pick and choose what I accept." I remember reading Song of Solomon 4:16, and I was shocked. I asked my mentor what this verse meant, and she said, "What do you think it means?" I admitted that it looked like it*

was talking about oral sex between the bride and groom, but that couldn't be true. After all, I had told my husband that oral sex wasn't just wrong … it was a horrid sin.

The more I read God's Word, the more I saw His picture of beauty and delight in sexual intimacy. But how could I get there? I had told God, If it is in Your Word, I'll believe it and do it. *I embraced God's view of sex in my mind and heart and told God I longed for His hand of blessing over us. So I re-created our wedding night. I sent our kids to some friends, pulled our mattress into the living room, and set out candles and draped fabric over the bed to create a canopy.*

Derek walked into the dream he thought would never be his reality and heard these words from the wife he had sacrificially loved all these years: "Honey, I've been concentrating for these years on how I was robbed, but I see now that you were severely robbed too. I never fully gave myself to you. Tonight I give you all of me. My body is yours to touch, kiss, fondle in any way you desire—and your body is mine."

That night I took what was mine and gave my husband what was his.

My friend Claire is my hero, a military wife I deeply respect. She cried out to the Lord for help and said, "I'll do anything." She made a secret choice to believe God's perspective on sex, and then she put into practice what she had learned by re-creating their wedding night.

Claire makes me ask hard questions. I didn't suffer sexual abuse. I didn't have my mind and body scarred. But do I seek God's truth about my sexual relationship like Claire did? Do I take hard steps because they are the right steps? Do you?

God gave the gift of sexual passion. It is His gift to you. Opening this gift will encourage your heart and bring you a step closer to being able to answer the question, *What is it like to make love with me?* with this response: "My husband is blessed to have me as his lover."

Insight 3: OPEN THE GIFT OF GOD'S BLESSING

Carly came up to me at an Intimate Issues Conference and said, "Linda, we have a big picture of Jesus over our bed. Every time we make love, we turn the picture around. It just doesn't seem right to have Jesus watching!" Right … and turning the picture around is sure to keep God out of the bedroom!

There is probably a little of this woman in all of us. No matter how we twist our mind around it, sex just seems too earthy to really have God's blessing. The sights, the sounds of sex, just don't square with the spiritual.

Did you know that God gives His blessing on your sexual oneness with your husband? Picture a shimmering violet gift bag, your name written across it in deep purple letters. This gift is for you, God's daughter. The gift of His blessing frees you to give yourself permission for passion.

We see God's blessing beautifully displayed in the Song of Solomon. In chapter 4 the bride and groom have just consummated their marriage. Their lovemaking has been steamy, very steamy. Listen to the bride's invitation to her lover. Somehow I don't think you'll have trouble figuring out what the word *garden* refers to.

> *Awake, north wind!*
> *Rise up, south wind!*
> *Blow on my garden*
> *and spread its fragrance all around.*
> *Come into your garden, my love;*
> *taste its finest fruits. (Song 4:16 NLT)*

The new husband answers that he has come into his garden and been enraptured with its delicacies (Song 5:1). Then something unexpected happens. A third presence is in the bridal chamber. The One who enters into this sacred chamber is the couple's Creator God. As He lovingly walks over to the bridal bed, the bride and groom lay naked and unashamed in one another's arms, delighting in the afterglow of lovemaking. It is as if their Holy God extends His hand of blessing over them and declares a benediction: "Eat, friends; drink and imbibe deeply, O lovers" (Song 5:1).[4]

Oh, I love God's blessing! In Hebrew, it literally means "to feast." The Almighty, Holy One of heaven and earth says:

> *Have a love feast!*
> *Eat! Drink! Taste deeply of the exquisite pleasures of loving one*
> *   another.*
> *Enjoy My gift to the fullest.*
> *I bless your sexual intimacy.*

The Holy God, the Redeemer and Healer, blesses *your* earthy, naked, and unashamed intimacy and ecstasy. Will you receive His personal blessing for you? Jesus' picture can stay over the bed. God sees. God knows. God blesses.

Are you wondering, *How can my husband and I receive God's blessing?* If so, it is not difficult. The next time you and your husband make love, as you are basking in the afterglow of your oneness, imagine together that your Creator walks over to your bed, extends His hand of blessing over you and says, "Feast, lovers! Taste deeply of the exquisite pleasures of loving one another." Thank Him for His blessing on your intimacy. (If you feel your husband could not enter into this blessing, you, alone, can imagine God coming to bless you and receive His hand of blessing.)

I have been surprised and excited to discover what happens when women open the gift of God's blessing on their sexual intimacy. Read what happened to Megan.

> *When we married, my husband was a virgin; I was not. Even*
> *when we were dating I often thought, I don't deserve this guy,*

because I'd had sex with several previous boyfriends. I was a Christian and knew that God reserved sexual intimacy for couples in a committed marriage relationship, but I had sex anyway. Then I got pregnant. I was furious! I didn't want a baby now. I had a budding career! Besides, if my mom and dad ever found out, they'd kill me. My boyfriend wanted to make things work, but as I marched off to an abortion clinic, I yelled over my shoulder at him, "Get out of my life. I never want to see you again."

After that I didn't want anything to do with men. Then I met Kirby at our church singles' group. He was such a godly man. We started dating. He made it clear that he was committed to waiting until marriage for sex, and so we did. During the first few years of marriage, sex was pretty good, but as time went by, I realized that I was just "going through the motions." After we had kids, my desire for sex all but vanished. I didn't understand this until a Right to Life Sunday at church, when they showed a picture of an eight-week-old baby in the womb. The baby waved her tiny hand, and it was as if she called out to me: "Hi, Mom." I lost it. The abortion had been years earlier, but it wasn't until that moment that I'd come face-to-face with what I'd done: I'd killed my own baby. I grieved for weeks. I cried out to God to forgive me. I'd asked Him to forgive in the past, and I believe He had, but truthfully, I'd never forgiven myself. I don't think I could have because I hadn't faced the breadth and depth of my sin. I'd stuffed my emotions and punished myself with subconscious thoughts like: I don't deserve this man. I don't deserve to enjoy sex because I am such a horrible person.

Grieving the full impact of my sin brought me to a place of healing. I actually fell more deeply in love with Jesus because I understood more fully what my sin had cost Him. And, I fell more deeply in love with my husband because he hadn't condemned me. It took many

more years, but finally, I gave myself permission for passion. My hus-
band will tell you that this decision has made all the difference in the
world. I'm a free woman now, both in bed and outside of it.

Megan makes me search my heart and ask hard questions. Like many (most?) women, I made wrong choices in the sexual area, but I never suffered the pain of aborting my baby. I didn't live with the consequences of that choice. I didn't have to relearn sexual intimacy after many years of marriage. I watched Megan work hard to come to the place of freedom she lives in today. Do I work as hard? Do you?

Have you received God's blessing? When you do, you'll be another step closer to being able to say that making love to you is *good*.

Insight 4: OFFER THE GIFT OF YOUR BODY

Again, picture a gift. This one is a brilliant red. The name across it is not yours, but your husband's. This gift, which will bring pleasure and delight to you both, is one you will give to him.

The apostle Paul discusses marriage in 1 Corinthians 7, and in the first five verses, he deals with sexual needs. For many years I have seen the beauty of the third gift hidden in the words of 1 Corinthians 7:4. Let's look at how different translations of the Bible render this verse for a deeper understanding of Paul's message:

> *The wife does not have authority over her own body, but the hus-*
> *band does; and likewise also the husband does not have authority*
> *over his own body, but the wife does. (1 Cor. 7:4)*

The Amplified Bible adds clarity:

> *For the wife does not have [exclusive] authority and control over*
> *her own body, but the husband [has his rights]; likewise also the*

husband does not have [exclusive] authority and control over his own body, but the wife [has her rights].

The Message adds special beauty and insight:

The marriage bed must be a place of mutuality—the husband seeking to satisfy his wife, the wife seeking to satisfy her husband. Marriage is not a place to "stand up for your rights." Marriage is a decision to serve the other, whether in bed or out.

Wow. One way a wife ministers to her husband is to delight him in the bedroom. I believe this deep ministry begins with giving your body as a gift to your husband. Ideally, a wife gives over authority of her body—gives it as a gift to her husband—on their wedding night, but the reality is that in many cases this does not happen. That was Kathy's story.

After telling her about the beautiful picture in 1 Corinthians 7:4, I asked Kathy if she had ever given over authority of her body to her husband. Her surprised look and silence said no. But I was the one surprised when Kathy told me that on Valentine's Day she had wrapped herself in ribbon and a bow and offered her body as a gift to her husband. She told him that before there had been lots of ifs and noes because she had control of her body, but no longer—her body was his. He was so touched by her gesture that he wept.

A wife can be creative in how she chooses to give her husband the gift of her body.

- Nancy more than shocked her husband when she presented her body in a red bow on their fiftieth anniversary. Jon said it was the best gift he ever received.
- Julie donned her wedding dress and said, "Let's start over.… I want to do it right."
- Mariah felt only a bow went too far for her, so she pinned a yellow bow to her nightgown. Later, her husband asked for the

yellow bow—took it to work and taped it on the inside of his desk, where no one could see it, but his foot would touch it and remind him. Who says men aren't sentimental?

- Becca planned a special romantic weekend away that included lovely music, candles, and a walk by the river. The menu of special food delighted their senses, and the dessert was Becca, wrapped in a chocolate-adorned ribbon.

What does it look like for you to give your body as a gift to your husband?

First, it is a secret choice between you and God. It is an act of your will.

Second, you choose the time, place, and way to give this gift.

What difference will it make in you if you offer this gift to your husband?

If you see your body as "mine," you decide when, where, and how much you'll give to your husband sexually. But if you give your body as a gift to your husband, you'll want him to enjoy the gift. It is *his*—a gift for him to delight in; it is no longer yours. This choice changes everything. For me, the offering of this gift has meant I hold nothing back. I open myself to experience fullness of joy in our sexual intimacy.

Some wives are *very* uncomfortable with the idea of giving authority or control of their body to anyone. Sometimes this stems from plain-old selfishness; however, women who have been sexually abused struggle with anyone having control of their body. Does the idea of your husband having control over your body stir strong emotions inside you? It did for my friend Sadie, and yet God healed her wounds and transformed their marriage. I've asked her to tell you her incredible story.

> *My husband's chest was wet with tears; mine, not his. This wasn't the first time in our thirteen years of marriage that tears had fallen after making love, but this night was different. These weren't tears flowing out of shame and horrific images of the sexual abuse I'd*

experienced through my growing-up years. These were tears of joy and thankfulness, springing from a grateful heart to my Savior and Redeemer—the One who could do anything, the One who had healed me.

After Charlie and I were married, it didn't take long for us to realize that intimacy wasn't going to be easy. Our first years of marriage were marked by his need and desire for something I couldn't and didn't want to give. My sexuality had been shattered, and my view of intimacy terribly distorted.

I experienced some healing, enough that we settled for tolerable intimacy. Tolerable was good considering where we had come from. I'd been told that sexually wounded women can't completely recover and to be glad for the progress I had made. There wasn't joy. There wasn't freedom. But at least we could have sex on a semiregular basis, and most times I didn't cry.

After living with tolerable intimacy for a number of years, I felt the Lord began to nudge my heart to believe Him for something beyond tolerable. I sensed He was asking me to believe that He could take me beyond tolerable to a place of complete freedom. I made a firm resolve that even though I couldn't imagine it, even though I had no strategy of my own to make it happen, I would at least believe my God could do it.

I began to memorize verses from the Song of Solomon that countered the thoughts and feelings that flooded me when Charlie and I were intimate. I went through the motions, silently reciting what I hoped I would actually feel someday. Time and time again I prayed, I cried, I struggled, I doubted, and then asked for faith to believe God again. But a little bit at a time, I began to notice a shift in my thoughts and attitudes. I began to feel desires I hadn't felt before. I began to find pleasure in things that before had made my skin crawl. And I watched my husband's eyebrows go up further and further as he asked things like, "Sooooo, is passionate Sadie here to stay?"

Finally a time came when I was able to make love with my husband without shame. I lay in Charlie's arms and wept over the Lord's mercy toward me. My Healer stood next to me. I felt His smile over me and heard the whisper I had longed for so many years to hear. "My sweet daughter, you are free." Little by little, the Lord did a miracle in my sexuality, and now I am free from tolerable intimacy.

Since these things many months ago, I've been able to stand before my husband wrapped in a bow and truly give myself to him without fear or shame. Charlie and I are delighting in what our Redeemer did for us—the impossible! We are having fun!

Sadie is my hero. She is a prayer counselor and a woman I deeply respect. She believed God for something beyond tolerable sex. She memorized verses from the Song of Solomon. She mentally repeated the verses during sexual intimacy. She prayed, she cried, she struggled and asked God for faith to believe again.

I have not lived through Sadie's deep pain. I have not had to live with tolerable sex. Sadie's journey causes me to search my heart. How many verses have I memorized about Jody's and my intimacy? Do I beg God for more in our sex life? Where would I be if I tried as hard as Sadie to make the most of God's gift of sex? Where would you be?

Giving your body as a gift to your husband is the third step you take so that when you ask yourself, "What is it like to make love with me?" your answer is, "Great! Amazing!"

Insight 5: WHAT DOES EVERYDAY LOVEMAKING LOOK LIKE?

I opened all three gifts, and I can say, "Jody thinks it is fun and exciting to make love with me." Does that mean that every day, through every season, sex is wonderful and that I do it all right? Of course not.

I remember one of the hardest times. Three small children in three years left me beyond exhausted. I was trying to be a good lover but still failed miserably. Jody used every creative bone in his body and made me a very special gift. He created a prescription bottle of fifty-two pills in capsule form, each empty capsule filled, not with medication, but with a creative sexual surprise for each week of the year. The label on the bottle read:

> *For Linda Dillow, prescribed by Dr. Joseph Dillow to alleviate stress.*
> *Take one each week.*

This gift took time to make:
- A trip to a drugstore to get fifty-two capsules. (I can just hear the pharmacist, "What do you want them for?")
- Much time, thought, and creativity to think up and type fifty-two clever ideas, one for each week of the year.
- Much more time and dexterity to cut fifty-two clever ideas into strips and roll them to fit in the tiny capsules. (And this from a husband whose strong suit is not the practical.)

No wonder Jody was disappointed and very hurt when I would forget to take my pill, when my excitement about his special gift was at the same level as my diminished sexual desire.

So I didn't handle this right. And you won't always do things right. But when your husband knows that you *want* to make your sexual intimacy fun and filled with delight, it doesn't hurt so much when you have a "bad sex day" now and then. Lots of times I did do it right. I wrote the following reflection in my journal about the total oneness I felt after a special time of lovemaking.

> *I awoke in the middle of the night. Everything was dark. I could hear Jody breathing next to me. I snuggled up to him and felt the*

warmth again of being close. I lay with my arm around him, reliving the beauty and incredible erotic feelings we had experienced together last night. It was as if our oneness reached a new height and depth. It's all so tied together. Talking and sharing our deep feelings for an hour before making love gave us such an emotional oneness that carried over to our physical oneness.

Experiencing the incredible physical ecstasy with one another is like the "frosting on the cake." It binds us close and adds spice to our spiritual, emotional, and intellectual oneness. I laugh inside at how some would not believe two—not so young people—a missionary and his wife no less!—could so love sex! The lingering feelings of joy and love, of deep satisfaction and peace, fill me with thankfulness for this man, my husband. I find myself here in the dark beside him praising God for His gift of oneness, thanking Him for the delights of sexual joy, and asking Him to show me anew how to cherish this man He has given me.

Lovemaking should include laughter, fun, teasing, joy, and variety. *God gave sex for pleasure, and pleasure is good.* It's not wrong or ungodly to delight in each other's bodies.

Listen to another woman's description of a night of fun and pleasure with her husband:

I woke up this morning laughing to myself. No one ever told me sex could be so much fun. It was hot out last night, so Dan and I decided to pull our mattress out onto our closed-in veranda. We brought glasses of cool lemonade and lay on the mattress sipping our drinks, looking at the stars and talking. I felt like a seventh grader at a slumber party! Dan said he was still hot, so off came his clothes. And then, he decided I'd feel cooler without mine. We buried our faces in our pillows because we were laughing so hard.

Making love in the fresh air was a new sensation. I liked it! We muffled our giggles for fear the neighbors would hear. The sensual feelings were so strong, the slight breeze on our bodies so nice after the hot apartment. I'm glad sex can be such fun and feel so good.

And for those who think life keeps getting in the way …

Our lives are so busy that lately we have to schedule sex—I never read this in a book but it works for us. We put sex down for Friday evening, but Zach's soccer game got rained out and rescheduled for that night. So we rescheduled sex for Saturday morning, but Lucy woke up screaming with an ear infection at 5:00 a.m., and then there was a mad rush to the doctor. On my way out the door I said to my disappointed hubby, "Maybe Sunday night?" But then, Saturday afternoon, a miracle occurred. One child was at a birthday party, and the other two went down for naps at the same time. I grabbed my husband, he grabbed me, and we raced into the bedroom for ten minutes of hot, steamy sex. All that delayed anticipation actually worked magic.

It makes me sad that some Christian women can't enjoy sex on the veranda. The sights, the sounds, the sensations are too *earthy*. And sex in the middle of the afternoon, with kids in the next room? No way! These women can enjoy sex only if they incorporate something spiritual into the physical, such as praying together before making love or singing the doxology together as they orgasm. (Yes, that is for real.)

Please understand. There is nothing wrong with singing praises to God, thanking Him for the gift of sex, or with praying before you make love. These spiritual actions can infuse deep meaning into the physical actions. I just want to emphasize that you don't have to "be spiritual" for God to bless your lovemaking. God has already given you permission to enjoy sex.

It's okay to tease all day long about what's coming later—to laugh, to take a shower together, and to slip into bed or on the floor and pleasure, pleasure, pleasure.

It's okay to grab your husband after he's been away on a trip and love one another quickly, saying, "More to come tonight after the kids are in bed."

It's okay to comfort your husband when he is stressed or depressed by giving love to him physically.

Give yourself permission to enjoy sex. Experiment. Enjoy variety. Don't expect or demand that there always be an hour of emotional sharing before lovemaking. Each time together takes on its own uniqueness, just as each time we talk with our best friend is a different conversation. Find new ways to talk with your husband about your lovemaking so you don't end up in a rut, like poor Emily, who wrote this on my survey:

> *Every time it's the same. He touches me for five minutes, always in the same way. I touch him briefly, he enters me, moves in and out, and it's over. Wham, bam, thank you, ma'am. It's no wonder I don't like sex.*

How awful! I'd be bored too! Lovemaking can be playful and fun, and it can be intense, with tears of deep release and emotion. Incredibly, it can create a child and bring deep oneness or great physical pleasure. It can bring comfort and release tension. Sex is God's gift to His people. Enjoy His gift. Use it wisely, use it freely—and use it often.

Dangerous Prayer!

> *God, I need You! Please show me how to embrace Your perspective from Your Word and give me the courage and strength by Your Spirit to take the hard steps. I long to give my husband the gift of my body, freely and without reservation—to give completely and never take it back again. Please show me practically how to do*

this. I want to be able to answer the Dangerous Question, "What is it like to make love to me?" with, "It is fun, filled with pleasure, and brings deep intimacy to our oneness."

The Worst Things I Did for My Marriage

I was selfish and had an affair. (Married twenty-one years)

I was busy with all that life, family, and ministry generates, so too tired to have energy for sex. (Married twenty-three years)

I settled for a level of intimacy that is far below what I want and what my husband needs. (Married twenty-four years)

I withheld my body from my husband as punishment. (Married twenty-four years)

I withheld sex from my husband because I didn't respect or understand what an important need this was for him. (Married twelve years)

I hung on to the romantic idea of my first boyfriend and lover for twenty-seven years. (Married twenty-seven years)

Been complacent with my husband sexually. (Married thirty years)

Watching porn with my husband. It is not good for our intimacy. (Married nine years)

Innocently "catching up" with an old friend of the opposite sex, which led to confusion and temptation. It made me wonder if maybe I had married the wrong guy. (Married ten years)

Not being sensitive to how long it goes between times of making love. (Married twenty-eight years)

Allowed my past to bind and hinder what God has for me in our sex life. (Married twenty years)

My husband is a doctor and has to get up early for work. He has asked me time and time again to get ready earlier for bed. I don't, and I know it hurts him. (Married thirty-three years)

The Best Things I Did for My Marriage

Been willing to meet his sexual need every other day or at least every third day (no longer) because we've discussed his needs. I had to have a small calendar in the night stand and draw a smiley face on the days we made love. (Married eighteen years)

I am willing and eager for sex every day (or more than once a day!). My question is … why not now? (Married nine years)

I put on my calendar specific times each week for having a rendezvous with my husband to meet his sexual needs, so that he can look forward to our time. If there is going to be a conflict on the schedule for these set times, I arrange another time ahead of the conflict. (Married thirty-seven years)

Realizing that his sexual needs are not selfish, but given from God, and not seeing it as just my duty to fill them, but rather something we experience together. (Married nine years)

Allowing my body to be a source of pleasure and comfort while doing my best to be responsive even when I'm not aroused. (Married five months)

Being willing to work on my issues and be healed of my own sexual sin. (Married thirteen years)

Being honest with my husband about temptation rather than letting it lead me into adultery. (Married ten years)

To ask for what I really need in making love. He really wants to please me. (Married thirty-three years)

Got my husband's porn addiction out in the open—been loving and shown grace toward him. (Married one year)

Got counseling and came under the healing authority of God's wings! (Married twenty years)

*Without a doubt the best thing was to agree early in the marriage to the "3 Ds" when we were apart. No **drinking**, no **dancing**, no **developing** friendships with people of the opposite sex. My husband was deployed a lot as a Special Forces soldier. By both of us following the 3 D rules, we never worried about falling into temptation because of long separations. We never wondered and worried. (Married twenty-three years)*

Why Do I Want to Stay Mad at You?

Over the long run, love's power to forgive is
stronger than hate's power to get even.
Lewis B. Smedes, *Forgive and Forget*

The Puritans called marriage "the little church
within the church." In marriage, every day
you love, and every day you forgive. It is an
ongoing sacrament—love and forgiveness.
Bill Moyers, *The Power of Myth*

Lord, when we are wrong, make us willing to change,
and when we are right, make us easy to live with.
Peter Marshall

Insight 1: IT FEELS GOOD TO HOLD A GRUDGE

Twenty young Texas wives sat around the room, unsure about what to expect. They were from different churches and didn't know each other, but had come together to read an early draft of this book and to do the Bible study. (See page 209.) During the weeks that they met together, the Spirit of

God came in an unusual way and opened their hearts to share some very private things with one another.

The week they studied forgiveness, the leader passed out 3 x 5 cards and asked these wives to write down their answers to the question *Why do I want to stay mad at you?* When I read their answers, I was amazed. These women were tuned into their emotions and their motives.

> *Staying mad is easier than forgiving. Anger justifies and comforts me after an offense. If I remain angry then I have no room in my mind to see fault in myself. If I remain angry, my heart can be so full of blame there's no room for conviction.*

> *U R unrepentant! U cheated—I forgave, I pursued you with God's love—you rejected me! I express my pain, U show no compassion. I stand by your side—U continue 2 pursue other women. I am willing 2 change—to do WHATEVER IT TAKES, U R willing 2 do NOTHING!*

> *I can't forgive you for constantly choosing work over me, because it makes me feel unloved and not appreciated; like you don't care enough about me.*

> *You have hurt me so deeply. I want to hurt you, too. I do not feel safe with you. When I stay mad I can just give up—it's never going to work or be different. It is hopeless. I think my anger gives me power over the hopelessness. If I stay mad, maybe one day it won't hurt so deeply. Maybe one day I won't care.*

> *It seemed staying mad (until reading this Dangerous Question) was my heart's way of protecting itself from being hurt or disappointed over and over again. I now see how much that decision*

robbed so much from our healing and marriage. Now I'm anxious
to begin learning how to forgive unconditionally and continuously.

These comments are from young women, some very wounded by their husbands. Several said it felt good to hold a grudge. I'm not a young woman, and I have a wonderful husband. I know God's Word and teach other women about forgiveness, yet there have been many times I wanted to hold on to my "mad" at Jody. These young women are right; it feels good.

Many of us have held a grudge against our husbands, but Rachel Jones takes the prize for being a champion grudge holder. She and her neighbor, David, had a lovers' quarrel. Every week for forty-two years, David slipped a love letter under Rachel's door in an attempt to mend the quarrel that parted them when both were thirty-two years old. Every letter was burned by the grudge-holding Rachel, and she repeatedly refused to speak to her suitor. Finally, despite the silent treatment, David summoned courage to knock on her door and propose and, to his surprise, she accepted. Both Rachel and David were seventy-four-years old when they finally got married.[1]

What did Rachel gain during her long years of silence? What did she achieve by failing to forgive? She gained loneliness, bitterness, and perhaps a sense of power over another person. Was her vigilant stance of "I'm right, and nothing will make me change my mind!" worth forty-two years of anguish? I wish she were still alive so we could ask her. I strongly suspect, however, that she would tell us that she had been a fool and had wasted years over an issue that mattered very little.

A happy marriage is the union of two good forgivers who commit not to hold a grudge and nurse a hurt, but instead to freely forgive their mate, even though sometimes he or she does not *deserve* forgiveness. This is easy to write, very difficult to accomplish, especially when you are the wounded or misunderstood party. It is difficult, because as Philip Yancey says, "forgiveness is an unnatural act."[2] Yet it is of vital importance, because it is the only way to break the cycle of blame and pain in a relationship. Yancey uses the story of a marriage that disintegrates over a bar of soap as told in the novel *Love in the Time of Cholera* to illustrate what happens when we don't forgive. In the book, it was the wife's job to keep the house in order, including the towels, toilet paper, and soap in the bathroom. One day she forgot to replace the soap, an oversight her husband mentioned in an exaggerated way ("I've been bathing for almost a week without any soap") but that she vigorously denied. Although she had indeed forgotten, her pride was at stake, and she would not back down. What was the outcome of one bar of soap not being in the bathroom? For the next several months, they slept in separate rooms and ate in silence. Author Gabriel Marquez writes that "even when they were old and placid they were careful about bringing it up, for the barely healed wounds could begin to bleed again as if they had been inflicted only yesterday."[3]

How can a bar of soap ruin a marriage? Because neither partner would say, *Stop! This cannot go on. I'm sorry for my part in this. Forgive me.*

Surely we would not be so petty and immature. I wish it weren't so, but I have counseled many women whose marriages were in shambles because they allowed an insignificant incident between husband and wife to blow up into a full-scale civil war—and I, too, have hung on to being "right" over unimportant issues. Over such trivialities, lifelong relationships crack apart, and only forgiveness can halt the widening fissures.

I can shake my head and laugh at a marriage blowing up into a civil war over a bar of soap. I can look at Rachel—holding a grudge for forty-two years—and think, *That is unbelievable.* But do I hold a grudge against my husband for forty-two days? Or forty-two hours? Do you?

What prompts a wife to hold a grudge?

Silly things—words spoken in haste, acts done unknowingly.

Sad things—a forgotten birthday or anniversary, an unkept
    promise, a sarcastic slam, or an unpaid bill.

Serious things—rage, vicious words, an emotional affair.

Sordid things—Pornography, adultery, abuse. Physically,
emotionally, or sexually harming a child.

When a friend, a colleague, or a family member hurts, misunderstands or wounds you, it is agonizing. But if your partner—chosen for life, the one who knows all your warts and failings—wounds you, the hurt is deeper, the wound more raw. This person is always around; you can't get away from him. You even sleep in the same bed!

I believe the only way you can forgive your intimate companion for silly, sad, serious, and sordid things is to cross over into the supernatural. The natural attitude says, "It is my right to stay mad at you. You deserve it." The supernatural attitude says, "I don't want to stay mad at you. I have forgiven you and reconnected with our love. Life is too short to stay mad." The only way a wife can move into the supernatural is to fall to her knees and cry out to her God, *I can't forgive. Give me the strength and power by the blessed Holy Spirit.*

God is by nature free from the pride and selfishness that by nature is our nature. God forgave us in Christ "while we were yet sinners" (Rom. 5:8)—when we were undeserving, when we turned our backs on Him. God asks us to forgive as He has forgiven us, not once or twice, but as Jesus says, forgive "seventy times seven" (Matt. 18:22). He must have had marriage in mind when He said this, because it is in this most intimate encounter that we are most vulnerable and open to hurt, and where we most often need to forgive.

My friend Dana can tell you about the power of forgiveness. She is an incredible woman who saturates herself in God's Word. She knows God's voice and says yes to God. For several years, she had been in and out of numerous hospitals (including Mayo Clinic and the Stanford Medical Center) for severe health issues. Over ten years of trauma had put deep strain on Dana and Adam's marriage. Adam couldn't see that his words of anger were uncalled for, and Dana waited for him to ask for her forgiveness for a long list of offenses. But he didn't. Soon months had shifted seasons.

Life went on. One evening Adam and Dana even had a date night. She was excited. She had finally gained some weight back after her surgeries. She had a new black dress, and she couldn't wait for Adam to tell her she looked beautiful. But the date turned into a disaster; no words of love, no "You look great!" Adam just wanted to hurry home to get back to work. The next morning Dana decided enough was enough. She stomped toward Adam's office with her list of his offenses. Everything she felt was justified. He was guilty! I'll let Dana tell you what happened:

> *With only five steps left before entering the battlefield, I heard a whisper, "Dana, keep your mouth shut. Do not say what you want to say." I knew who it was, and I didn't want to hear. What? Are You kidding me, Lord?*
>
> *This wasn't the first time God used spiritual duct tape to halt my babble. I knew I needed to obey. The door opened. My husband spun his chair around and said, "Hey, what's up?" All that came out was, "I just came in here to tell you I love you." It was a lie—well not the "I love you" part, because I do love my husband, but it certainly was not the reason I had come to see him. I stood there for a few seconds, not quite believing what had come out of my mouth. He smiled. "I love you, too," he said as I turned around and headed out the door.*
>
> *What just happened? The tears began to fall. I truly could not remember nine of the ten items that had been stuck in my brain for countless weeks. Okay—the black dress one, I remembered—it was only the night before. But the most amazing thing was that it held no power. My anger was gone. My self-righteousness was gone. My need for him to say, "Please forgive me" was gone. Obeying God— that's all it took—and the reward was a spiritual bath to my soul.*

I made it back to my bedroom and prayed, Lord, forgive me. Who am I to throw a punch at my husband? After all we've gone through and all he has sacrificed for me, I should be the one to ask him to forgive me. Would You help me, Lord?

So that night lying side by side, I took Adam's hand. The tears flowed, but so did my overwhelming love for this incredible man God had given to me. The words came easy: "Please forgive me, I'm sorry for …" Yes the list was long, but it was a list of what I needed to ask forgiveness for: my shortcomings, my quick judgments, the expectations I placed on him that made him feel burdened and defeated. How could I have been so blind? I told him of my great love for him. He, too, asked me to forgive him. God Himself was there: removing the weight of our unforgiving hearts.

I've learned to hear God's voice more clearly now. More often than not, He just whispers the words, "Spiritual duct tape," and I know that obedience is the only choice worth making.

Dana knew what God says about forgiveness in His Word. She listened to His voice, even when she didn't want to hear it. God longs for each of us to make a secret choice to forgive our husband quickly and completely of silly, sad, serious, and sordid things. Yes, staying mad may feel good, and it keeps conviction away, but it robs you and your husband of peace and healing. Think again, my friend. Do you really want to stay mad at your husband?

Insight 2: THREE SHOCKING TRUTHS ABOUT FORGIVENESS

One wife wrote this about why she can't forgive her husband:

I want to stay mad because you are clearly in the wrong and I'm not. If I give up being mad, then it's like I'm lying down and giving up—saying that you're right. I want to stay mad because then I have more ammunition stored up for the day I get to explode. Is this right? No! But it's so hard to let it go and give it up to the Father.

I agree; it is hard to let it go. To encourage you, let me share three shocking truths about forgiveness that have taken me deeper in never wanting to hold a grudge. If you understand them, they will cause you to run to the person who has hurt you and say, "I forgive you."

Hidden in the book of Second Corinthians is the first shocking truth about forgiveness.

1. Forgiving kicks Satan out! The apostle Paul exhorts you and me to forgive quickly and continually. Why? "So that *Satan will not outsmart us. For we are familiar with his evil schemes*" (2 Cor. 2:11 NLT). Outsmarted by Satan? No, thank you! I don't want to be outsmarted by anyone, but I definitely do not want the Deceiver, the Evil One, to outsmart me. Just the thought makes me mad! Do you realize that if you harbor resentment toward your husband, if you refuse to forgive, Satan gets the advantage over you?

Picture your adversary, Satan, squealing with delight because you chose to hold a grudge. He is dancing with glee that he has outsmarted you with his evil schemes. By harboring resentment toward your mate, you open wide a door for Satan. And what will he do? Take advantage of you, manipulate you, trick you, and weasel his wicked lies into your heart. Lies like:

- Why forgive him again, he doesn't deserve it.
- Stay angry, don't walk toward him.
- You'll be a pushover if you forgive him.

What Satan fails to tell you is that if you fail to freely forgive, he wins.

Kick Satan out! Don't let him win!

2. Forgiving invites intimacy with the Lord. You know the Lord's Prayer. Probably you could repeat it right now if asked. So let me ask you, what is the one conditional prayer in the Lord's Prayer? It's not, "Give us this day our daily bread," and not, "Lead us not into temptation." Open your Bible to Matthew 6:9–15 and read these familiar words. Did you see the one prayer that has a condition attached to it? "Forgive us our sins, *as we have forgiven those who sin against us*" (Matt. 6:12 NLT). When you pray this prayer, you ask God to grant you the same kind of forgiveness that you give to your husband. Is this really the kind of forgiveness you want? How free is your forgiveness? Do you hold a husband grudge or forgive freely?

The shocking thing is that God adds a P.S. to the Lord's Prayer. He repeats *only* this conditional prayer about forgiving. He even makes it more explicit. "If you forgive those who sin against you, your heavenly Father will forgive you. But if you refuse to forgive others, your Father will not forgive your sins" (Matt. 6:14–15 NLT). Are you thinking, *Wait a minute, Linda, I thought I was saved by grace through faith. What do you mean God won't forgive me?*

The Lord's Prayer is not about salvation; it is about intimacy and fellowship with the Father. The purpose of the prayer is to show us how to stay in fellowship with God: "If we walk in the Light as He Himself is in the Light, we have fellowship with one another, and the blood of Jesus His Son cleanses us from all sin" (1 John 1:7). R. T. Kendall says, "Walking in the light means following without compromise *anything God shows you to do.* But if He shows you something and you sweep it under the carpet, years later you will wonder why you haven't grown spiritually. The reason will be because you postponed obedience; there was no real fellowship with the Father."[4]

I long for deep intimacy with my Lord. Do you? Then be quick to forgive your husband. Forgiveness places you on the path of deeper fellowship.

3. Forgiving brings glory to you. This third shocking truth about forgiveness is hidden in the book of Proverbs. I have studied and taught the book of Proverbs, and I don't ever remember noticing this important verse:

> *A woman's wisdom gives her patience; it is to her glory to overlook*
> *an offense. (Prov. 19:11, author's paraphrase)*

Stop for a minute and ask yourself, *What would give me honor and glory?*

Getting your dream job?

Receiving the Nobel Peace Prize?

Being "The Mother of the Year"?

Have God tell you, "Well done"?

This verse tucked away in the book of Proverbs says something very different: You receive honor and glory when you forgive freely and overlook an offense.

Amazing.

Renowned Old Testament scholar Dr. Bruce Waltke says the glory a woman receives when she forgives the sin of another is like an "attractive adornment [she] wears." When a wife forgives, "people delight and rejoice in [her] and [she] wins … more fame, honor, praise, and distinction" through forgiving than in any other way.[5]

The adornment a forgiving wife wears is a sweet fragrance that reminds others of the Lord Jesus. Her calm and gentle spirit, her tender smile, radiates peace and joy because forgiveness has set her free from resentment and anger. I long to be clothed with this adornment.

My friend Katie already wears it. Eleven years ago, her world exploded without warning. The family she worked so hard to build and maintain was destroyed. It began with a phone call from the Children's Advocacy Center, asking her to come to the center about a matter involving her oldest daughter, Hannah. Once there, Katie received the worst news of her life. Hannah was accusing her father, Katie's husband, of sexually molesting her.

Katie called me to come to pray with her. The anguish was indescribable for her and for both her daughters. She says, "That first day I didn't know if I would even stay married to Craig, or what my future would look like, but I did know that I would have to cling to God and trust Him in a deeper way than I ever had before."

Craig was arrested, pled guilty, and was later sentenced to a half-way house for ninety days. Additionally, he was given probation for five years, which included attending weekly counseling and a group therapy program for sexual offenders. This sentence meant Craig could not come home for several years. Because he repented and immediately went to their pastor to confess, Katie believed she needed to be willing to walk toward him with forgiveness. Psalm 51:12 became her prayer: *Father, grant me a willing spirit!*

I'll let her tell you how God answered her prayer.

> *I learned a lot about forgiveness watching Hannah. It took her two years of sobbing, screaming, and fighting before she could give up her anger and say from the heart, "I forgive you, Dad." I was still struggling. I was trying to forgive, but the shock of my husband's betrayal was so great, and my trust so destroyed, it took seeing my own sin before I could take the necessary steps to forgive Craig. God showed me many things during my journey to forgiveness, but these three stand out in my memory:*
>
> *First, I had to "get the log out of my own eye" (Matt. 7:3–5) in order to see my own sin and how I had pushed my husband away from intimacy. God showed me in Romans 2:11 that He does not have favorites. He wanted my healing, but He wanted Craig's healing too. How could I want God to forgive me and yet punish him?*
>
> *Second, I learned firsthand that God's ways are above our ways (Isa. 55:9). He called me to repair the breach in this*

relationship, even though I was not the one who blew a big hole in the wall. God stripped everything away that was important to me and put me in a place where I was utterly dependent on Him.

Third, I committed to doing whatever I could to be a blessing to my husband (1 Peter 3:8–18). How many ways are there to do this? I truly did find countless ways to bless my husband, starting with "a soft word turns away wrath."

As I sought to give a blessing to Craig, God blessed me and my family. Many thought this betrayal was too hard to repair. Craig and I lived apart for over five years, and during that time he received counseling and demonstrated to me, our family, and to his counselor that he was truly on the road to healing, so I felt it was safe to invite him back into our home. Eleven long years later, I stand in awe of my God who is the Healer and the One who can heal anything! I'm moved to tears as I compile this list of God's many blessings on our family:

- My marriage is completely restored and flourishing in all areas.
- My daughter is completely reconciled to her father, and she even asked him to walk her down the aisle at her wedding!
- Both our daughters are happily married, and my husband is a father to our young sons-in-law.
- Our family all attend church together.
- My husband and I have served our church by leading financial workshops and now teach a marriage Bible study for couples.
- I have had the privilege of walking with many women who are suffering betrayal by their husbands.
- We are completely debt-free after years of financial hardship, job loss, legal and medical expenses. God has blessed us beyond our wildest dreams.

- *God has given us a heart for others, and we now comfort others with the same comfort with which we were comforted.*
- *AND this man who betrayed his whole family is today the beloved grandpa of Hannah's new daughter!*

God is so glorified, but let me tell you, I've never seen a woman in the agony Katie lived in for years. She made heart-wrenching choices daily. I remember her saying to me, "Linda, if I have to be in this pain, I hope God will make me into a gracious woman." I wish you could know Katie and see the peace and joy that radiates from her smile. Truly, her family is a walking miracle. And Katie is a gracious woman, all because she chose to forgive.

Not every husband is willing to repent and go through five long years of restoration and healing before being allowed to go back home. Craig is a man I call friend and deeply respect. He is proof that even in the most horrible of situations, when forgiveness is given and received, God can heal.

Insight 3: STRIP OFF ANGER, PUT ON FORGIVENESS

As I talk to women about their thoughts on forgiving, I see a new idea of forgiveness roaming around in hearts: Forgiveness is conditional. It comes across in comments like this:

- "My husband doesn't deserve forgiveness."
- "I don't think he is really sorry."
- "Look at the pain he's caused me—why should I let him off the hook?"
- "What he did was wrong!"
- "I'm always the one to forgive; it's his turn."

Let's return to Paul's statement in Ephesians 4:31–32. These are my all-time favorite verses on forgiveness. And they are very clear: We are commanded to strip off our anger and put on forgiveness.

Strip off! "Let all bitterness and wrath and anger and clamor and slander be put away from you, along with all malice." (Eph. 4:31)

Put on! "Be kind to one another, tender-hearted, forgiving each other, just as God in Christ also has forgiven you." (Eph. 4:32)

We are to strip off our old, harmful ways of relating. These six attitudes are to be tossed in the trash bin:

1. Bitterness. Nursing your wrath to keep it warm— brooding over insults, injuries, and slights that you've received. Aristotle spoke of bitterness as "the resentful spirit which refuses reconciliation."

2. Wrath. The flaring up of passion and temper, an outbreak of anger that springs from personal animosity.

3. Anger. A long-lived habitual anger, where it settles down and is at home in your heart.

4. Clamor. The loud self-assertion of an angry wife who wants everyone to hear her grievances.

5. Evil speaking. Slanderous or abusive speaking about one's husband.

6. Malice. Bad feelings of every kind that cause a wife to speak or do evil against her husband.

Bitterness, wrath, anger, clamor, evil speaking, and malice: six negative attitudes that we must strip off. Declare, "No more anger and slander for me!" Strip yourselves of your old selfish, angry ways of relating. Build a bonfire, and banish them forever!

Instead, put on a new wardrobe. Its shades of kindness, compassion, and forgiveness make your skin glow—your eyes sparkle.

The vibrant, yet soft, colors of your new garments are amazing.

1. Kindness. This is love in practical action. When you put on kindness, you are as concerned about your husband's feelings as you are about your own. You are as sensitive to your husband's sorrows, hurts, and struggles as to your own.

2. Tenderheartedness. The love in action that is kindness must be married to a tender heart of sympathy. The obstacle to kindness and compassion is often the sense of wrong done to you as a wife or a grievance nursed. So the overarching garment you must put on is forgiveness.

3. Forgiveness. The Greek word *charizoma*, translated as forgiving, means "to be gracious" or "to give freely."[6] The idea as expressed in *The Amplified Bible* is "forgiving one another [readily and freely], as God in Christ forgave you" (Eph. 4:32).

I love the way *The Message* describes your new wardrobe: "Be gentle with one another, sensitive. Forgive one another as quickly and thoroughly as God in Christ forgave you."

Colette had an agonizing decision to make about stripping off the old and putting on the new. After twenty-five years of marriage, she discovered her husband was very different from the man she had loved and trusted. As I was writing this book, I gave Colette the first Dangerous Question and encouraged her to write her Marriage Purpose Statement. She threw the manuscript in the trash. But God worked in her heart, and three months later Colette was ready to think about her marriage. She desperately needed God's wisdom, and He spoke to her from Exodus 34:1, where God told Moses He would rewrite His words on new tablets, replacing the tablets that had been shattered. Colette did not know if new words could ever be written, replacing the fragmented vows of her marriage, but God then spoke to her again, saying, "Trust Me."

She chose to obey, but she could commit to her marriage goals for only three months, and no longer. This is what she wrote:

> *I ask You, Jesus, to write on my heart new words that I can commit*
> *to. I cannot even begin to project a lifetime marriage statement,*

*though my face is resolutely set towards a long obedience to my
God, therefore to my husband. But I can commit to three months
of purposeful, prayed over, "I wills."*

- *I will forgive, and I will ask for forgiveness,
  purposefully and prayerfully each day. "As far as the
  east is from the west" I will not bring up forgiven hurts
  again. In my forgiving, I will release my husband of
  his "debts" so that he may walk in freedom and grow
  towards Light.*

- *I will relinquish all judging, self-righteous attitudes and
  my prideful heart. God alone is the righteous and holy
  Judge. It is not my job.*

- *I will be present in body and spirit to my husband, actively
  engaging with his needs. I will not manipulate him with
  absence of spirit, lack of attention, or withdrawal.*

- *I will be respectful, accepting his leadership.*

- *I will not dwell on the darkness in him, nor fear it. Rather,
  I will live out Philippians 4:8: Whatever is true, whatever
  is honorable, whatever is right, pure, lovely, whatever is of
  good repute, in my husband, excellent, worthy of praise,
  these are what I will discipline my mind to dwell on.*

- *I will be merciful to my husband, remembering the truth
  that my Father's mercies are new to us every morning.*

- *I will recognize, and celebrate, each decision for Life and
  Light my husband makes.*

- *I will not give up hope, for my hope is in God Himself,
  who is caring for me and protecting me.*

*These things, my Lord, I commit to You, fully understanding that
it is only through Your Holy Spirit and by Your incredible grace to
me that I can even pen these words. May You be praised!*

If you think the words Colette wrote flowed easily, you've never been in gut-wrenching pain. As I write, I can see her eyes; they overflow with sorrow. In her grief, this woman of faith stripped off her old clothes and put on her beautiful new wardrobe of kindness, compassion, and forgiveness.

Do you remember that Colette said she could not imagine committing to her "I wills" for a lifetime? Five months after writing her three-month Marriage Purpose Statement, she wrote: "May 15, 2010. Today I declare that this Marriage Purpose Statement is till death do us part."

P.S. Five months after Collette added "till death do us part" to her Marriage Purpose Statement, I received the following email from her.

> *God is beyond good! I'm not sure about the when, Linda, but my husband and I are in relationship again. I don't think I really thought this could ever happen.... God's exact kind of situation to His Glory! I big miss my husband when he's out of town.... I wait for him to come home at night with expectancy. I want to care for him again and spend time just because. And I am looking forward to a life together. CAN YOU BELIEVE IT?*

Who says God doesn't do miracles today? Collette's story qualifies as a miracle. I know. I watched it happen!

Insight 4: ANOINT WITH FORGIVENESS

Many women in my survey felt that offering the gift of forgiveness was the best thing they did for their marriage.

> *I decided to live in forgiveness. (Married forty years)*

> *FORGIVE! I forgave him for his affair, and God has restored our marriage! (Married twenty-three years)*

Six years ago, my husband confessed and repented of his infidelity to me of eleven years. At that point I had a choice to make—anger and bitterness or forgiveness. The BEST decision I made was to begin the process of forgiveness and restoration in my marriage. (Married thirty-seven years)

I learned to say, "I'm sorry." And this is RECENT! (Married twenty-four years)

I chose to forgive and let God restore our marriage, bringing beauty from ashes. (Married twenty-five years)

Learning to be the first to say "I'm sorry." (Married twelve years)

I forgave my husband, not only for the decisions he made that damaged our marriage, I forgave him for everything. (Married thirty years)

Thirty-one years ago he had an affair. The best thing I ever did was forgive him and begin changing my life. I chose to not look at his wrong but at my own problems. (Married thirty-five years)

Several of these wives forgave their husbands for sexual sins. All sin is difficult to forgive, but a husband's sexual sin touches a wife at the core of her being. There is a unique knowing when a wife opens herself up to her husband during sexual intercourse. She opens her soul, her body, and her emotions. Discovering her husband has "known" another woman pierces her in the core of her being. Connie knew this deep piercing.

She tried to forgive, but when the images came again and again, she wondered if she really had. She wanted out of the roller-coaster ride of questioning whether she had really forgiven him. To move forward, Connie decided to cement in her mind that she had made the choice to forgive by acting out her forgiveness in a beautiful way. Here is what happened:

> *I was shaking as I asked my husband to stand in front of me. I took off all of his clothes, and with a bottle of scented oil, I anointed his body.*
>
> *I touched his forehead: "I forgive your mind for thinking thoughts of her."*
>
> *I touched his ears: "I forgive your ears for listening to her."*
>
> *I touched his hands: "I forgive your hands for touching her."*
>
> *After anointing every part of his body, I came to his feet: "I forgive your feet for walking toward her." As the words came, tears cascaded down my face. Relief flooded me. The past was truly in the past—for both of us.*[7]

Sheryl heard me tell Connie's story of the Forgiveness Anointing at a conference. She wept bitter tears because she knew she could not be like Connie. Sheryl wrote me the following email:

> *In the immediate aftermath of learning that my husband had become sexually intimate with another, I allowed anger and unforgiveness to choke out the love of so many years. I surrendered to the pain, and I held him in contempt. Though he begged me to forgive him, I could not. So he walked away. Connie's story caused me to weep for what I had lost.*
>
> *My husband has moved and begun a new life, a life he has no desire to make me a part of. Still, I knew what I had to do. I called him and asked for a few minutes of his time. I traveled to his city and met him in a church. I had the CD of you sharing Connie's story and played it for my husband. I wept again and told him, "I'm sorry I could not be that woman. I'm sorry I didn't know how*

to forgive you sooner." I asked him if he would allow me to express my forgiveness in a similar physical act (except the "take off your clothes" part). He said yes.

Sitting beneath a tree, outside the church with anointing oil in hand, I touched my husband's eyes, his ears, his hands, his feet, and his heart. Through almost choking sobs, I managed to speak the words and give him the forgiveness he had begged me for so long ago. When I opened my eyes, this ever-strong man had tears tumbling down both cheeks. For a moment, neither of us spoke. Finally, I thanked him for forgiving ME, forgiving me for not being the woman I should have been when he came to me to repent of his sin. He then thanked me for forgiving him for not loving me and remaining faithful to our vows.

If only I could have done this sooner.

If only that moment would not have ended with us climbing into separate cars to return to our now-separate lives.

If only … words of regret, words of sorrow, for what might have been. I weep over Sheryl's loss.

Whatever barrier is between you and your husband, don't wait until it is too late. Don't let "If only I could have done this sooner" be your story. Forgiving is wrenching; it costs us. But not forgiving costs more. God commands us to forgive freely as we have been forgiven in Christ. There are blessings bestowed on the one who forgives. Today is the day to offer forgiveness!

Insight 5: BE A PROACTIVE FORGIVER

Think back to the last time you were blistering mad at your husband. Never heard *blistering* and *mad* together? It is when hot sparks of anger are erupting out of every cell in your body. If you've been there, you know what it is. This is not a time to consider forgiveness. Oh, you should consider it, but you can't. You're too spitfire indignant that your husband could be so dense, inconsiderate, irresponsible, inept, immoral, disgusting, _____ (you fill in the blank).

In the heat of the moment, forgiveness is the last thing you want to do. That is why I encourage you to make the decision to forgive *before* you need to forgive. You must be proactive about offering forgiveness for big things and for daily little things. Forgiveness is one of the most difficult parts of marriage and also one of the most important. So go before the Lord and pour out your heart NOW. Decide NOW to be a proactive forgiver!

Once you have made this secret choice, how do you forgive? What practical, physical symbol will substantiate to your mind and heart that you have forgiven?

Here are some ideas to consider:

1. Let your fingers do your forgiving. Consider the following story about Winston Churchill.

> *At a dinner party one night Lady Churchill was seated across the table from Sir Winston, who kept making his hand walk up and down—two fingers bent at the knuckles. The fingers appeared to be walking toward Lady Churchill. Finally, her dinner partner asked, "Why is Sir Winston looking at you so wistfully, and whatever is he doing with those two knuckles on the table?" "That's simple," she replied. "We had a mild quarrel before we left home, and he is indicating it's his fault and he's on his knees to me in abject apology."*[8]

2. Put "ISSUMAGJOUJUNGNAINERMIK" on your refrigerator. When missionaries first went to the Eskimos, they could not find a word in their language for forgiveness, so they had to compound one. This turned out to be ISSUMAGJOUJUNGNAINERMIK. It is a formidable looking group of letters that has a beautiful meaning for those who understand it. It means "Not-being-able-to-think-about-it-anymore."[9]

I have ISSUMAGJOUJUNGNAINERMIK posted in large letters on my refrigerator. I get some strange looks when people see it, but it reminds me to forgive freely, to not think about it anymore.

3. Let the leaves flutter away your offense. When I feel my body and soul holding resentment against my husband, I take a walk alone. I pick up leaves and hold them tightly in my closed hand. Then I pray, something like this: *My Father, You see my heart. You know I've clutched on to resentment toward Jody for how he's treated me. I'm opening my hand, Lord, and watching the leaves fall through my fingers. I give it up; I let go of holding on to the offense.*

4. Throw the rock of bitterness away. When I sense my heart is holding on to bitterness and anger, I go outside and find a quiet place alone, fall to my knees and tell my Father what He already knows: *Forgive me for hanging on in my heart. I'm throwing off the anger and bitter feelings toward Jody.* I pick up a rock, name it Bitterness, throw it as far as I can throw, and tell God I am banishing bitterness.

5. Exchange your anger with prayer. Stormie Omartian says, "Something amazing happens to your heart when you pray for another person. The hardness melts. You become able to get beyond the hurts, and forgive. It's miraculous! It happens because when we pray, we enter into the presence of God and He fills us with His Spirit of love. When you pray for your husband, the love of God will grow in your heart for him."[10]

I thank my Lord and Savior that He didn't look at me and evaluate whether I deserved forgiveness. What if He had said:

> Linda doesn't deserve it.
>
> I don't think she is really sorry.
>
> Look at the pain Linda's caused Me. Why should I let her
> off the hook?
>
> What Linda did was wrong.
>
> I'm always the One to forgive; it's Linda's turn.

Jesus' example humbles me and encourages me to follow in His steps. The beauty and glory of Christ's forgiveness is that it is unconditional. He paid the price for my sin, and I just say, "Thank You!" It is glorious to receive God's forgiveness, but then He turns to me and says, "Now, Linda, you extend forgiveness to Jody, the same unconditional forgiveness I've given you—and, Linda, remember to do it with kindness and compassion."

Dangerous Prayer!

Lord, I see why I want to stay mad at my husband. Teach me to be tenderhearted and forgiving toward him, just as God in Christ has forgiven me.

Is It Possible to Grow Together When Things Fall Apart?

My eyes are fixed on you, O Sovereign LORD; in you I take refuge.
Psalm 141:8 (NIV)

You will keep in perfect peace all who trust in you, all whose thoughts are fixed on you!
Isaiah 26:3 (NLT)

I always view problems as opportunities in work clothes.
Henry Kaiser

It doesn't matter ... how great the pressure is.
It only matters where the pressure lies.
Hudson Taylor

Insight 1: AN ANNIVERSARY ON THE BLUE DANUBE
1991—Home was in Vienna, Austria. With three kids in college that year and four the year before, our cupboards were beyond bare, and a camping

trip was the most I could expect for an anniversary celebration. What a wonderful surprise when our travel agent gave us two nights at the Budapest Hilton plus one three-course meal. I liked camping, but an anniversary atop the walled part of old Budapest overlooking the Danube and picturesque Parliament building definitely won over the old rusty camper in the romance department.

Visions of a candlelight dinner at a Hungarian restaurant, strolling musicians, and a view of incredible beauty filled my thoughts. I was ready for this. Jody and I had gone camping on our honeymoon. The Budapest Hilton overlooking the Danube was definitely a step up, and I liked the step.

The view *was* breathtaking, the Castle, Museum, Fishermen's Bastion, and Matthias Church, all amazing and otherworldly. The food and music was all I'd anticipated, the moonlight walk overlooking the river, breathtakingly romantic. Everything was just right, all the physical circumstances in place. There was romance, but the romance reflected the sadness of the romancers.

At one point Jody said, "I'm sorry this weekend has to be like this." When the anniversary getaway was planned, no one knew his father would have just died, that our future would be one big question mark. Amid the Old World beauty, we were experiencing one of the most difficult times of our life together. Not exactly an atmosphere conducive to an anniversary celebration. But as we drove home to Vienna, I told this man I'd loved for almost thirty years that I'd never felt closer to him than now. We had wept together, talked and prayed, been silent together, and shared an intimacy that goes beyond words.

What creates intimacy? Of course fun, laughter, intimate sharing, and abandoned sex do. But deep emotional bonding is also found in the hard times—when we cry, when answers evade us, when God seems far away, but we cling to Him and to each other. How glorious it would be if marriage were all picnics, parties, and glorious lovemaking. No pain, no problems, no perplexing circumstances. Yes, we could definitely get used to that. But it is not to be, not for me or for you. If it isn't already, crisis will be a part of your marriage.

Crises come wrapped in packages of all shapes and sizes. There are little boxes, in-between-size boxes, gigantic boxes, and boxes labeled personal crisis, couple crisis, kid crisis, job crisis, home crisis, everyday crisis, sexual crisis, health crisis, life crisis. Webster defines *crisis* as "a situation that has reached a critical phase; an unstable or crucial time."[1]

In a marriage, a crisis presents the potential for:

> *Danger that the crisis will tear us apart and destroy our oneness.*

> *Opportunity that the crisis will push us together and deepen our oneness.*

Since crisis will be part of your life and marriage, how do you turn it into an opportunity to grow closer to your husband?

1. *Know God's viewpoint.* Knowing God's perspective will enable you to not just survive but thrive in times of crisis. No place in Scripture are we promised a problem-free life—or marriage. In fact, Jesus said just the opposite: "Here on earth you will have many trials and sorrow. But take heart, because I have overcome the world" (John 16:33 NLT).

Mariah did not know God's viewpoint, and she listened to friends, not God. She shared her view with me at a conference.

> *I just don't get it. Marriage wasn't supposed to be this hard. I prayed about who to marry, we're Christians ... but every area of our marriage is a challenge: our finances, communication (we don't talk, we nag, sneer, and shout at each other), and sex. Don't even mention sex. My friend said that if you are really pleasing God that you won't have all the problems we're having.*

If the friend is right, Jody and I must not be pleasing God, because our marriage has been filled with trials. The friend has wrong thinking. Some Christians believe that if you're walking with the Lord, you will be delivered *from* trouble. But the promise of God is deliverance *in times of* trouble, which is quite different. God says there will be trials and sorrows. The blessing is, we have the Problem-Solver living within. He is our peace in the midst of panic and pain. But panic and pain *will come,* because crisis is no respecter of persons. Couples who love Christ and follow Him have deep trials. Couples who claim no God have deep trials.

2. Apply God's Word to the crisis. God's Word makes some unbelievable statements about how we are to respond in trials. One is found in James 1:2: We are to count it joy when we encounter trials.

Really? Did James really mean I was to say, "This is joy to us," when it feels like our world is falling apart in the midst of a romantic anniversary trip? I'm to count it joy when I feel grief over the death of Jody's father and complete confusion about our future?

A look at other translations and paraphrases confirms that this is indeed the meaning behind the Greek text:

> *Consider it all joy, my [sisters], when you encounter various trials.*

> *Consider it a sheer gift, friends, when tests and challenges come at you from all sides.* (MSG)

> *When all kinds of trials and temptations crowd into your lives, my [sisters], don't resent them as intruders, but welcome them as friends!* (PH)

All joy? A sheer gift? Pain as a friend? If you are like me, trials feel like intruders, not friends. Pain isn't the gift I want. Joy would be having the floods, fires, earthquakes, sexual pain, cancer, abuse, uncertainty—having *all* pain—*leave,* and the quicker the better. If we're honest, we don't welcome pain as a friend. We say: *"Get away from me! I don't want the process to go on. I hate distress, I hate tension. I just want it over."* In fact, I think most women count it all joy when they *escape* trials.

James said to count it all joy *in the midst* of trials. And there is a reason. Believe it or not, God says there are benefits to trials. Look with me at the next verses.

> *Consider it all joy … when you encounter various trials, knowing that the testing of your faith produces endurance. And let endurance have its perfect result, so that you may be perfect and complete, lacking nothing. (James 1:2–4)*

We are promised the benefit of endurance when we encounter a crisis. If we meet the testing in the right way, we will become stable, and our character will look more like Christ's character.

Looking like Christ is definitely a benefit!

James' message is this: Trials can be faced with joy because, if joy is infused with faith, endurance results—and if endurance goes full-term, it will develop a thoroughly mature Christian who lacks nothing. You will indeed be all God wants you to be.

So think on this. When a trial comes, you have a choice:

You can clench your fist and fight God. If this is your choice, you will become angry, griping, and bitter. Or …

You can open your hands and say, *God, this trial is very difficult. It feels unfair. But I want to trust You in it. Please work endurance in me. I want to become like Christ.*

As individuals and as marriage partners, we are to rejoice in the difficult things God allows in our life and relationship. I paraphrase James 1:2–4 like this for my marriage:

> *Rejoice in the trials you face as a couple; they will teach you per-*
> *severance and make your love and commitment to one another*
> *strong. They will produce character, a strength that will lead to*
> *intimacy.*

I will always remember the anniversary trip, not because of the beautiful Danube River but because of the closeness Jody and I experienced amid
the pain. Yes, it is possible to grow closer during crisis!

Insight 2: TRUSTING GOD WHEN LIFE HURTS

2010—Living in Monument, Colorado. In times of trial, God's perspective
is what we need most, yet our hearts and minds focus on what we can see
and touch. When what we are seeing goes from minor crisis to major crisis,
we get stuck in our own perspective. Rather than waiting on our Lord to
solve our dilemma in His own time, we want to step in and manipulate a
fast, painless escape.

When we are faced with a trial, we prefer a tangible way out to God's
telling us to trust Him to see us through. It is easier to escape with your
husband and put a moratorium on the problem—and even easier to try
to take control than it is to trust. Trusting God during a crisis is difficult,
because we don't know how long the crisis will continue or what the
outcome will be. We don't know how long we will have to trust. Trust
is the answer to worry, but when your child has cancer, your business is
bankrupt, or your beloved is deeply depressed, the logical perspective is
to worry.

This week, while editing this chapter, one phone call from a doctor
restructured our lives. Jody has cancer, and surgery is scheduled. The questions for Jody and me are:

Will the crisis of cancer tear us apart and destroy our oneness?

Or …

Will the crisis of cancer push us closer together and deepen our oneness?

And God has a personal question for me as a wife. *Linda, will you worry or trust?* So I turn once again to a much-loved passage of Scripture, and pray, *Lord, teach me in a fresh and new way how to trust You.*

In Proverbs 3:5–6, I am told how to trust in a practical way, what my part is in trusting and what God's part is. I have this passage glued to the crevices of my mind because it has been such an encouragement to me in times of crisis. And I need it today.

> *Trust in the LORD with all your heart and do not lean on your own understanding. In all your ways acknowledge Him and He will make your paths straight.*

Ask God to open your spiritual eyes to see this familiar passage in a new and deeper way. I see four verbs: Three are directed at me, one toward God. My part is to "trust," "lean not," and "acknowledge," and God's part is "to make my paths straight." One little word is mentioned four times in these two verses: the word *your.* Your responsibility in a crisis situation is to:

> *Trust with all YOUR heart*
> *Refuse to lean on YOUR understanding,*
> *Acknowledge Him in all YOUR ways,*
> *So that He might make straight YOUR paths.*

What do these four *yours* mean to me?

First, "Trust with all your heart." For me this means that I express my trust in God by thanking Him for what He will do in this crisis. I am asked to "give thanks in all circumstances" (1 Thess. 5:18 NIV), so in my current circumstances I am telling the Lord:

> *My Father, this situation makes no sense to me. I don't understand it, but I thank You for what You are going to accomplish because*

of it. By thanking You, I'm saying to You, I trust You to know bet-
ter than I know. I trust You even though I can't see what You are
doing. In Romans 5:3–5 You promise that the results of trusting
You in this situation are character, perseverance, and hope.

Second, "Lean not on your own understanding." I talk to myself:
"Linda, stay away from trying to figure it out. Throw out your own ideas
to fix it. Toss your creative manipulation in the trash." And then I pray,
Lord, instead of leaning on my clever plan to fix the mess, I want to lean, as on
a crutch, on You, my Father God.

I will rest the full weight of my problem on God—all the pressure off
of me and transferred onto Him.

Third, "In all your ways acknowledge Him." To *acknowledge* means "to
recognize." Rather than leaning on my finite understanding, I acknowledge
that God is the Blessed Controller of all things, even Jody's cancer. *Lord,*
I bow and worship You. You are the Blessed Controller of all things. I declare
this is true.

Fourth, "God will make your paths straight." The Hebrew word for
straight means "to make smooth, straight, right, and includes the idea of
removing obstacles that are in the way."[2] God says His part is to straighten
the stressful paths. He doesn't say when or how; He just promises He will.
So I thank Him: *My God, thank You that in Your infinite wisdom You see how*
to make smooth this stressful path. I praise You.

We need to practice trusting; we need to practice leaning; we need to
practice acknowledging—and we need to practice these things in times
of anxiety, in times of peace, in times of crisis, in times of joy. If we
wait until the crisis hits, we'll worry instead of trust. Our finite human
perspective will take front seat because it's more natural to us than God's
eternal perspective. Join me in memorizing Proverbs 3:5–6, and trust,
lean not, and acknowledge Him, knowing that He will straighten out
our paths.

The promise in these verses is wonderful. When I understand in my mind and heart what these passion-filled words in Proverbs 3:5–6 mean, then I can personalize them as a prayer to my Father God for help:

> *I will throw myself completely upon You, my Lord. I will cast all my present and future needs on You because You are my intimate Savior-God. I find in only You my true security and safety. I will do this with all my mind and feeling and will. I know I must refuse to support myself upon the crutch of my clever ingenuity. Instead, I recognize Your presence and concern for every minute detail of my problem. I know You will take full control of all that concerns me; You will remove all the rocks along the way and will smooth out and make straight my paths. Thank You, Abba, Father!*[8]

Jody and I have made our choice: The crisis of cancer is not going to pull us apart. We will trust Him in the crisis and cling to each other as we face this crisis together.

Insight 3: MARRIAGE CRISIS!

I want to introduce you to two special women who would tell you that even in a very difficult marriage crisis, it is possible for a couple to grow closer together. Both women have walked the hard road of abuse by their husband: Tabitha suffered the pain of pornography; Corina endured the pain of verbal abuse. Here are their stories:

Tabi's story. While Peter and Tabitha were dating, she discovered a stack of *Playboy* magazines in his closet. She thought they were gross and told him to toss them in the trash. Peter did as Tabi asked and threw the magazines away, but he admits that he thought she was overreacting. He didn't see any harm in porn. His parents took a picture of him looking at a *Playboy* when he was a boy of seven, and he'd been raised to think looking at porn was part of what it means to be a man. As Peter tossed the magazines in the trash can, Tabi thought, *Good riddance.* She had no idea how pornography affected a man's mind. She didn't know it changes a man's heart from who he wants to be to a man enslaved. She didn't know that pornography brings pain to more marriages than anyone can imagine.[4] And she didn't know that Peter continued to look at porn secretly.

Tabi had her own issues to deal with—a date rape in college. Because she was given the date rape drug, she remembered little of the sexual encounter. Though it left deep wounds in her heart, she thought if she couldn't remember it, she could pretend it didn't happen. Tabi had told Peter she was a virgin, but as she grew as a Christian, she realized she should have told him the truth, so two children and ten years into their marriage, she asked him to forgive her for not being honest. Peter couldn't have been sweeter or more understanding. He grieved for her pain.

Tabi sent me an email, telling me how her honesty brought about new oneness.

> *My honesty propelled us to study the Song of Solomon, and we did that with* Intimacy Ignited.[5] *When we got to the part about giving your body to your spouse as a gift, Peter read to me that for a man giving his body was to give his eyes. He was to commit to look only at his wife's body. I wasn't prepared for what happened next. He began sobbing and fell to his knees by the side of the bed. Out poured his continued addiction to porn. What really hurt were these words, "Sometimes when I'm with you, my mind is someplace else."*
>
> *I was so broken, so wounded. I didn't want to deal with this. I wanted to walk away and say, "I'm done! All men are disgusting!"*
>
> *Instead, I prayed and asked God to do something (like heal my husband now!). But God had something very different in mind. He said, "Tabi, make a commitment to never again refuse your husband sexually. Be totally available." Was God kidding? I*

thought this was very unfair and asked God, "Why did I have to do all the giving?" I was the one hurt here. Yet, every time I had my quiet time and was in the Word of God, He would whisper, "Make a commitment to never again refuse your husband sexually. Be totally available."

Finally I said yes to God. I was sure now He would pat me on the back and say, "Good job, Tabi, I'm really proud of you." Again God's response surprised me. "Tell Peter." "What? You can't be serious, God!" When I told Peter, he shouted, "YES!" I was amazed at what my gift did for him. And for me? It released me. I was no longer imprisoned by my past, always asking, "Do I want to do this tonight?" It freed me to give, and that freedom was so amazing. I was finally free to communicate during sex, to say what pleased me. By following God's personally tailored plan, I went from believing sex was a "necessary evil" in marriage to embracing God's beautiful gift of the one-flesh union.

Recently a couple we didn't know asked us if we were newlyweds. We laughed and said, "No." "Well, the way you look at each other, the way you are with each other made us think that."

Praise God for Tabi and Peter's renewed body, soul, and spirit intimacy. This wife chose to seek and obey God rather than allow her marriage crisis, while very painful and daunting, to come between her and her husband. This husband repented and sought help for his addiction. Tabi says, "The crisis of porn brought us even closer together. And I am so proud of my husband. He covenanted with God to give his eyes only to me—and that is what he is doing. At work recently, while waiting for a long download on the computer, the guys wanted to put on nude movies. Peter took the lead and said, 'We're not doing that. No nudity.'"

Corina's story. Corina came to me in tears after an *Intimate Issues* workshop and shared that she had suffered through years of verbal abuse from her husband, James. In his most recent verbal attack, he told her that he didn't find her attractive and that she needed to take better care of herself. (All I can say is, I wish I looked like Corina.) James didn't like anything she did. I cried with Corina and prayed for her. I had no answers but encouraged her to trust God and ask Him to show her what to do, and that is what she did. I'll let her tell you what God led her to do in her personal crisis.

> *After the retreat, I purchased* Intimate Issues *and read it. Not all of it related to me, but God taught me some new things about me and some creative ways to communicate with my husband.… I realized James wouldn't berate me if he felt connected to me. How can you put down someone you are intimately connected to? So, I tried it in various ways. God showed me to not just ask him, "How was your day?" but to ask specific questions and try to connect with him. Well, it worked. He opened up and we started dialoguing daily, and our communication improved and the way he talked to me improved.*
>
> *Eleven weeks ago, he left for six months [he's in the military]. Right after he left, he started a new relationship with Jesus Christ. He is Spirit-filled and Spirit-led and has a completely new relationship with God. He was adamant that I come visit him for a very short trip for our eleventh anniversary (even though I had to jump through hoops to get childcare, tickets, work covered, etc.). But I did it, and James surprised me with so many sweet and romantic things! Best of all—he wrote out for me (and read at dinner) 101 reasons why he loves me. It is my most treasured gift from him.*
>
> *The weekend was the best time of our marriage. He is a truly different person. I didn't demand for him to find God or to study the Bible. He came to it on his own and has stepped up to the plate as the spiritual leader of our home.*

I wish I could include all the 101 reasons James gave for why he loves Corina, but there isn't space here, so fifteen reasons will have to do. James really thought about these reasons.…

1. I love you because you truly are my best friend.

2. I love when you cross your leg over mine in bed.

3. I love you because you make me feel like a man.

4. I love you because you trust me with your body when we make love.

5. I love you because your hand fits just right in mine.

6. I love you because you have forgiven me.

7. I love you because you have always been the rock and foundation of our marriage and family.

8. I love you because you believe in the power of prayer.

9. I love you because you believe in me.

10. I love you because you always encourage me.

11. I love you because you never gave up on us.

12. I love you because you snort when I make you laugh.

13. I love you because you know how to touch me just right.

14. I love you because you have taught me what it means to truly experience love.

15. I love knowing that I will see you in heaven, and if I died today, my life was better because you loved me.

WOW! Truly what happened in Corina and James' marriage is as much a miracle as if God had healed them from a terminal illness. Their marriage was terminal, and God intervened.

Instead of walking away in anger or shutting their husbands out, both Tabi and Corina trusted God with their marriage crisis and asked Him to intervene and work in their hearts and in their husbands' hearts. God used a wife's loving perseverance to push Corina and James closer together. Through the crisis of pornography, God brought Tabitha and Peter closer together.

Are you facing a crisis in your marriage? God longs to show you how He can give you His peace in the midst of pain and crisis. Call out to Him, cast all your worry and anxiety on Him, and He promises to hold you and your problem. "You can throw the whole weight of your anxiety on Him for you are His personal concern" (1 Peter 5:7 PH).

The Amplified Bible says it like this:

> *Casting the whole of your care [all your anxieties, all your worries, all your concerns, once and for all] on Him, for He cares for you affectionately and cares about you watchfully.*

Today as your heart aches because crisis mode hurts, cling to the promise that your personal Father is caring affectionately about you, your husband, and your marriage. He loves you. While you sleep tonight, He will be watching through the night, carrying all that concerns you on His strong shoulders. He is your peace in times of crisis. He gives the strength you and your husband need to grow closer, even in times of crisis.

Insight 4: A LONG, DIFFICULT MARRIAGE

When Natalie and Paul married, they had planned to serve the Lord together, but this was not to be. Paul became very disillusioned by the sexual sin and double lives of ministry coworkers, and as a result, he has not been to church in fifteen years.

I asked Natalie to describe what her marriage to Paul is like, and this is what she said:

- Paul is not unlovable, but he is sometimes very difficult to love.
- Paul is harsh. I am convinced that my husband's heart is kind and good, but sometimes his expression is not. It hurts.
- Paul did several things that broke our vows and my trust in a major way. I confronted him, and he has never forgiven me for pointing out his sin.

- Paul does not want to share me with friends or family, and this makes me feel isolated.
- Paul does not want to be involved in the deepest things of my heart. For me, this is his most difficult rejection.

Natalie once asked the Lord, "If Paul is not following You, does that nullify my vows?" The response wasn't, "Well, a covenant is a covenant, and he's broken it." It was, "Natalie, what did you mean in your heart?" She knew that she'd vowed before God to join her life to this man, no matter what. A few years later she was ready to leave Paul on what she was sure were biblical grounds. Again she asked God, "Can I leave him now and still be in Your good graces?" She felt God say, "You are always in my good graces. You have grounds, and you may leave. But I wonder, Natalie, if you'd be willing to stay and see what I will do?"

Natalie believed that God asked her to stay and love Paul, so she chose to stay in the marriage. The staying has been painful, but she says, "The hope of seeing what God will do keeps me filled with anticipation." Jeremiah 17:7–8 says:

> Blessed are those who trust in the LORD
> and have made the LORD their hope and confidence.
> They are like trees planted along a riverbank,
> with roots that reach deep into the water.
> Such trees are not bothered by the heat
> or worried by long months of drought.
> Their leaves stay green,
> and they never stop producing fruit. (NLT)

Natalie gives testimony to the truth of this passage. Even in the midst of a very long drought, she and her leaves stay green. I asked her to share with you how this could be and what she would say to a woman in a hard marriage.

The first thing I had to do was forgive Paul. I couldn't do this until I heard a definition of forgiveness that made sense to me.

Forgiveness is releasing someone from your judgment.

First Peter 2:23 began to glow inside of me like an ember. It says, "When they hurled their insults at him, he did not retaliate; when he suffered, he made no threats. Instead, he entrusted himself to him who judges justly" (NIV). Forgiveness means I let go of my own judgment, and I trust God to judge justly.

First I had to forgive, and then I had to walk out love. My Marriage Purpose Statement is a letter I wrote to Paul, stating how I want to live out my love for him. I read it often, asking God to show me how to live it.

My Paul,

I give you my heart, my respect, my acceptance, and my love always regardless of our circumstances or my feelings, for richer, for poorer, in sickness and in health, in agreement and in discord, in peace and in chaos, in joy and in despair.

I will seek to know what is important to you and let that become important to me.

I will tell you the truth to the very best of my ability, and when I find myself hiding, omitting, or distorting the truth, I will return to the simplicity of telling you the truth and trust you and Jesus to handle the ramifications or repercussions. This includes our finances, my emotions, my failures, our children, and my joys.

I will follow our Jesus passionately, fervently, joyfully so that I can be whole in my love for Him and you. I will share with you my discoveries in and with God.

I will let you know me, all of me, every bit that you are willing to know, doing my very best to be transparent for you, that you might find me a trustworthy, safe lover who is without unpleasant secrets.

I will enjoy you just as you are and let any changes that might be necessary in your life be between God and you. I will do my best to allow the Holy Spirit to be your teacher and me to be your cheerleader.

When romance dims, I will do my best to rekindle it, but even if romance burns out, I will continue to love you and be your beloved and friend.

I will keep myself as fit and healthy as I can, that you might find delight in me physically, for I know it is important to you.

I will do my best to make you laugh and never stop singing. I will find joy in you, but do not hold you accountable for my happiness. I will dance and joke and play with you in the good and bad times and will cry and pray and struggle with you in the hard and dark times. I will not leave you or reject you … ever.

And above all, I will ask my Abba for His help and strength always to live and love in the way that is best for us, for you and me as one.

You will be my one and only earthly lover, always.

Your Natalie

I choose to live my Marriage Purpose Statement and to love Paul. Believe me, I don't get to a godly place easily; usually I have a really good gripe first. There are still days I say, "I'm done now, God." But I made a secret choice to stay and watch what God would do. It has been a long, slow walk of loving a man who is not always easy to love. I have peace that I am making a difference, peace that in ten years, twenty years, I will be happy with my choices. BUT today I can see positive change:

- *We are growing as companions.*
- *"Grandma" and "Grandpa" are together and enjoying our first grandchild.*
- *Our marriage is better than it has ever been.*
- *I have hope it will be even better as time goes on.*

What would I say to a woman in a hard marriage? I would encourage her to: Be gentle with yourself. Give yourself grace. Loving someone is not something you achieve. It is something you live, day by day.

Is your marriage in a period of drought where it seems the trial will never end? Plant Jeremiah 17:7–8 in your mind and heart, and make it your prayer to the Lord. I love *The Message*'s paraphrase of these verses:

> *Blessed is the [woman] who trusts me, God,*
> *the woman who sticks with God.*
> *They're like trees replanted in Eden,*
> *putting down roots near the rivers—*
> *Never a worry through the hottest of summers,*
> *never dropping a leaf,*
> *Serene and calm through droughts,*
> *bearing fresh fruit every season.*

Beth Moore writes: "A bruised heart that chooses to beat with passion for God amid pulsing pain and confusion may just be the most expensive offering placed on the divine altar." Natalie has a bruised heart, yet she has slowly seen God pull her and Paul closer together. It hasn't happened in one year; it has been many years, but there is progress and growth toward intimacy. Natalie has chosen to trust God, and she ministers to me and many others with her green leaves. Oh, how God delights in Natalie's expensive offering!

Insight 5: THE INTEGRITY WALK

Tina leaned in close and said, "You would think after so many years of marriage that you'd moved beyond times of crisis. We had many seasons of trials when we were younger, but I thought we'd gotten marriage more together now. Boy, was I wrong."

Jack and Tina had what I call a smooth marriage. They moved easily together without a lot of friction. Then one of their daughters left her husband and moved in with her three children, and a frictionless union became a very uneasy one. As parents, Jack and Tina had agreed on how to raise the children, but they could not agree on their role with the live-in grandchildren. Tension erupted with their daughter. It was no longer a peaceful home.

Beth and Jim had also moved through marriage without too many bumps. Then Jim lost his job. Beth became the "job hunter supervisor," continually checking to make sure Jim was applying for every possible position. Quarrels over money erupted often. The stress of a year with no job threatened to pull Beth and Jim apart.

I can relate to what these couples who have been married many years are going through.

After years of speaking and writing on marriage, I thought I had Jody's and my relationship figured out, and that as we grew older, our intimate oneness would flow easily. But we, too, hit a bump in the road. Children and grandchildren did not move in with us, no one lost a job. After thirty-five years of marriage, we found an area of conflict that we couldn't resolve. It wasn't a moral issue. One of us changed our perspective on something that we had been in agreement about all of our married life. This change disrupted our equanimity and threatened to erode our emotional and spiritual intimacy. Neither Jody nor I ever saw this coming. Marriage wasn't supposed to be like this. It was supposed to get easier. Ha!

God was calling me to trust Him. I promised to choose trust and so I said, *Lord, I choose to trust You for:*

> *What I don't understand*
> *What doesn't make sense to me*
> *What I can't see.*

Was it easy to live with tension at age fifty-five? What do you think? Did I ever feel like giving up? What do you think?

But I couldn't give up. I wouldn't give up! I had promised to be faithful, to walk in my house with a heart of integrity.

We don't often hear the word *integrity*. It seems like something from George Washington's and John Adams' era. But *integrity* is a word of deep meaning; a biblical word. One dictionary defines *integrity* as "the quality of being honest and upright in character."[6]

The psalmist David said, "I will walk within my house in the integrity of my heart" (Ps. 101:2). This verse speaks of fixed determination. The original Hebrew term translated *integrity* means "to be finished, whole, and complete." It carries with it the idea of being "totally honest, thoroughly sound."[7]

Job offers us the most profound picture of integrity I have ever seen. Almighty God describes Job as "a man of complete integrity" (Job 1:8; 2:3 NLT). He maintained his integrity even when catastrophic trials assailed him (2:3). After all was taken from him—food, property, health, all ten of his children—he still kept his integrity. His wife did not. Job sat with boils covering his body, in physical, emotional, and spiritual agony, and his wife came and asked him, "Are you still trying to maintain your integrity? Curse God and die" (2:9 NLT).

What did Job say to his wife? "You talk like a foolish woman. Should we accept only good things from the hand of God and never anything bad?" (2:10 NLT). Job's idea of maintaining his integrity meant:

> *Accepting the bad things in life as well as the good.*

Do you realize how amazing Job's statement is? In one day he had a tsunami sweep over his possessions and his family, one devastating crash after another. I can't imagine losing one child—and Job lost ten children in one day! He was physically ill, emotionally spent, and questioning spiritually, yet he says, "How can I only accept good? I have been blessed in this life and now the bad has come. I will worship God and bow to Him still" (Job 1:20–21, author's paraphrase).

Job amazes me. I understand why God called him a "man of complete integrity." I want to walk in my house with a heart of integrity. I want to be like Job and worship God, in good times and in hard times.

When I am in pain about something in my marriage, I declare my trust in the Lord out loud to Him. I go to my favorite Scriptures for spiritual help and pray them out loud to God:

> *My Father, I choose to trust You with all my heart, to lean only on You, thanking You that You will straighten out the rough path (see Proverbs 3:5–6).*

> *Lord, I will receive this "irresolvable issue" between Jody and me as a gift. Work endurance and maturity in my life. I want to be like Jesus (see James 1:2–4).*

> *Lord Jesus, thank You that You care affectionately and watchfully for all that concerns me (see 1 Peter 5:7 AB).*

> *Lord, my trust is in You alone. You are my hope and confidence. Oh, please let my leaves stay green … let me continue to bear fruit! (see Jeremiah 17:7–8).*

> *My God, like Job, I will accept the bad along with the good. I will hold fast to my integrity. I trust You! Blessed be Your holy name! (see Job 1:20, 2:10).*

I go to God's Word, and then I take hold of practical helps to fight against trials:

- I put on my Gripes Be Gone bracelet.
- I get out my Thankful Journal and read all the reasons I'm thankful I'm married to this man.
- I practice Philippians 4:8: "I will remember what is true, worthy of respect, honorable, just, pure, lovely. I will dwell on what is excellent and praiseworthy in my husband."
- I get on my knees and read my Marriage Purpose Statement as a prayer to God.

Then I get up off my knees, sigh, and say, *Okay, God, I've got my head on straight now. Show me today how to trust You, and show Jody and me how to grow closer in crisis.*

The story is told of a Green Beret who came up to a speaker after listening to him speak about facing trials together as a couple and said, "In the Green Berets we train over and over, and then over and over again. We repeat some exercises until we are sick of them, but our instructors know what they are doing. They want us so prepared and finely trained that when trials and difficulties come on the battlefield, we will be able to fall back upon that which is second nature to us. We literally learn to do things by reflex action."

Like the Green Berets, let's be prepared for crisis. There are seasons of marriage that seem like a battlefield, but God has given us the battle plan. We are to trust Him, even when we can't see what He is doing. This is what Job did, and his faith in God became worship: "Blessed be the name of the LORD" (Job 1:21).

In the last few years, Jody and I have faced several crises, including my brain injury, his cancer, and this seemingly irresolvable issue. Remember what I said at the beginning of this Dangerous Question about a crisis? We can choose to see a crisis as:

Danger that the crisis will tear us apart and destroy our oneness.

Or we can choose to see ...

Opportunity that the crisis will push us together and deepen our oneness.

Jody and I choose that each crisis in our marriage will be an opportunity to grow closer to the Lord and closer to each other. May it be true for you and your husband too!

P.S. Jody and I have now been married forty-six years. Our difference of perspective is still an issue, but we have grown in trusting God. We've gone deeper in accepting and loving each other. That, my friend, is what marriage is all about.

Dangerous Prayer!

My Father, teach me how to trust You. I want crisis to bring my husband and me closer together. I'm up when things are good and down when they're bad. I do want to walk in my house with a heart of integrity.

The Woman in the Mirror

One [woman] has enthusiasm for 30 minutes, another
for 30 days, but it is the [woman] who has it for
30 years who makes a success of [her marriage].
Adapted from Edward B. Butler, *Scientist*

Every job is a self-portrait of the person who did it.
Autograph your work as a wife with excellence.
Author Unknown

The quality of a person's life is in direct
proportion to their commitment to excellence,
regardless of their chosen field of endeavor.
Vincent T. Lombardi

Love never fails. Money, youth, and motorboats all fail.
Waistlines stretch, teeth vanish, eyes weaken. Skin wrinkles,
heads bald, arches drop. Love and love alone never gives up.
William Coleman

Insight 1: LOOK AT YOU ... A WIFE BY DESIGN!

National Football League coach John McKay said, "I am a big believer in the *mirror test.* All that matters is if you can look in the mirror and honestly tell the person you see there, that you've done your best." I find the word *best* confusing because some of us feel like we can never live out our definition of "best." If I were writing the above quote, it would sound different—it would go like this:

> *I am a big believer in the mirror test. All that matters is if you can look in the mirror and honestly tell the wife you see there, that you've been faithful.*

Faithfulness is what God asks of me as a wife.

> *It is required that a wife who has been given a trust must prove faithful. (1 Cor. 4:2, author's paraphrase)*

The "trust" I have been given is one man, Jody Dillow, and God asks me to prove trustworthy in carrying out my assignment as a wife to him.

Have you taken this verse into your heart? God doesn't say you have to be the best wife in the world. He doesn't ask you to be successful or popular. You don't have to be like Super Wife down the street. You don't have to be the best lover or best anything. You just have to be the "newly designed you" who says, "Yes, God, I'll ask these Dangerous Questions. Show me what it's like to be married to me." You have taken your assignment as a wife seriously.

Do you know why I respect you? Lots of wives would have put this book back on the shelf and thought, *No way am I asking what it's like to be married to me!* You didn't run from the Dangerous Questions. I think you're brave. I think you're smart. And I just bet you're creative. God is taking brave, smart, creative you and showing you how to love your unique husband. It doesn't happen overnight—it is a process—but you are on the road, headed toward the goal. You, my friend, are becoming a wife by design. You've chosen to live not by default, but by design.

Your design for you as a wife is your Marriage Purpose Statement. You've read the Marriage Statements written by many wives in this book. Every one is special because it is the picture of who each wife longs to become. Your Marriage Statement is unique only to you, designed by God through you to guide you in your journey as a wife. My Marriage Statement has changed over the years, and yours probably will too. Keep it close by, as it is your guide on your journey through the seasons of life as a wife.

I live my years as a wife knowing that one day the Lord will ask me, "Linda, were you faithful?" Faithful wives prove trustworthy in carrying out their assignments. I want to do my part to love Jody, to make the right choices, because one day God will evaluate my life at the judgment seat of Christ. I long to hear the Lord say to me, "Linda, you have loved and encouraged Jody. Well done, My good and faithful servant."

These verses from Psalm 119 have encouraged me as I reflect on walking faithfully as a wife. They encompass all the seasons of my marriage journey: past, present, and future.

> *I have chosen the faithful way....*
> *I cling to Your testimonies....*
> *I shall run the way of Your commandments,*
> *For You will enlarge my heart. (Ps. 119:30–32)*

In the past: **"I have chosen** the faithful way." *Chosen* in Hebrew means to "take a keen look at."[1] It is a choosing that has ultimate and eternal significance. If your choice in the past has been to set your heart on God's desire for your marriage, your choice has eternal significance. God rejoices over your choice! If this has not been your choice in the past, it can be your choice today. Consider writing today's date here:_____.

By doing this, you declare: *From this day forward, I choose God's way. I want to be a wife by design, to live by my Marriage Purpose Statement.*

In the present: "**I cling** to your testimonies." *Cling* is a strong word that means to "stick like glue."[2] This special word is translated as *cleave* in Genesis concerning marriage: "Therefore shall a man leave his father and his mother, and shall cleave unto his wife: and they shall be one flesh" (Gen. 2:24 KJV). I love this; I cling to my husband in intimate oneness, and I cling to God's Word.

In the future: "**I shall run** the way of your commandments." The word *run* fails to capture the energy of the Hebrew word. It means to charge into battle.[3] Your God desires that you have a "charging into battle" mentality as you walk out each day as a wife. With a steadfast heart, determine to keep on keeping on, running purposefully along the track of His commands. Every day you can join me and pray something like this:

> *Okay, God, another day to choose Your way. Give me a charging-into-battle mentality as a wife. Today I will live by my Marriage Purpose Statement.*

Your part is to cling to the faithful way and charge into the battle of becoming all God desires you to be as a wife—to continue running toward who you want to become. This is your part. But the wonderful thing is, God has a part too.

> *I shall run the way of Your commandments,*
> *For You will enlarge my heart. (Ps. 119:32)*

God knows I am weak, and He says to me, "Linda, as you charge into battle, running on My path, I will enlarge your heart by expanding your understanding of Jody. I will multiply your insight into Jody as a man. I will increase your knowledge of how to love and encourage Jody. I will give you skill so you can live your marriage as a thing of beauty." And God's promise is for you, too!

God will enlarge your heart of love for your husband.

God will expand your heart to understand and appreciate him.

God will pump more power into your heart so you can keep on keeping on.

Some people want to give up, but I firmly believe there is no marriage beyond God's healing touch. People give up on marriage, but God doesn't. Sometimes He even takes what we have given up on and re-creates it.

Insight 2: GOD IS THE RE-CREATOR!

Cris and Nick Palafox have personally experienced God's re-creation in their marriage. They *undid* their sacred vows, and then *redid* them again.

> *We were married for nine years.*
> *We were divorced nearly three years.*
> *We remarried April 1998.*
> *We have been given a second chance.*
> *To God be the glory!*[4]

Listen to the sweet messages Nick and Cris wrote to each other. See the joy of God's re-creation!

Nick wrote:

> *Cris, my love, my heart,*
>
> *Thank you for giving me another chance to be your husband, to share our children's lives and our walk with the Lord. Thank you for giving me and the kids so much—no book would have enough room to hold my thanks for who you are and what you mean to me.*

Cris wrote:

> *Nick, my husband, my love,*
>
> *Thank you for opening your heart to the Lord and to me. I feel*
> *your love, your tender touch, and your forgiveness. You teach,*
> *guide, and help me grow. I thank you for accepting His leadership*
> *for our family, and for allowing me another chance to be your wife*
> *and to make memories with our children as we build our future*
> *together.*[5]

God is the Re-Creator!

Proverbs 24:3–4 contains a powerful message of hope to wives who want to restore their marriages. It says:

> *By wisdom a house [of marriage] is built,*
> *And by understanding it is established;*
> *And by knowledge the rooms are filled*
> *With all precious and pleasant riches.*

What insight can this passage give you if you want God to restore your marriage? You need to understand three nouns in this verse, but the verbs speak of the possible re-creation of marriage and are even more important.

First, look with me at the nouns: *wisdom, understanding,* and *knowledge.*[6]

"By *wisdom* [a marriage] is built." A wife with wisdom has skill in living life. The Hebrew word used in this passage for wisdom is *hokmah.* In the Old Testament, this word was used to describe the skill of craftsmen, artists, and counselors (Ex. 28:3; 31:3, 6; 35:26; 36:1). Wisdom is skill, a skill in living life as a thing of beauty. A wife who lives skillfully helps create a marriage of lasting value.

"By *understanding* [a marriage] is established." A wife with understanding listens to her husband's heart. She weighs her words on the balance scale of love.

"By *knowledge* the rooms are filled with all precious and pleasant riches." A wife with knowledge studies her husband and asks, "Who is he today, my Lord? Who is he becoming? Show me what encouragement looks like during this season of his life."

Now for the exciting part—the three verbs: *built, established,* and *filled.*

"By wisdom [a marriage] is *built.*" The Hebrew word translated here as *built* suggests the idea of restoring. It is the idea of "*re*"building something so that it flourishes once again.[7] When you said, "I'll look in the mirror and ask, *What's it like to be married to me?*" you took a step to begin the rebuilding process.

"By understanding [a marriage] is *established.*" The word *established* means to "set in order."[8] It's the idea of putting something back into an upright position, something that was once leaning, falling, or twisted. This is exactly what you have been doing. You've taken each Dangerous Question and said:

> *Change me, God. Take me from griping to gratitude.*
> *Change me, God. I long to give my body as a gift to my husband.*
> *Change me, God. I want to forgive freely as Christ forgave me.*

"By knowledge the rooms are *filled* with all precious and pleasant riches." The word *filled* suggests fulfillment and abundant satisfaction. These riches are not of this world but are found in the precious and pleasant joy of a deep intimacy between you and your husband. I pray this is growing in your marriage.

My friend, do you understand this message of hope? It isn't about already-perfect relationships. This is about restoring and rebuilding a relationship so it can once again flourish. It is about taking a marriage that has been leaning, almost falling over, and re-creating it so it can stand strong. So it is lasting.

Oh, I hope you see. This passage is saying that there is always hope. If you feel discouraged about your marriage, STOP! There is hope! If you feel like it is impossible to be the wife God asks you to be, STOP! There is hope! *God is in the re-creation business. That means there is hope for you and for your marriage.*

God says hope comes through His Word and through the Holy Spirit (Rom. 15:4, 13). Read God's promises from His Word again on the previous pages. They are for you! Wherever your marriage is today, there is hope because God breathes hope through the Word and the Spirit. He is the God of hope!

Insight 3: THE CHANGING SEASONS OF YOUR MARRIAGE

Every couple travels on a journey though the changing seasons of their marriage. Some seasons we skip through as they are joyous and filled with delight. Others we stomp through, hoping they are quickly over. And some we walk through on tippy toes because we long to embrace every moment of the tender intimate oneness.

Jody and I began our marriage journey as young, idealistic college students. We were new Christians and convinced that with Christ as Lord of our marriage, it would be a walk in the park. So, we wrapped our arms around one another and began walking through the seasons of our lover/best-friend intimacy together. Quickly, we learned that all seasons were not a stroll in the park. So, we whispered words of encouragement to one another. Sometimes, when our partner struggled, we shouted words to build them up: "I love you; I'm here for you; we'll get through this together."

I began writing to you about Dangerous Questions on Jody's and my forty-fifth anniversary. Amazingly enough, another year has passed. God gives us anniversaries as milestones, significant points in the passing of time, specific yet mute reminders that more sand has passed through the hourglass. He builds them into our calendar once every year to enable us to make an annual appraisal—not of the length of time we've been married but the depth of our intimacy. Not just to remind us we've been married longer, but to help us determine if we are now married deeper.

Jody and I have grown deeper in our intimate oneness, and I thank and praise God. I wrote a letter to God on our last anniversary to express my gratitude for His molding of two very different people into one. Even though the letter was to God, I gave it to Jody in his anniversary card.

My Father,

It is our forty-sixth anniversary, and my heart is filled with thankfulness to You. I woke up this morning wanting to write You, precious Lord, to thank You for Your abundant wisdom. I am so grateful for this husband You brought to me. You knew, You saw, that even though we were so different, that we would learn to complement and complete one another.

I laugh when I think how the first year of our marriage I said to Jody, "You should have a wife more like you; an intellect, someone interested in deep theology." And I really believed that. And Jody was convinced I needed a husband who was more social, more structured, more of everything he wasn't.

How beautiful it is to look back over the seasons of our marriage and see the beauty of Your choice for me. Would marriage have been a smoother ride through the decades with someone else? Maybe. But together Jody and I have learned to live the words adapt, accept, respect, and love—as Christ loved, with no strings attached. We have grown more intimate with You, our God, as we have begged You for answers, listened to Your gentle whispers as

You painted a picture of just what love looked like for our mate that very day.

Oh, look at the lover/best-friend intimacy we have forged! It takes my breath away!

On this day when I pledged to love, honor, and respect Jody Dillow, I bow and thank You, my God. I am so blessed!

Your Linda

I think it is helpful for each of us to see how other couples walk on their marriage journey, to reflect on how other wives live by intentional design. So, I want to introduce you to three couples at different places in their journey together: one in the morning of their marriage, one in the late afternoon, and the last in the midnight hours of their marriage. Each couple has committed to be forever faithful, although what that means looks different for each of them. Each has experienced seasons of difficulty and grown more in love through the hard times.

Heidi and Scott White are a picture of young love. They have been married six years. Below is Heidi's Marriage Purpose Statement, which is based on a passage from the Song of Solomon:

Place me like a seal over your heart,
Like a seal on your arm;
For love is as strong as death,
Its jealousies unyielding as the grave.
It burns like blazing fire,
Like a mighty flame.
Many waters cannot quench love;
Rivers cannot wash it away.
If one were to give all the wealth of his house for love,
It would be utterly scorned. (Song 8:6–7)

My marriage goal is that I would choose every day of my life to
intentionally see Scott through the lens of the love described in
Song of Solomon 8:6–7.

- *I will prioritize Scott as first in all my human*
  relationships.
- *I will listen to Scott.*
- *I will study Scott.*
- *I will honor Scott in word and action.*

Heidi and Scott are basking in the morning sunshine of their marriage, yet they think on deep things. We see in the passage Heidi used for her Marriage Purpose Statement that nothing can quench this love. Why? "Its flashes are flashes of fire, the very flame of the LORD" (Song 8:6).

May the flame of the Lord light a fire in your heart for your husband.

The second couple, Bev and Gary DeSalvo, are in the afternoon of their marriage. They have been married thirty-two years. Here is Bev's Marriage Purpose Statement:

When I look into the mirror I see an image of myself. It is an
exact likeness of Bev DeSalvo, and it's the only way I know if my
makeup is smooth and if the cowlick in the back of my hair is
filled in. In fact, it is the only way that I can know what I look
like from the chest up.

Ephesians 5:31–32 tells us that our marriage is to be a mys-
terious reflection of Christ and the Church. So when people look
at my marriage, I want them to see a divine representation of the
love relationship between the Beloved Bridegroom and His bride,
whose hearts are knit together so tightly that God sees them as one.
My desire is to become so close to my husband that we are spiritu-
ally, emotionally, and physically one. So I choose to trust Gary
DeSalvo and allow him to lead me in a holy, romantic dance for
all the days that we have left on earth together. I surrender to the

Holy One so that I can hear Him tell me how to listen to Gary's heart when he speaks, and not just his words. I will keep my eyes on my Beloved so that I will know when, where, and how to step in time with Gary as our bodies, hearts, and minds become so closely woven together that Abba sees us as one flesh. I pray that as He mysteriously knits us together we will reflect an image of the passionate love relationship between Christ and His bride. Who knows? This may be the only way someone will know what that looks like.

I love Bev's word picture of God mysteriously knitting husband and wife together so their union will radiate the joyous and passionate intimacy between Christ and His bride. It's as if God elevates the marriage bond by declaring, "Look at Bev and Gary—look at Jody and Linda—and catch a glimpse of Me—Jesus—with my bride, the Church." I am humbled. Can the world see holy love in the way I love Jody—in the tone of my voice when I speak to him, in the joy of my smile when I look at him?

May the world see the mysterious reflection of Christ and the Church in your intimate oneness and mine.

Young love is vital and energizing, love in the afternoon years is stable and secure, but the question is asked:

Is there anything more beautiful in life than a boy and a girl clasping clean hands and pure hearts in the path of marriage? Can there be anything more beautiful than young love? And the answer is given. "Yes, there is a more beautiful thing. It is the spectacle of an old man and an old woman finishing their journey together on that path. Their hands are gnarled, but still clasped; their faces are seamed but still radiant; their hearts are physically bowed and tired, but still strong with love and devotion for one another. Yes, there is a more beautiful thing than young love: old love."[9]

The third couple, Mark and Anita Bubeck, are in the midnight of their marriage. They show us a portrait of the beauty of old love. Mark is a Christian leader and author, yet God has given him a new job, caring for his wife of sixty years. For the last ten years, Alzheimer's has slowly been taking Anita away. Mark is still able to care for her in their home.

The Bubecks' daughter, my friend Judy Dunagan, wrote this touching poem after visiting her parents:

The Dance

Their dance took my breath away.
Heads bowed toward each other, face to face.
She in a pink bathrobe, her hands gripped on her walker.
He is gently coaxing her to take steps toward him as he guides the
    front of her walker.
He is guiding her toward her hospital bed,
Placed recently at the foot of the bed they've shared for almost 60
    years of marriage.
She is breathing heavily as if she's run a marathon,
Taking only ten steps from the bathroom where her
Husband just helped her like she helped me when I was a
    toddler.
He gently helps her into her new bed.
She looks at him with frightened, childlike eyes and says,
"I am afraid." He says, "Don't be afraid, Jesus is here."
He tucks her in while they quietly sing "His Name is
    Wonderful!"
She still remembers most of the words of this favorite hymn.
Her voice is still beautiful and she sings on key.
He brushes her cheek with a gentle kiss,

And covers her with his prayers.
He then goes to their bed alone.
With his bride in her hospital bed at the foot of his bed,
She soon falls asleep, safely under the shelter of him.[10]

I can't read "The Dance" without tears. What a precious picture of lifetime love. Judy says that the first night of her visit she couldn't take her eyes off of them as her dad so lovingly cared for his bride. While cleaning their home, Judy found a note her mom probably wrote two years ago, before Alzheimer's stole her beautiful handwriting. On a yellow sticky note she had written, "I'm fading away, but Jesus is keeping me every day."

May we experience the precious joy of "Old Love."

In the beginning of your marriage journey you pledged:

For better or worse, for richer or poorer, in sickness and in health.

When we are young, beautiful, and vital, our ears are attuned to BETTER, RICHER, and HEALTH. But each couple will enter into seasons of WORSE, POORER, and SICKNESS.

Jody and I have known sickness. He sat by my bed for five days in the trauma hospital in California after my fall and brain injury. I was "not there," so he sat and held my hand and prayed. I've had my turn to pray as I followed the ambulance in the middle of the night to the emergency room when Jody's heart wasn't working right, when his pacemaker failed. In a week, I will hold his hand and pray after his cancer surgery.

When you are young and strong, it doesn't sound difficult to say, "In sickness and in health." Health is definitely more fun than sickness, for better is lots more fun than for worse, and we all know richer is more fun than poorer. But I committed to the bad as well as to the good. Jody and I have known both.

Marriage is a journey. I want to walk through the seasons of my marriage with a forever-faithful mentality. So I brand the words of 1 Corinthians 13 on my heart and make a secret choice to live them:

> *Love never gives up, never loses faith, is always hopeful, and endures through every circumstance. (1 Cor. 13:7 NLT)*

There is glorious hope for those who choose to faithfully endure through every season of marriage. I believe this will be your choice!

Insight 4: LOOK AT YOU: LEARNING! GROWING! CHANGING!

Ten women, married seven to fifteen years, sat around the table holding their Marriage Purpose Statements. As they each read the portrait of who they wanted to become as a wife, I was unprepared for their waves of emotion. As Renee began reading hers, tears fell, and she stopped. She gathered herself together and read, only to stop a second time. Renee's good friend tried to come to the rescue—"I'll read it for Renee." I smiled at sweet Renee and said, "I think Renee can read it."

Here is what she read:

> *I pray that one day soon I can be this person for my God and for my husband.*

As Read by David

> *You raised me up, so I could stand on mountains,*
> *You made me want to be a better man.*
> *My head turned only in your direction and*
> *your laughter made me stare with delight.*
> *Your confidence made my breath escape*
> *And your passion for GOD and me was so great.*

Your heart always growing
the capacity never full
the kindness you showed was unconditional.
You were perfect from your head all the way to your toes.
You raised me up more than you'll ever know.
The Lord was her love and I was her lover.

As Renee finished reading, she looked up at the group and said through her tears, "I read this to David last night. My poem to him was about how I wanted him to see me by the end of my life, but when I read it, David was so sweet. He was really touched by the poem and looked at me as if to say, 'I already think of you that way,' where I feel like I still have a long way to go."

Two days later, her husband flew to Haiti with Compassion International to film children in Haiti's villages. When the earthquake of 2010 hit Haiti, David had just walked into Hotel Montana. An unending month later, David's body was found among the rubble. He was one of more than two hundred thousand who perished.

During David's memorial service, the pastor called Renee up to the stage. He told the five hundred gathered to celebrate David's life that Renee had written her Marriage Purpose Statement and read it to David before he left for Haiti. As the pastor read Renee's poem, there wasn't a dry eye in the sanctuary. Here was a wife who lived intentionally in her marriage—who thought about what was really important to her and who verbalized who she wanted to become to God and to her husband.

After her husband's death Renee said, "I'm so grateful that one of the last things David heard from me was my Marriage Purpose Statement. He knew who I wanted to be to him as a wife and that I was walking toward that goal."

David Hames was forty years old when he died. We don't expect life to end when we're young, when our sons are ages three and six. We all feel like we have all the time in the world, but God's Word tells us differently.

LORD, remind me how brief my time on earth will be.
  Remind me that my days are numbered—
  how fleeting my life is.
You have made my life no longer than the width of my hand.
  My entire lifetime is just a moment to you;
  at best, each of us is but a breath. (Ps. 39:4–5 NLT)

This life is short, and so we want to grow every day toward who we want to become. The minutes of our marriage pass so quietly, so consistently, that we fail to realize the time is ticking away, so I go back to where I started: We must live our marriage by design. We only have this year, this month, this moment to grow in intimate oneness.

Can you remember back to the first chapter where you thought about what was really important to you? I asked you to think about your funeral, thirty years in the future, and imagine what you would want your husband to say about you as a wife. Then you wrote your Marriage Purpose Statement. Why don't you get your Marriage Statement and read it now. I wonder, as you think back to all the Dangerous Questions you have asked yourself as you have read this book—is there anything you would change in what you wrote? Ask the Lord if there is anything He wants you to change.

Think deeply, because "one of these days, much sooner than you want to face, one of you is going to be sitting beside the deathbed of the other, holding a frail, clammy hand. You'll look into each other's misty eyes during those aching, final hours, and the memories will flood through your grieving minds in a raging torrent.

- You will not regret a single dreamy walk you took together in the park.
- You will not regret the time you stayed up so late talking and holding each other that you were both zombies at work the next day.

- You will not regret all the times you made love and let the housework go."[11]

And more than that—

- You will not regret writing your Marriage Purpose Statement and sharing it with your husband.
- You will not regret telling your husband why you respect him.

But I'll tell you what you will regret.

- You will regret the hundreds of hours you spent fighting.
- You will regret the times you held a grudge or gave the silent treatment.
- You will regret griping, venting, and complaining.
- You will regret saying, "Maybe next year sex will get better."
- You will regret not really believing that your time as lovers was limited.

I don't think you will regret looking in the mirror. I am a big believer in the *mirror test*. All that matters is if you can look in the mirror and honestly say to yourself these three words: *I've been faithful.*

Look in the mirror! I think you will see a "newly designed wife," a brave woman who is intentionally becoming her picture of a faithful wife. Keep on learning. Keep on growing. Keep on changing. Your intimacy with that special man, your husband, will just get better and more beautiful!

Know that I will be praying for you as you keep on keeping on.

A Ten- (or Twelve-) Week Reflective Bible Study

To the Women in This Study:

I'm excited that you are willing to ask, *What's it like to be married to me?* and to reflect on the other Dangerous Questions. You are taking a step forward in becoming a wife by design. This is exciting!

I've called this a reflective Bible study, because it is a bit different from a normal Bible study. It is:

- A time to think deeply about who you are as a wife—and who you are becoming.
- A time to be in God's Word, reading, pondering, and memorizing.
- A time to think, search your soul, pray, and plan.
- A time to do practical projects that will reveal to you much about you, your husband, and your marriage.

Before you begin, here are some things you need to know:

1. Each Bible study has the questions divided under five days. Some of these line up with the Dangerous Questions' insights; others do not. You can do the study all at once or over five days or three days or seven days, whatever works for you.

2. Some sections have personal projects for you to do. If so, I alert you at the beginning of the study so you can have the entire week to work on the project.

3. What you put into the Bible study and the projects is what you will get out—growth takes work, reflection takes quiet, time, and thought.

Thank you for setting these weeks aside to reflect on your marriage and who you are becoming as a wife. I am asking the Lord to meet with you, to send His Blessed Spirit as Teacher, Encourager, Comforter, and Transformer!

I am praying for you!

Linda Dillow, 2010

To the Bible Study Leader:

I'm excited you are going to lead the reflective Bible study on *What's It Like to Be Married to Me?* Let me give you a little of my thinking about a few things in the study.

I stress memorizing God's Word because our minds are renewed when they are filled with God's truth.

I ask the women in the study to write out Scripture because when we write, we see things we missed by simply reading. For the same reason, I often ask the women to read the Word out loud.

In the first three studies I assign some projects. Be sure to alert the women in your study to the project so they will have the entire week to reflect, practice, and complete the project. In the second Bible study, the women are to wear a "Gripes Be Gone" bracelet all week. Every time they gripe, they have to change the bracelet to the other arm. Each day they journal about what they learn about themselves and about *when* they complain. In the third study, they will keep a "Thankful Bookmark" in their Bible or book to remind them to learn the language of gratitude. Both the bracelet and bookmarks are available at www.LindaDillow.org. The bracelet and bookmark will bring life changes but also add an element of fun.

I encourage wives to have a Thankful Journal where they can record what they are learning about growing in God gratitude and in husband gratitude. You can either buy some journals and have the women pay you, or let them get their own. In the future, I hope to have Thankful Journals available on the website. On the website, you will find additional examples of Marriage Purpose Statements plus comments from women who have taken the Bible study. Please email the website with anything you or your group feel would be helpful for other Bible study groups.

The study can be either ten or twelve weeks. Ten of the lessons correspond to the Dangerous Questions in the book. The two additional studies are a time of thanksgiving, reflection, and celebration. These optional studies fall after weeks five and ten. My hope in having the study be ten or twelve weeks was to make it adaptable for every group, but if possible, I encourage you to do the two additional studies, as I believe they push God's truth deeper into hearts.

When I led the pilot studies for this book, I told the study groups that they could share anything about themselves as a wife, but they could *not* share anything about their husbands—unless, of course, it was positive. This study is for wives. It's an invitation for them to ask themselves Dangerous Questions, to seek God and His perspective. It is a place to begin to live, not by default, but by design. To look ahead and decide who you want to become, and then begin to grow toward that picture.

Know that I am praying for you as you lead your precious women to all God desires them to be as wives.

I trust the Lord to lead you as you lead them!

Linda Dillow, 20-10

Week 1

What Is Really Important to Me?

Read "What Is Really Important to Me?", Insight 5 now so you can be reflecting on it all week.

"By Design, Not Default," Day 1: By Design or Default?

1. What did you learn (both positive and negative) in your childhood home about marriage?

2. Describe a woman who was a role model to you as a wife.

3. Why did you choose this woman as your picture of a wife?

Memorize and meditate on Song of Solomon 5:16

> *"His mouth is full of sweetness*
> *And he is wholly desirable.*
> *This is my beloved and this is my friend."*

4. Write a paragraph amplifying what this verse says to you personally.

"What Is Really Important to Me?", Day 1: What Do My Choices Say?

1. What do you say is most important to you? List your priorities.

2. How would your husband list your priorities?

3. How would it help you to ask yourself, *Will I be happy with my choice in five years or twenty years?*

Day 2: Marriage Matters and The Treadmill Won't Stop

> *It is because the* Lord *is acting as the witness between you and the wife of your youth, because you have broken faith with her, though she is your partner, the wife of your marriage covenant.*

Has not the LORD made them one? In flesh and spirit they are his.... So guard yourself in your spirit, and do not break faith with the wife of your youth. (Mal. 2:14–15 NIV)

1. How would you explain these verses to a young woman about to marry?

2. How can you "guard yourself in your spirit"?

3. Reflect on Bethany and Chris's marriage vows on pages 23–24. When you read these precious vows, do you feel joyful, sad, encouraged, or discouraged? What do your feelings say to you?

4. Which of the comments on pages 26–27 do you identify with? Why?

5. What can you do to get off the treadmill?

Day 3: Live with the End in View

1. Do you agree with Emily's statement in the play *Our Town* that no one ever realizes life while they live it? Explain your answer.

2. Are you living in reality, valuing each day with your husband, or are you walking through marriage as in a fog?

3. Read Psalm 90:12 and Ephesians 5:15–16. Write a paragraph describing how living these verses will help you realize life while you live it.

4. Find a block of time and a quiet place. Reflect on what you would want your husband to say at your funeral thirty years from now. (Refer to the questions on page 30.) Write your thoughts in a notebook or journal.

Day 4: Aim for the Goal

1. Define a goal

2. Define a desire

3. Have you had your goals and desires mixed up? If so, how?

Day 5: Get a Vision for Your Marriage

Now it is your turn to write your unique Marriage Purpose Statement.

Find a quiet place and time to reflect. Review what you wrote about what you want your husband to say at your funeral thirty years from now. These words describe who you hope to become. Think, pray, and form your thoughts into a Marriage Purpose Statement. It can be a:

- Resolution or declaration
- Prayer
- Scripture
- Poem or song
- Letter you write to yourself
- Acrostic
- List or paragraph

Come prepared to share your personal Marriage Purpose Statement at the Bible study.

Week 2

What Does It Feel Like to Be My Husband?

Read "What Does It Feel Like to Be My Husband?", Insight 5 now. Begin wearing your bracelet and journaling today.

Day 1: Sophisticated Venting
Memorize Philippians 2:14 in any translation of the Bible (and 15 and 16 if you can!).

> *Do everything without complaining and arguing, so that no one can criticize you. (v. 14–15 NLT)*

> *Live clean, innocent lives as children of God, shining like bright lights in a world full of crooked and perverse people. (v. 15 NLT)*

1. What are your thoughts as you read what wives said was the worst thing they had done in their marriage (see pages 44–45)?

2. Do you think you are a positive person, a griping nag, or somewhere in between? Explain your answer.

3. If you haven't already, begin wearing your bracelet and journaling today. What do you learn about yourself as you wear and switch the bracelet? Be specific.

Day 2: Where Did I Catch the Griping Disease?

1. Read page 47 and then write your own translation of Philippians 4:8.

2. List at least five things you learn from Jean's story on pages 48–49.

3. Do you think Christian women think it is okay to whine and complain? Give an example.

Day 3: God—on Griping

1. Read Proverbs 27:15–16 and write the verses here.

2. Read Proverbs 25:24 and write it here.

3. Give an example of when you have been "the nag."

4. Read Proverbs 12:4 and write it here.

5. Read Proverbs 31:11–12 and write it here.

6. Give an example of when you have been "the crown."

Day 4: Gripes Be Gone!

1. Read 1 Corinthians 10:1–13. Write your own paraphrase of this passage.

2. Who were the Israelites really griping about? How do you do this?

Day 5: Put on a Bracelet

1. Read Psalm 142:1–5. List your complaints before the Lord. Write them here.

2. Read Romans 15:5–7. Apply these verses by writing a prayer about accepting your husband.

3. Read Matthew 7:3–5. Pray and ask God to show you how to fill in the following chart.

4. Write a prayer, giving God permission to change you (instead of asking Him to change your husband).

Using a "Gripes Be Gone" bracelet, take the challenge for a week. Every time a gripe or complaint escapes your lips, switch the bracelet to your other wrist. Be sure to journal every day about what you are learning about yourself through this project.

Day 1

Day 2

Day 3

Day 4

Day 5

Day 6

Day 7

Week 3

Am I Willing to Change My Attitude?

Buy a special journal to be your Thankful Journal, or use any journal or notebook. Keep a Thankful Bookmark in your Bible or in this book.

Day 1: Building a House of Gratitude

  1. Memorize Psalm 92:1–2. Write Psalm 92:1–2 here.

  2. Read about Kaye on page 65. If you were going to list three things you would do to nurture an attitude of gratitude, what would they be?

Day 2: Growing in God Gratitude

Make Psalm 92:1–2 your daily practice this week. Thank and praise God in the morning for His lovingkindness and in the evening for His faithfulness. Journal what you are learning each day in your Thankful Journal.

Day 3: Growing in Husband Gratitude

Read about the Thankful Journal on pages 75–76. Chose one day this week to write in your journal about why you are thankful for your husband. (Consider sharing what you write with your husband.)

Read "Dwell on the positive" on page 76. Then list the following words from Philippians 4:8 in your Thankful Journal: *true, worthy of respect, right, pure, lovely, excellent, worthy of praise.* Each day of the week, dwell on one of these attributes and ask God the Spirit to reveal how your husband displays this quality. Write your thoughts in your Thankful Journal.

1. Gratitude creates an atmosphere where emotional sweetness can flourish. Write a paragraph describing what it looks like in your marriage when sweetness reigns.

Day 4: Offer a Sacrifice of Thanksgiving

1. Read Emma's story of offering a sacrifice of thanksgiving on pages pages 82–83. Write a paragraph that describes the feelings and thoughts you have as you read this.

2. Read Psalm 50:14–15, 23 and Hebrews 13:15. Write a summary of the four verses and how they apply personally to you and your marriage.

Day 5: A Dangerous Prayer!

The book of Colossians has four chapters, and each one talks about being thankful. Read each of these references: Colossians 1:3, 12; 2:7; 3:15–17; 4:2. In your Thankful Journal, personalize the thankful message to your husband.

1. What does it look like for you to devote yourself to prayer for your husband with an alert mind and a thankful heart? Write your answer here.

Week 4

What Will It Take for Me to Get Close to You? Part 1

Day 1: Surprise! Men and Women Are Different!

1. Memorize Genesis 2:18. Write it here.

2. Write your description of emotional intimacy.

3. Consider asking your husband how he would define emotional intimacy. Write his answer here.

4. List three ways you can move closer to your "shoulder to shoulder" husband.

Day 2: We Both Have Gaps

Prayerfully read Ephesians 5:25–32.

1. Do you see any conditions the wife must meet before her husband loves her sacrificially?

2. Do you see any conditions the husband must meet before the wife respects him unconditionally?

3. Fill in the commands you find in Ephesians 5:25–32 in the chart below.

Commands	Commands to Wife

4. Whose commands are the most difficult to live out, the husband's or the wife's? Why?

Day 3: A Wife's Divine Calling

1. How do you describe your "love gap"? Use at least five adjectives.

2. How do you describe your husband's "respect gap"? Use at least five adjectives.

3. Memorize Ephesians 5:33 in *The Amplified Bible:*

> *And let the wife see that she respects and reverences her husband [that she notices him, regards him, honors him, prefers him, venerates, and esteems him; and that she defers to him, praises him, and loves and admires him exceedingly].*

4. It is very difficult for some wives to live out this description of the word respect. Give five reasons why you think it is hard.

Day 4: A Wife's Divine Calling

1. What did you learn in your childhood family about being a "helper"?

2. Write out the following verses about God being our Ezer, our strong Helper: Psalm 121:1–2; 124:8; 146:5. Then read them out loud as a prayer of thanksgiving to God.

3. Write a paragraph describing what it looks like practically for you to respect your unique husband unconditionally.

Day 5: A Wife's Divine Calling

1. Does learning about the word Ezer (page 97) help you with being called a "helper"? Give five reasons why.

2. What do you learn from Tamra about being a helper (page 98)?

3. Write a letter to your daughter, niece, granddaughter, or other special young woman in your life. Share with her about a wife's divine calling to be an Ezer—a helper to her husband.

Week 5

What Will It Take for Me to Get Close to You? Part 2

Day 1: Fill His Gaps with Encouragement and Respect

1. Memorize Ephesians 4:29. Write it here.

2. In Ephesians 4:29, there is one negative command and three positive commands. List them.

3. Tell about a time when you encouraged your husband with your words.

4. Read 1 Thessalonians 5:11 out loud. Ask God to show you at least five ways you can build up and encourage your special husband with your actions. List them.

TAKE THE RESPECT TEST!

- Find a quiet place.
- Spend ten or fifteen minutes making a list of things you respect about your husband.
- When your husband is not distracted, say, "I was thinking about you today and several things about you that I respect, and I just want you to know that I respect you."
- Leave the room, and leave the response up to God.
- How did your husband respond? Describe how your words and actions impacted your husband.

Look at the acrostic of the word respect on page 105, then make your own acrostic of respect. Perhaps you would like to frame it or keep a copy in your Bible where you can reflect on it often. Consider sharing your acrostic with your husband and telling him you want to learn to live it.

Day 2: Who Will Fill My Gaps?

1. What do you think are your husband's five most basic needs?

2. What are your five greatest needs?

3. Do you think you and your husband understand each other's needs?

Consider sharing the lists you wrote with him and asking for his input.

4. Read Matthew 20:28. How does this verse relate to you as a wife?

5. Read about changing your perspective from my right to God's gift on page 106. Write a paragraph explaining this concept to a friend.

Day 3: Who Will Fill My Gaps?

1. Read Michelle's story at least two times (pages 107–109). If you were making a list of things you were giving to God, what would be on your list?

2. Write an email to a friend expressing what you learned from Michelle's story. Explain what difference you think this will make in your marriage.

3. Read Philippians 2:3–4. If possible, read these verses in other translations. Write the verses here.

4. Meditate on Philippians 2:3–4. Then write your own paraphrase of these verses, applying them to your role as a wife.

Day 4: Who Will Fill My Gaps?
1. Read "What Will It Take for Me to Get Close to You?", Insight 6, "A Wife Can Set the Stage for Intimacy" (pages 109–114). Ask the Lord to speak to you personally from this insight.

2. Read the description of emotional sweetness on page 109. What do you think your husband would say is the opposite of emotional sweetness? Consider asking him.

Day 5: A Wife Can Set the Stage for Intimacy

Read again "A Wife Can Set the Stage for Intimacy" (page 109–114). You are a wife, and that means that just like Krista, *you* can set the stage for intimacy.

Pray, and ask the Lord to speak to you and reveal what will speak love to your husband.

Ask God to show you if a weekend away, a day hike, a once-in-a-lifetime vacation, just you two, or a day of cross-country skiing will build emotional intimacy between you and your husband.

1. Krista ministered to Caleb body, soul, and spirit. Write down how she did this, and ask God to show you if any of these ideas are right for your husband.

You, dear wife, with God's guidance set the stage for intimacy. Step out and do it!

Optional Lesson for a Twelve-Week Study

A Time of Thanksgiving, Reflection, and Celebration

You have been asking yourself Dangerous Questions for the last five weeks. You have searched God's Word and reflected on who you want to become. You are on the road to becoming a wife by design, not default, and that is exciting! This week will be a time of thanksgiving, reflection, and celebration.

THANKSGIVING (TO BE DONE ON YOUR OWN, PRIOR TO THE MEETING)
Reflect on Psalm 92:1–2, the verses you memorized the week you reflected on the Dangerous Question *Am I willing to change my attitude?* In the morning, you thanked and praised God for His lovingkindness and in the evening for His faithfulness. Make this your habit again this week.

REFLECTION (FOR YOUR STUDY DURING THE FIVE DAYS OF THE WEEK)
Day 1: Look through the first Dangerous Question, *What is* really *important to me?* Read through the first Bible study, thanking and praising God that you are living not by default, but by design. Ask God to show you one way you've grown because you asked, *What is really important to me?*

Day 2: Reflect on the second Dangerous Question, *What does it feel like to be my husband?* Page through the chapter and read over the Bible study. Put on your "Gripes Be Gone" bracelet and thank God that your venting and complaining is different than it was five weeks ago. Ask God to show you one way you've grown because you asked, *What does it feel like to be my husband?*

Day 3: The third Dangerous Question was about attitude: *Am I willing to change my attitude?* Think about how you've grown in God gratitude and husband gratitude. Be sure your Thankful Bookmark is where you will see it every day. Look through the entries in your Thankful Journal and thank God that gratitude is growing in you. Ask God to show you one way you've changed because you asked, *Am I willing to change my attitude?*

Day 4: Reflect on the fourth Dangerous Question, *What will it take for me to get close to you?* Scan-read the chapter again and read through the Bible study. Remember that God has a special calling on your life—to be an *Ezer*, a helper to your husband. Encouragement and respect are beginning to flow from you to him. You are learning to fill his respect gap. Ask God to show you one way you are different because you asked, *What will it take for me to get close to you?*

Day 5: Continue to reflect on how to set the stage for intimacy. Reread how Krista set the stage and filled her husband to overflowing, body, soul, and spirit (page 110). Ask God to show you how you can set the stage for intimacy with your husband.

CELEBRATION (TO BE DONE PRIOR TO AND DURING YOUR GROUP TIME) As you look back and thank God and reflect on what He has been teaching you, think of something to prepare to share with the group during your celebration time.

Your time of celebration will be during your next Bible study. Decide in advance as a group how this time will look. You could have a brunch or luncheon or meet outside if the weather is nice. Allow time for each woman to share how this study has impacted her view of God and of her marriage. Here are six suggestions for what you could do to prepare:

1. Read something you wrote for an assignment.

2. Write a letter to your daughter (daughter-in-law, grand-daughter, niece, special friend), expressing what you have learned as you've reflected on the first five Dangerous Questions.

3. Make an acrostic using a word like marriage, intimacy, or wife.

4. Recite memory verses that have been meaningful to you.

5. Draw a graph that shows how you have grown.

6. Write a poem or a song or paint a picture that reveals what God has taught you.

End with a time of worship and prayer, celebrating what God has done. And you still have four more Dangerous Questions ahead!

Week 6

What Is It Like to Make Love with Me? Part 1

This week you will ponder and reflect on:

    1. How your sexual mind-set developed, and what it is today.

    2. What the Song of Solomon teaches about God's perspective of sexual intimacy.

Day 1: How Did We Get Where We Are?

1. What did you learn in your home about sexual intimacy in marriage?

2. How did this influence you when you married?

3. "A mind-set is a collection of individual thoughts that over a period of time influence the way we perceive life."[1] How have your individual thoughts over the past twenty years (or more) contributed to the sexual mind-set you have today?

4. Which of Satan's lies about your sexuality did you listen to (page 118)?

5. How were you influenced by the media (page 118)?

6. Did Christians influence you in a positive or negative way (page 119)?

7. After reading this chapter, how do you think your sexual mind-set differs from God's perspective?

Day 2: Open the Gift of Sexual Passion

God gave the gift of sexual passion for an intimate oneness.

    1. Read and memorize Ephesians 5:31–32. Write it here.

    2. Paraphrase these verses here.

3. Ephesians 5:31–32 says that your sexual intimacy is a picture of the spiritual intimacy the Lord desires with you. How does this change how you view intimacy with your husband?

God gave the gift of sexual passion for exquisite pleasure.

4. Read Proverbs 5:15, 18–19. Paraphrase Proverbs 5:19 here.

Day 3: Open the Gift of Sexual Passion

1. Read Proverbs 5:15, 18–19 again. List five to ten adjectives that describe this wife as a sexual partner.

2. Read Song of Solomon 7:1–9. Write a paragraph describing what you see in this bride as a lover.

3. Make a list of what Claire did to open the gift of sexual passion.

4. If you put as much thought, prayer, and creativity into your sexual intimacy as Claire did, where would you be as a lover to your husband?

Days 4 & 5: Open the Gift of Sexual Passion

Read the Song of Solomon. If possible, read it in a modern version like the New Living Translation.

The theme of the Song is found in Song of Solomon 8:6:

> *Put me like a seal over your heart,*
> *Like a seal on your arm.*
> *For love is as strong as death,*
> *Jealousy is as severe as Sheol;*
> *Its flashes are flashes of fire,*
> *The very flame of the LORD.*

"This, the key verse of the Song, speaks of a love between a husband and wife that is white-hot, passionate, burning, and unable to be extinguished because it comes from God."[2]

Here are three reasons given for why the Song of Solomon can be confusing:[3]

1. We don't understand how to read Hebrew poetry. It helps to realize that you are reading poetry and not prose. The beauty of God writing this love poem through Solomon exactly the way He did in poetic symbols is so precious; a child can pick up the Song of Solomon and not be offended.

2. The scenes in the drama are not in chronological order. The bride is seeing the scenes as a series of flashbacks so

you will read about a sexual encounter before the couple is married.

3. Sexual references are explained through illusive imagery and symbolism. The word garden refers to the special place the husband enters. Mandrakes and pomegranates speak of fertility. Honey and wine convey intense, erotic desire.

What do you learn about God's view of sexual intimacy in the Song?
1. Write a letter to a young woman about to marry, detailing God's perspective in the Song.

Week 7

What Is It Like to Make Love with Me? Part 2

Day 1: Open the Gift of God's Blessing
Memorize Proverbs 5:18–19:

> *Let your fountain be blessed,*
>   *And rejoice in the wife of your youth.*
> *As a loving hind and a graceful doe,*
>   *Let her breasts satisfy you at all times;*
>   *Be exhilarated always with her love.*

1. Would you feel strange if you had a picture of Jesus over your bed? Why do you think you would feel this way?

2. Read Song of Solomon 4:16—5:1. Describe God's blessing in 5:1 in your own words.

3. Have you received God's blessing on your sexual intimacy? If not, how could you do this?

4. What did you learn from Megan's story (page 129)?

5. Write a paragraph describing what it looks like for you to be able to say:

- I am forgiven!
- I am free!
- I can delight in God's gift of sex!
- I can leave Jesus' picture over the bed!

Day 2: Offer the Gift of Your Body

1. Read out loud the three versions of 1 Corinthians 7:4 on page 131. Choose one of the versions, write it here, and memorize the verse.

2. What were your feelings when you read about Kathy wrapping herself in a bow (page 132)?

3. Have you given the gift of your body to your husband? If not, how might you do this?

4. Sadie moved beyond tolerable intimacy. Do you believe God can redeem the horror of sexual abuse in you or in your friend? Explain your answer.

5. Where would you be if you believed God, if you prayed to and begged God like Sadie did? Write a prayer asking God for more in your sexual intimacy with your husband.

Day 3: What Does Everyday Lovemaking Look Like?

1. Write a paragraph describing how you felt when you read the quotes on page 132 about the fun, closeness, and planning for sexual intimacy these wives enjoyed with their husbands?

2. Describe a time you "did sex right" and how it impacted your intimate relationship with your husband.

3. Describe a time you "did sex wrong" and how it impacted your intimacy.

4. Write your own Dangerous Prayer to God about your intimacy with your husband.

Day 4: Pondering God's Word

Read through the Song of Solomon again. Ask the Holy Spirit, your Teacher, to reveal what it was like for Solomon to make love with his bride. Make a list of all you discover about her attitude, her creativity, how and when she communicated. (You will discuss this and make a combined list of what all the women found at the Bible study.)

Day 5: Pondering God's Word

Find a quiet time to be alone. Reflect on what you have learned from the Song of Solomon. Remember what you learned in the Dangerous Question "What Is It Like to Make Love with Me?" Write your declaration to God of who you desire to become as a lover to your husband.

Week 8

Why Do I Want to Stay Mad at You?

Day 1: It Feels Good to Hold a Grudge

Memorize Ephesians 4:31–32 and write it here. Also, write it on two 3 x 5 cards, and put one:

- In your purse (to pull out and meditate on at a doctor's office or waiting for your car at the repair shop).
- On the mirror where you put on your makeup each morning so you can get beautiful on the inside as you get beautiful on the outside!

1. On pages 144–145, five women expressed why it feels good to hold a grudge. Which woman do you relate to, and why?

2. What did you learn in your childhood home about forgiving? Spend time alone with God, seeking His wisdom about this for you, and then journal your thoughts.

3. Describe a time you overreacted to your husband over an insignificant incident (like a bar of soap).

4. List three to five things God revealed to you through Dana's forgiveness story on page 147.

Day 2: Three Shocking Truths about Forgiveness

1. Read 2 Corinthians 2:11. Write it here, then pray it back to God.

2. Has Satan outsmarted you? Explain how.

3. List several things you can do to kick Satan out.

4. Read the Lord's Prayer (Matt. 6:9–15) out loud. What does it look like for you to forgive your husband?

5. Is there anything you need to change about how you forgive?

6. Write a paragraph to a friend about the connection between forgiveness and intimacy with the Lord.

7. Read Proverbs 19:11 and write it here. What would give you honor and glory?

8. Make a list of the many things you learned from Katie's story on pages 152–155.

Day 3: Strip Off Anger, Put On Forgiveness

1. Go over your memory verses—Ephesians 4:31–32. List the six pieces of clothing in Ephesians 4:31 that you are to strip off, and give a definition of each one.

2. Which one is the hardest for you to "strip off"?

3. List your three new pieces of clothing in Ephesians 4:32, and give a definition of each one.

4. Which one is your "strong suit"?

5. Which one is hardest for you to "put on"? Why do you think this is difficult for you?

6. Write a short letter to a friend, expressing what you learned from Colette's story on pages 157–159.

Day 4: Anoint with Forgiveness

1. Describe the joy you feel over Connie's forgiveness anointing (pages 160–162). What delights you the most?

2. Describe your feelings about Sheryl's forgiveness anointing on pages 161–162. What grieves you the most?

3. Meditate on your memory verses, Ephesians 4:31–32. How will you be certain that you will never be saying, *If only I could have done this sooner...* ?

4. Read over quotes on pages 159–160 regarding the best things various women did for their marriages. Which one spoke to you and why?

Day 5: Be a Proactive Forgiver

1. Write a paragraph to a teenage girl sharing what a proactive forgiver is and why she should be one.

2. Write a prayer, telling God that you want to become a proactive forgiver.

3. Chose two of the practical physical symbols of forgiveness listed on pages 163–164, and explain how you will apply them in your relationship with your husband.

4. Ask yourself: What does it look like for me to be kind, tenderhearted, and forgiving toward my husband, just as God in Christ has forgiven me?

Spend some time (ten minutes or more) alone with God talking to Him about this Dangerous Question, *Why do I want to stay mad at you?*

5. Is there anything you need to ask your husband forgiveness for? How will you do this?

Week 9

Is it Possible to Grow Together When Things Fall Apart?

Day 1: An Anniversary on the Danube

1. Write James 1:2 from the three translations on page 170. Choose one of the versions to memorize.

2. Read John 16:33, Psalm 141:8, Psalm 112:7, and Isaiah 26:3. Write your view of God's perspective of trials from these verses.

3. Copy my paraphrase of James 1:2–4 for my marriage on page 170. What would you add to this paraphrase?

Day 2: Trusting God When Life Hurts

1. Read Proverbs 3:5–6 several times out loud. Write it down.

2. Describe what "trust in the Lord with all your heart" means to you personally.

3. Write a paragraph about how you live out "lean not on your own understanding."

4. What does it look like practically for you to "acknowledge God in all your ways"?

5. Write a prayer expressing your gratitude to God for His promise to make your paths straight.

Day 3: Marriage Crisis!

1. What three things did you learn from Tabi's story on page 175?

2. How was Corina creative in a hard situation (page 177)?

3. What did you feel when you read what James wrote on pages 179 about why he loves Corina?

4. Read 1 Peter 5:7 out loud. Write this verse as a prayer, thanking God that your marriage is His personal concern.

Day 4: A Long, Difficult Marriage

1. What did you learn from Natalie's story on page 180?

2. Which of Natalie's "I wills" from her Marriage Purpose Statement do you want to write out and remember?

3. What does Natalie's encouragement to a woman in a hard marriage mean to you (pages 181–183)?

4. Write Jeremiah 17:7–8 here.

5. How were these verses a reality in Natalie's life?

6. How can they be true in your life?

7. Write a note to a friend, sharing how hiding Jeremiah 17:7–8 in her heart can encourage her during time of trial.

Day 5: The Integrity Walk

1. Write out all the "I wills" you find in Psalm 101. Why do you think this psalm might have been David's Life Purpose Statement?

2. Write a paragraph sharing how Job's statement about integrity (Job 2:9–10) can impact you in times of trial in your marriage.

3. How would praying the Scriptures from this chapter help you during a trial? Write a prayer to God, based on what you read in James 1:2–4, Proverbs 3:5–6, 1 Peter 5:7, Jeremiah 17:7–8, and Job 2:10.

4. How can the four practical helps at the end of the insight (put on a "Gripes Be Gone" bracelet, write in a Thankful Journal, read the reasons you are thankful you're married to your husband, and so on) on page 188 encourage you during times of trial?

Week 10

The Woman in the Mirror

Day 1: Look at You … a Wife by Design!

Bring your Marriage Purpose Statement to the Bible Study to share.

Read 1 Corinthians 4:2. Then memorize it.

1. What does it look like for you to look in the mirror and say, "Yes, I've been faithful. I have fulfilled my assignment as a wife to _____"?

2. Read Psalm 119:30–32. Write it here.

3. Write a paraphrase of these verses, applying them to your marriage.

4. God says as you run the faithful road, He will enlarge your heart. List three ways you need God to expand your heart toward your husband.

5. Read 1 Corinthians 4:2, write it here, and memorize it.

Day 2: God Is the Re-Creator!

1. Read pages 195–196, which talk about God being the Re-Creator. Write Proverbs 24:3–4 here.

2. What are the "precious and pleasant riches" that fill the rooms of your marriage?

3. Do you need God to re-create your marriage? Write a prayer with your specific requests for God, the Master Marriage Builder.

Day 3: The Changing Seasons of Your Marriage

1. Where are you on your marriage journey?

2. In this insight, three couples shared about their marriage journeys. Which couple did you connect with, and why did you connect with this particular one?

3. Write 1 Corinthians 13:7 here. Explain how this verse applies to you as a wife.

Day 4: Look at You: Learning! Growing! Changing!

1. What were your thoughts as you read Renee's story and Marriage Purpose Statement?

2. Read Psalm 39:4–5. Write the verses here.

3. If you really believed these verses, what difference would it make in how you loved your husband today?

Read your Marriage Purpose Statement out loud to God. Spend fifteen to thirty minutes praying about your Marriage Purpose Statement. Ask God if there is anything He wants to add to your Statement.

4. Now that you have spent these weeks reflecting on Dangerous Questions, is there anything you want to add to your Statement?

Get your calendar or PDA and write yourself a "to do" on your anniversary. On this special day, take time to reflect on your Marriage Purpose Statement. Make this your yearly anniversary habit.

Day 5: Questions to Ponder

Who asks you the hard questions? Questions like:

> Are you living your Marriage Purpose Statement?
>
> Are you walking toward your husband in love, devotion, and faithfulness?
>
> Are you being tempted to enter into an emotional or sexual affair?
>
> Are you growing in deeper intimacy with the Lord?
>
> Are you growing in deeper intimacy with your husband?

Who asks you the hard questions? A mentor? A friend? A Bible study leader or an accountability partner? If no one does, talk to God about this. Ask Him and your leader how you go about choosing someone who will.

Optional Lesson for a Twelve-Week Study

A Time of Thanksgiving, Reflection, and Celebration

For the past several weeks you've been reflecting on the question *What is it like to be married to me?* and other Dangerous Questions. You have searched God's Word and reflected on who you want to become. You are now at the end of this study, it is time to praise and thank God. This week will be a time of thanksgiving, reflection, and celebration.

THANKSGIVING (TO BE DONE ON YOUR OWN, PRIOR TO THE MEETING)
Reflect on Psalm 92:1–2, the verses you memorized the week you reflected on the Dangerous Question *Am I willing to change my attitude?* In the morning, you thanked and praised God for His lovingkindness and in the evening for His faithfulness. Make this your habit again this week.

REFLECTION (FOR YOUR STUDY DURING THE FIVE DAYS OF THE WEEK)
Day 1: Look through the chapter on the Dangerous Question *What is it like to make love with me?* Read through the Bible study, thanking God that you have new understanding about how your sexual mind-set was formed. Rejoice that you are learning new and exciting things about God's perspective about sexual intimacy—and that you are getting creative and setting the stage for intimacy with your husband.

Day 2: Continue to reflect on *What is it like to make love with me?* Page through the chapter and read over the Bible study. Thank God that you are growing in all it means to receive His blessing on your intimacy. You've laughed about wrapping yourself in a bow but been serious about the deep meaning of giving your body as a gift to your husband. Ask God to show you one way you have grown as a lover to your husband.

Day 3: The next Dangerous Question was about one of the most important parts of marriage, *forgiveness.* Read through "Why Do I Want to Stay Mad at You?" again, and remember why it is so important to freely forgive. You are learning how to strip off the negative and put on the positive. Forgiveness is not always easy to give or to receive, but marriage is the union of two good forgivers. Ask God to reveal one way you've grown as a "forgiver."

Day 4 is about facing trials together and asks the Dangerous Question *Is it possible to grow together when things fall apart?* Reflect on the stories of couples who have grown closer in crisis. Meditate on the many Scriptures in the Bible study that will encourage you during difficult times. Reflect on what it means to walk the Integrity Walk. Ask God to continue to reveal how you and your mate can grow closer in crisis. Write one way you can see you have grown closer to your husband during a trial.

Day 5: God is a God of hope, and He says there is hope for you and your husband. Remember that God is the Re-Creator. He loves to bring beauty out of ashes. Reflect on what you will regret and what you will not regret as a wife. Thank God that you are becoming a wife by design!

CELEBRATION (TO BE DONE PRIOR TO AND DURING YOUR GROUP TIME)
As you look back and thank God and reflect on what He has been teaching you, think of something to prepare to share with the group during your celebration time.

Your time of celebration will be during your final Bible study. Decide in advance as a group how this time will look. You could have a brunch or luncheon or meet outside if the weather is nice. Allow time for each woman to share how this study has impacted her view of God and of her role as a wife. Here are six suggestions for what you could do to prepare:

1. Read something you wrote for an assignment.

2. Write a letter to your daughter (daughter-in-law, granddaughter, niece, special friend) expressing what you have learned as you've reflected on the last four Dangerous Questions.

3. Make an acrostic using a word like faithful, forgiving, or forever.

4. Recite memory verses that have been meaningful to you.

5. Draw a graph that shows how you have grown.

6. Write a poem or a song or paint a picture that reveals what God has taught you.

End with a time of worship and prayer, celebrating what God has done. God is faithful, and you are on the road headed toward the wife you long to become!

Notes

BY DESIGN, NOT DEFAULT

1   Attributed to the Atlanta Humane Society.

2   Author unknown.

3   Dr. Bill Bright's 1964 message.

WHAT IS REALLY IMPORTANT TO ME?

1   Thornton Wilder, *Our Town: A Play in Three Acts* (New York: HarperCollins, 2003), 100.

2   Ibid., 108.

3   Ibid., 109.

4   Ibid., 108.

5   Stephen R. Covey, *The Seven Habits of Highly Effective People* (New York: Simon and Schuster, 1989), 96.

6   Lawrence J. Crabb, Jr., and Dan Allender, *Encouragement: The Key to Caring* (Grand Rapids, MI: Zondervan, 1984), 52.

7   Used with permission.

WHAT DOES IT FEEL LIKE TO BE MY HUSBAND?

1   Author unknown.

2   Dr. Laura Schlessinger, *The Proper Care and Feeding of Husbands* (New York: Harper-Collins, 2004), 40.

3   Author unknown.

4   Schlessinger, 51.

5   Barbara Johnson, *I'm So Glad You Told Me What I Didn't Wanna Hear* (Dallas, TX: Word, 1996), 163.

6   Joyce Meyer, *The Battlefield of the Mind* (New York: Warner Faith, 1995), 69.

7   Earl D. Radmacher, *You and Your Thoughts* (Wheaton, IL: Tyndale House, 1977), 15.

8   Nancy Cobb and Connie Grigsby, *The Best Thing I Ever Did for My Marriage* (Sisters, OR: Multnomah, 2003), 83-85.

9   Charles Haddon Spurgeon, "Psalm 142:2," *The Treasury of David,* ed. Roy H. Clarke (Nashville, TN: Thomas Nelson, 1997), 654.

10 Stormie Omartian, *The Power of a Praying Wife* (Eugene, OR: Harvest House, 1997), 25–26.

11 Adapted from Will Bowen, *A Complaint Free World* (New York: Doubleday, 2007).

12 Will Bowen, *A Complaint Free World* (New York: Doubleday, 2007).

AM I WILLING TO CHANGE MY ATTITUDE?

1   Adapted from Schlessinger, *The Proper Care and Feeding of Husbands,* 12–13.

2   Nancy Leigh DeMoss, *Choosing Gratitude* (Chicago, IL: Moody Press, 2009), 50.

3   Leslie Brandt, *Psalms Now* (St. Louis, MO: Concordia, 2004).

4   Daniel Block, *The New American Commentary: Vol. 6, Judges—Ruth* (Nashville: Broadman & Holman, 1999), 605–6.

5   Beth Moore, *Living Beyond Yourself* (Nashville, TN: Lifeway Press, 1998), 157.

6   Ibid.

7   Ruth Myers, *Thirty-One Days of Praise* (Sisters, OR: Multnomah, 1994), 27.

8   Merlin Carothers, *Prison to Praise* (Escondido, CA: Merlin R. Carothers, 1970), 85.

WHAT WILL IT TAKE FOR ME TO GET CLOSE TO YOU?

1   David Minkoff, *Oy Vey: More!* (New York: St. Martin's Press, 2008), 6.

2   C. S. Lewis, *A Grief Observed* (New York: HarperCollins, 2001), 7, 47.

3   Dr. Emerson Eggerichs, *Love and Respect* (Nashville, TN: Thomas Nelson, 2004), back cover.

4   More modern words describing your important role might be *creative counterpart, completer, competent complement.*

5   *Merriam-Webster's Collegiate Dictionary,* 11th ed., s.v. "Helper."

6   Paul Lee Tan, *Encyclopedia of 7700 Illustrations* (Rockville, MD: Assurance Publishers, 1979), 71.

7   Eggerichs, *Love and Respect,* 185.

8   Ibid., 186.

WHAT IS IT LIKE TO MAKE LOVE WITH ME?

1   Eric Fuchs, *Sexual Desire and Love* (New York: Seabury Press, 1983), 108.

2   Quoted in Tim Stafford, *Sexual Chaos* (Downers Grove, IL: InterVarsity, 1993), 37.

3   Ruth Smythers, "Instruction and Advice for the Young Bride," *The Madison Institute Newsletter* (New York: Spiritual Guidance Press, Fall 1894).

4   *The Ryrie NASB Study Bible* (Chicago, IL: Moody, 2008).

WHY DO I WANT TO STAY MAD AT YOU?

1   Tan, *Encyclopedia of 7700 Illustrations,* 284.

2   Philip Yancey, *What's So Amazing About Grace?* (Grand Rapids, MI: Zondervan, 2002), 84.

3   Gabriel Garcia Marquez, *Love in the Time of Cholera* (New York: Penguin, 1989), 29–30.

4   R. T. Kendall, *Total Forgiveness* (Lake Mary, FL: Charisma House, 2007), 84.

5   Dr. Bruce K. Waltke, *The Book of Proverbs: Chapters 15—31* (Grand Rapids, MI: Eerdmans, 2005), 105.

6   Lawrence O. Richards, *Expository Dictionary of Bible Words* (Grand Rapids, MI: Zondervan, 1985), 289.

7   Dr. Joseph Dillow, Linda Dillow, Dr. Peter Pintus, and Lorraine Pintus, *Intimacy Ignited* (Colorado Springs, CO: NavPress, 2004), 215–216.

8   Allen T. Edmunds, *Reader's Digest,* January 1982, 90.

9   Tan, *Encyclopedia of 7700 Illustrations,* 456.

10 Stormie Omartian, *The Power of a Praying Wife,* 29.

IS IT POSSIBLE TO GROW TOGETHER WHEN THINGS FALL APART?

1   *Merriam-Webster's Collegiate Dictionary,* eleventh ed., s.v. "Crisis."

2   Charles R. Swindoll, *Living Beyond the Daily Grind: Book 1* (Dallas, TX: Word Publishing, 1988), 181.

3   Adapted from a prayer by Swindoll, *Living Beyond the Daily Grind: Book I,* 181.

4   Doug Weiss, one of the leading experts on sexual addition, believes that 50 percent of Christian men are involved in pornography.

5   I cowrote this book with Jody and our good friends Lorraine and Peter Pintus. It takes you on a verse-by-verse exploration of the Song of Solomon, the Bible's manual on sex and intimacy.

6   *The Oxford English-Reader's Dictionary,* s.v. "Integrity."

7   Swindoll, *Living Beyond the Daily Grind: Book II,* 289.

THE WOMAN IN THE MIRROR

1   R. Laid Harris, Gleason L. Archer Jr., Bruce Waltke, *Theological Wordbook of the Old Testament* (Chicago: Moody Press, 1980), s.v. "bahar."

2   The Hebrew word translated "run" is *ruts,* and it means "to hasten." While the word is simply the common word for "run," interestingly, it is sometimes used of soldiers charging into battle (e.g., Joshua 8:19).

3   Ludwig Koehler, Walter Baumgardner, M.E.J. Richardson, and Johann Jakob Stamm, *The Hebrew and Aramaic Lexicon of the Old Testament* (Leiden, New York: E.J. Brill, 1999), 209.

4   Ray Boltz, *Thank You* (Nashville, TN: Thomas Nelson, 1998), 43.

5   Ibid.

6   Adapted from Swindoll, *Living Beyond the Daily Grind: Book I,* 240–41.

7   Swindoll, *Living Beyond the Daily Grind: Book I,* 241.

8   Ibid., 241.

9   Author unknown.

10   Used with permission.

11   Stephen and Judith Schwambach, *For Lovers Only* (Eugene, OR: Harvest House, 1991), 19–20.

TEN- (OR TWELVE-) WEEK REFLECTIVE BIBLE STUDY

1   Linda Dillow and Lorraine Pintus, *Intimate Issues* (Colorado Springs, CO: WaterBrook Press, 1999), 25.

2   Dr. Joseph Dillow, Linda Dillow, Dr. Peter Pintus, and Lorraine Pintus, *Intimacy Ignited* (Colorado Springs, CO: NavPress, 2004), 15.

3   Adapted from Dillow and Lorraine Pintus, *Intimacy Ignited,* 14–15.

INTRODUCTION TO
CALIFORNIA
PLANT LIFE

California Natural History Guides

Phyllis M. Faber and Bruce M. Pavlik, General Editors

Introduction to

CALIFORNIA PLANT LIFE

Robert Ornduff

Revised by Phyllis M. Faber and Todd Keeler-Wolf

UNIVERSITY OF CALIFORNIA PRESS

Berkeley   Los Angeles   London

We dedicate this revision to the memory of Robert Ornduff
(1932–2000), plant lover par exellence and friend.

California Natural History Guides No. 69

University of California Press
Berkeley and Los Angeles, California

University of California Press, Ltd.
London, England

© 2003 by the Regents of the University of California

Library of Congress Cataloging-in-Publication Data

Ornduff, Robert.
    Introduction to California plant life / Robert Ornduff; revised by Phyllis M.
Faber and Todd Keeler-Wolf.—Rev. ed.
        p. cm.—(California natural history guide series ; 69)
    Includes bibliographical references and index.
    ISBN 0-520-23702-1(hardcover : alk. paper).—ISBN 0-520-23704-8 (pbk. : alk.
paper)
    1. Botany—California.   2. Plant ecophysiology—California.   3. Plants—
Identification.   I. Faber, Phyllis M. II. Keeler-Wolf, Todd. III. Title. IV. Series

QK149.O73   2003
581.9794—dc21   2002032078

Manufactured in China
10   09   08   07   06   05   04   03
10   9   8   7   6   5   4   3   2   1

The paper used in this publication meets the minimum requirements of
ANSI/NISO Z39.48-1992 (R 1997) (Permanence of Paper). ∞

The publisher gratefully acknowledges the generous
contributions to this book provided by

the Moore Family Foundation
Richard & Rhoda Goldman Fund
and
the General Endowment Fund of the
University of California Press Associates.

———————

Grateful acknowledgment is also made to
the California Academy of Sciences.

CALIFORNIA
ACADEMY OF
SCIENCES

CONTENTS

PREFACE

An Introduction to California Plant Life, written by Professor
Robert Ornduff and published in 1974, has in the intervening
years introduced many thousands of students to California's
unique flora. During the nearly 30 intervening years, however, a number of new findings have occurred in the field of
botany. Changes in the taxonomic treatment of plants have
resulted in the reclassification of several plants, , and studies
have led to new information regarding several aspects per-
taining to the plants of California.

Dr. Ornduff died in September of 2000 before he could
make needed revisions to his book. Since his death, Dr. Todd
Keeler-Wolf, vegetation ecologist with the California Department of Fish and Game, and I have taken on the assignment to
update it. Our goal throughout has been to maintain the integrity of Bob's original work, as his extensive knowledge and
love of the California flora remains unmatched.

In light of recent taxonomic changes, scientific plant
names in this revised edition conform to *The Jepson Manual:
Higher Plants of California* (Hickman 1993), and the common
names used are preferentially from the *Jepson Manual,* the
*CNPS Inventory of Rare and Endangered Vascular Plants of
California* (Tibor 2001), or *A California Flora* (Munz 1968).

Todd has added a discussion of "vegetation type," a term
more currently in use than "plant community." A controversy
over these terms was noted even in the first edition of this
book. We have retained the selection of plant communities

Ornduff described because they continue to represent in broad terms the basic assemblages of plants found in California.

The seven chapters of the 1974 edition have been increased to 10, with discussions of biological and physical influences on plant life and plant ecotypes separated into two chapters, and the evolution of the California flora and present human influences also in two chapters. We have added a chapter, chapter 9, on early explorers and plant collectors, the first part of which was written by Dr. Elizabeth McClintock of the California Academy of Sciences. Her material originally appeared in the *California Horticultural Society Journal* (McClintock 1967). The full chapter appeared with minor changes in a syllabus, prepared by Dr. Ornduff for the University of California Extension course, Integrative Biology x113 in 1992. Chapter 10 contains an expanded discussion of plant conservation topics and some of the impacts of human activities on native plants and plant communities. A reference list, originally provided for each chapter with an additional general list, has been merged into a single reference list and updated. We also have added a short, supplemental reading list and a small glossary.

Many people have helped to make this revision better. Richard Moe from the University of California Herbarium has assisted with taxonomic nomenclature and species numbers, and Roxanne Bittman from the Natural Diversity Data Base helped with rare plant information. A number people have reviewed parts or all of the manuscript: an anonymous reviewer saw three versions of the manuscript; Frank Almeda and Paul di Silva both reviewed an early version, Diane Renshaw critiqued chapter 10; and Pam Muick and Emily Roberson each added information to chapter 10. All have been generous with their knowledge, time, and suggestions, and we thank each of them.

Because of better printing technology, many new photographs have been added to this edition, some from the Ornduff collection but many from other sources. John Game and Wilma and Bill Follette deserve special mention for graciously providing numerous photographs on short notice. Drawings in the original publication were redrawn by Peter Gaede, map 1 was provided by Paula Nelson, maps 2, 3, and 4 were redrawn by William Nelson, and water color illustrations are by Virginia Bates.

We hope that those who read and learn from this book will appreciate and enjoy California's unique plants and natural landscapes and will play an active role in preserving them.

Phyllis M. Faber
June 2002

PREFACE FROM
THE 1974 EDITION

To many Californians, the wealth of the state lies in its gold, its petroleum, its timber, or its fertile valleys. To those of us who are amateur or professional botanists, or who simply enjoy "plant watching," the riches of California are also reflected in the diversity of wildflowers, shrubs, and trees that occur throughout the state. California is isolated from the rest of North America by deserts or mountains that have allowed the development within its boundaries of one of the most varied floras that occurs anywhere on earth. The plant cover ranges from the forests of the northern coast and the mountain slopes, to the woodlands and scrublands of the foothills and deserts, to the grasslands of the valleys. Our plants range in size from the stately Coast Redwoods of the fog-shrouded coast to the minute belly plants of the southern deserts, and in age from the venerable four-thousand-year-old Bristlecone Pines to the diminutive ephemeral annuals whose life span can be counted in weeks.

This small book introduces you to the plant life of California and tells you something of how plants are grouped into communities and what environmental influences determine the pattern of distribution of these communities in the state. It also discusses the origin of our flora, how plants are adapted to the diverse climates of the state, and how they respond to forest and chaparral fires, to unusual soils, to man, and to each other.

The contents of this book are adapted from a syllabus that I wrote for an Independent Study course developed for the University of California, Berkeley. Because most of my botanizing has been in northern California, the contents of the book are perhaps unevenly weighted toward this portion of the state. Drafts of portions of the manuscript were read by L. R. Heckard, J. R. McBride, D. R. Parnell, and a few other friends and colleagues to whom I am indebted for helpful suggestions. I am also grateful to S. C. H. Barrett, R. Benseler, S. Carlquist, D. Hafner, L. M. Moe, and A. C. Smith for allowing me to reproduce their slides, to C. Mentges for executing the line drawings, and to P. Watters for her assistance in preparing the manuscript. Several of the color illustrations have been taken from the slide collection of the Jepson Herbarium, University of California, Berkeley. I am also indebted to my students, who have proven time and again that there is still a great deal that I have to learn about California plants, and that most of this will be gained by studying the plants themselves and not what is written about them in books.

Map 1. Major topographical features of California. The portion of the state in the California Floristic Province is to the coastward side of the hatched line.

Robert Ornduff
June 1974

INTRODUCTION

Nearly one-fourth of the plants found in North America north of Mexico, and more than are found in any other state, grow in California. Around 6,000 species, subspecies, and varieties of native flowering plants, conifers, and ferns grow in woodlands, deserts, mountains, and wetlands of California, some from the days when dinosaurs roamed the earth and some of far more recent origin. California is home to the world's tallest trees, the coast redwood *(Sequoia sempervirens)*, the world's largest trees, the giant sequoia *(Sequoiadendron giganteum)*, and the world's oldest trees, the western bristlecone pine *(Pinus longaeva)*.

The extraordinary diversity found in California's native plants is a reflection of the complex geologic history, diverse topography, and climate of the area now called California that has changed dramatically over the eons. Particles eroded from base rocks combine with organic matter to slowly form soils. Where an area is wet and warm, soils form faster, where dry and hot, soil formation can be almost nonexistent. Today's vegetation is a reflection of environmental conditions found in years past together with conditions found today. As conditions change, some plants can persist, whereas others cannot and become extinct. Fan palms *(Washingtonia filifera)*, for example, are relics from 60 million years ago when the region was less mountainous and the climate tropical; the coast redwood and the giant sequoia are remnants from 40 million years ago when the climate was cooler and wetter; and some of the oaks and desert shrubs we see today are descendents of species that evolved in the warmer, drier period of 10 million years ago.

Because plants occur where environmental conditions meet their needs, understanding the subtle factors that affect plant distribution can be interesting and a challenge. Noting features such as slope direction, soil depth, history of disturbance, intensity of shade, and availability of moisture enable prediction of the assemblages of plants that might be expected, or the understanding of why certain plants so often grow together.

California'a landscape is rich and varied, with dozens of vegetation types ranging from those found on coastal bluffs and dunes to towering montane forests. The stunning beauty of the annual spring wildflower displays on coastal terraces and on valley slopes alone brings visitors from around the world. As the population of this state continues to expand rapidly, being good stewards of this rich resource becomes a daunting challenge. Gaining an understanding and enjoyment of the plant life found in this state is a good place to begin.

The Californian Floristic Province

California is a large state with a complex topography and a great diversity of climates and habitats, resulting in a very large assemblage of plant species that vary in size and include both the world's largest trees and some of the smallest and most unique plant species. In order to create manageable units for plant investigations, botanists have divided the continental landform into geographic units called floristic provinces. These units reflect the wide variations in natural landscapes and assist botanists in predicting where a given plant might be found. Within the borders of California, there are three floristic provinces, each extending beyond the state's political boundaries.

The California Floristic Province includes the geographical area that contains assemblages of plant species that are more or less characteristic of California and that are best developed in the state. This province includes southwestern Oregon and northern Baja California but excludes certain areas of the southeastern California desert regions, as well as the area of the state that is east of the Sierra Nevada–Cascade Range axis (map 1). The flora of the desert areas and those east of the Sierra Nevada crest are best developed outside the state, and therefore, parts of the state of California are not in the California Floristic Province. The Great Basin Floristic Province includes some of the area east of the Sierra Nevada and some regions in the northeastern part of the state, although some botanists consider the latter area to belong to another distinct floristic province, the Columbia Plateau Floristic Province. A third floristic province partly located within California is the Desert Floristic Province, which makes up the southeastern portion of California. The climate in this province is unpredictable from year to year, but rainfall is uniformly scarce.

Map 1. Major topographical features of California. The portion of the state in the California Floristic Province is to the coastward side of the hatched line.

N

Diversity of the Flora

The Jepson Manual: Higher Plants of California (Hickman 1993), the current authority on the higher plants of California, includes 7,000 vascular plant taxa (species, subspecies, and varieties) as occurring in California outside of cultivation. Of these, 5,862 are considered native, and 1,023 are presumed to have been introduced during the immigrations of the eighteenth through twentieth centuries. *The Jepson Manual* defines vascular plants as having a well-developed vascular system to transport water, dissolved minerals, and other substances throughout the plant body. Club mosses, horsetails, ferns, gymnosperms, and flowering plants are vascular plants; fungi, algae, mosses, and liverworts are not. These 7,000 taxa are distributed in *The Jepson Manual* among 1,227 genera and 173 plant families, with 19 families consisting entirely of naturalized (nonnative) species. Of the 5,862 native taxa, 4,693 are considered distinct species, and 1,169 are considered varieties or subspecies. There are 1,416 species endemic to California—that is, they are found nowhere else in the world—and 737 endemic varieties or subspecies. At least 26 endemic species are presumed extinct. The large number of endemic species is the result of the great diversity of climate, soils, and topography found in California.

TABLE 1. Six Largest Families in California

Family	Alternative Family Name	Number of Genera	Number of Species
Asteraceae (sunflower family)	Compositae	185	907
Poaceae (grass family)	Gramineae	106	438
Fabaceae (pea family)	Leguminosae	44	400
Scrophulariaceae (figwort family)		30	313
Brassicaceae (mustard family)	Cruciferae	56	279
Cyperaceae (sedge family)		14	210

In the 10 years since *The Jepson Manual* went to press, scientific understanding of California plants has continued to advance, and botanical collections from previously unvisited locations have led to new discoveries. As a result, the numbers of species given in the 1993 manual are already somewhat out of date. The California Native Plant Society's *Inventory of Rare and Endangered Plants of California* (Tibor 2001), which uses somewhat different definitions or limitations defining rarity than does *The Jepson Manual,* estimates that there are 6,300 California native plants. The Jepson Herbarium located at the University of California, Berkeley, has begun a program, the Jepson Interchange, that is intended to follow and evaluate proposed changes in the taxonomy of California higher plants. The six largest plant families, with approximate numbers, are listed in table 1.

A simple analysis of the numbers in table 1 reveals that 40 percent of the species of vascular plants in California belong to only six families. You can simplify the task of identifying plants in any part of the state by learning the distinguishing characteristics of these six families, listed here.

In the sunflower family (Asteraceae) (fig. 1, pl. 1), flowers are in a dense head and have disk florets, ray florets, or both. The heads are surrounded by bracts, and the anthers are generally fused into cylinders around the style. The calyx is

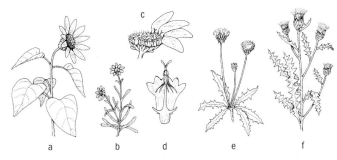

Figure 1. Sunflower family (Asteraceae). (a) Sunflower, (b) goldfield, (c) portion of flower head, (d) details of disk floret, (e) dandelion, (f) thistle.

Plate 1. Sunflower family (Asteraceae), balsam-root (*Balsamorhiza sagittata*).

represented by a scaly or bristly pappus on the one-seeded inferior ovary. Members of the sunflower family include sunflowers (*Helianthus* spp.), asters (*Aster* spp.), ragweeds (*Ambrosia* spp.), sagebrushes (*Artemisia* spp.), goldfields (*Lasthenia* spp.), pineapple weed *(Matricaria matricarioides)*, thistles (*Cirsium* spp.), balsam-root *(Balsamorhiza sagittata)*, tarweeds (*Madia* spp. and *Hemizonia* spp.), and dandelions (*Taraxacum* spp.).

In the grass family (Poaceae) (fig. 2, pl. 2), flowers are very small, greenish, and inconspicuous, and the stamens, pistil, or

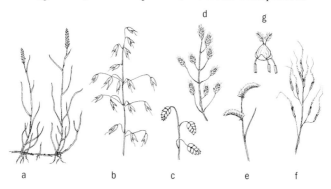

Figure 2. Grass family (Poaceae). (a) Rye grass, (b) flower stalk of oats, (c) three spikelets of rattlesnake grass, (d) spikelet clusters of brome, (e) grama grass, (f) needle grass, (g) details of flower.

both are clustered in spikelets. The perianth is greatly reduced or absent. The ovary is superior. The stem is hollow and round in cross section, and the leaves are two ranked. Members of the grass family include cheat grass *(Bromus tectorum),* brome *(B. carinatus),* rye grass *(Elymus glaucus),* and pampas grass *(Cortaderia* spp.).

In the pea family (Fabaceae) (fig. 3, pl. 3), flowers have stamens and a pistil and are generally bilaterally symmetrical. They usually have 10 separate or fused stamens, and the ovary is superior. The leaves are alternate and usually divided into

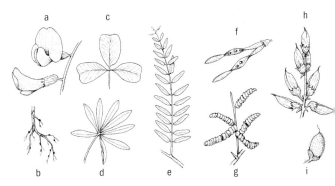

Figure 3. Pea family (Fabaceae). (a) Typical flower, (b) roots with bacterial nodules, (c) clover leaf, (d) lupine leaf, (e) vetch leaf, (f) open vetch pod, (g) pods of mesquite, (h) pods of locoweed, (i) pod of lupine.

Plate 3. Pea family (Fabaceae), Bentham's lotus *(Lotus ben-thamii)*.

three or more leaflets. The roots have bacterial nodules. The fruit is a pod. Examples of plants in the pea family include palo verde (*Cercidium* spp.), lupines (*Lupinus* spp.), clovers (*Trifolium* spp.), locoweeds or milk vetch (*Astragalus* spp.), vetches (*Vicia* spp.), western redbud *(Cercis occidentalis)*, and mesquites (*Prosopis* spp.).

In the figwort family (Scrophulariaceae) (fig. 4, pl. 4), leaves are undivided into leaflets and usually opposite. Flowers are often showy, have both stamens and pistils, and are weakly to strongly bilaterally symmetrical. The ovary is superior, and the fruit is a capsule. Members of the figwort family include penstemons (*Penstemon* spp.), monkey flowers (*Mimulus* spp.), Indian paintbrushes (*Castilleja* spp.), Chinese houses *Collinsia heterophylla)*, elephant's head *(Pedicularis groenlandica)*, and owl's clover (*Castelleja* spp.).

Plate 4. Figwort family (Scrophulariaceae), showy penstemon *(Penstemon speciosus).*

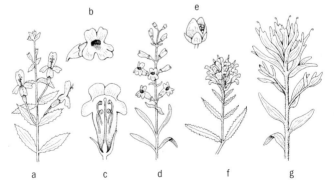

Figure 4. Figwort family (Scrophulariaceae). (a) Monkey flower, (b) flower of penstemon, (c) detail of penstemon flower, (d) flowering stalk of penstemon, (e) open penstemon capsule, (f) lousewort, (g) Indian paintbrush.

Plate 5. Mustard family (Brassicaceae), Menzies's wallflower *(Erysimum menziesii* subsp. *concinnum).*

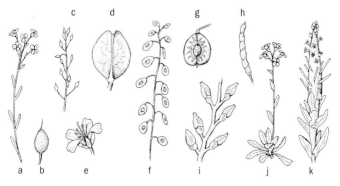

Figure 5. Mustard family (Brassicaceae). (a) Flowering stalk of bladder pod, (b) fruit of bladder pod, (c) fruiting stalk of bladder pod, (d) peppergrass fruit, (e) typical flower, (f) fruiting stalk of fringe pod, (g) fringe pod fruit, (h) rock cress fruit, (i) fruits of sea rocket, (j) rock cress, (k) desert candle.

Plate 6.
Sedge family
(Cyperaceae),
umbrella
sedge *(Cyperus involucratus)*.

In the mustard family (Brassicaceae) (fig. 5, pl. 5), the leaves are alternate and undivided into leaflets but often deeply lobed. Flowers have both stamens and pistils, typically with four petals and sepals. There are six stamens, and the ovary has two chambers. Members of the mustard family include mustards (*Brassica* spp.), wallflowers (*Erysimum* spp.), peppergrass (*Lepidium* spp.), desert candle (*Starleya* spp.), sea rocket (*Cakile* spp.), water cress (*Rorippa* spp.), and shepherd's purse (*Capsella* spp.).

The sedge family (Cyperaceae) (fig. 6, pl. 6) contains grasslike herbs that live in damp places. The flowers have stamens and pistils or are unisexual, are inconspicuous, and are clustered in spikelets. The perianth is represented by scales or bristles, and the ovary is superior, often enclosed in a sac. The stem is usually solid and triangular in cross section. Leaves are

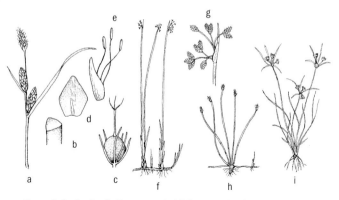

Figure 6. Sedge family (Cyperaceae). (a) Flower stalk of sedge, (b) stem cross section of sedge, (c) detail of typical pistillate flower, (d) flower scale, (e) detail of staminate flower, (f) common tule, (g) flower clusters of common tule, (h) spike rush, (i) umbrella sedge.

usually three ranked. Members of the sedge family include tules (*Scirpus* spp.), sedges (*Carex* spp.), and umbrella sedge (*Cyperus involucratus*).

If you remember the simple characteristics of these six families, plant identification will be greatly simplified because almost half the plants that you find in the field belong to these families. If you recognize members of these families on sight, you can spend considerably less time on identification.

About 10 percent of the vascular plant species in California belong to six genera: *Carex* (sedges, Cyperaceae); *Astragalus* (loco-

Plate 7. Carex *(Carex obnupta).*

weeds, Fabaceae); *Phacelia* (most without common names, Hydrophyllaceae); *Lupinus* (lupines, Fabaceae); *Eriogonum* (wild buckwheat, etc., Polygonaceae); and *Mimulus* (monkey flowers, Scrophulariaceae) (pls. 7–12).

Plate 8. Astragalus *(Astragalus whitneyi* var. *siskiyouensis).*

Plate 9. Phacelia *(Phacelia californica).*

Plate 10. Yellow bush lupine *(Lupinus arboreus).*

Plate 11. Eriogonum *(Eriogonum lobbii* var. *lobbii)*.

Plate 12. Mimulus *(Mimulus lewisii)*.

Naming Plants: Latin Binomials and Common Names

Naming plants began in prehistoric times when early humans' knowledge of plants consisted of which plants to eat and which plants would cure sicknesses. As more information accumulated, it was important to put the information into some kind of order. The modern classification of plants provides the relationship of an individual plant to all the other plants in the world. By a long-standing general agreement among botanists, every plant has two Latin names, also called its scientific binomial name. Latin names are universal and are identical in an English, German, or Chinese text. The first name is the genus, or generic, name, and the second is the species, or specific, name. It is easy to remember which is which because of the similarity of the word "generic" to "general" and because the word "specific" means just what it says.

A large number of plants also have common, or vernacular, names. Common names are more familiar to more people than are scientific binomial names. However, some serious problems arise in calling plants only by their common names. One problem is that a common name applied to a plant in one area may apply to different plant in another area. For example, "white pine" in the western United States refers to *Pinus monticola;* in the eastern United States it refers to *Pinus strobus.* In the Pacific Northwest, the name "skunk cabbage" refers to *Lysichiton americanum,* but in California this name is often applied to species of the unrelated genus *Veratrum.* In short, you should be wary of common names because one common name may apply to two or more very different plants, which can lead to serious communication problems.

A second objection to using common names for plants is that one plant may have many common names (but it always has only one generic and specific name pair). In California, the names California bay, California laurel, or even pepperwood are unambiguous, and there is little difficulty in using any one of them for *Umbellularia californica*. Once you cross over the border into southwestern Oregon, however, the name of this evergreen tree changes to Oregon myrtle. I doubt whether most southern Oregonians would recognize the names "bay" or "laurel," but if you mentioned "myrtle," they would immediately know which species you meant. Also note that the often repeated story that Oregon myrtle grows only in Oregon and the Holy Land is untrue, unless you assume that the latter designation refers to California. Perhaps an extreme example of multiple common names is the number of common names applied to Douglas-fir *(Pseudotsuga menziesii* var. *menziesii),* which is an exceptionally important timber tree in western North America. At least 26 different common names are in use for this coniferous tree. You might expect such situations to exist for economically useful, widespread, and conspicuous species, but communication is not enhanced by having to remember 26 different names for one tree that has a single, unambiguous name pair (pls. 13, 14).

In the binomial nomenclature system, every plant has two names, the genus name and the species name. The genus de-

Plate 13. California bay *(Umbellularia californica)* is known as Oregon myrtle in Oregon, although it is the same species.

Plate 14. Douglas-fir *(Pseudotsuga menziesii* var. *menziesii)* cones are easily recognizable by their little "mouse-tail" bracts.

notes a related group of plants, all with a set of similar characteristics. A genus may include as few as one species (as is the case with *Umbellularia,* which consists only of the aforementioned California bay, or many, as in the pine genus *(Pinus),* the species of which all have needlelike leaves and seeds in cones—*P. ponderosa, P. jeffreyi, P. contorta, P. radiata, P. coulteri,* and so on. The generic name is always capitalized and is generally treated as a Greek or Latin noun, even though the word may have originated from Japanese *(Tsuga),* Cherokee *(Sequoia),* or another language. Such a name has gender, that is, it is masculine, feminine, or neuter. This is not particularly important to remember for present purposes, except to say that the species name of a plant must agree in gender with the genus.

Standard conventions are followed in this book. Species names of plants are not capitalized. Binomial names are italicized; however, when a variety or subspecies name follows the species name, the abbreviations for these words, "var." and "subsp.," respectively, are not italicized. Family names are also not italicized.

Specific names are used to define one and only one plant species in a genus. The specific name by itself is meaningless, but when combined with the genus name, it forms a binomial plant name that is unique for that species. Species names are generally treated as Latin or latinized names; sometimes, this leads to curious consequences, as shown below. The examples of generic and specific names in table 2 demonstrate the often descriptive nature of the specific name.

You will probably find that pronouncing these binomials gives you some difficulty. The best advice on pronunciation is to listen to an expert; your expert may mispronounce the words, but at least he or she tries, and that is the first thing to do. Say the names out loud—to yourself if need be—in a comfortable, euphonious way. Chances are that you will pronounce the words correctly; if not, at least you will be understood, and if you are off base, then more experienced listeners may correct you. Discussions of correct pronunciation of binomials are usually good-natured, with each side citing an authority. The pronunciations of many generic names of plants are given in *Webster's Unabridged Dictionary* and other books such as E.C. Jaeger's *Source Book of Biological Names and Terms.* It is easy to be intimidated by generic and specific names, but remember that only a very small proportion of the 290,000 species of flowering plants on this earth have com-

TABLE 2. Examples of Descriptive Generic and Specific Names

Common Name	Genus	Species
Coast Redwood	*Sequoia*	*sempervirens*
Ponderosa pine	*Pinus*	*ponderosa*
Ocotillo	*Fouquieria*	*splendens*
Joshua tree	*Yucca*	*brevifolia*
Basin sagebrush	*Artemesia*	*tridentata*
California-poppy	*Eschscholzia*	*californica*

mon names. Therefore, for communication and identification purposes, the only name that exists for most plants is a binomial. Also, remember that most people can pronounce *"rhododendron," "eucalyptus,"* and *"chrysanthemum"* correctly, and these generic names are probably more complex than the majority of the generic names of the California flora; at least they are no more difficult. W. T. Stearns's *Botanical Latin* (1983) states, "Botanical Latin is essentially a written language, but the scientific names of plants often occur in speech. How they are pronounced really matters little provided they sound pleasant and are understood by all concerned."

The Meanings of Plant Names

What do the binomials mean? How are they derived? Specific names of plants may be taken from several sources. Often, but by no means always, they tell you something about the plant. Following are some examples of specific names for some native plants of California:

Aesculus californica (California buckeye): *Californica* means "Californian." One might suspect that because other buckeye species are found in the Old World and in North America, whoever named this species was giving it a geographical designation to distinguish it from its relatives elsewhere (pl. 15).

Plate 15. California buckeye *(Aesculus californica)* is designated as a California native species by its species name, *californica.*

Fragaria chiloensis (coast strawberry): *Chiloensis* means "from Chiloe," an island off the coast of Chile. The *-ensis* suffix means that plants are from whatever place is designated by the prefix. We have species in other genera named *idahoensis, utahensis, canadensis,* and so on. Coast strawberry is a native of both California and Chile; several other plant species have this particular distributional pattern (pl. 16).

Plate 16. Coast strawberry *(Fragaria chiloensis),* considered a native species here, is named as coming from Chiloe Island in Chile, as indicated by the ending *-ensis.*

Pinus monticola (western white pine): *Monticola* means "living in the mountains." Several other pines grow in the California mountains, so this specific name is not as appropriate as it might be. Nevertheless, only one pine is named *Pinus monticola.*

Sequoia sempervirens (coast redwood): *Sempervirens* means "evergreen." Because most conifers are evergreen, you might ask how this name came to be attached to our redwood. When it was first named, the coast redwood was assigned to *Taxodium,* the bald cypress genus. *Taxodium* species are all deciduous, that is, they lose their leaves seasonally, usually in fall. Had the coast redwood really been a *Taxodium,* it would have been an unusual one because of its evergreen characteristics. But it is not a "bald" cypress. Later, the plant was transferred to a different genus, *Sequoia,* but because of the international code governing nomenclature of plants, the specific name carried across from one genus to the other. Thus, *Taxodium sempervirens* became *Sequoia sempervirens* (pl. 17).

Plate 17. Coast redwood *(Sequoia sempervirens)* remains evergreen year-round, as its name indicates.

Pinus albicaulis (whitebark pine): The common name parallels the binomial; *albicaulis* means "white stem" and refers to the whitish bark of this montane pine (pl. 18).

Plate 18. Whitebark pine *(Pinus albicaulis)* means "white-stemmed pine," referring to its whitish bark.

Pinus edulis (pinyon pine): *Edulis* means "edible," in reference to the edible pine nuts gathered from this tree.

Pinus torreyana (Torrey pine): This pine was named after John Torrey, an important nineteenth century American botanist who resided in New York. Torrey named a number of California plant species (although the Torrey pine was named in his honor by someone else). The California-nutmeg genus *(Torreya)* is also named after John Torrey (pl. 19).

Generic names also follow the general descriptive pattern discussed above, with a few exceptions. *Osmorhiza* (sweet cicely) means "odorous root" in reference to the fragrance of the crushed root of this relative of the carrot; *Lithocarpus* (tanoak) means "stone fruit" in Greek, an allusion to the hard

Plate 19. California-nutmeg *(Torreya californica)* and Torrey pine *(Pinus torreyana)* (not shown) are named for John Torrey, a nineteenth century botanist.

acorns that actually are probably no harder than acorns of the true oaks (*Quercus* spp.). *Rhododendron* means "red tree" in Greek, and this generic name was probably chosen because the first species described in this large genus has red flowers. Many genera also bear commemorative names: *Jepsonia* is named after an early professor of botany at the University of California, Berkeley, and author of *The Jepson Manual* (Hickman 1993). *Eschscholzia californica* (California-poppy) is named after a nineteenth century Russian explorer who first collected this flower; The genus *Munzothamnus* is named after P. A. Munz, author of *A California Flora* (1959). The genera *Lewisia* and *Clarkia* (lewisias and godetias, respectively) are named after the pair of early nineteenth century explorers of the American northwest; *Rafinesquea* and *Schmaltzia* are both named after the eccentric botanist of the nineteenth century, Constantine Rafinesque-Schmaltz. Some generic names have geographical connotations, for example, *Hesperolinon* means "western flax" and refers to a group of species in a western genus closely related to the widespread flax genus *Linum*. Many generic names, particularly those of Old World plants, are taken from mythology, such as *Cassiope, Adonis,* and *Phoenix*.

Still other generic names refer to supposed medicinal properties of the plants. The figwort, *Scrophularia,* was named because of its use in treating scrofula; *Salvia* comes from the Latin *salveo,* meaning "I save," in reference to the purported lifesaving abilities of this plant. Other names are from traditional usages that predate scientific botany; in essence, these are common names that have come into scientific usage. Among these are *Acer* (maples), *Quercus* (oaks), and *Pinus* (pines). A final category could perhaps be called whimsical; these names suggest that some taxonomists have a sense of humor, or at least a certain amount of ingenuity in devising taxonomic names. *Muilla* is a western genus that looks like an onion (*Allium* spp.), although it differs from onions in that it is odorless, among other things. *Muilla* is *Allium* spelled backward. *Tellima* (fringe cups) is a western saxifrage whose name is an anagram of that of another genus in the same family, *Mitella* (mitrewort). Perhaps the ultimate is the curious generic name for a rare California aquatic plant named *Legenere limosa.* Its generic name is an anagram derived from the letters of the name E.L. Greene, another early professor of botany at the University of

Plate 20. *Muilla maritima*'s name spelled backward is *Allium,* which is a closely related genus of onions. Both genera are in the lily family.

California, Berkeley, and a noted, indeed controversial, figure in the botanical history of the state (pls. 20, 21).

Some generic and specific names are truly misnomers resulting from historical accident. Goatnut *(Simmondsia chinensis),* also called jojoba, a desert shrub of the American

Plate 21. The onion fragrance of *Allium campanulatum* is lacking in the genus *Muilla*.

Southwest, is not found in China. Apparently, the specimen upon which the name is based was involved in a mix-up of labels with a group of plants that had indeed been collected in China. You may wonder how many Chinese plants are called *californica* as a consequence of this accident! Nevertheless, inappropriate as it is, the specific name of this shrub must remain. Thimbleberry *(Rubus parviflorus)* has a specific name that means "small flowered," yet it has one of the largest flowers of any member of the blackberry genus *(Rubus)* (which includes blackberries, blackcaps, etc.). How this name came to be applied to thimbleberry is uncertain, but it is possible that the specimen upon which the name was based was atypical in some respect. Lastly, if you have traveled up the northern California coast in Mendocino County, you may have visited the Mendocino White Plains, where several dwarfed conifers, including pygmy cypress *(Cupressus goveniana* subsp. *pigmaea)* are found. Although this tree is truly a small one when it grows on the ancient, well-leached soils in these areas, when it occurs elsewhere it grows to a good-sized tree.

A Hierarchy of Classification

Taxonomy is the classification or ordering of plants or animals. Every species belongs to a more inclusive group, a genus, and every genus belongs to a still more inclusive group, a family. There is only one sugar pine *(Pinus lambertiana),* although many other species of pines exist, such as *P. torreyana, P. contorta, P. ponderosa,* and *P. aristata.* (Note that once a generic name is used in a chapter, a single letter in subsequent usage may abbreviate it. Specific names are not abbreviated, however.) Because every genus belongs to a family, the taxonomic hierarchy continues upward. For example, the rose genus *(Rosa),* blackberry genus *(Rubus),* the strawberry genus *(Fragaria),* the bitterbrush genus *(Purshia),* the chokecherry genus *(Prunus),* the cinquefoil genus *(Potentilla),* and their genetic relatives all are members of the rose family (Rosaceae).

Despite the differences in the general appearance of these plants, close examination of the flowers reveals that they have a number of basic similarities that indicate they are related and should be placed together in a single family. Likewise, pines *(Pinus),* true firs *(Abies),* hemlocks *(Tsuga),* and a number of other coniferous tree genera are placed together in the pine family (Pinaceae). The family name, like the generic name, is always capitalized. Family names terminate with the suffix *-aceae.* Examples of common families include the sunflower family (Asteraceae), the grass family (Poaceae), the pea family (Fabaceae), the mint family (Lamiaceae), and the carrot family (Apiaceae).

In one respect, the taxonomic hierarchy is like an accordion in that various categories can be inserted at appropriate levels by using the prefix *sub-.* Subspecies are common; subgenera and subfamilies are less common in botanical nomenclature. For example, one of the perennial composites belonging to the goldfield genus *(Lasthenia)* has three subspecies. The most widespread of these is *Lasthenia macrantha* subsp. *macrantha,* which occurs in a couple of localities on the California coast south of San Francisco Bay; it is common from Point Reyes northward into Mendocino County. A second subspecies is *L. macrantha* subsp. *bakeri* (named after Milo Baker, an important botanical explorer of the North Coast Ranges), which is restricted to shaded localities that occur slightly inland from those occupied by *L. macrantha* subsp. *macrantha*. The third subspecies is *L. macrantha* subsp. *prisca,* which is restricted to a few coastal headlands in southern Oregon (pl. 22).

Plate 22. Goldfields *(Lasthenia macrantha* subsp. *macrantha)* are common spring wildflowers from Point Reyes in Marin County into Mendocino County.

Table 3 presents the hierarchical nature of the taxonomic system.

Using the characteristics presented in table 3, you can guess that, although some other pine species have leaves with one vascular strand (vein), or five leaves per cluster, or sharp-pointed leaves, or unarmed cones, only sugar pine has all of these characteristics combined. Its long cones are probably unique in the genus. The three characteristics listed at the generic level occur only in the genus *Pinus* and thus in all species of pines. The two traits given at the family level are

TABLE 3. The Hierarchical Nature of the Taxonomic System

Taxonomic Unit	Characteristics Members Have in Common	Taxonomic Category
Sugar pine (*Pinus lambertiana*)	Leaves with one vascular strand Five leaves per cluster Cones unarmed Cones 10 to 16 inches long Leaves sharp pointed	Species
Pines (*Pinus* spp.)	Leaves of two kinds Cones maturing after first year Cone scales with minute bracts	Genus
Pine family (Pinaceae)	Cone scales overlapping Cone scales with two seeds	Family
Coniferales	Cone dry, with several scales One to several seeds per cone Leaves needlelike (or scalelike)	Order

present in the Pinaceae (pine family) but not together in other families. The order (Coniferales), which is the next higher and more inclusive taxonomic rank, is defined, among other things, by the concurrence of the three characteristics listed.

The pine genus contains many species; the pine family has many genera; and the order Coniferales has a few other families in addition to the pine family. In practice, we are generally concerned mostly with the family, genus, and species of a plant.

At a very high taxonomic level, flowering plants are divided into two groups. Members of Dicotyledoneae, or dicots, are flowering plants that have flower parts in fours or fives, vascular bundles of the stem arranged in a ringlike pattern, and, as the name implies, two seed leaves, or cotyledons. Members of Monocotyledoneae, or monocots, have flower parts arranged in threes, scattered vascular bundles, and one seed leaf. Exceptions exist to almost all of these characteristic patterns, but nevertheless, the dicots and monocots are distinctive and evolutionarily well-separated groups of plants.

Some familiar dicots are California-poppy, meadowfoams (*Limnanthes* spp.), fiddlenecks (*Amsinckia* spp.), lupines, and filarees (*Erodium* spp.). Monocots include trilliums (*Trillium* spp.), grasses (Poaceae), sedges (*Scirpus* spp.), yuccas (*Yucca* spp.), palms (Arecaceae), blue-eyed-grass (*Sisyrinchium* spp.), irises (*Iris* spp.), lilies (*Lilium* spp.), and various other familiar genera and families.

Naming New Plant Species

Taxonomists name plants (the root word *tax-* is Greek for "to arrange"). Naming plants is not completely arbitrary but must follow a series of rules laid down in the International Code of Botanical Nomenclature. The code does not tell taxonomists what name they must give to a plant or how to determine whether a species is undescribed; it simply provides the procedure to be followed in naming a plant that is believed to be a new species. Although the code is a fairly lengthy legalistic document, it contains common-sense rules and in general is a practical guideline for taxonomists. Despite the fact that the California flora is rather well known, botanists regularly comb the state, and each year an amazing number of rediscoveries of species thought to have been extirpated (eliminated), as well as some entirely new species, are described.

Many of the species in California that have been collected for the first time in recent years have come from the North Coast Ranges, the Klamath Mountains, or from other more remote, less explored areas. A species of meadowfoam (*Limnanthes vinculans,* Limnanthaceae), for example, was first described in 1969 by Robert Ornduff. It was found in several populations just north of San Francisco Bay in Sonoma County in vernal pools that occur in a fairly densely populated area. Ornduff used a form of the Latin noun *vinculum,* meaning "a confining band," to describe this species that forms colorful floral rings around vernal pools. In 1973, a distinctive, previously uncollected species of the mariposa-lily genus, *Calochortus*, Tiburon mariposa-lily *(C. tiburonensis)* was discovered by an amateur botanist and physician, Dr. Robert West, on a hilltop of the Tiburon Peninsula in Marin County, where a small population of the plant grows amid the millions of residents of the San Francisco Bay Area. No one had collected specimens of this plant until then, although we have reason to believe the species has occurred in this heavily populated region for thousands of years. In southern California, several plants, among them *Allium shevockii* and *Mimulus shevockii,* have been named for James R. Shevock, a botanist with the U.S. Forest Service, who spent his free time in the 1980s and 1990s exploring and discovering new plants along the rugged eastern crest of the southern Sierra Nevada. In 1992, Shasta snow-wreath *(Neviusia cliftonii)* (pls. 23, 24), a plant whose nearest relative grows in Virginia, was discovered in 1992 by two botanists, Glen Clifton and Dean Taylor, searching for limestone endemics near Lake Shasta. It was later named Neviusia cliftonii after one of its discoverers.

Plate 23. Sebastopol meadowfoam *(Limnanthes vinculans)* was discovered only a few years ago in Sonoma County and was named by the author, Robert Ornduff.

Plate 24. The Tiburon mariposa-lily *(Calochortus tiburonensis)* was discovered only in 1973, although it grows just across the bay from the densely populated city of San Francisco.

Other newly named species have been known for many years but have been confused with other closely related species. Intensive studies of godetias, or farewell-to-spring, (*Clarkia*, Onagraceae) have shown that several plants that have long been recognized as a particular species are in fact each composed of more than one species. As a result of these studies, a number of new species have been described in recent years.

In many manuals that cover the California flora, the binomial may be followed by a surname or an abbreviation of the surname of the person who named the species. Examples include *L. vinculans* Ornd. (for Robert Ornduff), *Astragalus nutans* Jones (for Marcus E. Jones), and *Angelica tomentosa* Wats. (for Sereno Watson). Although these surnames are technically a part of the plant name, they are not a part of the binomial and are not used in verbal communication, although they often appear in technical botanical writing.

Rarity and Endemism

Plants can be rare for a wide variety of reasons, some natural and some human-made. Some species have been rare throughout their evolutionary history, and others have been made rare by human activities. Plant species considered to be rare are either broadly distributed but never abundant where found, such as the little orchid California lady-slipper *(Cypripedium californicum)*, or narrowly distributed or clumped in a small locale but abundant where found, such as blennosperma *(Blennosperma nanum)* (pl. 25).

Plate 25. In early spring, blennosperma *(Blennosperma nanum)* can carpet hillsides in a few areas such as at the tip of the Point Reyes peninsula.

In 1992, Fiedler and Ahouse identified 13 general categories of factors that probably contribute to rarity: 10 were related to the biology of rare species and three were related to human activities (Fiedler, 1992). The latter included specific causes such as horticultural trade, aboriginal uses, uses in ancient or modern medicine or industry, and the demographic and environmental causes of urbanization, agriculture, and weed invasions.

One striking feature of the California flora is the high percentage of endemism: about 3.4 percent of the genera and 30 percent of the species of vascular plants of California are endemic. An endemic species is a plant species that is restricted to a specific locality or habitat. This term can be applied to species restricted to a state, a county, or a particular acreage or site. This percentage of endemism in California is unusually high for a continental area. The genera with the largest number of endemic species are *Mimulus* (monkey flowers), *Astragalus* (locoweeds), *Lupinus* (lupines), *Eriogonum* (wild buckwheats), *Arctostaphylos* (manzanitas), and *Ceanothus* (wild-lilacs). Most of the genera on this list are also on the list of the largest genera in the state. Monterey cypress *(Pinus radiata)* is endemic to the Monterey peninsula. Coast redwood is endemic to the California Floristic Province but not to the state of California because it also occurs in extreme southwestern Oregon. *Senecio clevelandii* is endemic to serpentine soils.

In California, most plants are rare because they are either new species, neoendemics, or old species, paleoendemics. Neoendemics are frequently found on geologically youthful habitats and have not had time to expand their range to their climatic and geological limits. Butte County meadowfoam *(L. floccosa* subsp. *californica),* found in vernal pools, and Eureka Dunes evening primrose *(Oenanthera californica* subsp. *eurekensis),* found in the Mojave Desert, are examples of these. Many of the newly described, highly restricted species of godetia from the southern Sierra Nevada foothills are recently evolved. This is also true of several species of tarweeds (*Madia* spp. and *Hemizonia* spp., both Asteraceae) in California. Their restricted distribution is probably a result of recent speciation. They have not yet developed the genetic variability to allow them to expand their ranges, and in many cases today, it is unlikely that they will expand their ranges because of the unavailability of suitable habitats (pl. 26).

At the other end of the spectrum, some of California's most famous rare species have extensive fossil records and are considered paleoendemics that were once more widely distrib-

Plate 26. The restricted distribution of different species in the genus *Madia*. *Madia madioides,* from Monterey County, is shown here and is probably a result of recent speciation.

uted but have retreated to their current range in response to dramatic climatic changes. Examples include the bristlecone fir *(Abies bracteata),* known only from the Santa Lucia Mountains, and tree-anemone *(Carpenteria californica),* which has only seven recorded occurrences near Fresno and Santa Cruz. California ironwood *(Lyonothamnus floribunda)* is found only on Santa Cruz Island, coast redwood is found along foggy coastal areas, and giant sequoia *(Sequoia gigantea)* is restricted to about 75 groves in the western Sierra Nevada. In southern California, a relative of the mountain-mahogany *(Cercocarpus betuloides)* is known only as six or seven surviving plants on Santa Catalina Island. This small tree, Catalina Island mountain-mahogany *(Cercocarpus traskia),* in the rose family, has a fossil history that goes back several million years. It is likely that this species (like a number of island endemics) has been unable to adjust to the climate of modern California, which is why it is so rare and unsuccessful. Recovery efforts are being made to preserve this rare species, but fortunately, it thrives in cultivation, and if it does become extinct in the wild, it may persist in botanical gardens.

Some endemics in the California Floristic Province are widespread and are rather well known. Perhaps the most famous endemic of the province is coast redwood. Because of the measures that have been taken to preserve this tree, the coast redwood has been saved from extinction from logging and habitat loss, and large tracts of this species have been set aside in perpetuity. Other more widespread endemics are California buckeye and gray pine *(P. sabiniana)*.

A number of other less spectacular endemics, however, are faced with extinction, and some plant species have already become extinct as a result of human activity. In the San Francisco Bay Region, for example, the endemic species presidio manzanita *(Arctostaphylos hookeri* subsp. *ravenii)* is known from only a single shrub. Because pollen from another plant is necessary to pollinate its flowers and set seed, it is the end of the line for this species. *Limnanthes douglasii* subsp. *sulphurea* is endemic to a few meadows and seeps along the coast in Point Reyes, Marin County (pl. 27). It is an abundant annual where it grows but is found in only a few places and is thus considered an endangered species. Another endemic in the San Francisco Bay Area is a member of the fiddleneck genus *(Amsinckia,* Boraginaceae). Some species of this genus are widespread and somewhat weedy, but the attractive, large-flowered fiddleneck *(Amsinckia grandiflora)* is now known to occur in only three populations: two within the fences of the Lawrence Livermore Laboratory installation near Livermore and one on private land nearby (pl. 28). Two or three reintroduction attempts are growing also but are not faring well. In northern California, the attractive Pine Hill flannelbush *(Fremontodendron decumbens)* is known only from fewer than 10 individual plants at Pine Hill,

Plate 27. Only a few populations of the rare Point Reyes meadowfoam *(Limnanthes douglasii* var. s*ulphurea)* occur on Point Reyes in Marin County.

Plate 28. Large-flowered fiddleneck *(Amsinckia grandiflora)* is seriously threatened by competition from nonnative weeds.

El Dorado County, and one near Grass Valley, Nevada County (pl. 29).

Munz's iris *(Iris munzii)* occurs only along the Tule River and near Springville in Tulare County. Another southern California endemic, one that occurs in the Mojave Desert, is the diminutive annual poppy *Canbya candida*. It is threatened by increasing development and nonnative plants. In the vernal pools found on the coastal terraces around San Diego, about 40 percent of the known occurrences of the San Diego thorn-mint *(Acanthomintha ilicifolia)* have been extirpated, and many others are severely threatened by development and habitat degradation from roads, motorcycles, trampling, and invasive weeds. In spite of the federal and state listings of this plant as threatened and endangered, its future is at considerable risk.

The largest number of plant species endemic to the state is found in southern California, where development pressures are most intense, followed by the central coastal area. Relatively few endemics occur in the desert areas, the northern Sierra Nevada–Cascade Range, and the Central Valley. A number of California rare and endemic plant species are being preserved in state parks, national forests, or other areas. In addition, native plant gardens at Rancho Santa Ana (Claremont), Santa Barbara, University of California (Berkeley), and East Bay Regional Park Botanic Garden (Berkeley) also contain a num-

Plate 29. The Pine Hill flannelbush *(Fremontodendron decumbens)* grows in serpentine soils in Eldorado and Nevada Counties, where only two populations remain.

ber of rare and endangered species. Although it is relatively easy to maintain perennial plants in these gardens, maintaining stocks of annuals is difficult because these must be grown from seed each year.

The California Native Plant Society, headquartered in Sacramento, is an organization that maintains and intermittently publishes a list of the rare and endangered vascular plants of California and their approximate location, habitat, and degree of endangerment. During the year, members keep track of known populations of rare or threatened species. The society is actively involved in the preservation of the native flora of the state, particularly its native habitat. Although botanic gardens can maintain rare species, they are always subject to administrative changes that may result in the loss of an employee who has expertise with a particular species. Populations in the wild are more likely to have greater genetic diversity and be able to respond to climatic and other changes. On the other hand, gardens have been effective at rescuing plants on the brink of extinction and reintroducing them to the wild when their habitat has been secured into the future.

Darwin (Allan, 1977) wrote that rarity is linked inseparably with the extinction process. With so many rare species in California, however, and such a vast array of causes, both natural and human-made, and a combination of both, it is abundantly evident that a greater understanding of the biology of individual species is essential to preserve our unique flora.

Topographical Features of California

The area of California is about 160,000 square miles, and most of this land supports plant life. The state is approximately 1,200 miles long and about 200 miles wide. Elevations range from about 279 feet below sea level in Death Valley to approximately 14,491 feet on the top of Mount Whitney, not far from Death Valley. The area is topographically diverse, but its major feature is two mountain systems that extend in a north-south direction, the Coast Ranges on the west side of the state and the Sierra Nevada and Cascade Range on the east (map 1). The two systems join in the north in the vicinity of Mount Shasta and in the south at the southern end of the San Joaquin Valley. The relatively flat valley delimited by this ring of mountains, the Central Valley, is made up of the Sacramento Valley in the north and the San Joaquin Valley in the south. The two great rivers of these valleys, the Sacramento and San Joaquin Rivers, join east of San Francisco Bay and flow westward through the bay into the Pacific Ocean.

The Coast Ranges consist of the North Coast Ranges north of San Francisco Bay and the South Coast Ranges south of the bay. At the northern end of the state, the Coast Ranges merge into the Klamath Mountains, which in turn merge with the southern end of the Cascade Range. This complex of mountains forms an important climatic and phytogeographical barrier at the northern end of the Sacramento Valley. In the southern portion of the state, the South Coast Ranges are joined with the southern Sierra Nevada via the Transverse Ranges, which include the Tehachapi Mountains. In extreme southern California are the Peninsular Ranges, which extend across the Mexican border well into Baja California.

Because California is a large state with great topographic complexity and a wide range of climatic and habitat diversity, dividing it into geographic ranges instead of political units is more useful for botanists. *The Jepson Manual* (Hickman 1993) divides the state into 50 geographic units based on topogra-

Plate 30. A valley in the Santa Lucia Mountains, part of the South Coast Ranges in Monterey County.

phy and features of the natural landscape, including natural vegetation types to increase the predictiveness of species range descriptions. For our purposes, the important aspects of the chief topographic features of the state are listed in the following sections.

The Coast Ranges

The Coast Ranges extend over 500 miles from near the Oregon border southward to the Santa Barbara area. In general, the Coast Ranges are a relatively old range of rather low mountains (below 6,000 feet elevation) that rise abruptly at the immediate coastline of the Pacific Ocean. The orientation of these ranges is north to south. Between the major north-south ridges are numerous valleys. These valleys range in size from very small to sizable (such as the Napa, Sonoma, and Salinas Valleys). The Coast Ranges are interrupted at San Francisco Bay: the mountains of this system that occur north of the bay are called the North Coast Ranges, and those south of the bay are called the South Coast Ranges (pl. 30).

Sierra Nevada and Cascade Range:
The Sierra-Cascade Axis

Geologically the Sierra Nevada and Cascade Range have different origins, but because they form a continuous north-south high mountain range, they can be considered together. The Cascade Range, which is extensively developed in Oregon and Washington, reaches its southern limit in northern California and is terminated there by Lassen Peak (10,453 feet elevation). The range is volcanic in origin throughout most of its area. The Sierra Nevada is exclusively a California range and is generally nonvolcanic in origin and characterized by the oc-

Plate 31. Large blocks of granitic rocks form a north-south ridge in the southern Sierra Nevada, the result of an uplift that occurred between 10 and 12 million years ago.

currence of immense expanses of granitic rocks. These mountains originated by faulting. They rise gradually to a crest that is frequently well above 10,000 feet, and the range drops off very sharply to the east. Unlike the Cascade Range, the Sierra Nevada consists of a series of ridges with major peaks such as Mount Whitney (14,496 feet elevation). Mount Whitney is the highest peak in the contiguous 48 states, yet it is rather poorly differentiated from the surrounding peaks. Evidence exists of extensive glaciation in the higher reaches of the Sierra Nevada, and this glaciation is believed to have had an important effect on the present distribution of some woody plants in these mountains.

The Sierra-Cascade axis is heavily vegetated, with various forest types on the lower slopes and with alpine or other montane herbaceous or shrubby vegetation in the upper regions. Despite the difference in geological origin between the ranges, relatively good continuity has developed in the vegetation types running from one range into the other (pl. 31).

Klamath Mountains

The Klamath Mountains, in northwestern California and adjacent southwestern Oregon, are a geologically and topographically complex series of mountain ranges that vary from 5,000 to 7,000 feet. These mountains are topographically rather rough, frequently accessible only with difficulty, and floristically very interesting. A variety of soils are present in this area, including serpentine and limestone, which results in a relatively high number of plant species endemic to these moderately high mountains (pl. 32).

Plate 32. A view of Sawtooth Mountain in the Trinity Alps from Boulder Creek Lake.

Plate 33. Mount San Bernardino lies across the San Andreas fault from the San Gabriel Mountains, where the Cajon Pass separates the two ranges.

Transverse Ranges

The Transverse Ranges consist of relatively low mountains that run in an approximately east-west direction, unlike most mountain ranges in North America. They extend from near the Pacific Ocean eastward across the southern end of the San Joaquin Valley, forming the northern border of the Los Angeles Basin and ultimately joining with the southern Sierra Nevada. From west to east the ranges are the Santa Monica, San Gabriel, and the San Bernardino Mountains, which are bordered on their eastern flanks by the Mojave Desert. The highest peak in southern California is Mount Gorgonio, at 11,502 feet in the San Bernardino Mountains (pl. 33).

Peninsular Ranges

The Peninsular Ranges, in the extreme southwest section of the state, form the northern end of Baja California, a long peninsula off southern California, and are considered a southern extension of the South Coast Ranges, although their continuity is obscured by the intrusion of the Transverse Ranges

Plate 34. A view over the Mendenhall Valley looking at Palomar Mountain (5,202 feet elev.) where the famous 200-inch telescope was built because of the lack of urban light pollution and the usually clear skies.

discussed above. These mountains are relatively low, and like the Sierra Nevada, offer extensive areas of granitic soils. From north to south are the San Jacinto, Santa Rosa, and Laguna Mountains. These mountains are separated from the Santa Ana Mountains by broad valleys. San Jacinto Peak, at 10,805 feet, is the second highest mountain in southern California. As in the Sierra Nevada, the eastern scarps of these mountains are steeper and drier than the western slopes (pl. 34).

Central Valley

This wide, flat valley occupies the central portion of the state between the Coast Ranges and the Sierra-Cascade axis. In some areas, this valley has extensive marshes. Many of these marshes have been drained for agricultural purposes, but remnants still may be seen in various parts of the valley. Before the development of intensive agriculture, the Central Valley contained a number of interesting plant communities, but these are now largely a thing of the past, and we must rely on historical records concerning their nature and extent. Remnants of the once great wildflower shows are still found in places such as Bear Valley in Colusa County and the Carrizo

Plains in San Luis Obispo County. The soils of the Central Valley are variable and may consist of peat, sands, rich alluvial soils, alkaline clays, or rather sterile, hard soils such as those that occur in some of the oil-producing areas of the San Joaquin Valley (pl. 35).

Plate 35. Central Valley, often called the Great Valley, of California was once characterized by sheets of wildflowers in early spring, similar to this wildflower display still seen in Bear Valley, Colusa County.

Deserts

The southern portion of the state and adjacent regions have two major deserts: the Colorado Desert and the Mojave Desert. The Colorado Desert is a low desert in California located east of the Peninsular Ranges and is presently dominated by the Salton Sea. It is a part of the more extensive Sonoran Desert that extends beyond the California border and into Mexico (pl. 36). The Mojave Desert is a somewhat higher desert than the Colorado Desert and is broken up by a number of small mountain ranges. This desert extends into adjacent Nevada. It is rather poorly drained, and as a consequence, numerous periodically inundated low areas are now highly saline because of the influx of water during very wet years followed by evaporation of this water in subsequent years (pl. 37).

Plate 36. The Colorado Desert is low, between 0 and 500 feet elevation, and characteristic vegetation includes low shrubs, agave *(Agave deserti)*, and species of cactus such as teddy bear cactus *(Opuntia bigelovii)*.

Plate 37. The Mojave Desert lies at higher elevations than the Colorado Desert. Its characteristic vegetation is small, widely spaced shrubs and sometimes stands of the Joshua tree *(Yucca brevifolia)*.

Great Basin and Related Areas

North of the Mojave Desert and east of the Sierra Nevada are occasional valleys or upland areas that are basically the west-ernmost reaches of the Great Basin, a large, relatively high area that lies between the Sierra Nevada (and Cascade Range) and

Plate 38. The gray green Basin sagebrush *(Artemisia tridentata)* produces a memorable fragrance that extends across the Great Basin from California to across Nevada.

the Rocky Mountains and has its center in Nevada. To the north, in northeastern California, the Modoc Plateau is an area in which extensive areas are covered by lava (pl. 38).

Climate

California's climate is strongly influenced by the physiography of the state. Botanically, climate may be defined as the sum of atmospheric conditions that influence the growth and reproduction of plants. In much of the United States, the latitude approximately fixes the regional climate. Although this may be true in a general sense for California, the tremendous variation in topography exerts an influence that is equal to, if not more important than, the latitude. In California, the major factors determining the climate are the Pacific Ocean and the presence of mountainous masses of land.

Much of California has a maritime climate, which is in contrast to the continental climate of montane or inland areas. Table 4 shows the extremes between these two climatic regimes.

TABLE 4. Differences between Maritime and Continental Climates

Maritime Climate	Continental Climate
Coastal location	Inland location
Winters warm	Winters cold
Summers cool	Summers hot
Small daily temperature range	Large daily temperature range
Small seasonal temperature range	Large seasonal temperature range
High relative humidities	Low relative humidities

The climate of most of cismontane California, that is, of the part of California that lies west of the Sierra Nevada–Cascade Range crest, is Mediterranean: summers are cool and dry, and winters are relatively warm and wet. Some genera, such as rock rose (*Helianthemum* spp., Cistaceae), sage (*Salvia* spp., Lamiaceae), and tree mallow (*Lavatera* spp., Malvaceae) are even common to similar climatic zones in Mediterranean lands, although different species occur in each of the two regions (pl. 39).

The climatic influences of the ocean are manifold. Low-pressure areas that develop in the Pacific Ocean in the vicinity of the Gulf of Alaska are stationary during some parts of the year, but in winter they frequently move southeastward and bring cold weather, strong winds, and rain to much of Cal-

Plate 39. Some genera, such as the sage *(Salvia)* (*S. spathacea* shown here), rock-rose *(Helianthemum),* and tree mallow *(Lavatera)* are found both in the Mediterranean climate areas of California and around the Mediterranean Sea.

ifornia. In summer, these Pacific lows are generally centered to the north, and as a result, summer rainfall is rare in California, except for local thunderstorms in the mountains. During summer, the moisture present in the cold, oceanic air often condenses when this air meets the warm, dry air over the land. The result is the development of the coastal fog belt that is typical of much of the California coastline during summer months.

In most of the central and eastern United States, climatic zones tend to follow roughly latitudinal lines running from east to west across the continent. In California, however, the climatic zones generally run in a more or less north-south direction. This is due to the strong influence of the Coast Ranges and the Sierra-Cascade axis; because these mountains run in a north-south pattern, so does the climate over which they exert such a strong influence. For example, the winter storms that bring rain to California generally come into the state from the Pacific Ocean. The distribution of this rain within the state, however, is largely determined by topography. Much of the moisture in the Pacific air has been dropped by the time it reaches the crest of the Coast Ranges, and a second portion of moisture is lost by the time the air reaches the crest of the Sierra Nevada–Cascade Range. As a result, the immediate coast and the westerly slopes of both ranges have a higher precipitation rate than do areas slightly east of each. Because the Sierra-Cascade axis is considerably higher than the Coast Ranges, rather little moisture-laden air reaches beyond it, and the result is that the Great Basin has a considerably lower winter rainfall than does that portion of California immediately to the west of these mountains.

In the same fashion that these mountains act as a barrier to the passage of moisture-laden winds, they also act as barriers to the passage of hot or cold air masses. During summer, the Sierra Nevada–Cascade Range protects much of California from the hot, dry air masses that develop over the central United States. This, combined with the proximity to the cool Pacific Ocean, explains why California has a generally cool summer climate. During winter, these mountains serve to insulate California from the cold, dry air masses that develop over the inland portion of the continent. As a consequence, California has winters that are, in general, milder than might be expected at its latitude.

On the western side of the Sierra Nevada, annual (mostly winter) precipitation increases with elevation up to a point, and then it begins to drop off as elevation continues to increase. The zonation of vegetation in the mountains reflects this variation in precipitation patterns. In the lowest portions of the foothills, the vegetation types are characteristic of a relatively arid climate. In middle elevations, the vegetation reflects the rather favorable precipitation patterns. Above the middle elevations, however, the vegetation acquires a more arid aspect. As you go southward in the Sierra Nevada, these climatic zones move up in altitude, and in the southernmost Sierra Nevada, the zone of highest precipitation is considerably higher than it is in the northern Sierra Nevada.

Of chief importance to the distribution and nature of the plant cover of California is the amount and seasonal distribution of rain or other precipitation. The wettest portions of California are in the northwestern part of the state. Wet areas also occur on the western slopes of the Sierra Nevada and in the Santa Lucia Range of Monterey County. On the western slopes of the Coast Ranges, from coastal Monterey County northward to southern Oregon, the average annual rainfall exceeds 50 inches per year. This is also true for much of the western slopes of the Sierra Nevada–Cascade Range. On the other hand, the Sacramento Valley averages below 20 inches of rain per year, and the San Joaquin Valley averages less than 10 inches per year. The southeastern deserts receive an average of less than five inches per year, and in a few areas, such as Death Valley, some years may pass by without any measurable rainfall. The extremes in average annual rainfall range from an excess of 110 inches in parts of Del Norte and Siskiyou Counties to less than two inches per year at Furnace Creek Ranch in Death Valley.

Most of the rainfall that occurs in California falls during winter months. The rainy season in southern California generally occurs during a period of five months between November and March; in northern California it occurs during a seven-month period between October and April. As many as 100 days of measurable rain occur on the average in parts of northern California; as few as 10 days occur in some desert regions. In the calendar year 1909, over 153 inches of rainfall was recorded at Monumental in Del Norte County; during one season (July 1–June 30), over 160 inches of rain was recorded at one station in Monterey County. Southern California has frequent intense seasonal storms during which very heavy amounts of rain fall. For example, one storm in Los Angeles County in late January 1943 dropped nearly 26 inches of rain in 24 hours. On another occasion, over 11 inches of rain was recorded in 80 minutes at Campo, San Diego County. Obviously, such heavy amounts of rain during very short periods are of little value to plants and may result in damaging floods in lowland areas.

Although the average rainfall for much of the state is so low that few plants would be expected to survive such conditions (because the rain falls mostly during winter months), many arid areas provide shows of spectacular annuals that flower in early spring. Such displays are conspicuous in the southern end of the San Joaquin Valley and also in portions of the Mojave and Colorado Deserts. The average rainfall figures for a particular area may not be very helpful in estimating what sort of a vegetation is present in the region, however, because of the yearly fluctuations in rainfall and the seasonal distribution of the rain. Prolonged periods of drought may have a negative effect on the survival of woody plants; for example, shrubs or trees might be absent from areas where they are expected to be present. Also, because of the prolonged summer drought in much of the state, plants that are unable to survive long periods without rainfall do not become established. In general, winter rains are more or less dependable, but there are some notable exceptions to this reliability. For example, in the winter of 1850–1851, San Francisco received only slightly over seven inches of rain, which is about one-fourth its average rainfall. Clearly, that year was a bad one for the plants. Also, prolonged drought during winter may exert a negative influence on plants, even though early winter and late winter rains may produce an average total amount of rain for the year. It is these seasonal or yearly bottlenecks in rainfall that have a very important local effect on plants.

As mentioned above, the rain in California tends to be highly seasonal, and summers are generally very dry and rainless. In northern California, the occurrence of heavy fogs along the coast has a twofold beneficial effect in alleviating some of the effects of summer drought. One of these effects is that the fogs reduce the amount of water loss from plants and from the soil so that what little water there is can be conserved. A second effect is seen in the familiar so-called fog drip that occurs from the foliage and branches of tall trees along the coast. This is particularly noticeable in redwood forests but also occurs in other coniferous forests, as well as in eucalyptus groves in some areas. The fog that condenses on the upper portions of the trees drips down to the soil and in some areas has been estimated to be equivalent to an extra 10 inches of rainfall per year.

Snow is another important source of moisture for plants and also serves as an important insulator for many plants in areas that have severe cold and strong winter winds. Snowfall in winter can be expected in the Sierra Nevada at any elevation above 2,000 feet. Above 4,000 feet the snow may remain on the ground for long periods of time, and at higher elevations snow remains on the ground during the entire winter. The coastal region is mostly free of winter snow, although peaks in the Coast Ranges and the southern California ranges may have snow on the ground for weeks or months at a time. The snow season in the Sierra Nevada is between October and June, the actual length of time depending on the season and the elevation. Snowfall may be extremely heavy during some years. For example, at Tamarack, Alpine County, a total of 884 inches of snow was recorded during the winter of 1906–1907. This is equal to almost 74 feet of snow!

Although the temperature regime over much of California is moderate, extreme temperatures have been recorded for various localities. The lowest temperature recorded in the state was −45 degrees F at Boca, Nevada County, which is east of Truckee. This amazingly low temperature was recorded on January 20, 1937. Because Boca is at only about 5,500 feet elevation, it is quite probable that even lower temperatures have occurred in the state but have been unrecorded. The highest temperature in the state (and almost the highest temperature for any station on earth) was 134 degrees F in Death Valley. Both temperature extremes occurred in areas that are well vegetated, so some plant species are able to tolerate them.

The frost-free season, which agriculturalists call the growing season, varies in length from place to place. The longest growing season is 365 days along parts of the extreme southern coast of California. In the Central Valley, the season is about 260 days long. In northeastern California, it is 100 to 120 days long, and at elevations of 6,000 feet or above, it rapidly drops off to below 100 days. Some areas in the state, therefore, rarely, if ever, experience a frost; other areas in the high montane region may have nighttime temperatures that frequently drop to freezing or below, even in midsummer.

The average climate of a region is important in determining what sort of vegetation and plant communities occur there. However, extreme deviations from the average climate may also have a striking effect on the plants of an area and may exert a determining role if these extremes occur frequently. For example, in parts of northern California, a very hard freeze with unprecedented low temperatures occurred in December 1972. This killed or damaged large plantings of orchard crops and ornamentals and also damaged a number of native trees and shrubs. Similar freezes in the southern part of the Great

Basin have been known to kill or damage vast acreages of the native creosote bush (*Larrea tridentata,* Zygophyllaceae) at the northern edge of its range. In addition, prolonged droughts, such as occurred in 1976–1977, may also be effective in reducing or eliminating populations of certain perennial plants.

In general, winds in California are relatively unimportant in their influence on plant life, but in many coastal areas the persistent and occasionally very strong winds may have an effect in influencing the growth patterns of woody plants. For example, at Point Reyes, Marin County, just north of San Francisco, winds in excess of 75 miles per hour are recorded regularly during each month from January through May. Although few trees grow on the coastward portions of Point Reyes, the trimming or pruning effect can be seen in the sculptured pine and bay forests that occupy the exposed ridges just inland from the coast. In southern California, the occasional dry, gusty Santa Ana winds may blow toward the coastal regions from the north or northeast. Likewise, the Sacramento Valley has periods during which the dry "northers" blow. If these strong winds occur during the growing season, they may contribute to a rapid drying of the soil, which in turn results in poor growth of native annuals. If these winds occur during summer months, they considerably increase the danger of grass, brush, or forest fires and also aid in spreading fires once they start.

At one time in the geological history of California, the state had a mild, wet climate with abundant rainfall distributed throughout the year. Since the Pliocene, however, the summer season has become longer, warmer, and drier. Total rainfall has decreased and become limited to winter months. This increasing aridity over a long period of time resulted in striking vegetational changes in the state and was associated with the rather rapid evolution of a large number of plant species adapted to the modern, warmer, drier climate of the state. At the same time these species were evolving, some plant species and entire plant communities became extinct in the state.

About half of the plant communities present in California are strongly characteristic of the state and are closely adapted to its present Mediterranean climate. Some of these plant communities are restricted to California or extend only slightly into adjacent areas. Other more ancient plant communities are adapted to wetter conditions or are better developed and more extensive outside the boundaries of the state.

Geology and Soils

The geological events of volcanic eruptions spewing ash and lava onto the land and the mixture of rocks brought about by faulting, mountain uplifting, glaciation, and erosion all directly influence soil development. In addition to their mineral content, the amount of organic matter present, abundance of water, and degree of aeration all influence the properties of soils. Some other features of soils that reflect the presence and nature of these properties are the soil texture (sand or clay), proportion of mineral nutrients present, availability of nutrients, heat-exchange capacity, presence of salts, level of the water table, moisture-retaining capacity, presence of microorganisms, soil depth, and so on. The complex interactions among these various factors influence the overall nature of the soil, and this, in turn, has an important effect on the plant cover present in that soil type.

In addition to the factors listed above, the nature of the parent rock from which the soil has been derived is also important. California has large expanses of granitic rock, basalts, serpentine, and even limestone. Climate, too, has an important effect in determining soil types. In very wet climates, the soil that results from the weathering of limestone may be quite different from that which develops in an arid climate. Topography is also important; deep soils may never form in steep areas.

One soil property that has an important effect on plants is degree of salinity. Many areas of the deserts of California, and

Plate 40. Goldfields *(Lasthenia chrysantha)* thrives next to an alkali scald where salinities are high and few other plants can grow.

even the Central Valley, have tracts of land that are sometimes called alkali flats. In such areas, the soil contains high amounts of various salts of potassium, sodium, or both, as well as other soluble minerals. When these soils are dry, the minerals (alkali) may leave a whitish or grayish crust on the soil surface. In small depressions or other low areas where water collects during the rainy seasons, the salt concentration may become so high that growth of most flowering plants is inhibited. The higher the salt concentration, the fewer the number of plant species that can tolerate the soil. After a certain concentration has been reached, no vascular plants can grow, which results in patches of soil devoid of vegetation. These barren areas are sometimes called alkali scalds. In the Central Valley, these areas may be only a few square feet, but in drier, desert regions they may cover several acres or even square miles (pls. 40, 41).

Although limestone is not as abundant in California as it is in many other states, extensive outcrops of this rock are present in various parts of the state, and certain peculiarities in plant distribution are associated with these outcrops. In 1992, two botanists, Dean Taylor and Glen Clifton, were exploring a limestone area near Lake Shasta and found a plant

Plate 41. Tracts of land, such as this mineral-encrusted, dry lake bed in Borrego Springs, where salt buildup exceeds the tolerance of any plant species, are called alkali sinks, or alkali flats.

that turned out to be an entirely new genus to California, *Neviusia*. Its nearest relative is in the southeastern United States. This new plant, called Shasta snow-wreath, was named *Neviusia cliftonii* after one of the discoverers (pl. 42). It is a limestone endemic, an ancient genus that had a wider distribution in the deciduous forests that spanned the continent during the Tertiary era. Two other relic genera with similar disjunct distributions are leatherwood (*Dirca* spp.) (pl. 43) and spicebush (*Calycanthus* spp.) (pl. 44), the latter sometimes growing with Shasta snow-wreath.

Plate 42. In 1992, an ancient limestone endemic, Shasta snow-wreath *(Neviusia cliftonii)* was discovered on a remote limestone outcrop.

Plate 43. Leatherwood *(Dirca occidentalis)* is an early spring–blooming ancient endemic that is found only in the Bay Area.

Plate 44. Spicebush *(Calycanthus occidentalis)* is another ancient endemic that sometimes grows with Shasta snow-wreath.

Although the rocks of the central Sierra Nevada are largely rather sterile granitics, in the Convict Creek basin area, south of Mammoth Lakes, in Mono County, are some marble deposits located between 8,000 and 12,000 feet. These alkaline rocks are mostly not forested because rather little soil is associated with them. However, in the creek basin, several plant species occur on limestone and are slightly to extremely out of their normal geographical range. Among these are bear berry *(Arctostaphylos uva-ursi),* a low shrub of the heather family (Ericaceae), which occurs otherwise in California only along the coast north of San Francisco Bay and is not known to occur elsewhere in the Sierra Nevada; *Kobresia bellardii,* a small sedge (Cyperaceae) whose nearest populations are in the Wallowa Mountains of northeastern Oregon and the Uinta Mountains of Utah; and *Scirpus pumilus,* another small sedge whose other populations occur about 750 miles away in the mountains of Colorado and Montana. The explanation for these unusual plant distributions associated with the Convict Creek basin marble deposit is not clear, but it is apparent that in some way the peculiar local soil allows these plants to grow in an area where they otherwise would not be expected.

In the arid regions of California, subtle differences in soil characteristics may have striking effects on the distribution and assemblages of vegetation and plant communities. The various soil types found in California are associated with vegetational effects that range from the undetectable to the very dramatic. To illustrate the effect that soil factors may have in influencing plant distribution, the vegetation of serpentine soils is discussed next in some detail.

Serpentine Soil

In California, the term "serpentine" is generally applied to a class of rocks that are essentially magnesium silicate. Serpentine rocks tend to be greenish or gray green, rather glossy, and occur in outcrops that range from a few square feet to many square miles. Serpentine outcrops are common in the North Coast Ranges, particularly in Lake County, and appear in many locations around the Bay Area, such as the Berkeley and Oakland Hills, Mount Tamalpais, and even the Presidio in San Francisco. Serpentine is perhaps less common south of the bay than north of it, although extensive outcrops occur near San Jose at Jasper Ridge, at Pacheco Pass, in the region of Idria in San Benito County, as well as in various other portions of the South Coast Ranges (pl. 45).

Serpentine also occurs in various portions of the foothills of the Sierra Nevada and can be seen in many areas near and along Highway 49 (pls. 46, 47). Although the raw outcrops are

Plate 45. In this aerial view of Jasper Ridge in Santa Clara County, an area of serpentine soil and flowering serpentine-tolerant plants is easily distinguished from the surrounding green slopes.

generally greenish in hue, weathered serpentine and the soil derived from it are often red. Many of the mountains in the state named Red Mountain bear reddish soil derived from serpentine. Serpentine is so sufficiently distinctive and widespread in California that in 1965 the legislature designated it as the official state rock. The discontinuity between serpentine vegetation and the vegetation on adjacent nonserpentine soils generally is very striking. Where the two soil types meet, dense forest may give way abruptly to open chaparral or even to large expanses of ground that support only a few shrubs interspersed with occasional herbs. In the North Coast Ranges, serpentine often supports chaparral in a climatic region that, on other soils, favors the development of coniferous forest (pl. 48).

Serpentine soils are unproductive from an agricultural standpoint. Few crops can be grown successfully on them, and these soils do not support the growth of good forage grasses

Top: Plate 46. The author, Robert Ornduff, standing in front of a serpentine outcrop in the foothills of the Sierra Nevada.

Center: Plate 47. Serpentine rock, with high magnesium and low calcium content, often has a shiny, greenish appearance and is toxic to many plant species.

Bottom: Plate 48. A vegetational discontinuity is clearly visible between serpentine-tolerant conifers and shrubs and a deciduous nonserpentine community in fall color in the foothills of the Sierra Nevada.

for grazing animals. Because trees usually occur only rather sporadically and thinly on serpentine, such areas also are not useful for timber purposes.

Professor Art Kruckeberg has made extensive studies of the relationship of serpentine soils and plants in the western states and has summarized the following characteristics of serpentine soils in California that are so unfavorable to plant growth.

1. Serpentine soils have a very low calcium content and correspondingly high magnesium content. Calcium and magnesium are both essential nutrients in the metabolism of plants, but plants are unable to take up sufficient calcium through their roots when magnesium is present in excessive quantities. The result of this imbalance may be stunted growth of plants due to a combination of calcium deficiency and magnesium toxicity. Addition of calcium salts may render serpentine soils relatively amenable to agricultural use.

2. Serpentine soils also frequently have a high nickel and chromium content. These mineral elements are not only unnecessary for plant growth but are toxic to plants even in small quantities.

3. Serpentine soils are low in nutrients such as nitrogen that are required in relatively large quantities by most plants for adequate growth. In addition, serpentine soils are deficient in many other nutrients, such as molybdenum, which are equally essential to plants but are needed in smaller quantities.

4. Serpentine soils are often waterlogged in winter and excessively dry in summer. The transitional periods between being very wet and very dry may be quite short, with the result that a perennial plant growing on serpentine soil must be able to tolerate very wet soil during some seasons of the year and very dry soil during other seasons. Such extremes in water content also may be characteristic of other soil types in California, but few other soils offer the peculiar set of characteristics of mineral composition as well.

Serpentine soils have a very high proportion of endemic plant species restricted to them. For example, Sargent cypress (*Cupressus sargentii*, Cupressaceae) is found only on serpentine deposits in the Coast Ranges from Mendocino County southward to Santa Barbara County. It is therefore termed an obligate serpentinophile. Many species of jewelflower (*Streptanthus* spp., Cruciferae) (pl. 49) likewise occur only on serpentine, and some of these species are known strictly from a single serpentine outcrop. These species, too, are obligate serpentine endemics.

Fidelity to serpentine ranges from 100 percent to nil. Some species, such as leather oak (*Quercus durata*, Fagaceae) of the North Coast Ranges, are commonly found on serpentine, but populations also occur on volcanic soils in Napa and Sonoma Counties. Similarly, Macnab cypress (*C. macnabiana*, Cupressaceae) is also generally, although not always, found on serpentine. Clearly, neither of these tree species is a serpentine endemic, although both usually occur on serpentine soil. Next in line are species such as knobcone pine (*Pinus attenuata*, Pinaceae) that frequently grow on serpentine but commonly occur on other soils as well. The fidelity of knobcone pine to serpentine is perhaps only about 50 percent. Species such as *Jepsonia heterandra* (Saxifragaceae) often occur immediately adjacent to serpentine rocks but rarely on serpentine. Only a few, rather unhealthy individuals of this species are established on serpentine soil even though abundant seed is dispersed on this soil type. Finally, many plant species in California never occur on serpentine. In summary, some species in the state's flora are true serpentine endemics; others may be found on serpentine in some areas; and still others are not known to occur on serpentine anywhere in their range. Further information on serpentine can be found in publications in the reference list.

Plate 49. The endemic Tiburon jewelflower *(Streptanthus niger)* grows only on serpentine soil and is found only on Tiburon ridge in Marin County.

The different assemblages of plant species found in a given area are determined by a combination of physical and biological factors. The previous chapter describes California's setting—its geology, climate, and soils. This chapter discusses some of the physical factors that determine plant distribution, such as soils and their physical and chemical composition; topographic features including slope, terrain, and elevation; and climatic factors including temperature, sun exposure, wind, water, and fire. Biological factors result from interactions with other living organisms such as microorganisms, plants, and animals, including humans. Biological influences on plants are numerous and complex, and many are still poorly understood. Some plants interact with their environment passively, whereas others interact aggressively, for example, through competition between same and different species, particularly invasive weeds, or through defenses such as synthesis of chemicals to repel animals or other plants. Although their roots fix individual plants to a given location, they are far from passive organisms. Plants exhibit a wide range of adaptations that enable them to grow and reproduce under a wide range of environmental conditions. The sum of environmental conditions, physical and biological, directly affects not only the distribution of species but an individual plant's vigor and resulting reproductive success. In a very real way, every plant becomes an indicator of the particular environmental conditions in which it lives and reproduces.

Soil and Topography

Soils develop from their base rocks very slowly over many years as the rocks weather. Organic materials such as lichens, fallen leaves, roots, dead insects or other animals decay and become integrated over time with the rock fragments to form soil. This process is greatly accelerated by the presence of soil organisms, particularly earthworms. Because there are so many types of rocks and conditions under which soil is formed, countless types of soils exist. For example, limestone soils are derived from limestone rocks (an accumulation of the shells of once-living organisms, formed under the sea), whereas granitic soils may be accumulations of crumbling rock material containing little organic matter. Limestone soil is usually alkaline, whereas granitic soil is often more acid. Soils differ in their ability to hold water because of their texture. Soils composed largely of sand, gravel, or cobble take in moisture quickly but do not retain it well. Coarse soils are more easily penetrated by roots; however, fine-grained clay takes up water more slowly and retains it over longer periods of time. Clay soils also hold nutrients better than sand and gravel. Soils found on valley floors typically are deeper, contain a mix of clay and silt, retain moisture well, and are rich in nutrients. These soils typically support forests or woodlands that cannot grow on drier, thinner soils.

Topography also plays an important part in the distribution of species because slope direction and wind exposure affect temperature and drainage. California is in the northern hemisphere, so south-facing slopes get more direct sunlight and are thus hotter, whereas north-facing slopes are more shaded and thus cooler. Because north-facing slopes are more moist and cooler, they support forests or denser growth. Winds are slowed, evaporation is reduced, and over time more leaf litter accumulates, leading to greater soil development. Chaparral stands tend to be on south-facing slopes and have little leaf litter and dry, humus-poor soils.

The addition of organic matter and moisture to soil brings a rich assortment of soil microbes (bacteria and fungi) and other soil organisms such as springtails, mites, and millipedes that can number in the trillions per acre of temperate soil. The interactions of rock type, climate patterns, vegetation type, and associations of soil organisms are complex but determine the nature of the soil and hence the distribution of plant species. Soils develop slowly under conifer trees and tend to be more acid, whereas soils developing in grasslands are deeper, richer in organic matter, and less acid (pl. 50).

Plate 50. Vegetation on the north slopes of hillsides or mountains is larger and lusher because of reduced exposure from the hot afternoon sun.

Sun and Wind

Although plants need light to carry on photosynthesis, high temperatures, direct sun, and wind can nonetheless be sources of moisture stress. These factors can cause a plant to wilt, shred, or even die. Along the coast or high up in the mountains where winds tend to be strong, one can see wind-pruned trees and plants that have special adaptations such as prostrate growth forms or reduced leaves. Some desert plants have abandoned leaves and carry on photosynthesis in their trunks, such as the various cactuses or ocotillo *(Fouquieria splendens)* that leafs out only after rain. Chaparral plants tend to have small, tough leaves that often grow upright to reduce solar exposure, whereas riparian plants have soft, horizontally growing, large leaves. Other kinds of defenses of leaves to wind and sun include increased hairiness, grayness, succulence, tough waxy coverings, and reduced surfaces.

Effect of Shade

The most obvious effect of shade is seen in the differences between north- and south-facing slopes in the Northern Hemisphere. Here in California, north-facing slopes often are covered by forests, whereas south-facing slopes are covered by grasslands or some form of chaparral or scrubland. Where slopes are cooler, soil moisture is higher, soil development is greater, and seed germination and growth favor larger plants. In a redwood forest or other forest type, the intense shade cast by large trees is a prime influence in preventing the establishment, growth, or maturation of other plant species. Even the light shade cast by a deciduous tree standing in a field, or taller plants such as grasses may have an important effect on determining what understory plants can become established and grow.

All plants need sunshine or strong light; some are adapted to manage with less direct sunlight, as are many ferns, whereas some are adapted to having more direct sunlight, as are oaks (*Quercus* spp.), cactus, and many annual wildflowers. A riparian (streamside) corridor visually stands out against a hillside of trees growing in more mesic, or moist, conditions because the trees along a watercourse have greater access to water year-round. They tend to be deciduous (shed their leaves in winter), but they struggle to gain enough light to support their growth. Leaves tend to be larger, softer, horizontal in aspect, and often compound, giving each leaf maximum exposure to available light.

Competition for Water and Light

Competition for water and light strongly affect plant behavior and hence distribution. Sometimes the search for water is on a "first come, first served" basis, that is, the oldest individuals in a community may have well-established and pervasive root systems that prevent the establishment of either their own seedlings or seedlings of other species because these systems are so efficient in taking up water. This effect is particularly important in arid regions where water supplies are generally at a premium. It is probable that the wide, orchardlike spacing of blue oaks *(Quercus douglasii)* and gray pines *(Pinus sabiniana)* on valley foothills and of many desert shrubs is a by-product of competition for water. Competition for light is particularly apparent in a riparian corridor, where leaves grow large and trees reach for light, or in a successional stage of woodland formerly occupied by chaparral plants, where Douglas-fir *(Pseudotsuga menziesii* var. *menziesii)* trees now create a canopy. Before dying from lack of adequate light, the enveloped chaparral plants, such as manzanita *(Arctostaphylos* spp.) or madrone *(Arbutus menziesii),* grow tall, rangy, and sparse (pl. 51).

Plate 51. The wide spacing of gray or foothill pine *(Pinus sabiniana)* occurs where there is severe competition for water.

Water and Salinity

Although water scarcity limits plant diversity and distribution, the presence of a lot of water either seasonally or in standing bodies presents plants with a physiological challenge. Root cells need oxygen to remain healthy. In standing water, air in the soil is replaced by water, and roots of plants not adapted to these conditions will rot. Plants such as cattails *(Typha* spp., Typhaceae) and sedges *(Scirpus* spp.) have hollow vessels in their stems that allow air to diffuse into the roots to maintain them in a healthy condition. The number of plant species that can tolerate standing water and tidal inundation is quite limited.

The variety of plants found in tidal salt marshes is further limited because of the salinity of seawater. Plants that can tolerate salt in the soil are called halophytes, and they have special adaptations that allow them to concentrate salt in their root cells to maintain a flow of water into the plant, a kind of reverse osmosis. Both salt marsh and desert plants share this adaptation that is found only in a small number of plant families, grasses (Poaceae) and members of the goosefoot family (Chenopodiaceae) being the most common. Because of the adverse impact of high salt levels on cell metabolism, these plants have also evolved ways of maintaining tolerable levels of salt. Grasses that grow in a salt marsh—cordgrass *(Spartina foliosa)*, salt grass *(Distichlis spicata)*, and marsh rosemary *(Limonium californicum)*, for example—all have glands along their leaves that enable them to excrete salt. In late summer, sizeable crystals can be seen on the underside of leaves. Pickleweed *(Salicornia virginica)* manages salt by storing excess amounts in its outer joints, which turn red as the salt interferes with the green chlorophyll pigment and eventually drop off.

The Presence of Fire

Fire can have a significant effect on plant distribution over time and space. Fire caused by lightening has been a constant in the California landscape, presumably for millions of years, although fire probably became more widespread with the coming of the Native Americans, who used it to flush game and perhaps to manipulate plant communities such as grasslands and oaks. Different species have evolved a number of adaptations to withstand the ravages of fire. Grasslands are little damaged by fire and recover rapidly, particularly if a fire occurs after annual species have set their seed. Perennial grasses are quite immune as their roots are safely protected underground.

Plate 52. Fire poppy *(Papaver californicum),* the only true poppy native to California, is seen only in the Coast Ranges during the spring following a brush or forest fire.

In coastal California the mosaic pattern of vegetation is considered by plant ecologists to be the result of past fires. Following a fire, regenerating scrub and chaparral areas first have a period when grasses and annuals become established from seed that has lain dormant for years. Following a fire, soils are fertilized by ash from burned plants, speeding up a recovery process. Species sometimes appear that may not have been seen for years, such as the fire poppy *(Papaver californicum),* which is seen only after a brush or forest fire in the Bay Area, or a blue variant of bush lupine *(Lupinus arboreus)* that formed dense thickets on the Inverness Ridge after the 1995 fire, presumably from seed that lay dormant for 30 or 40 years (pl. 40).

Each vegetation type has its own rate of recovery. Grasslands, which have a relatively small amount of fuel, recover within a year or two. Chaparral types of brushlands can recover in a decade or more, depending on the timing of the fire. In fall when everything is dry, fires burn fast and heat does not penetrate the ground very much, so seeds and roots are not damaged. Winter burns, unlikely in nature but sometimes attempted for vegetation management, can be more damaging because the moisture absorbed by seeds can heat up and destroy it. Redwood trees *(Sequoia sempervirens* and *Sequoia-*

dendron giganteum) are often not damaged extensively in a fire because of the tannin in their bark and the extensive duff below the trees burns slowly. Bark grows over burn scars and stumps sprout readily. Fire's effect on chaparral is discussed at greater length in chapter 6. Most forests can take a 100 years to regain their diversity and magnificence.

Fungi and Bacteria

Fungi and bacteria present in the soil or duff have an effect on the nature of both soil and vegetation. Fungi come in many forms, but in general they do not make their own food as green plants do but derive energy from the decay process of plants and animals. Usually we see only the fruit—the mushroom—because the vegetative part of the fungus is a mass of threads growing underground or in the duff and not very visible. Fungi are classed as saprophytes (plants that obtain much of their nutritional requirements from decomposing organic material, such as dead leaves or wood) and are now placed in the Protist Kingdom.

In warm, wet regions, decomposition of leaves that fall from trees is very rapid and occurs largely by means of soil bacteria and soil animals (invertebrates); in cooler or drier areas, particularly in coniferous forests, this decomposition—the result of bacterial and fungal action—may be slowed down so considerably that a thick layer of duff accumulates. The presence of duff may prevent the establishment of seedlings simply because it is so loose and well aerated that the roots of newly germinated seedlings dry out before they reach the soil surface. The soil itself may become quite acidic because of the sluggish decomposition of tough needles. This acidic soil favors the growth of some plants, especially saprophytic orchids and relatives of the heather family (pl. 53).

A curious relationship exists between some plants and a fungus known as mycorrhizae, or fungus roots. The tree or shrub roots form many short knobbed branches, which are

Plate 53. Mushroom mycelia are like threads that grow beneath the ground, and their fruit, a mushroom, emerges above ground, enabling their reproductive spores to disperse.

mantled with a fungus and appear to replace root hairs in gathering moisture and nutrients for the host. This partnership is being widely studied and seems to be more prevalent on species growing on nutrient-poor soils. It may in fact be present on most species and make it possible for species to expand their range of suitable habitats.

Fungi also cause disease in plants. In 1986 a fungus causing pitch canker in Monterey pine *(Pinus radiata)* was identified as *Fusarium subglutinans* and is transmitted by beetles. The concern is that it will eliminate trees growing on the Monterey Peninsula that are endemic to the peninsula. More recently a number of native trees in central coastal California—tan-oak *(Lithocarpus densiflorus),* madrone, and, particularly, coast live oak *(Quercus agrifolia)*—suddenly died for no apparent reason. The cause of sudden oak death was established by two California researchers, David Rizzo and Matteo Garbelotto, to be a new pathogen, a previously unknown member of the genus *Phytophthora,* a type of fungus or water mold. This organism has two forms of spores: one type has flagellae that enable it to swim; and another type, a drought-resistant, resting spore, enables it to survive for many years. The sudden oak death *Phytophthora ramorum* is a close relative of the organism that nearly decimated the French wine industry and caused the

Irish potato blight, both in the late 1800s. The long-term survival of these infected trees is in question, as hundreds have died since 2000.

Plant Competition and Allelopathy

The closer the ecological niches occupied by plant species, the stronger the competition will be. In a vernal pool where several species grow together, this can be seen in the annual variation in the population size of the various species. Years of heavy rainfall may favor one species over another, so there will be a fluctuating equilibrium over the years. Another plant-plant interaction has received much attention in recent years. This is the phenomenon called allelopathy, which can be defined fairly accurately as chemical warfare among plants. Recent work on various native and introduced California plants indicates that certain species produce chemical compounds that are toxic to other plants (and in some instances are toxic also to seedlings of the same species). An example of a genus that demonstrates allelopathic behavior is *Salvia*, a member of the mint family, commonly known as sage (not sagebrush). *Salvia* shrubs produce volatile odorous chemicals called terpenes. These terpenes diffuse into the air and also diffuse or wash into the soil, which inhibits the establishment of seedlings in the immediate vicinity. As a result, stands of *Salvia* contain individuals that are rather uniformly spaced, much as if humans had planted them. The advantage of allelopathic inhibition of other plants is probably that, by preventing other plants from growing in their vicinity, the *Salvia* shrubs insure themselves access to the local groundwater supply.

Another plant that exhibits allelopathy is chamise *(Adenostoma fasciculatum)*, a shrubby member of the rose family that is an important constituent of chaparral in California. Creosote bush *(Larrea tridentata)*, a common desert shrub, causes an allelopathic inhibition of root growth in burro-weed *(Ambrosia dumosa)*; however, burro-weed appears to have a detection and avoidance system, rather than producing a secondary chemical, that allows it to avoid nearby plants and grow roots in unoccupied soil spaces. The California flora has numerous examples, which suggests that allelopathy may be an important factor in influencing the presence and distribution of various plant species in California plant communities (pl. 54).

Herbivory

Plants synthesize chemicals to repel insects and to reduce herbivory (plant tissue damage from animal consumption). For example, redwoods synthesize tannins that repel bark beetles and fungi, making it a long-lived decay-resistant lumber tree. Gum plants (*Grindelia* spp.) growing in salt marshes advertise to insects for pollination with bright yellow daisylike flowers, but at the same time, they also produce a white gummy substance in their flower buds that discourages seed beetles from laying eggs in gum plant seeds. The strong odors that some plants, for example, sages and mints, synthesize are presumed to reduce the amount of damage they sustain by insects and other animals munching on them. In addition to chemicals, plants have evolved structural adaptations to reduce herbivory, such as hairs, thorns, prickles, and indigestible fibers in the leaves of forbs, shrubs, and trees. The ongoing interactions between plants and animals are endless, fascinating, and ever changing (pl. 55).

Pollination

Although the association of bees and plants was known in biblical times and has been described by Aristotle and Virgil, it was not until the late seventeenth and eighteenth centuries that the sexual parts of flowers and the role of bees in pollination (the transfer of pollen to female flower parts) were first described. Functionally, a flower is a compound organ in

Plate 54. Creosote bush (Larrea tridentata) produces chemical compounds that are toxic to other plants, thus inhibiting their growth and reducing competition for water.

Plate 55. Gumplant *(Grindelia stricta)* produces a gummy substance on its flower buds to reduce seed predation by beetles.

which all of its structural parts are presumably adapted to sexual reproduction. Some plants are self-fertile, but most have evolved strategies leading to outcrossing, which permits greater levels of genetic variation and change. The outer whorls of a flower (sepals and petals) are important for advertising and protection of inner parts. The inner parts (anthers, stigma, style, and ovary) are the reproductive organs. Pollen is formed in the anther, and eggs are formed in the ovary. Pollen that lands on the stigma grows down into the ovary to fertilize an egg. The arrangement and diversity of these parts vary considerably and are the basis for plant identification.

Many plants such as grasses and many trees are wind pollinated and thus have no need for showy flowers. Wind carries an abundant supply of pollen to female parts. Other plants, however, have evolved in ways to attract pollinators by producing nutritive rewards (nectar and/or pollen) and advertisements (colorful and showy petals and sepals, and attractive fragrances) that assure repeated visits by pollinators. Pollen, rich in protein, is the most common reward for insects and bats, and nectar, rich in sugars, is a calorific reward altered in volume, concentration, and rhythm of secretion for specific pollinators. Pollination efficiency that increases reproductive success is important to the long-term viability of plant populations and their distribution.

Butterflies and moths, flies, beetles, and bees are the largest groups of pollinating insects. Many flower forms are pollinated by several different species of insects, that is, by insect generalists (pl. 56). Today, agriculturalists raise bees just to ensure higher pollination success for their crops. Some species have evolved flower shapes that are distinctive for the size and shape of a specific pollinator, as, for example, long tubular

Plate 56. Many flower forms are pollinated by insect generalists such as this acrocerid fly, which pollinates the stigma as it searches for a nectar reward.

Left: Plate 57. The red color of keck-iella *(Keckiella breviflora)* flowers attracts hummingbirds, which are effective pollinators in flowers that have evolved to accommodate these birds' beak shape.

Below: Plate 58. The white, tubular-shaped flowers of jimson weed (*Datura* spp.) flowers open toward dusk in the desert and attract large hawk moths that seek nectar deep in the floral tube.

flowers have evolved to accommodate the long proboscis of butterflies and moths, and red tubular shapes attract and suit hummingbirds (pl. 57). The open throat shapes of jimson weed (*Datura* spp.) flowers found in the desert accommodate large hawkmoths. These whitish flowers open toward dusk, making them more visible in the fading light and freshly receptive for pollination (pl. 58).

Some flowers have guidelines showing insects the route to their nectar reward, or they have strong fragrances, whereas others have evolved clusters of flowers to better attract insect pollinators. Martha Weiss at Georgetown University has shown that plants sometimes signal their pollinators that pollination has already taken place and rewards have ceased by

Plate 59. Newly opened flowers of the blue lupine (Lupinus nanus) fade to pink and signal insects they no longer produce a nectar reward because they are pollinated.

Plate 60. The Mojave yucca (Yucca schidigera), shown here, and the Tegiticula moth have a mutualistic relationship that assures the yucca of pollination and the moth larvae a food supply.

flower color changes. For example, once pollinated, the banner petal spot fades from white to pink in the lupine *Lupinus nanus* (pl. 59). Certain orchids have evolved with flower shapes and colorings to mimic female bees so that male bees mistakenly try to copulate with the orchid flower, incidentally getting a pollen packet attached in the process. A visit to the next orchid may result in pollination. Jerry Powell at the University of California, Berkeley, has worked out the mutualistic relationship between moths and desert yucca (*Yucca* spp.) plants. Female *Tegeticula* moths have special mouthparts to gather yucca pollen. They pack pollen on the yucca stigma to insure pollination and the development of seed before laying eggs in the developing fruit of the flower. The Tegetula moth thus assures an adequate source of food for her developing larvae and the development of abundant yucca seed. This specialized pollination has led to an obligatory mutual dependence between the yucca and the moth. Fig species (*Ficus*

Plate 61. Dutchman's pipe *(Aristolochia californica)* lures gnats into its complex flower to assure its pollination.

spp.), too, have a mutualistic relationship with particular species of wasps that are essential to fig pollination, development of fruit, as well as development of wasp larvae (pl. 60).

Since the 1970s, Robbin Thorp at the University of California, Davis, has been gathering evidence linking the annual flowers found in vernal pools with species of specialized native bees. He has found that relocated or restored vernal pools fail because the pollinators, andrenid bees that nest in adjacent uplands, are not brought along with soil and seeds to those relocated pools; thus, annual flowers may grow the first year or two but fail to be pollinated and set seed for following years. A complex plant-insect relationship can be found in the Dutchman's pipe *(Aristolochia californica)* that grows near streams in forests and chaparral areas. The pipe-shaped flowers lure fungus gnats into the flower entrance by emitting an attracting odor. Once inside, the gnats cannot get out but are attracted to light patches at the top of the flowers that falsely suggest escape, where they interact with receptive stigmas. After two or three days of feeding on nectar, the anthers have matured and covered the gnats with pollen, and the flower droops allowing escape. The gnat then goes forth to the next flower (pl. 61).

Birds and bats, too, are flower pollinators, each gaining access to a floral reward by visiting a floral shape specifically evolved to accommodate a vertebrate visitor. Tubular red flowers are sometimes referred to as hummingbird flowers because the birds can insert their long bills and tongues successfully to obtain nectar. The flaring, short-tubed flower of night blooming cactus *(Selenicereus grandiflorus)* or of jimson weed has evolved to better accommodate the slender muzzle of bats that perform as effective pollinators.

Plant populations fluctuate naturally from year to year as a result of a number of factors including weather patterns that affect pollination success, and this, in turn, affects seed production. Cold, rainy weather reduces the ability of bees to fly, for example. Pollinators depend on a year-round source of food, so severe or unusual weather patterns can reduce effective pollination. With habitat destruction, pollinators die out or move to other areas, and plant populations dependent on specific pollinators may also die out. Plant diversity that provides a seasonal sequence of flowering thus encourages pollinator diversity. If the population of a specific species is already small, a combination of perturbations can endanger the species in a single given year.

Seed Dispersal

Many seeds are distributed by wind or moving water. Seed shape, such as the winged samara of maples (Acer spp.), and tufts of hairs, such as are found on dandelion (*Taraxacum* spp.) seeds, accommodates this passive dispersal. Among the numerous activities of animals that benefit plants is movement of their seeds away from the parent plant. Different animals have different roles in seed dispersal. For example, ants collect seeds of a number of plants because, in some, the seed bears an appendage, a food body called an elaiosome, that induces the ant to carry seeds to its nest where the seed may in time germinate. This phenomenon of ant dispersal of seed has been described in the chaparral shrub Pine Hill flannelbush *(Fremontodendron decumbens)* in the early spring–blooming plant fetid adder's tongue *(Scoliopus bigelovii),* and in the desert flower yellow saucers *(Malocothrix sonchoides)* (pls. 62, 63).

Left: Plate 62. Following pollination, fetid adder's tongue *(Scoliopus bigelovii)* flowers drop their developing seed close to the ground where ants become important dispersal agents.

Below: Plate 63. *Malacothrix sonchoides* flowers in early spring in the desert on an anthill where seed-collecting ants gathered the seeds.

In other kinds of plants, seed coats are covered with barbs or sticky substances so they stick to animals that then carry the seeds to new places. Some fruits such as cherries and berries are covered by sweet, fleshy tissue readily eaten by birds or other animals, only to be scattered far and wide in their droppings. The late evolutionary geneticist G. Ledyard Stebbins referred to the transport of seed from one hemisphere to another by the long-distance migration of a bird he called "the sloppy phalarope" bearing seed stuck to its feet or in its gut. Scrub jays and woodpeckers bury acorns where some will serve as a food reserve but some will germinate and grow into trees.

Adaptations to Aridity

How do California plants cope with a Mediterranean climate with its prolonged periods of summer drought, as well as unreliable winter rains? Plants respond to this climatic regime in several ways, with specific adaptations in their form or lifestyle.

Many Mediterranean species have tough, drought-resistant (sclerophyll) leaves that are thick and have a waxy protective coat, or cuticle. The leaves of some drought-tolerant plants decrease the direct exposure to sunlight by permanently orienting themselves to a near vertical position. Many species of manzanita demonstrate this adaptation. Some species such as the California buckeye *(Aesculus californica)* can be summer drought deciduous, although if they grow in a streambed and have access to water, they will retain their leaves throughout the summer. Other trees, such as the coast live oak and the California bay *(Umbellularia californica)*, remain evergreen and lose their leaves only a few at a time year-round. In early spring, when moisture is in the ground and the ground temperature warms, they can amass the energy to produce flowers and a new set of leaves. Many Mediterranean shrubs, particularly in the chaparral community, have dual root systems with a thick tap root and a mat of finer roots closer to the soil surface. Young seedlings typically have a rapidly growing taproot that penetrates downward through the soil to keep ahead of progressive summer drying. Survivors of the first dry season add a network of lateral roots that grow near the surface of the soil where they find ready access to any available moisture from coastal fog or early rains.

Annuals are plants that circumvent summer drought by

completing their life cycle before it begins, that is, their seeds germinate and the plants grow, flower, and set seed in less than 12 months. Many California annuals have evolved interesting mechanisms that are direct adaptations to growing in areas with a highly seasonal rainfall. Studies by a number of workers, in particular a group of biologists who worked at the California Institute of Technology in Pasadena some years ago, have investigated these adaptations. For example, the seeds of several annual species do not germinate unless they have been drenched with more than half-an-inch of rainfall (or its simulated equivalent in the laboratory). This water must come from above and actually wash over the seeds; placing the seeds in a bed of wet soil does not induce them to germinate. The basis of this behavior is the leaching of chemical inhibitors from the dormant seeds of these annuals, or the leaching of germination-inhibiting salts from the soil. A desert plant that germinates after the first slight rain in the autumn has a very low chance of continuing to survive and grow to maturation, and some desert annuals do not germinate immediately after the first heavy rains but exhibit delayed germination. The adaptive value of this trait is that such a delay, until after one or more heavy rainfalls, increases the chance that the seedlings will be growing during a period of good soil moisture. All the germination patterns that have been studied in desert annuals are explicable in terms of the average pattern of winter rains in desert areas. Obviously, any species that is unable to respond to this average pattern has a poor chance of survival over a period of many generations (pl. 64).

Some of the southern California deserts receive summer rains in addition to winter rains. It is of interest to note that at a lowland, cismontane (west of the Sierran crest), nondesert station such as Berkeley, for example, the average monthly rainfall for the month of August is only 0.05 inch; in Indio, in the desert, the August rainfall averages 0.38 inch. Summer rains generally are less reliable than winter rains, and the amount of rain that falls during the summer in these desert

Plate 64. Many arid areas have spectacular spring displays of annual wildflowers, such as this one with sheets of goldfields (*Lasthenia* spp.) in the San Joaquin Valley.

areas usually is much lower than that which falls during the winter. As a result, some areas of the Colorado Desert (particularly that portion located in Arizona) support two somewhat different sets of annual plant species. Winter annuals germinate and grow during the winter and flower in the spring; these species provide the spectacular displays in areas such as the Anza-Borrego Desert in southern California. Less well known is the smaller number of summer annuals that germinate after summer rains and flower during summer months.

The winter annuals that have been studied germinate only when the temperatures are relatively low, thus being prevented from germinating during the summer rains. In addition, such plants do not flower until the days reach a critical length in the spring, after the cool, wet winter season. These winter annuals are "informed" that spring has arrived by day length rather than by temperature or moisture conditions, perhaps because over the long run, day length is a more reliable indicator of season than are other environmental conditions. In contrast, summer annuals germinate only at a warm temperature and thus appear during summer but not winter. These plants have no photoperiod requirement for flowering; they flower when the plants have reached a suitable size for the production of flowers. Because these plants carry out their growth during the relatively benign temperature regimes that exist in the summer, they do not require a further mechanism to delay their flowering until a specific season has been reached.

The phreatophyte is another type of plant that lives in arid regions. Phreatophytes are perennial plants that have extensive and deep root systems that enable them to tap underground sources of water. Blue palo verde *(Cercidium floridum)*

Plate 65. Blue palo verde *(Cercidium floridum),* found along desert washes, is a phreatophyte sending its roots down into the water table.

is an example of a phreatophyte that occurs in desert regions. The young seedlings of most phreatophytes produce extensive root systems very rapidly during the winter growing season, and if these roots reach the permanent underground water supply, further growth of the plant is not directly dependent on local rainfall. However, most seedlings produced by phreatophytes are not successful in reaching ground water supplies, and as a consequence, seedling mortality is generally very high (pl. 65).

Plate 66. Most cacti such as this *Opuntia basilaris* in the Anza-Borrego Desert are leafless and adapted to minimize water loss.

Xerophytes include succulents, which are plants such as cacti and members of other families having fleshy stems and leaves that enable them to store water for long periods of time. Succulent xerophytes frequently have shallow root systems and thus are able to utilize the soil moisture that results from a light rainfall or from heavy dew. Such plants take advantage of what little precipitation falls in desert regions and store this water for months or years, during which time it is slowly and economically used in the metabolism of the plant. Many succulents, such as most cacti, are leafless and are so shaped that they present a minimum surface area from which water loss can occur (pl. 66).

Nonsucculent xerophytes, such as some species of the sagebrush genus *Artemisia* (Asteraceae), creosote bush, and ocotillo, have developed various means other than water storage in succulent tissue to endure long periods of drought. The means by which xerophytes deal with the scarce water supply vary. Some of these plants are able to obtain water from the soil even when it is present in very low amounts, because they have a high diffusion pressure deficit within their root cells, thus enabling the roots to take up what little water is present in the soil long after rains have fallen. Many of these xerophytes have developed combinations of other characteristics that enable them to economize on water. These include the presence of a heavy, waxy cuticle on the leaves and stems, which reduces water loss from these tissues; presence of dense mats of hairs, which have the same function; vertical orientation of leaves, which places the leaves at such an angle that they receive the sunlight obliquely rather than directly, and thus do not become heated; grayish color of leaves and stems due to pigmentation, waxes, or hairs, which also reduces heating of plant tissues; leaves curling (or dropping) during drought periods to reduce the surface area from which water loss may occur; sunken stomates (pores) on the leaves to reduce water loss; and wide spacing of plants, perhaps in response to the low water supply. Further, a variety of thorns, spines, or essential oils may serve to discourage browsing animals from eating the leaves and stems of xerophytic plants.

Reading the Landscape by Indicator Species

In the 1920s the American ecologist F. E. Clements, who dominated the American ecological scene for many years, developed the idea of an indicator species, meaning that every plant is a product of the conditions under which it grows and is, therefore, a measure of environment. Although many of Clements's ideas have fallen into disrepute in recent years, he was an original thinker and made a number of useful contributions to the development of ecological theory. The idea that certain plant species may be restricted exclusively to a single soil type or, by extrapolation, may occur in only a certain climatic regime, as does the coast redwood *(Sequoia sempervirens)*, brings up the concept of an indicator species. Using this theory, one can state that a species such as Sargent cypress

Plate 67. Cattails *(Typha latifolia)* indicate the presence of standing water, a fresh or brackish pond, or a ditch.

is an indicator of serpentine soils. The goldfield *Lasthenia maritima* is an indicator of the presence of seabird guano. Cattails are an indicator of ponded water or of prolonged (or permanent) flooding (pl. 67). The greasewood of the Great Basin (*Sarcobatus vermiculatus,* Chenopodiaceae) is an indicator of saline soils. The presence of sedges or cattails in a salt marsh indicates more brackish than saline conditions, that is, a source of freshwater supplements saline ocean water. In many areas of the West, various species of brome grass (*Bromus* spp., Poaceae) are indicators of overgrazing, as is Basin sagebrush (*Artemisia tridentata,* Astereaceae). Clumps of rushes (*Juncus* spp.) in a pasture or meadow often indicate seeps. Knobcone pine *(Pinus attenuata)* is an indicator of fire within recent decades. Thus, the presence of certain species in an area provides insights into the ecological status (soil type, drought tolerance, etc.) and history of the area. The same is true of a fire-induced plant community. For example, areas on Mt. Tamalpais in Marin County covered by chaparral vegetation today indicate a history of fire in the area because Douglas-fir or redwoods eventually crowd out chaparral species. The appearance of light-starved, scraggly chaparral species, manzanitas in particular, growing under Douglas-fir is not an uncommon sight and suggests a history of fire on that particular site where postfire chaparral plants are giving way to taller trees.

The presence of coast redwood indicates the likelihood of coastal fogs essential to the tree's survival over dry summers. The Alkali Sink Scrub with its characteristic assemblage of desert shrubs, is, as its name implies, an indicator of alkaline, or at least saline, soils. Pickleweed invariably indicates the presence of salt in the soil. The presence of certain species often tells a great deal about the general physical and ecological characteristics of an area and can be used to in a sense "read the landscape." This concept of indicator species is particularly important to agriculturalists that may be interested either in the future agricultural prospects of an area or in whether a plot of land is being properly managed. Sanitary engineers use the presence of stinging nettles (*Urtica* spp.) to indicate overflowing septic systems, and geologists use a weedy grassland plant, red-stem filaree *(Erodium cicutarium),* to indicate hairline faults or cracks in the earth.

Many species of plants are variable throughout their range. This variability may be expressed in morphological characteristics such as height of plant or size of leaves; in "behavioral" characteristics such as time of flowering or season of leaf fall; or in subtle physiological characteristics such as tolerance to specific soil conditions, for example, serpentine soil. Some environmental characteristics—soil type, for example—show a discontinuous distribution, and plants respond accordingly. However, one important environmental feature that shows a graded variation is the complex of phenomena that we call climate. Climatic factors such as average rainfall, average temperature, and so forth tend to show rather gradual changes from one area to the next. The difference in the average annual climate between a locality at 3,000 feet in the Sierra Nevada or San Gabriel Mountains and one at 4,000 feet in the same mountains may be very slight. The difference between 3,000 and 5,000 feet is stronger. Obviously the difference between the average climate at sea level in coastal California and the top of Mount Dana in the Sierra Nevada or Mount San Jacinto in southern California is very great. Few plant species occupy such a diversity of habitats, but some plant species in California are widely distributed and occur in a variety of climatic regimes. In the 1930s, scientists posed the following question: What adaptations to climatic differences can we expect in diverse plant species that grow in a wide variety of habitats in California? The resulting studies have been landmarks in understanding plant speciation and distribution and are discussed in the following sections.

Climatic Ecotypes

In the 1930s, a trio of botanists in California began a long series of investigations aimed at answering the question about expected adaptations to climatic differences posed above. Their results were published primarily in a monographic series entitled *Experimental Studies on the Nature of Species*

(Clausen, Keck, and Hiesey 1940). The trio consisted of Jens Clausen, a Danish cytologist (a biologist who investigates chromosome number, structure, and behavior), William Hiesey, a plant physiologist, and David Keck, a plant taxonomist. These three men worked at the Carnegie Institution of Washington's Division of Plant Biology housed on the Stanford campus. The Carnegie group established three gardens that provided the growing grounds for some of their experimental plants. These gardens are located at Stanford, Mather, and Timberline.

The Stanford garden is situated in the South Coast Ranges at an elevation of about 90 feet. The natural vegetation of this area is (or was) oak savanna, which belongs to the Valley and Foothill Woodland plant community. The average growing season here is about 280 days. There is no snow, and freezing temperatures are uncommon. The average rainfall is about 12.5 inches per year, most of which falls in winter. Summer is dry and relatively warm.

The second garden, at Mather, is on the western slope of the Sierra Nevada. The elevation of this garden is somewhat over 4,000 feet. It is located in a well-developed coniferous forest that belongs to the Montane Forest plant community. The growing season here is 145 days long and there are moderate winter snows. The annual precipitation averages 38.5 inches and, although July, August, and September are generally dry, occasional rains may fall during these months.

The third garden is at Timberline, which is just east of the crest of the Sierra Nevada at an elevation of over 9,000 feet. This is an alpine area located in a montane meadow near the vegetational timberline. The growing season here is only 67 days long, and there are heavy and prolonged snows in the winter months. Precipitation is 29 inches of rain and snow per year, with no distinct dry season during summer.

The Carnegie group was interested in learning how certain widely distributed plant species are adapted to the climatic regime that occurs over much of California. They selected as

Plate 68. The Carnegie Group selected the widely distributed yarrow (*Achillea* spp.) to study climatic ecotypes, or plant adaptation to climatic conditions.

their experimental plants some relatively widely distributed species that included yarrow *(Achillea millefolium)* (pl. 68).

Yarrow seeds were collected from natural populations distributed across California from the sea coast to the high alpine regions. Seedlings from these wild plants were grown at Stanford, and each of 60 seedlings was subdivided into three rooted cuttings. One cutting from each seedling was planted in the Stanford garden, one at Mather, and one at Timberline. The three individual plants obtained in this manner from a single parent together constitute a clone, which is a term that refers to all individuals vegetatively propagated from a single "mother" plant. The result was that each of the 60 individuals at Stanford had a genetically identical clone at Mather and at Timberline. Use of the clone method enabled Clausen, Keck, and Hiesey to study the behavior of 60 "individuals" grown in three different places at once.

After a suitable time interval, the Carnegie group started the first of a series of measurements of the plants in the three gardens to determine the plants' responses to the different climatic conditions that prevail in these three localities (fig. 7).

Although several characteristics were measured and several populations were studied, table 5 gives measurements for

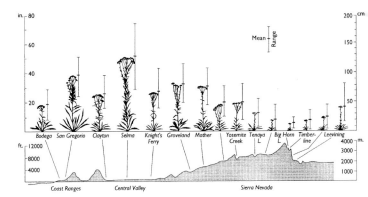

Figure 7. Diagrammatic transect across central California showing origin of several yarrow (*Achillea* spp.) populations studied by the Carnegie group. Plant specimens represent the mean height of each population grown at Stanford.

three characteristics of four sample populations; this condensed version of the extensive experiments suffices for illustrative purposes. All figures given in the table are means. The Bodega population refers to plants that originated near Bodega Bay, Sonoma County, an area on the immediate coast of northern California not far from San Francisco. The Clayton population came from the vicinity of Clayton, Contra Costa County, near Mount Diablo, which is at the edge of the Central Valley east of San Francisco. The Mather population originated at Mather in the vicinity of the Mather garden in the Sierra foothills. Big Horn Lake is over the crest of the Sierra Nevada at approximately 11,000 feet. Its climatic regime is similar to that of Timberline.

Before commenting on the results, some explanation must be given. In nature, yarrows native to coastal areas grow actively all year-round. These areas have cool, foggy summers and cool, rainy winters. Frosts are uncommon. Because of frequent exposure to sea winds, many of the coastal plants are dwarfed in stature. In contrast, yarrows native to the valley areas grow rapidly during the wet winter and become dor-

TABLE 5. Carnegie Group Experiments

Characteristic Measured	Stanford	Mather	Timberline
BODEGA POPULATION			
Stem length	48.9 cm	30.8 cm	died
Number of stems	19.3	18.2	–
Time of first flowers	May 21	July 11	–
CLAYTON POPULATION			
Stem length	70.0 cm	37.3 cm	died
Number of stems	16.0	7.5	–
Time of first flowers	April 13	June 17	–
MATHER POPULATION			
Stem length	79.6 cm	82.4 cm	34.3 cm
Number of stems	7.2	28.3	0.7
Time of first flowers	May 15	June 30	Sept. 20
BIG HORN LAKE POPULATION			
Stem length	15.4 cm	19.5 cm	23.6 cm
Number of stems	2.9	3.3	3.7
Time of first flowers	April 29	June 6	August 14

All measurements are means.

mant with the onset of drought in late spring. The plants that occur naturally at Mather generally become dormant in winter because of the cold weather, although plants from slightly lower elevations are winter active, just as the valley plants are. Plants that occupy alpine areas (such as Big Horn Lake) are dormant during the long, cold winters and during much of winter are covered by heavy layers of snow. Such plants grow and flower only during the short summer months after the snow has melted. In nature, therefore, yarrows show a diversity of responses that are more or less obviously related to the climatic regime in which various natural populations of the plants grow. One question the Carnegie group asked is whether these local differences in plant "behavior" have a genetic basis or if they merely represent a plastic response to the ecological differences among the various habitats occupied. A second question was whether the plants from various localities would be able to tolerate environmental conditions outside their locality of origin, and if so, to what extent they were tolerant of these conditions. The stem length and stem number that I have chosen to list table 5 may be taken as a measure of the general vigor of plants in the various transplant localities. The time of flowering may provide some basis for estimating whether a plant that is able to thrive vegetatively in an area can actually reproduce in the area via seeds.

The figures given in table 5 provide some interesting insights into the genetic and ecological nature of yarrow. The Bodega population obviously did best at Stanford in view of its stem characteristics there, although it also did relatively well at Mather. However, the plants of this population flowered at Mather in July, whereas at Stanford they flowered in May. No Bodega plants survived at Timberline. The response of the Clayton population was similar to that of the Bodega population. However, the Clayton population was taller than the Bodega population at both Stanford and Mather, indicating that some genetic differences affect plant height in the two populations. The two races were also different in flowering time. The Mather population did best at Mather, which is no surprise. It also produced tall stems at Stanford, although the number of stems was reduced. The two gardens also had a six-week difference in flowering time. Mather plants survived at Timberline and even flowered there; however, because they flowered in late September, it is doubtful whether the Mather plants could have reproduced successfully at Timberline, because maturation of seed would be stopped by the first killing frosts. The Big Horn Lake population survived and flowered at all three sites. The plant height and vigor were best at Timberline, however, suggesting that for all the rigors of the alpine climate, the Big Horn Lake plants "liked" their native climate better than the relatively gentle climate of Stanford. There was a difference of four months between the time of flowering of the Big Horn Lake plants at Stanford and their time of flowering at Timberline. The early flowering at Stanford was probably a result of the fact that the plants were able to develop sufficient food reserves during the mild winter to produce flowers in early spring; at Timberline, the plants required about two months to produce flowers after the snow disappeared. Presumably, August flowering is generally early enough to develop seeds before the first killing frost of fall, although there must be numerous years when seeds do not develop because of early severe freezes.

The observations of the Carnegie group on yarrow and some other, unrelated plant species that are also widely distributed in California suggest that each of these species is able to occupy a wide range of habitats, not because of the great plasticity of a single genetic type, but because each of these species is subdivided into a number of local, climatically adapted, genetically different races. These climatic races are called climatic ecotypes, in the same way that serpentine-tolerant and -intolerant races of blue- or white-flowered gilia *(Gilia capitata)* are called edaphic (soil) ecotypes.

The Carnegie group concluded that in California yarrow is made up of 11 statistically different climatic ecotypes that occur along the 200-odd-mile transect running from the Pacific coastline to the eastern boundary of the state. They suggested that probably hundreds of ecotypes of yarrow exist over its entire range in Europe and North America. Here is a summary of some of the major conclusions of the Carnegie workers based on their transplant work:

1. An intricate balance exists between a plant and its environment.
2. Species consist of ecotypes, each of which is in equilibrium with its environment. However, the transplant work indicated a fair amount of variability of response within each population. Although the figures given in table 5 are aver-

ages, they are averages of a range of responses. This variability suggested to Clausen, Keck, and Hiesey that each populations of yarrow has the potential for responding to gradual changes to its environment, that is, these populations have not become so closely and invariably adapted to their immediate habitat that they would become extinct as a result of slight environmental change.)

3. A species is widespread only if diversified into local ecological races or ecotypes. This generalization may not be true of weedy plant species or some forest trees.

One practical consequence of an understanding of the genetic complexity of wide-ranging plant species is that now, when foresters choose seeds of forest trees to provide seedlings for reforestation of logged or burned areas, an attempt is made to select seeds originating from populations growing near the area to be reseeded, or at least from a population occurring under similar ecological circumstances.

Soil Ecotypes

In the early 1950s, A.R. Kruckeberg, then a graduate student in the Department of Botany of the University of California, Berkeley, devised a series of experiments aimed at testing the presence of ecological races within certain plant species of California that were known to occur both on serpentine (in some areas) and off serpentine (in other areas). Kruckeberg filled several planter boxes with serpentine soil and others with ordinary garden soils. Among the plants Kruckeberg worked with was an annual blue- or white-flowered gilia. This species has populations that occur on serpentine and others that occur on other soil types; plants from the two soil types are indistinguishable morphologically. Kruckeberg collected seed from serpentine and from nonserpentine populations and grew the offspring on both serpentine and nonserpentine soils. In general, seedlings from nonserpentine populations grew very well on nonserpentine soils but did very poorly on serpentine soils. The latter either died shortly after germination or grew very slowly. A few managed to make it through to flowering, but only as dwarfed plants. Seedlings from serpentine populations grew very well on serpentine soils and also did very well on nonserpentine soils. One conclusion that was drawn from this set of simple experiments is that this species is made up of at least two genetically different ecological races adapted to different soils. One of these races is a serpentine race that tolerates serpentine soil (as well as nonserpentine soil), and the other is a serpentine-intolerant race that can grow only on nonserpentine soils (pl. 69).

Plate 69. Blue-flowered gilia *(Gilia capitata* subsp. *chamissonis)* has a serpentine-tolerant race that is adapted to serpentine soils and a non-serpentine race that is not.

One question that might be asked, however, is that if the serpentine races can grow not only on serpentine soils but off serpentine soils as well, why is it that apparently all gilia plants that occur off serpentine in the wild are, in fact, serpentine intolerant? The answer to this seems to be that, for some reason, the serpentine races are not only tolerant of serpentine soils, but they are generally restricted to these soils because they are susceptible to pathogenic soil fungi that occur in nonserpentine soil. Whenever seeds of the serpentine race stray over to nonserpentine soils, the resultant seedlings die because they are attacked by pathogenic soil fungi present under field conditions, or are otherwise unable to compete successfully with plants on these soils. In contrast, the serpentine-intolerant races are not only intolerant of serpentine but are tolerant of the soil fungi. One might characterize this species as made up of serpentine-tolerant, fungus-intolerant races and serpentine-intolerant, fungus-tolerant races. R. B. Walker, a contemporary of Kruckeberg's, suggested that the physiological basis of serpentine tolerance lay chiefly in the ability of serpentine-tolerant races to extract sufficient calcium for their metabolic needs against the magnesium gradient.

Regardless of the physiological interpretations that can be made from the series of experiments and observations described above, it is clear that soils do have an important influence on plant distribution, and it can be demonstrated clearly that some species or races of plants can survive only on specific soil types and are genetically and physiologically adapted to them.

Another example of the effect that a peculiar soil type may have on the distribution of a plant species is seen in the distribution of Ione manzanita (*Arctostaphylos myrtifolia*. Ericaceae). This small shrub is restricted to the Ione formation, which is a highly acid soil that is a mixture of clay, sand, and ironstone. The Ione formation occurs in a small area in the vicinity of Ione, Amador County, about 40 miles southeast of Sacramento. Another endemic of the Ione formation is the Ione wild buckwheat (*Eriogonum apricum,* Polygonaceae). The ecological reasons behind the restriction of these two plant species to the Ione formation are not clear, but they nevertheless provide another example of endemism that is related to soil type.

A rather peculiar example of endemism to another soil condition comes from the goldfield genus, *Lasthenia* (Asteraceae). Many species of this genus form large and colorful populations in the valley regions of mainland California. However, maritime goldfields *(L. maritima)* is restricted to the guano-rich soils of offshore islands, ranging from the Farallon Islands west of San Francisco northward to some islets at the northern tip of Vancouver Island. So far as is known, this species grows only on nitrate-rich seabird guano. Tests of its foliage indicate that this plant is a nitrate accumulator, which suggests that it is able to tolerate the high concentration of nitrates in soils that are toxic to most other plants. It is probable that the distribution of this species is aided by the migration or casual flights of sea birds from island to island along the Pacific coast. In cultivation, this plant grows well on normal garden soil, but in the field it seems unable to compete with other plant species on any substrate but the highly friable and malodorous seabird guano.

The serpentine investigations of Kruckeberg, Walker, and others, plus the investigations of a number of other biologists and soil scientists, suggest the following general conclusions concerning plants and soils:

1. Where soil patterns are complex, the vegetation patterns are correspondingly complex.
2. The presence of certain atypical soils (serpentine, acid clays, etc.) may result in the presence of a plant community that is not typical of the general area.
3. The restriction of a plant species or a race to a specific soil type may be due to genetically determined physiological adaptation to this soil, as well as to an inability of the plant to survive naturally on other soil types.
4. The absence of a plant species (or race) from a soil type present within its geographical range is probably due to a genetically determined intolerance to this soil type.

5. A plant species that occurs on a wide variety of soils can do so because it is made up of ecological races that are individually adapted to these soils.

Each ecological race may have a narrow adaptation, and one result of this is that the ecological amplitude exhibited by a species is a rough reflection of its ecotypic richness. That is, a species that occupies a wide range of habitats is likely composed of more ecological races than is a species, which occurs in a more restricted variety of habitats. Thus, in general, the ability of a species to occupy a wide range of habitats is due to the presence in the species of ecological races, otherwise called ecotypes.

The term ecotype is a useful one but must be used with three qualifications in mind. The first of these is that it must be used with some sort of qualifier indicating what ecological condition is involved. We must speak of seasonal, climatic, soil, or other ecotypes. Second, an ecotype is something that can be identified initially only by experimental methods. We cannot look at a plant in a specific habitat and term it an ecotype in the absence of any information concerning the plant. Third, the term ecotype is used only at the infraspecific level. We cannot speak of Ione manzanita as an ecotype adapted to Ione clay, because the term ecotype is used only when two or more ecological races occur *within* a species. Also, it would be incorrect to call gilia an ecotype because it contains at least two soil ecotypes, one of which is a serpentine ecotype and the other of which is a nonserpentine ecotype. It may have climatic ecotypes, too, although these have not yet been demonstrated.

Vegetation and Flora

The term vegetation refers to the life forms or general aspect of the plants growing in an area, such as a pine forest or chaparral or salt marsh. Vegetation gives the general look of the area. On the other hand, a flora of an area provides a list of the specific plant species that occur there: some may be large trees, some tiny and hard to find. An area's flora may not communicate much information concerning the "looks" of the plant cover of an area. For example, the flora of California's Kern County consists of slightly over 1,700 plant species, but the list of these species does not give much of an idea concerning the nature of the plant cover of the county. The vegetation of Kern County, however, consists of a variety of different vegetation types such as grassland, pine forest, and freshwater marshes, and these descriptive terms provide more information as to what the dominant plants of the area are (e.g., grasses vs. pine trees) and a general image of what the county looks like. However, note that "pine forest" as a term can refer to forests dominated by pine trees found over much of the northern hemisphere: the kinds of pine trees at Point Reyes (Bishop pine [*Pinus muricata*]), for example, are different from those of the Sierra Nevada (ponderosa pine [*P. ponderosa*]). Thus, with respect to pines, the floras (pine species) of these two areas are different even though their vegetation type (pine forest) might be considered the same.

Although vegetation is classified by the name or names of dominant plant species, such as pine or willow or sagebrush, the lines for these vegetation types are not strongly defined. Transitional boundaries or gradients exist where plants from two or more vegetation types can be found; these are sometimes called ecotones. Current views of vegetation suggest that environmental variables such as soil, water availability, and shade affect the individual requirements of species and explain the presence of a particular species in adjacent plant communities or vegetation types, rather than its belonging to a particular plant community, which is a human-made construction. Sword fern *(Polystichum munitum),* for example, can be found in the understory of a redwood forest or in an adjacent oak woodland.

Concepts of Plant Community and Vegetation

In the first edition of this book, a plant community was defined as a regional assemblage of interacting plant species characterized by the presence of one or more dominant species. The concept of the community has been the subject of considerable argument in past decades, and no uniform application of the term exists even today. The composition of plant species in a given area has most to do with each plant species's individual requirements for moisture and temperature, and little to do with any specific dependence of one species on any other. Factors such as the amount of shade a particular specie provides affect soil moisture levels and in turn soil development rates, nutrient levels from leaf or bird droppings, seed germination conditions, and so on. The relationships of species within a given vegetation type are complex and not well understood. However, practical reasons exist for recognizing plant communities, now more commonly called vegetation types, in California as a basis for discussing the plant life of the state. The ecological patterns of vegetation are readily apparent across all landscapes in California, and the composition of plants forming these patterns indicates distinct physical and biological settings. These vegetation types, or plant communities, are useful for describing the natural environments of the state. It is easy, for example, to distinguish a redwood forest from an oak woodland or a coastal salt marsh.

Over the years, several efforts have been made to synthesize these patterns of vegetation in California. Each of these efforts has attempted to summarize information about vegetation for different reasons. Some, like Munz and Keck's approach are very simple (only 29 communities for the entire state) and were used as general habitat units for plant species in *A California Flora* (Munz and Keck 1968). Other systems evolved to serve more detailed purposes. Cheatham and Haller developed a more detailed approach to help the University of California identify major habitats and communities for representation in the University's Natural Reserve System. This classification further divided the state into about 145 communities, adding a number of riparian, chaparral, alpine, and other types not present in the Munz and Keck system.

Cheatham and Haller's classification was further refined by Holland (1986) and others working at the California Natural Diversity Database (California Department of Fish and Game) to serve as the means to identify rare natural communities for recognition and conservation. This system recognized 260 plant communities, or vegetation types. More recently the California Native Plant Society undertook a mission to classify the vegetation of the entire state so that all vegetation types, particularly rare types that went unrecognized when lumped into a more general category, would be recognized. This classification is meant to be an evolving system in which quantitative data based on measurements of the diversity and cover of plant species are used to define vegetation types that serve as ecological units for conservation and resource management. The first edition of this classification system was published in 1995 (Sawyer and Keeler-Wolf). In this edition, plant communities were refined into about 400 vegetation types. A table is provided in table 7 showing the relationships between several vegetation types in various classification systems.

A classification system for vegetation, thus, is subjectively defined and serves only as a tool for descriptive or conservation and management uses. A particular plant community can be termed rare because of a narrow habitat requirement or special

Plate 70. Sycamore alluvial woodland, early spring aspect, along Arroyo Seco in central Monterey County.

adaptation such as a soil type or the presence of fog (as for redwoods), but the assemblage of species may or may not include any rare plant species. An example of one of the rare communities is the Sycamore Alluvial Woodland, which is defined as an open woodland dominated by California sycamore *(Platanus racemosa)*. This vegetation community exists in localized settings in the foothills of the southern Sierra Nevada and in the central California Coast Ranges and exists nowhere else. It is restricted to intermittent streams by its specific need for seasonally fluctuating water tables, and to deep alluvial gravels where streams debauche out of the hills and hit the relatively flat valley floors of the San Joaquin, Salinas, and other large internal valleys. The community is rare, although this particular vegetation type has no rare plant species (pl. 70).

A Classification System

A classification of California plant communities that is relatively simple and useful as an introduction to the complexity of California vegetation is given in table 6. This classification of California plant communities is a modification of one developed by J.R. Haller of the University of California, Santa Barbara, which was modified by Dan Cheatham and J.R. Haller and used for the University of California Natural Reserve System. This list of 23 communities, or vegetation types, includes many associations in more recent classification systems, so that the example given above, for example, the rare vegetation type Sycamore Alluvial Woodland, is lumped into Riparian Woodland. Each of these vegetation types is discussed later in the text, including characteristic plant species for each vegetation type. In table 6, the names given in parentheses following the plant community name indicate their equivalent according to the Munz and Keck system. The distribution of these plant communities in California is given in Maps 2–4.

Coastal Prairie
Valley Grassland
Freshwater Marsh
Coastal Salt Marsh
Coastal Strand

Map 2. Approximate distribution of herbaceous vegetation types in California.

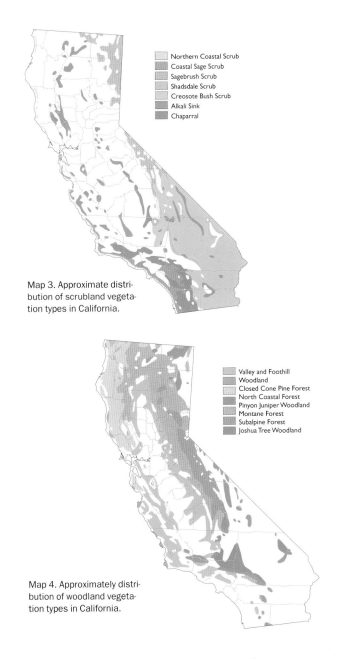

	Northern Coastal Scrub
	Coastal Sage Scrub
	Sagebrush Scrub
	Shadsdale Scrub
	Creosote Bush Scrub
	Alkali Sink
	Chaparral

Map 3. Approximate distribution of scrubland vegetation types in California.

	Valley and Foothill
	Woodland
	Closed Cone Pine Forest
	North Coastal Forest
	Pinyon Juniper Woodland
	Montane Forest
	Subalpine Forest
	Joshua Tree Woodland

Map 4. Approximately distribution of woodland vegetation types in California.

TABLE 6. California Vegetation Types (Plant Communities)

CISMONTANE REGION (Areas Found West of the Sierra Nevada Crest)

Coastal Strand (same in Munz)

Coastal Prairie (same in Munz)

Coastal Salt Marsh (same in Munz)

Northern Coastal Scrub (same in Munz)

Closed-Cone Pine Forest (same in Munz)

North Coastal Forest (includes North Coastal Coniferous Forest; Redwood Forest; Douglas-fir Forest; and Mixed Evergreen Forest) (all in Munz)

Coastal Sage Scrub (Soft Chaparral) (same in Munz)

Chaparral (Hard Chaparral) (same in Munz)

Valley and Foothill Woodland (includes Northern, Southern Oak Woodland; and Foothill Woodland)

Valley Grassland (same in Munz)

Riparian Woodland (not in Munz)

Freshwater Marsh (same as Munz)

Montane Chaparral (not in Munz)

MONTANE REGION (High Mountain Areas)

Montane Coniferous Forest (mostly Yellow Pine Forest in Munz)

Montane Chaparral (not in Munz)

Subalpine Forest (includes Red Fir Forest; Lodgepole Forest; Subalpine Forest; Bristlecone Pine

Montane Meadow (not in Munz)

Alpine Fell-field (same in Munz)

TRANSMONTANE REGION (Areas East of the Sierra Nevada Crest and the Deserts)

Pinyon-Juniper Woodland (includes Northern Juniper Woodland; Pinyon-Juniper Woodland) (both in Munz)

Sagebrush Scrub (same in Munz)

Shadscale Scrub (same in Munz)

Alkali Sink Scrub (same in Munz)

Joshua Tree Woodland (same in Munz)

Creosote Bush Scrub (same in Munz)

Ecological Dominance

Some plant communities are named for the tree or shrub species that are dominant in them. The term dominant refers to one or more plant species that may be the largest or most abundant plants in a community, or those that account for the greatest coverage in the community. Because of the foliage cover or the extent of their root systems, dominants have a strong influence on the local ecology of the community of which they are members. Perhaps the most straightforward and familiar example of the idea of dominance is that which exists in the Redwood Forest, which is recognized by Munz and Keck as a distinct community, although here it is included in the North Coastal Forest plant community. This plant association is named after its sole dominant, coast redwood *(Sequoia sempervirens)*. Because of the large size of these trees and the influence that they have on the moisture and shading relationships under them, redwoods exert a strong influence on determining which plants can grow under them and are clearly the dominant species in this community. Redwood forests tend to be densely shaded at the ground level and also to have thick mats of semidecomposed fallen redwood leaves and twigs. Because of the shading and the dense cover of fallen leaves, rather few herbaceous plants can flourish under redwood trees. Among these are redwood sorrel *(Oxalis oregana)*, inside-out flower *(Vancouveria parviflora)*, sword fern, and a few shrubs such as salal *(Gaultheria shallon)*, evergreen or California huckleberry *(Vaccinium ovatum)*, and some other species (pl. 71).

Certain features of the Redwood Forest also support the contention of some plant ecologists that in many instances the idea of "community" is rather arbitrary. Obviously, wherever you encounter a large natural stand of redwoods you are, by definition, in a redwood forest. A redwood forest is defined by the presence of a single dominant species. One might assume, however, that a number of "fellow travelers" of the coast red-

Plate 71. Salal *(Gaultheria shallon)* is among the few herbaceous plants that can grow under redwood trees because of the dense shade and thick duff. Note its thick, waxy leaves.

Plate 72. A red fir *(Abies magnifica)* casts heavy shade on the ground and creates a thick duff layer, which restricts the growth of most understory plants.

wood *(Sequoia sempervirens)* also are generally restricted to redwood forest. But this is not true. If you examine the distribution of all other plant species that generally are associated with redwoods, you will find that each of these is widespread in areas where the coast redwood does not occur, and furthermore, no striking parallels among the ranges of these individual species are found.

Examples of other Coniferous Forest plant communities dominated by one or a few tree species are the Closed-Cone Pine Forest (dominated in various areas by Bishop pine or Monterey pine [*P. radiata*]), or the Montane Forest (dominated in various areas by the ponderosa pine, Coulter pine [*P. coulteri*], sugar pine [*P. lambertiana*], incense-cedar [*Calocedrus decurrens*], Douglas-fir [*Pseudotsuga menziesii* var. *menziesii*], red fir [*Abies magnifica*], and a few other coniferous tree species) (pl. 72).

Plant Succession

Change is a natural part of vegetation and has been recognized as part of plant ecology for many years. Succession may be defined as the change in vegetation that may occur on a given site over a period of time. Succession, as it was once defined, may occur after gross ecological disturbances such as storm damage or fire or may result from more subtle changes such as the gradual filling in of a pond with the consequent replacement of an aquatic community by a terrestrial one, or from the occupation of a bare rock surface by lichens, mosses, and ultimately other plants. Vegetation once was considered to proceed to a "climax" stage as it matured in one place over time. However, relatively recently, over the past decade or so, new concepts have been advanced that suggest the term succession, implying a unidirectional progress toward some ultimate state, is overly simplistic.

Climax vegetation is defined as the final, self-perpetuating vegetation type that occurs in an area under stable ecological conditions. The idea of climax goes back to Frederick Clements, an American ecologist who invented the term because of its similarity to the word climate. As a Midwesterner it was probably natural that Clements believed that climate was the chief determining influence in the stable vegetation that occurs in any area, but in California other influences (such as soil type and fire history) may be extremely important in influencing the distribution of plants. However, whenever a plant community is severely disturbed by fire, glaciation, or other ecological influences, it may not be replaced immediately by reestablishment of the same plant species that were present before the disturbance. For example, the first plants to occupy an area in California after a hot forest fire are generally not seedlings of the tree, shrub, or herbaceous species that previously occupied the site, but are seedlings of other species that typically occur after fires sweep through an area. In the upper-middle Montane Forest of the western slope of the Sierra Nevada, we find a characteristic forest flora that is subject to frequent burning. After the fires sweep through these forests, the first plants to appear in the following year are various herbaceous annuals and perennials. Later, shrubs become established and eventually provide the shade that is necessary for the establishment of seedlings of the climax forest trees. Seedlings of pines and firs become established under these shrubs and eventually grow up through the shrub layer. After a period of several years, the large trees cast sufficient shade to inhibit further establishment of shrub seedlings and to allow the establishment of seedlings of additional forest trees (pl. 73).

Under Clements's hypothesis, the plant community reaches a climax stage in which it does not undergo a directional change in species composition but, instead, has achieved a sta-

Plate 73. A pond eventually is filled by decaying vegetation and siltation to become a meadow, which, over time, may be invaded by trees and shrubs to become a forest.

Plate 74. Species such as the giant sequoia *(Sequoia giganteum),* shown here, and the Jeffrey pine *(Pinus jeffreyi)* have declined in an era of active fire prevention.

bility that is reflected by the fact that the youngest plants in the area are the same species as the oldest ones. This concept has at least indirectly led to some serious mismanagement of vegetation in California. For example, the mixed coniferous forest of the Sierra Nevada was far too successfully protected from fires for about 100 years from the late 1800s to the late 1900s. During this time this so-called climax forest continued to change, primarily by the proliferation of shade-tolerant species such as incense-cedar *(Calocedrus decurrens)* and white fir *(Abies concolor)* and the reduction of shade-intolerant ponderosa pine, Jeffrey pine *(Pinus jeffreyi),* sugar pine, and the giant sequoia *(Sequoiadendron giganteum)* (pl. 74). It was only in the 1970s that researchers began to understand that the continual disturbance by fire was the process by which these forests maintained their diversity and their species composition. Without regular fire of low intensity, the forest becomes dense and certain species do not germinate successfully. The risk also exists of a stand-destroying fire, which severely alters species composition. In major fires, all or most of the trees of all sizes burn, which results in a higher than natural representation of montane chaparral and other brush species. These brushlands are likely to catch fire more frequently and are thus likely to reduce the likelihood of mixed conifer forest recolonizing the area.

Because change is a major factor for all vegetation, the term climax becomes relative and in many cases outmoded. As the old adage goes, nothing is constant except change. Vegetation is no exception to this. Although many vegetation types have a tendency to proceed toward some state in which larger and older plants dominate the stand, these plants will be interrupted in their idealized linear progression to the "ultimate" climax in many ways. Because fires or other disturbances such as floods, avalanches, disease, and pest outbreaks are the natural rule among most vegetation types in California and elsewhere, a wealth of potential states of vegetation exist, depending on the type, frequency and intensity of the disturbance. This catalog of states may be, and usually is, interrupted in many ways that make the actual process of transition very complex and variable.

Change operates in many temporal and spatial scales from local-scale occurrences that affect individuals within stands, or stands themselves, to entire regions. Picture, for example, the extent and frequency of disturbance by local flash floods or individual lightning strikes, versus large landslides or forest fires, versus global climate change or prolonged drought. Each of these is indicative of large- to small-scale events that occur at different time and geographic scales, and yet each has a profound effect on the composition and structure of stands of vegetation.

New terms such as "stand dynamics" and "state transitions" have come to replace the term "succession." These terms more realistically reflect the truly variable and complex web of interactions between vegetation and time and space.

Plate 75. Successional events over varying periods of time following a fire may include stages of grassland, chaparral, conifer or hardwood invasion, and finally a forest.

For example, for vegetation such as coast live oak woodland and California annual grassland there exists a catalog of possible states and transitions between them. These states represent visually distinct vegetation types—grassland, grassland with shrub and oak seedlings, dense cover of shrubs and oak saplings with little grass—all in the same area. The transitions represent change from one state to another brought about by changes in environmental conditions (moist versus dry, slopes, shallow versus deep soil), by disturbance events (fire, disease), or by the inevitable growth of new species overtopping the previously tallest plants (oaks versus shrubs and grasses). Meadows are often successional stages between a pond filled in by vegetative decay and siltation and an invasive forest. Depending on the interplay between environment, disturbance, and growth, these states can be reset, skipped, or interdigitated in many ways. The variety in the plant cover of California is a reflection of the richness of the flora of the state and of the remarkable diversity of ecological conditions that interact to influence the patterns of distribution of each plant species (pl. 75).

Life Zones

A discussion in chapter 3 considered factors that affect the distribution of plant species in California. Any factor that influences the distribution of a plant species also has an influence on the distribution of plant communities, because a plant community is an aggregation of several plant species.

An early attempt to describe the biotic composition of North America was made by the American biologist C. Hart Merriam in the 1890s. Merriam recognized that as one ascends a mountain, the vegetation is stratified into horizontal zones, or bands, that are characteristic of certain elevations. In a very general way, these changes in the vegetation as one ascends a mountain are similar to the latitudinal vegetational changes that occur from sea level in the southern parts of North America to sea level in the northern parts of the continent. For example, the tundra vegetation of mountain tops in the central Rocky Mountains bears a general similarity to the vegetation of the arctic coast of Alaska—or at least this similarity seemed to be a real one to Merriam. As a consequence of these general observations, Merriam formulated the life zone concept. The essence of this idea is that North America can be divided into life zones that, according to Merriam, represent a vegetational response to temperature.

The following discussion of life zones in California is adapted from the introduction to W.L. Jepson's *A Manual of the Flowering Plants of California,* published in 1923–1925. Considering the time at which Jepson's observations were published, they exhibit a remarkably modern insight into fundamental ecological principles. Although Merriam's life zone concept is no longer taught in more advanced ecology classes, it nonetheless provides a valuable general, overall description of the vegetation of California.

As a result of the varying combinations of climatic factors in the state, intensified by distance from the ocean and by altitude, the vegetation of California is markedly stratified into horizontal bands called life zones. Six life zones are recognized: (1) Lower Sonoran, (2) Upper Sonoran, (3) Transition, (4) Canadian, (5) Hudsonian, and (6) Boreal. The isothermal lines of a temperature chart of California correspond in a general way with these life zones, and a contour rain chart shows similar correspondence. Annual rainfall, which is slight in the deserts of the Lower Sonoran, increases half-an-inch for every 100 feet as you proceed up the west slope of the Sierra Nevada. Insolation (exposure to sun) increases toward the south and also increases markedly with altitude. Humidity is greatest along the coast and diminishes toward the interior and in the south.

The Lower Sonoran comprises three distinctive areas: (1) the Colorado Desert, or Colorado Sonoran; (2) the Mojave Desert, or Mojave Sonoran; and (3) the Great Valley, or Valley Sonoran. The two deserts are characterized by a typical desert climate. They have low humidity and low rainfall; the annual precipitation varies from zero to about five inches. They have high summer temperatures, averaging from 90 to 130 degree F; they have low winter temperatures, varying from about 15 to 50 degrees F; and they have a great annual temperature range and a great diurnal range. Drying winds of gale force are prevalent. The vegetation of the Lower Sonoran has the characteristic aspect of plants of desert regions; that is, there is everywhere exhibited a marked development of structures to inhibit transpiration or physiological devices for the conservation of water.

The Colorado Desert lies at a low altitude, between zero and about 500 feet. Characteristic species are members of the goosefoot family (Chenopodiaceae), a few low bushes, and several herbs. Only a few species of trees occur, such as desert ironwood *(Olneya tesota),* mesquite *(Prosopis juliflora* var. *torreyana),* and screw bean *(P. pubescens),* these being limited to streambeds and the borders of springs or low-lying valleys. This desert passes gradually into the Mojave Desert.

The Mojave Desert lies at a higher elevation than the Colorado Desert, the altitudes ranging from about 2,000 to 5,000 feet, and the rainfall is usually somewhat greater. In other respects it has a desert climate similar to that of the Colorado Desert, and its vegetation presents a similar desert aspect. Hundreds of square miles exhibit the dark green of creosote saltbush *(Larrea tridentata),* a shrub commonly three to six feet high with very small, resin-covered evergreen leaves; the individuals are widely but rather regularly spaced in response to the meagerness of soil water (or perhaps allelopathy) (pl. 76). Low shrubs or bushes of gray hue are abundant and include various widely distributed species common to the desert valleys and belonging to the salt-bush genus *(Atriplex)* and several members of the sunflower family (Asteraceae). Bladder sage *(Salazaria mexicana)* and box thorn *(Lycium andersonii* and *L. cooperi)* are roughish or spiny shrubs. Seep weed *(Suaeda* spp.) is characteristic of alkaline valleys, whereas turpentine broom *(Thamnosma montana)* is a small switch plant of the arid slopes. We find several characteristic desert herbs as well. Extensive groves of Joshua tree *(Yucca brevifolia),* the individuals 16 to 30 feet high, lend an added touch of strangeness to the xerophytic populations. Save for this one species, true trees are mainly absent, except that along stream courses, about springs, or in low valleys where roots may go down 20 to 70 feet to a low-lying water stratum, a few species occur, for example, the mesquites *Prosopis juliflora* var. *glandulosa* and *P. pubescens.*

Plate 76. Creosote bush *(Larrea tridentata),* a dark green, medium-sized shrub, covers hundreds of miles of the Mojave Desert.

The Valley Sonoran, or Great Valley, comprises the plain of the Central Valley of California except for the lower, or central delta, portion. It is a grassland formation, varying in altitude from 10 to 500 feet, with greater rainfall and fewer extremes of temperature than occur in the desert areas. In its primitive condition it is characterized by vast numbers of annuals that germinate with the winter rains and flower in spring; characteristic perennial herbs are California-poppy *(Eschscholzia californica)* and gum plant *(Grindelia camporum)*. Large areas of alkalai flats are encountered, especially on the west side of the valley. On the valley floors or undulating plains the traveler finds small depressions, a few feet or yards square and a few inches or feet deep, which fill with water in the rainy season. When a little deeper, more well-defined, and more numerous, they take the name " hog wallows." With the coming of the dry season the water evaporates, and the beds of these pools in late spring or early summer give rise to a distinctive flora composed of several species of mostly annual plants (pl. 77). A narrow curtain of trees along streams of the Central Valley is composed of California sycamore *(Platanus*

Plate 77. Spring wildflowers blooming in the basin of a hog wallow.

racemosa), Fremont poplar *(Populus fremontii)*, and a few willows *(Salix* spp.)—although the willows are not confined to the valley floors.

The Upper Sonoran may often be divided into a lower foothill belt and a chaparral belt. The lower foothill belt is a grassland formation, sometimes with a scattered growth of blue oak *(Quercus douglasii)* and Engelmann oak *(Q. engelmanii),* plus several characteristic herbs (pl. 78). Above the lower foothill belt is the chaparral belt, or hard chaparral. It has an average altitude of 100 to 400 feet and is characterized by the presence of extensive brushlands. Most of the species represent extreme arid land types and possess various markedly xerophytic structures, such as small or reduced

Plate 78. In the Upper Sonoran life zone, blue oak *(Quercus douglasii)* grows widely spaced at higher elevations. At lower elevations, as the climate grows hotter and drier, the vegetation shifts to a chaparral community.

leaves, entire leaves, thickened epidermis, hard and very dense wood, vertically placed leaves, small flowers, and seeds adapted to xerophytic conditions. The most widely spread and characteristic species are three species of California-lilac *(Ceanothus)*, several manzanitas *(Arctostaphylos* spp.), and mountain-mahogany *(Cercocarpus betuloides)*. Many of the species characteristic of chaparral inhabit rocky or gravelly slopes or ridges and grow on well-drained slopes.

Plate 79. In coastal southern California in the Upper Sonoran life zone, matilija-poppy *(Romneya coulteri),* shown here, grows with species of buckwheat *(Eriogonum* spp.), and mariposa-lilies *(Calochortus* spp.).

Coastal southern California, below about 4,000 or 5,000 feet, lies mostly in the Upper Sonoran life zone. Some of the more important species are goldenbowl mariposa *(Calochortus concolor)* and the related Plummer's mariposa-lily *(C. plummerae);* Engelmann oak; the buckwheat *Oxytheca trilobata; Clematis pauciflora;* matilija-poppy *(Romneya coulteri)* (pl. 79); the jewelflower *Streptanthus campestris;* laurel sumac *(Malosma laurina)* and lemonadeberry *(Rhus integrifolia);*

Ceanothus megacarpus and red-heart *(C. spinosus);* and the monkey flower *Mimulus brevipes.*

The Transition life zone is well defined, especially on its lower borders. The Sierra Transition lies between average altitudes of 2,000 and 5,000 feet and has a mean temperature of 55 to 60 degrees F and an average rainfall of 25 to 35 inches. It includes the main forest belt and is repeated in the mountains of southern California and in the Coast Ranges where the latter rise to sufficiently high altitudes. This life zone is distinctive and, on the whole, rather definitely circumscribed. It contains, for California, a greater number of species of trees and shrubs than any other life zone and has, in addition, a very large population of herbs.

Widely developed in some parts of the state and very narrow in others, the Arid Transition of the Great Basin underlies the lower margin of the main Humid Transition and Sierra Transition. It is, in California, a drier and more exposed subarea, often with a preponderance of brush slopes and scattered trees. Its most characteristic species are ponderosa pine, Basin sagebrush *(Artemisia tridentata),* the manzanita *Arctostaphylos patula, Garrya fremontii,* and the plum *Prunus subcordata.*

The Sierra Transition is well developed and forms a broad band. It carries the less open part of the forest belt. The dominant forest species are ponderosa pine and sugar pine; incense-cedar, and white fir (pl. 80). The giant sequoia *(Sequoiadendron giganteum)* is a marked feature of this zone in the southern part of the Sierra Nevada. The dry or more open forest or forestless slopes present many shrubs of wide range, such as California hazelnut *(Corylus cornuta* var. *californica),* thimbleberry *(Rubus parviflorus),* service-berry *(Amelanchier alnifolia),* three species of *Ceanothus,* mountain dogwood *(Cornus nuttallii),* and a few other shrubby species. On the dry flats or open wet meadows or swamps, as well as on the forest slopes, various characteristic herbs occur. The Redwood Transition, which comprises the coastal redwood belt, extends from sea level to 2,000 or sometimes to 3,000 feet. It has, there-

Plate 80. The Sierra transition portion of the Transition life zone supports a wide variety of forest species including white fir *(Abies concolor),* shown here.

fore, a very much lower altitude than the Sierra Transition and a somewhat higher rainfall, varying from 25 to 122 inches. From the standpoint of temperature, it enjoys a lower annual range and smaller diurnal range. Being wholly within the coastal fog belt and lying next to the ocean, it has much greater humidity. Proceeding from the Central Valley to the coastal edge of the redwood belt, you pass through formations similar, in an ecological view, to those met within ascending the Sierra Nevada from the Central Valley, because you meet, successively, the dry barren plains, the barren foothills, the chaparral, and finally a narrow band of ponderosa pine and California black oak *(Q. kelloggii),* which is characteristic of the Arid Transition. In its greatest development, coast redwood forms pure stands. In other parts of the belt it is dominant but associated with tan-oak *(Lithocarpus densiflorus)*, Douglas-fir, and other conifers. On the inner side of the redwood belt is a marked band of madrone *(Arbutus menziesii)* and Douglas-fir. Herbs include fetid adder's tongue *(Scoliopus bigelovii)*, *Clintonia andrewsiana*, false lily-of-the-valley *(Maianthemum dilatatum)*, western trillium *(Trillium ovatum)*, wild-ginger *(Asarum caudatum)*, inside-out flower, vanilla leaf *(Achlys triphylla)*, saxifrage *(Saxifraga mertensiana)*, and redwood sorrel. Certain shrubs form a very low understory and often occur in heavy stands, for example, blue brush *(Ceanothus thyrsiflorus)*, evergreen huckleberry *(Vaccinium ovatum)*, and salal.

The Canadian life zone is not well defined in the Sierra Nevada and has, as a separate zone, only a shadowy or wavering existence. Its natural place is, on the average, between 5,000 and 7,000 feet where the mean annual temperature is 50 to 55 degrees F and the average rainfall is 40 to 50 inches.

Plate 81. The Canadian life zone is not clearly delineated in the Sierra Nevada, but Jeffrey pine *(Pinus jeffreyi)*, shown here, red fir *(Abies magnifica)*, western white pine *(P. monticola)*, and lodgepole pine *(P. contorta* subsp. *murrayana)* are characteristic.

The most useful indicator species in this life zone are red fir, Jeffrey pine, western white pine *(P. monticola)*, and lodgepole pine *(P. contorta* subsp. *murrayana)* (pl. 81). The first three species are, however, often found in the upper part of the Transition zone, associated with typical Transition species, whereas the fourth is frequently a characteristic species of the next life zone higher, the Hudsonian. The following herbs and shrubs may be considered as belonging to this zone: bitter cherry *(Prunus emarginata)*, pinemat manzanita *(Arctostaphylos nevadensis)*, *Nama lobbii*, *Hesperochiron californicus*, the monkey flower *(Mimulus lewisii)*, and the lousewort *(Pedicularis semibarbata)*.

The Hudsonian life zone is the timberline zone and has fairly well defined upper borders. It has an average altitude of

Plate 82. The Hudsonian life zone is at timberline, where tree species such as the western white pine *(Pinus monticola)*, whitebark pine *(P. albicaulis)*, and western juniper *(Juniperus occidentalis)* are commonly found.

7,000 to 9,000 feet, a mean annual temperature of 45 to 50 degrees F, and an average rainfall of 50 to 55 inches. The most important index species are whitebark pine *(P. albicaulis)*, western juniper *(Juniperus occidentalis)*, and various herbaceous species.

The Boreal life zone is a true alpine zone. Its altitude range varies from 9,000 to 14,500 feet, with a mean annual temperature of 40 to 45 degrees F and an average rainfall of 60 to 70 inches. The characteristic species are almost exclusively herbs. The Boreal zone presents marked plant formations on the Salmon Mountains, Mt. Shasta, Lassen Peak, and the high Sierra Nevada. It recurs (although represented by few species)

Plate 83. In the Boreal or Alpine life zone, where winds are strong and insolation great, plants such as this phlox *(Phlox diffusa)* become reduced to cushion forms.

on Mt. San Gorgonio in the San Bernardino Mountains and feebly on Mt. San Jacinto in the San Jacinto Mountains.

Merriam's classification of life zones in North America was an early attempt to subdivide the biota of the continent in a biologically meaningful manner and is no longer presented in courses in ecology. His assumption of the all-controlling influence of temperature conditions is a naive one in view of the other variables that affect plant distribution. In other words, Merriam's scheme was too simple in its approach, although it was a valuable pioneer attempt to classify the vegetation of North America according to ecological principles.

Table 7 demonstrates the complexities in the meanings of different classifications of vegetation. The five different classifications have been developed for different purposes, stressing different types of vegetation, and likewise some are generalized and some are moderately to very specific when applied to the specific floristic composition of a given stand of vegetation. Comparing the terms and their meaning across the columns gives you a sense of the different classifications' value for different needs. Several of these classifications are hierarchical, meaning that they have their own internal systems of specificity or generality. A complete walk-through of these vegetation types is found in the *Manual of California Vegetation* (Sawyer and Keeler-Wolf, 1995).

In table 8, a simple classification of California plant communities with characteristic plant species of each vegetation type is listed along with their distribution in California.

TABLE 7. Relationships between Several Different Vegetation Types and Their Classification California

Floristic Characterization (Sawyer and Keeler-Wolf 1995)	Munz (1968)	Holland (1986)
A forest dominated (>50% relative cover) by white fir	Yellow pine forest	Desert mountain white fir, Sierran mixed conifer forest, Sierran white fir forest
A scrub dominated (>50% relative cover) by chamise	Chaparral	Chamise chaparral, gabbroic northern mixed chaparral, northern north-slope chaparral, northern maritime chaparral, southern maritime chaparral
A forest or woodland dominated (>50% cover) by California black oak	Northern oak woodland	Black oak forest, black oak woodland
A shrubland dominated (>50% cover) by black sage	Coastal sage scrub	Central Lucian coastal scrub, Diablan coastal scrub
A grassland dominated (>25% relative cover) by purple needlegrass	Valley grassland	Valley needlegrass grassland
A meadow with >50% relative cover of Rocky Mountain sedge	Subalpine forest	Wet montane meadow, freshwater seep

Wildlife Habitat Relationships (Meyer and Laudenslayer 1988)	Manual of California Vegetation (Sawyer and Keeler-Wolf 1995)	CALVEG (Gordon, 2002)
White fir	White fir forest, woodland alliance complex; includes 32 individually defined plant associations	White fir, mixed-coniferous forest
Chamise-redshanks chaparral	Chamise shrubland alliance; includes 12 individually defined plant associations	Chamise
Montane hardwood, montane hardwood-conifer	Black oak forest alliance; includes 16 individually defined plant associations	Black oak
Coastal scrub	Black sage shrubland alliance; includes six individually defined plant associations	Mixed soft scrub chaparral
Perennial grass	Purple needlegrass grassland alliance; includes five individually defined plant associations	Perennial grass/forbs
Wet meadow	Rocky Mountain sedge herbaceous alliance; includes five individually defined plant associations	Wet meadow

COASTAL STRAND (Same in Munz)

Abronia spp.	Sand-verbena	Nyctaginaceae	Widespread
Ambrosia chamissonis	Silver beachweed	Asteraceae	Widespread
Atriplex spp.	Saltbush	Chenopodiaceae	Widespread
Camissonia (Oenothera) cheiranthifolia	Beach evening primrose	Onagraceae	Widespread
Lupinus arboreus and others	Bush lupine	Leguminosae	Widespread

COASTAL PRAIRIE (Same in Munz)

Various genera of grasses		Poaceae	
Heterotheca villosa var. shevockii	Golden aster	Asteraceae	N. Cal. only
Iris douglasiana	Douglas iris	Iridaceae	Widespread
Pteridium aquilinum	Bracken fern	Pteridaceae	Widespread
Sanicula arctopoides	Yellow mats	Umbelliferae	N. Cal. only

COASTAL SALT MARSH (same in Munz)

Distichlis spicata	Salt grass	Poaceae	Widespread
Frankenia salina	Frankenia	Frankeniaceae	Widespread
Salicornia spp.	Glasswort, pickleweed	Chenopodiaceae	Widespread
Suaeda californica	Seep weed	Chenopodiaceae	Widespread

NORTHERN COASTAL SCRUB (Same in Munz)

Anaphalis margaritacea	Pearly everlasting	Asteraceae	Widespread
Artemisia suksdorfii	Suksdorf's sagebrush	Asteraceae	N. Cal. only
Baccharis pilularis var. consanguinea	Coyote brush, chaparral broom	Asteraceae	Widespread
Erigeron glaucus	Seaside daisy	Asteraceae	Widespread
Eriogonum latifolium	Coastal eriogonum	Polygonaceae	Widespread
Eriophyllum staechadifolium	Seaside woolly sunflower	Asteraceae	N. Cal. only

Gaultheria shallon	Salal	Ericaceae	Widespread
Heracleum lanatum	Cow parsnip	Umbelliferae	Mostly N. Cal.
Rubus ursinus	California blackberry	Rosaceae	Mostly N. Cal.

CLOSED-CONE PINE FOREST (Same in Munz)

Cupressus spp.	Cypress	Cupressaceae	Scattered
Pinus contorta	Beach pine	Pinaceae	N. Cal. coast
Pinus muricata	Bishop pine	Pinaceae	Widely scattered on coast
Pinus radiata	Monterey pine	Pinaceae	Scattered, central coast

Associated Species

Arctostaphylos spp.	Manzanitas	Ericaceae	Widespread
Baccharis pilularis var. consanguinea	Coyote brush, chaparral broom	Asteraceae	Mostly N. Cal.
Myrica californica	Wax-myrtle	Myricaceae	Mostly N. Cal.
Pteridium aquilinum	Bracken fern	Pteridaceae	Widespread
Quercus agrifolia	Coast live oak	Fagaceae	Widespread
Rhamnus californica	Coffeeberry	Rhamnaceae	Widespread
Toxicodendron diversiloba	Poison-oak	Anacardiaceae	Widespread
Vaccinium ovatum	California huckleberry	Ericaceae	Mostly N. Cal.

NORTH COASTAL FOREST (Includes North Coastal Coniferous Forest, Redwood Forest, Douglas-fir Forest, and Mixed Evergreen Forest)

Abies grandis	Lowland grand fir	Pinaceae	N. Cal. only
Acer macrophyllum	Bigleaf maple	Aceraceae	Widespread
Cupressus lawsoniana	Lawson cypress, Port Orford–cedar	Cupressaceae	N. Cal. only
Chrysolepis (Castanopsis) chrysophylla	Giant chinquapin	Fagaceae	N. Cal. only
Lithocarpus densiflorus	Tan-oak	Fagaceae	Mostly N. Cal.
Picea sitchensis	Sitka spruce	Pinaceae	N. Cal. only
Pseudotsuga menziesii	Douglas-fir	Pinaceae	N. Cal. only
Sequoia sempervirens	Redwood	Taxodiaceae	N. Cal. only

continued ➤

TABLE 8. *Continued*

Thuja plicata	Canoe- or western red-cedar	Cupressaceae	N. Cal. only
Tsuga heterophylla	Western hemlock	Pinaceae	N. Cal. only

Understory Species

Acer circinatum	Vine maple	Aceraceae	N. Cal. only
Gaultheria shallon	Salal	Ericaceae	N. Cal. only
Oxalis oregana	Redwood sorrel	Oxalidaceae	N. Cal. only
Polystichum munitum	Sword fern	Aspidiaceae	N. Cal. only
Rhododendron macrophyllum	California rose bay	Ericaceae	N. Cal. only
Rubus parviflorus	Thimble berry	Rosaceae	Mostly N. Cal.
Vaccinium ovatum and others	Huckleberry	Ericaceae	Mostly N. Cal.

Drier Margins of the North Coastal Forest (Mixed Evergreen Forest)

Acer macrophyllum	Bigleaf maple	Aceraceae	Widespread
Arbutus menziesii	Madrone	Ericaceae	Mostly N. Cal.
Lithocarpus densiflora	Tan-oak	Fagaceae	Mostly N. Cal.
Quercus chrysolepis	Canyon oak	Fagaceae	Mostly N. Cal.
Quercus garryana	Oregon or Garry oak	Fagaceae	N. Cal. only
Quercus kelloggii	California Black oak	Fagaceae	Widespread
Quercus wislizenii	Interior live oak	Fagaceae	Widespread
Toxicodendron diversiloba	Poison oak	Anacardiaceae	Widespread
Umbellularia californica	California bay	Lauraceae	Widespread

CHAPARRAL (HARD CHAPARRAL) (Same in Munz)

Adenostoma fasciculatum	Chamise, greasewood	Rosaceae	Widespread
Arctostaphylos spp.	Manzanita	Ericaceae	Widespread
Ceanothus spp.	California-lilac	Rhamnaceae	Widespread
Cercocarpus betuloides	Mountain-mahogany	Rosaceae	Widespread
Heteromeles arbutifolia	California-holly, toyon	Rosaceae	Widespread

Malosma laurina	Laurel sumac	Anacardiaceae	S. Cal. only
Prunus ilicifolia	Holly-leaf cherry	Rosaceae	Widespread
Quercus dumosa	Scrub oak	Fagaceae	Widespread
Rhus ovata	Sugar bush	Anacardiaceae	S. Cal. only
Toxicodendron diversiloba	Poison-oak	Anacardiaceae	Widespread
Yucca whipplei	Yucca, Spanish bayonet	Agavaceae	S. Cal. only

VALLEY AND FOOTHILL WOODLAND
(Includes Northern, Southern Oak Woodland, Foothill Woodland)

Aesculus californica	California buckeye	Hippocastan-aceae	Widespread
Juglans californica	S. Cal. walnut	Juglandaceae	S. Cal. only
Pinus sabiniana	Gray pine	Pinaceae	Widespread
Quercus agrifolia	Coast live oak	Fagaceae	Widespread
Quercus douglasii	Blue oak	Fagaceae	N. Cal. only
Quercus engelmannii	Engelmann oak	Fagaceae	S. Cal. only
Quercus garryana	Oregon or Garry oak	Fagaceae	N. Cal. only
Quercus lobata	Valley oak	Fagaceae	Mostly N. Cal.
Quercus wislizenii	Interior live oak	Fagaceae	Widespread

Understory consists of Valley Grassland species and occasional Chaparral species

VALLEY GRASSLAND (Same in Munz)

Native

Aristida (many species)	Three-awn	Poaceae	Widespread
Poa (many species)	Bunch grass	Poaceae	Widespread
Stipa (many species)	Needle grass	Poaceae	Widespread

Introduced

Avena (many species)	Wild oats	Poaceae	Widespread
Bromus (many species)	Brome grass	Poaceae	Widespread
Festuca (many species)	Fescue	Poaceae	Widespread

continued ➤

TABLE 8. *Continued*

RIPARIAN WOODLAND (Not in Munz)

Acer macrophyllum	Bigleaf maple	Aceraceae	Widespread
Acer negundo subsp. *californicum*	California box elder	Aceraceae	Widespread
Alnus rhombifolia	White alder	Betulaceae	Widespread
Platanus racemosa	California sycamore	Platanaceae	Widespread
Populus fremontii	Fremont cottonwood	Salicaceae	Widespread
Populus balsamifera subsp. *trichocarpa*	Black cottonwood	Salicaceae	Widespread
Salix (many species)	Willow	Salicaceae	Widespread
Umbellularia californica	California bay	Lauraceae	Widespread

FRESHWATER MARSH (Same as Munz)

Carex spp.	Sedge	Cyperaceae	Widespread
Scirpus spp.	Bulrush or tule	Cyperaceae	Widespread
Typha spp.	Cattail	Typhaceae	Widespread

MONTANE FOREST (Mostly Yellow Pine Forest in Munz)

Abies concolor	White fir	Pinaceae	Widespread
Calocedrus decurrens	Incense-cedar	Cupressaceae	Widespread
Pinus coulteri	Coulter pine	Pinaceae	S. Cal. and S. Coast Ranges
Pinus lambertiana	Sugar pine	Pinaceae	Widespread
Pinus ponderosa	Ponderosa pine	Pinaceae	Widespread
Pseudotsuga macrocarpa	Bigcone spruce	Pinaceae	S. Cal.
Pseudotsuga menziesii	Douglas-fir	Pinaceae	Central Cal.
Quercus chrysolepis	Canyon oak	Fagaceae	Widespread
Quercus kelloggii	California black oak	Fagaceae	Widespread
Sequoiadendron giganteum	Giant sequoia, Sierra bigtree	Taxodiaceae	Sierra Nevada

Understory Species

Chamaebatia foliolosa	Mountain misery	Rosaceae	Sierra Nevada
Pteridium aquilinum	Bracken fern	Pteridaceae	Widespread
Ribes spp.	Currant, gooseberry	Grossulariaceae	Widespread
All species from Montane Chaparral			

Upper Margin of the Montane Forest

Abies magnifica	Red fir	Pinaceae	Sierra Nevada
Pinus jeffreyi	Jeffrey pine	Pinaceae	Widespread
Pinus contorta subsp. *murrayana*	Lodgepole pine	Pinaceae	Widespread

---

MONTANE CHAPARRAL (Not in Munz)

Arctostaphylos spp.	Manzanita	Ericaceae	Widespread
Ceanothus cordulatus	Snow bush	Rhamnaceae	Widespread
Chrysolepis (Castanopsis) sempervirens	Chinquapin	Fagaceae	Widespread
Quercus chrysolepis	Canyon oak	Fagaceae	Mostly S. Cal.
Quercus vacciniifolia	Huckleberry oak	Fagaceae	Central Sierra Nevada north

---

SUBALPINE FOREST (Includes Red Fir Forest; Lodgepole Forest; Subalpine Forest; Bristlecone Pine Forest)

Abies magnifica	Red fir	Pinaceae	Sierra Nevada
Juniperus occidentalis	Sierra juniper	Cupressaceae	Mostly Sierra Nevada north
Pinus albicaulis	Whitebark pine	Pinaceae	Sierra Nevada north
Pinus longaeva	Bristlecone pine	Pinaceae	High desert ranges
Pinus balfouriana	Foxtail pine	Pinaceae	S. Sierra Nevada and Scott Mountains
Pinus flexilis	Limber pine	Pinaceae	S. Cal. and E. Sierra Nevada
Pinus monticola	Western white pine	Pinaceae	Sierra Nevada north

continued ➤

TABLE 8 *Continued*

Pinus contorta subsp. *murrayana*	Lodgepole pine	Pinaceae	Widespread
Populus tremuloides	Quaking aspen	Salicaceae	Sierra Nevada
Tsuga mertensiana	Mountain hemlock	Pinaceae	Central Sierra Nevada north

Understory

Artemisia spp.	Sagebrush	Asteraceae	Widespread
Ledum glandulosum	Labrador tea	Ericaceae	Sierra Nevada north
Penstemon spp.	Penstemon	Scrophulariaceae	Widespread
Phyllodoce breweri	Red heather	Ericaceae	Mostly Sierra Nevada north
Ribes spp.	Currant	Grossulariaceae	Widespread
Salix spp.	Willow	Salicaceae	Widespread
Vaccinium spp.	Huckleberry	Ericaceae	Sierra Nevada north

Many species from Montane Meadow

MONTANE MEADOW (Not in Munz)

Veratrum californicum	Corn-Lily	Liliaceae	Widespread

Many species of mostly perennial grasses and sedges (especially *Carex* spp.); many species of annual and perennial broad-leaved herbs

---

ALPINE FELL-FIELD (Same in Munz)

Many species of perennial herbs and dwarf woody plants

PINYON-JUNIPER WOODLAND (Includes Northern Juniper Woodland; Pinyon-Juniper Woodland)

Cercocarpus ledifolius	Mountain-mahogany	Rosaceae	Widespread
Juniperus californica	California juniper	Cupressaceae	S. Cal. only
Juniperus occidentalis	Sierra juniper	Cupressaceae	Widespread
Juniperus osteosperma	Utah juniper	Cupressaceae	Nevada border region
Pinus monophylla	Single-leaf pinyon	Pinaceae	Widespread
Purshia spp.	Antelope brush	Rosaceae	Widespread

Quercus turbinella	Desert scrub oak	Fagaceae	S. Mojave and Colo. Deserts

All species of Sagebrush Scrub

SAGEBRUSH SCRUB (Same in Munz)

Artemisia tridentata	Basin sagebrush	Asteraceae	Widespread
Atriplex spp.	Saltbush	Chenopodiaceae	Widespread
Chrysothamnus nauseosus	Rabbitbrush	Asteraceae	Widespread
Coleogyne ramosissima	Blackbush	Rosaceae	Widespread
Purshia spp.	Antelope brush	Rosaceae	Widespread
Tetradymia spp.	Cotton thorn	Asteraceae	Mojave Desert north

COASTAL SAGE SCRUB (SOFT CHAPARRAL) (Same in Munz)

Artemisia californica	Coastal sagebrush	Asteraceae	Widespread
Baccharis pilularis var. *consanguinea*	Coyote brush, chaparral broom	Asteraceae	Widespread
Eriogonum fasciculatum	Wild buckwheat	Polygonaceae	Widespread
Toxicodendron diversiloba	Poison-oak	Anacardiaceae	Widespread
Rhus integrifolia	Lemonadeberry	Anacardiaceae	S. Cal. only
Salvia leucophylla	Purple or white-leaved sage	Lamiaceae	Mostly S. Cal.
Salvia mellifera	Black sage	Lamiaceae	Widespread

SHADSCALE SCRUB (Same in Munz)

Artemisia spinescens	Spiny sagebrush	Asteraceae	Mojave Desert north
Atriplex spp.	Saltbush, shad-scale	Chenopodiaceae	Widespread
Coleogyne ramosissima	Blackbush	Rosaceae	Widespread
Ephedra spp.	Mormon tea	Ephedraceae	Widespread
Krascheninnikovia lanata	Winter fat	Chenopodiaceae	Mojave Desert north
Grayia spinosa	Hop sage	Chenopodiaceae	Mojave Desert north

continued ➤

TABLE 8. *Continued*

Gutierrezia spp.	Matchweed	Asteraceae	Mojave Desert north
Hymenoclea salsola	Burrobrush	Asteraceae	Widespread

ALKALI SINK SCRUB (Same in Munz)

Allenrolfea occidentalis	Iodine bush	Chenopodiaceae	Widespread
Atriplex spp.	Saltbush	Chenopodiaceae	Widespread
Salicornia spp.	Pickleweed	Chenopodiaceae	Widespread
Sarcobatus vermiculatus	Greasewood	Chenopodiaceae	Widespread
Suadea spp.	Seep weed	Chenopodiaceae	Widespread

JOSHUA TREE WOODLAND (Same in Munz)

Atriplex spp.	Saltbush	Chenopodiaceae	Widespread
Ephedra spp.	Mormon tea	Ephedraceae	Widespread
Eriogonum fasciculatum	Wild buckwheat	Polygonaceae	Widespread
Haplopappus spp.	Bristlewood	Asteraceae	Widespread
Juniperus californica	California juniper	Cupressaceae	Widespread
Lycium spp.	Box thorn	Solanaceae	Widespread
Opuntia spp.	Cholla, prickly pear	Cactaceae	Widespread
Salazaria mexicana	Bladder sage	Lamiaceae	Widespread
Tetradymia axillaris	Cotton thorn	Asteraceae	Mojave Desert north
Yucca brevifolia	Joshua tree	Agavaceae	Mojave Desert
Yucca schidigera	Mojave yucca	Agavaceae	Mojave and Colo. Deserts

Most species of Shadscale Scrub

CREOSOTE BUSH SCRUB (Same in Munz)

Encelia farinosa	Brittle bush	Asteraceae	Mostly Colo. Desert
Fouquieria splendens	Ocotillo	Fouquieriaceae	Colo. Desert
Ambrosia dumosa	Burro-weed	Asteraceae	Very widespread
Hymenoclea salsola	Cheese bush	Asteraceae	Widespread in washes

Larrea tridentata	Creosote bush	Zygophyllaceae	Very wide-spread
Opuntia spp.	Cholla, prickly pear	Cactaceae	Widespread on rocky slopes

MONTANE CONIFEROUS FOREST

Pinus ponderosa	Ponderosa pine	Pinaceae	Widespread
Abies concolor	White fir	Pinaceae	Widespread
Pinus coulteri	Coulter pine	Pinaceae	S. Cal.
Calocedrus decurrens	Incense-cedar	Cupressaceae	Widespread
Quercus kelloggi	California Black oak	Fagaceae	Widespread
Pinus contorta subsp. *murrayana*	Lodgepole pine	Pinaceae	Higher ele-vations
Pinus flexilis	Limber pine	Pinaceae	Above 9,500 feet

This chapter presents a synopsis of the composition and distribution of the California vegetation types listed in chapter 5 that are encountered along the coastal and valley areas of northern and central California, the cismontane region found west of the Sierra Nevada crest. Also included is some discussion of outstanding characteristics of the communities or of certain of their component species. As mentioned in the previous chapter, these vegetation types remain a simplified but useful overview of the California landscape. Most of the vegetation types in this part of the state tend to be distributed in a pattern that is related to climatic patterns that are strongly influenced by the position of mountain ranges in a north-south series. The following chapter is concerned with vegetation types found in montane areas and areas east of the Sierra Nevada and in the deserts.

The Cismontane Region (West of the Sierra Nevada Crest)

Coastal Strand (Map 2)

The first terrestrial vegetation type encountered above the high tide line in much of California is the Coastal Strand community. As plants establish, they hold the sand, which keeps it from drifting and results in dune formation (pl. 84). Common plants in the Coastal Strand community are the silver beach-weed *(Ambrosia chamissonis)*, in the sunflower family; various species of the saltbush genus *(Atriplex)*; various lupines such as the beautiful yellow bush lupine *(Lupinus arboreus)*; the colorful sand-verbena *(Abronia* spp.); and beach evening primrose *(Camissonia cheiranthifolia)*. Also found growing in the Coastal Strand are the introduced dunegrass *(Ammophila arenaria)* and species of succulent ice plants *(Carpobrotus edulis, Mesembryanthemum nodiflorum,* and *M. crystallinum,* all Aizoaceae); and the attractive beach morning glory *(Calystegia soldanella)*. All these members are widespread in this com-

munity, and most of them occur only in this distinctive vegetation type. The Coastal Strand vegetation type occurs in loose
sand above the high tide line on Pacific coast beaches along the
entire length of California and extends both south and north

Plate 84. Dunes are stabilized where dune plants become established.

of the state's borders. Some of the species in this community
are very widespread outside California. For example, beach
morning glory is found all along the Pacific coast of North
America and in South America and the Old World as well
(pls. 85–87).

The climate of the area occupied by the Coastal Strand vegetation type in California is variable. Rainfall varies from an
average annual total of about 15 inches to a total in excess of
70 inches. Many parts of the coast have extensive fog during
summer and winter. The growing season along the immediate coast is very long and even in extreme northern California exceeds 350 days. Because of the tempering effect of the
adjacent ocean, diurnal as well as seasonal temperature fluctuations are relatively small. Summers are cool and winters are
relatively warm.

Plate 85. The Coastal Strand plant community is found along sandy beaches and dunes scattered along the entire coast. Between open patches of sand, most plants have a creeping prostrate growth form and often grayish foliage. There is low species diversity in this harsh environment.

Plate 86. Sand-verbena *(Abronia latifolia)* grows a very large and deep root that enables it to survive hot, dry, and windy summer days. This plant was first collected by early Russian explorers.

Despite the relatively benign climatic conditions, the environment of the Coastal Strand vegetation type is a harsh one. This may explain why so few plant species occur in this community. During much of the year it is subjected to strong

Plate 87. Beach evening primrose *(Camissonia cheiranthifolia)* displays the low, sprawling growth form typical of dune plants. Its bright yellow flowers attract insect pollinators.

winds, which carry salts that are deposited on the plants and the soil. Because of these salt-laden winds and occasional high tides during winter storms, the sand occupied by the plants has a high concentration of sea salts. Besides being salty, the sand is often very unstable and blown about by the winds. The level of plant nutrients is generally very low; from a nutritional standpoint these sands are infertile. Furthermore, during summer months the surface of the sand may become extremely hot, to the extent that it is very uncomfortable to the human touch.

Although the plant species that occur in the Coastal Strand are taxonomically unrelated, many of them share similar adaptive characteristics. For example, many of the plants in this community are prostrate and have creeping stems that hug the sand. In some species, these stems may produce roots at the nodes and eventually form a large colony derived from a single individual. Sexual reproduction of some of the perennial species may be relatively rare, perhaps because of the great difficulties that seedlings have in becoming established in the continually shifting and generally inhospitable sands. Also, many Coastal Strand plants have grayish foliage; this is probably an adaptation to the frequent extreme daytime heat to which these plants are subjected and undoubtedly serves to reflect heat from the plant and thus reduce the temperature of internal tissues. Plants in this community are frequently succulent and may have sufficiently high salt concentrations in their tissues that the salt is detectable to human taste. Possibly, this succulence is an adaptation to the occasional dry periods to which strand plants are subjected, and it may also enable these plants to take in water whose salt content would dehydrate most nonsucculent plants of other communities. Needless to say, Coastal Strand plants are notably resistant to salt and to wind.

Coastal Prairie (Map 2)

Immediately inland from the Coastal Strand vegetation type are the grasslands known as Coastal Prairie. This vegetation type occurs sporadically along the northern California coast from the Oregon border to the San Francisco Bay area. At one time, some of the hills behind Oakland and Berkeley were occupied by Coastal Prairie, as well as by patches of Valley Grassland. Some of the "balds" on the northern California coastal hills—which may be several miles from the ocean—represent

Plate 88. Coastal Prairie occurs on the rich, stable soils immediately inland and is species rich compared to Coastal Strand. Vegetation is usually dense, rather low, and dominated by herbaceous species.

Plate 89. A white wallflower *(Erysimum concinnum)* and the yellow coastal form of the California-poppy *(Eschscholzia californica)* add spring color in the Coastal Prairie.

the Coastal Prairie vegetation type. Extensive areas along the coast of northern California have been cleared to encourage the growth of grasses for grazing animals; such areas would seem to belong to the Coastal Prairie vegetation type. Because of their unnatural origin, however, and their component of introduced plant species, these artificial grasslands should be excluded from a definition of the Coastal Prairie vegetation type. Coastal Prairie was originally covered with a number of native perennial bunch grasses mixed with several other herbaceous plants. Shrubs and trees are missing. The soils of Coastal Prairie areas are typical prairie soils similar to those found in the grasslands of the American Midwest, indicating that these coastal areas have been occupied by prairie for hundreds of years or more and are not of recent origin. For this reason, Coastal Prairie can be considered to be a climax vegetation type in California.

Typical plants of the Coastal Prairie are perennial grasses that belong to the genera fescue *(Festuca)*, oat grass *(Danthonia)*, reed grass *(Calamagrostis*, hair grass *Deschampsia)*, and others. Bracken fern *(Pteridium aquilinum)* also is a common inhabitant of this area. Monocots such as blue dicks *(Dichelostemma capitatum)*, Douglas iris *(Iris douglasiana)* in blue and white forms, blue-eyed-grass *(Sisyrinchium bellum)*, and yellow butterfly tulip *(Calochortus luteus)*, all of the family

Plate 90. Blue-eyed-grass *(Sisyrinchium bellum)*, in the iris family, is another common plant in the Coastal Prairie.

Plate 91. In early spring, coastal bluffs are brightened by the light green and yellow of footsteps-of-spring *(Sanicula arctopoides)*.

Brodiaea, add a colorful display of flowers in late spring months. Also present are California buttercup *(Ranunculus californicus)*, two lupines *(Lupinus variicolor* and *L. formosa)*, the peculiar prostrate yellow mats called footsteps-of-spring *(Sanicula arctopoides)*, golden aster *(Heterotheca villosa* var. *shevockii)*, and a few other members of the sunflower family (Asteraceae) (pls. 88–91).

Because Coastal Prairie areas are naturally treeless and because they occur in temperate and relatively well watered areas of California, the majority of the area occupied by the Coastal Prairie vegetation type has been subjected to grazing by sheep and cattle since the settlement of California by agriculturalists. Many of the areas along the coast that are being developed for summer housing tracts also occur in areas occupied by the Coastal Prairie vegetation type. On bluffs overlooking the Pacific, plants such as thrift or sea-pink *(Armeria maritima* subsp. *californica)* have adapted to the harsh conditions of wind and salt spray and are succulent and tough (pl. 92).

Plate 92. Thrift or sea-pink *(Armeria maritima* subsp. *californica)* is common on ocean bluffs and coastal strands in northern California and less common in the south.

Coastal Salt Marsh (Map 2)

Coastal salt marsh is a vegetation type that exists under some of the same climatic conditions as the Coastal Strand community, although there are some striking differences in the ecology of the two communities. As the name implies, the Coastal Salt Marsh community occurs along the Pacific coast of California, although it is a much less frequently encountered community than is the Coastal Strand. The Coastal Salt

Marsh community is found in tidal areas of estuaries, bays, and other areas that are protected from the wave action and strong winds of the open rocky coast. This community is widely scattered; in California it occurs primarily at the edges of Humboldt Bay, Tomales Bay, San Francisco Bay, Elkhorn slough, Morro Bay, the Carpenteria Marsh south of Santa Barbara, the Ballona wetland in Los Angeles, Bolsa Chica near Huntington, and the lagoons in the San Diego area.

Tidal wetlands are periodically inundated with saltwater, and plant distribution is determined, in part, by length of tidal inundation. As a consequence of the water-saturated soils (which are often heavy clays), the roots of salt marsh plants live in a soil with a very low oxygen concentration. Because of the salinity of the salt marsh soils and of the water that reaches the plants growing on these soils, these plants are all halophytes, that is, plants that are adapted to live in saline soils. The halophytes of the Coastal Salt Marsh community are mostly low perennial herbs with fleshy stems and leaves, often very reduced, and specially adapted roots. Salt marsh plants are frequently rhizomatous and, like strand plants, may reproduce vegetatively. Except for the showy yellow flowers of salt marsh gumplant *(Grindelia stricta),* in the sunflower family, the flowers of most salt marsh plant species in California are inconspicuous.

Typical Coastal Salt Marsh species in California include the peculiar glasswort or pickleweed genus *(Salicornia),* and sea blite or seep weed *(Suaeda* spp.), both in the goosefoot family; cord grass *(Spartina foliosa);* salt grass *(Distichlis spicatae);* marsh rosemary *(Limonium californicum);* alkali heath or frankenia *(Frankenia* spp.); jaumea *(Jaumea carnosa):* and arrow grass *(Triglochin* spp.). The number of plant species represented in the Coastal Salt Marsh is small because of the harshness of the environment. Pickleweed is the predominant species in marshes in this Mediterranean climate where no rainfall occurs for several months. It has historically, as its name suggests, been used for making pickles because of its

Plate 93. Coastal Salt Marshes are found in bays and estuaries along the coast from sea level up to 10 feet. These tidal areas are inundated twice daily and drained by meandering channels. Because of the harsh physical conditions, there is low species diversity.

Plate 94. Many plants growing in salt marshes have succulent stems and leaves and a varying tolerance for tidal inundation. The leaves of pickleweed (*Salicornia virginica*), the most common salt marsh plant, are reduced to bracts. Its flowers have no petals, and salt is stored in distal "joints" that turn red and fall off in the fall.

high salt content, particularly by early pioneers who had few other sources of salt. Although few people today use it for making pickles, this practice is still fairly common in northern Europe. Because of the high content of sodium (from salt) in the tissues of the plants, in times past, large quantities were

Plate 95. *Jaumea carnosa,* in the sunflower family, has relatively succulent leaves and is found in the mid to upper zones of a salt marsh.

burned for soda ash, which in turn was used for making glass. Thus, the two common names for *Salicornia,* pickleweed and glasswort, are derived from actual uses of the genus. During May and continuing into summer months, in some places plants of coastal salt marshes become infested with the colorful, bright orange strands of dodder (*Cuscuta salina,* Cuscutaceae), a parasitic relative of the morning glory (pls. 93–97).

Some portions of the Coastal Salt Marsh vegetation type are subjected to daily inundation from tidal action, whereas higher portions of the marsh are only occasionally inundated, although the soil may be saturated with saltwater. Some plant species characteristic of this vegetation type are able to tolerate periods of immersion in saltwater, and others are less tolerant. The result is frequently a zonation pattern of plants in a Coastal Salt Marsh that is related to the tolerance of the plants to inundation. For example, cord grass tolerates inundation, but salt grass is intolerant of frequent inundations and is found only on the upper margins of a marsh. Frankenia and jaumea are found in small patches of the middle and upper marsh. It is not surprising that many genera of plants that occur in Coastal Salt Marsh also reappear in saline areas of the desert. Both salt grass and pickleweed have related species in desert regions that have the same adaptations for managing life in a salty environment.

The area covered by the Coastal Salt Marsh vegetation type

Plate 96. Crystalline iceplant *(Mesembryanthemum crystallinum)* is found growing at the margins of saline wetlands in San Francisco Bay and in southern California.

Plate 97. Salt marsh bird's beak *(Cordylanthus maritimus* subsp. *maritimus)* is an endangered plant found in a few salt marshes in southern California and shown here at the edge of Newport Bay.

is relatively small and, in California, is mostly in regions with high concentrations of human population. In the San Francisco Bay Area, hundreds of acres of salt marsh have been lost, first, by diking for agricultural land use in the late 1800s, and later, in the 1900s, by bay-fill projects for industrial and residential uses. Likewise, in southern California a number of salt marshes have been reduced in size or filled. From a zoological standpoint, this community is valuable because it provides feeding and nesting areas for a large number of resident or migratory water birds, but it also provides the base of a large food web in bays and estuaries for fish and invertebrate organisms. Today, a considerable amount of effort and money are being directed toward the preservation of existing wetlands and learning how to restore diked areas to their former productivity.

Northern Coastal Scrub (Map 3)

Continuing in an eastward direction inland across the coastal portion of northern California, immediately inland from the beaches and dunes and along coastal bluffs, is the Northern Coastal Scrub, which is dominated by a maritime climate but differs conspicuously from Coastal Prairie or Coastal Strand vegetation types in that shrubs are present. This vegetation type occupies a narrow and discontinuous strip of land running from the Oregon border south to Santa Cruz County, reappearing briefly south of Monterey Bay from Pacific Grove to Point Sur. It lies between the Coastal Prairie and the North Coastal Forest or the Closed-Cone Pine Forest discussed below. Other areas of Northern Coastal Scrub are found in drier habitats in the Inner Coast Ranges from Mt. Diablo south. Northern Coastal Scrub is characterized by the presence of low shrubs, generally one to five feet in height, intermixed with grassy meadows. These small meadows contain plant species that are characteristic of the Coastal Prairie. Northern Coastal Scrub is sometimes called Soft Chaparral because the twigs and leaves of shrubs are flexible in contrast to the stiff twigs and leathery leaves of true Chaparral, and it gives a softer appearance across the landscape. Shrubs occurring in the Northern Coastal Scrub include coyote brush *(Baccharis pilularis)* (a prostrate coastal form of this species is becoming increasingly popular as a ground cover plant for planting in dry, sterile, ground), blue blossom *(Ceanothus thyrsiflorus)*, bush monkeyflower *(Mimulus aurantiacus)*, seaside woolly sunflower *(Eriophyllum staechadifolium)*, salal *(Gaultheria shallon)*, coastal eriogonum *(Eriogonum latifolium)*, coffeeberry *(Rhamnus californica)*, and coastal mugwort

Plate 98. Northern Coastal Scrub is dominated by a maritime climate and differs from Coastal Prairie by the presence of low, dense, woody shrubs, particularly coyote brush *(Baccharis pilularis)*. Often this vegetation is shaped by strong winds; in other words, it is wind pruned.

(Artemisia suksdorfii). Blackberry *(Rubus ursinus),* thimbleberry *(R. parviflorus),* and salmonberry *(R. spectabilis)* all thrive in this environment. Herbs include the large-leaved and lush-growing cow parsnip *(Heracleum lanatum),* pearly everlasting *(Anaphalis margaritacea),* Indian paintbrush *(Castilleja* spp.), and seaside daisy *(Erigeron glaucus)* (pls. 98–100).

Closed-Cone Pine Forest (Map 4)

One interesting vegetation type that occurs inland from the vegetation types of the immediate coast is the Closed-Cone Pine Forest. This coniferous vegetation type is sporadically distributed along the coast from extreme northern California southward to Santa Barbara County. In the northern part of its range, the Closed-Cone Pine Forest occurs on the seaward side of the North Coastal forest and often extends well out on the coastal bluffs. The climatic regime of this vegetation type is similar to that of the coastward portions of the North Coastal Forest. Winters and summers are temperate, frosts are rare, and rainfall varies from 20 to 60 inches per year. Ad-

Plate 99. Seaside woolly sunflower *(Eriophyllum staechadifolium)* is common on coastal terraces.

Plate 100. Seaside daisy *(Erigeron glaucus)* is found on coastal bluffs and sandy flats.

ditional precipitation may occur as a result of fog drip, particularly in the northern portion of the area occupied by this vegetation type. Soils of the Closed-Cone Pine Forest generally are somewhat less fertile than those of the North Coastal Forest.

Characteristic coniferous tree species of the Closed-Cone Pine Forest vegetation type are Bishop pine *(Pinus muricata)*, beach pine *(P. contorta)*, Monterey pine *(P. radiata)*, and various cypresses such as pygmy cypress *(Cupressus goveniana* subsp. *pygmaea)*, Gowen cypress *(C. goveniana)*, and Monterey cypress *(C. macrocarpa)*. Bishop pine, beach pine, and pygmy cypress commonly occur in this community north of San Francisco Bay, and Monterey pine, Monterey cypress, and Gowen cypress occur only south of the Bay. The term *closed-cone* comes from the fact that the cones of the pines in this forest do not open at maturity but remain closed for several years after maturation and then gradually open and disperse seeds (pls. 101, 102).

Plate 101. Closed-Cone Pine Forest is sporadically distributed along the coast where dense fogs augment annual rainfalls of 20 to 60 inches. This Bishop pine *(Pinus muricata)* forest grows densely on the Inverness Ridge in Point Reyes National Seashore in Marin County.

Plate 102. The cones of several species of pine and cypress remain closed until a fire or a very hot day causes them to open and release their seed. The cones of the knobcone pine *(Pinus attenuata)* are shown here.

Although generally not a member of the Closed-Cone Pine Forest, another closed-cone pine in California is knobcone pine *(P. attenuata)*, a species that mostly occurs in inland localities and is particularly common on burned-over lands. The cones of knobcone pine open during the heat of a fire; thus, this species has a built-in mechanism that allows it to reseed itself after a fire.

The closed-cone pines have an extensive fossil history that provides an insight into their evolutionary background. The ecological distinctiveness of the coastal species compared with knobcone pine is associated with the fact that the fossil record of knobcone pine is essentially a separate one back into the Pliocene, a geological period that began about 10 million years ago. In other words, the genealogy of knobcone pine indicates that its ancestry has been separate from that of its close relatives for several million years. In contrast, the coastal closed-cone pines were derived from a common ancestor that prevailed in the Pleistocene, a period that began about one million years ago. (The Pleistocene is sometimes called the Ice Age in allusion to the great glaciations that occurred during that time.) All closed-cone pines are connected to a common ancestor *(P. masonii)* that became extinct in the early Pleistocene, although some of its traits persist in its modern descendants. The fossil record also indicates that Monterey pine was once considerably more widespread in California than it is at present. Like some other tree species in California, Monterey pine has had its day, evolutionarily speaking, and is on the road to natural extinction. As a matter of fact, the only closed-cone pine that seems to be holding its own in contemporary California is knobcone pine. It is an interesting and somewhat puzzling contrast that both Monterey pine and Monterey cypress—rare and remnant species that are ecologically unsuccessful in their natural habitat—are widely planted as windbreaks and timber trees in many areas of the world, particularly in New Zealand and Australia, and that in some of these southern regions these trees are invasive weeds that have spread from areas in which they have been planted into adjacent native vegetation types.

A particularly interesting local phase of the Closed-Cone Pine Forest occurs in the Mendocino White Plains area of Mendocino County in northern California. This phase is locally known as the Pygmy Forest and occurs on the highly acid, sterile soils a few miles inland from the immediate coast. The soil acidity and the sterility are coupled with the fact that these soils are underlain with an impervious hardpan and are waterlogged for much of the winter rainy season. This combination of unfavorable ecological characteristics results in the presence of an assemblage of dwarfed trees, or natural bonsai, hence the name Pygmy Forest. Trees of pygmy cypress (*Cupressus goveniana* subsp. *pygmaea)* and Bolander pine *(P. contorta* var. *bolanderi)* that occur on this soil may reach a mature height of only one or two feet in 50 or 60 years. These dwarfed trees occur with a few other plant species, some of which are nearly restricted to the White Plains soils (e.g., the Fort Bragg manzanita *[Arctostaphylos nummularia]*). However, if pygmy cypress or other tree species that occur on these soils break through the hardpan or become established on more normal soils, they grow to the usual treelike proportions that one expects. In this case, therefore, the dwarfing is induced by the unusual soil characteristics and is not a part of the genetic makeup of the plants that occur in the area.

North Coastal Forest (Map 4)

The greatest difference between the Munz and Keck treatment of California vegetation types and that presented here is in the interpretation of the North Coastal Forest. Munz and Keck broke up this vegetation type into several: the North Coastal Coniferous Forest, Redwood Forest, Douglas-Fir Forest, and Mixed Evergreen Forest. Arguments can be offered pro and con regarding the conservative treatment used here, but it is simpler to treat this complex and variable assemblage of woody plants as a single vegetation zone. The North Coastal Forest occurs over much of the North Coast Ranges, in the Siskiyou and Klamath Mountains, and in the Santa Cruz Mountains. It continues northward along the Pacific coast into southern Alaska; patches of this vegetation type occur in the

Plate 103. A North Coastal Forest is dominated by one or more species of coniferous trees and have coastal fog and annual rainfalls from 40 to 60 inches. Here, a redwood forest is shown along the Eel River. The coniferous community increases in importance northward.

vicinity of Mount Shasta as well, although in this last area most of the typical conifers are absent and the plant species are those characteristic of Munz and Keck's Mixed Evergreen Forest.

Over most of its area of distribution, the North Coastal Forest is dominated by one or more species of coniferous trees. These include majestic species such as coast redwood *(Sequoia sempervirens)*, Douglas-fir *(Pseudotsuga menziesii* var. *menziesii)*, western hemlock *(Tsuga heterophylla)*, the lowland grand fir *(Abies grandis)*, Sitka spruce *(Picea sitchensis)*, canoe-cedar or western red-cedar *(Thuja plicata)*, and Port Orford–cedar *(Cupressus lawsoniana)*. Also present are the giant chinquapin *(Chrysolepis chrysophylla)*, tan-oak *(Lithocarpus densiflorus)*, and bigleaf maple *(Acer macrophyllum)*, which are hardwood trees associated with the conifers. Understory species consist of small trees or shrubs such as vine maple *(Acer circinatum)*, evergreen or California huckleberry *(Vaccinium ovatum)*, salal *(Gaultheria shallon)*, California rose bay *(Rhododendron macrophyllum)*, thimbleberry *(Rubus parviflorus)*, sword fern *(Polystichum munitum)*, and redwood sorrel *(Oxalis oregana)* (pls. 103–105).

Plate 104. Rose bay *(Rhododendron macrophyllum)* grows well in the understory of a redwood forest.

Plate 105. Tan-oak *(Lithocarpus densiflorus)* often grows with redwoods where conditions are drier and are also an important component of a Mixed Evergreen Forest.

Climatically, the area occupied by the North Coastal Forest is variable. Average rainfall varies from over 100 inches in redwood areas to as little as 25 inches in inland areas occupied by forests of Douglas-fir or the phase of the North Coastal Forest that Munz and Keck designated as the Mixed Evergreen Forest. Where this vegetation type occurs on the immediate coast, it is in a cool area dominated by coastal fog during much of the summer; inland, summer temperatures become increasingly higher and the winter temperatures increasingly lower. These gradients in moisture and rainfall are reflected in differences in the species composition of the North Coastal Forest throughout its area. In the wetter portions of its range, this forest is dominated by the coast redwood, Sitka spruce, western hemlock, canoe-cedar, or Port Orford–cedar. In somewhat drier areas, Douglas-fir is the dominant tree species. In even drier, warmer areas—usually on the inland slopes of the North Coast Range—conifers give way to various broad-leaved trees such as Kellogg oak *(Quercus kelloggii),* canyon oak *(Q. chrysolepis),* tan-oak, madrone *(Arbutus menziesii),* California bay *(Umbellularia californica),* California hazelnut *(Corylus cornuta* var. *californica),* mountain dogwood *(Cornus nutttallii),* and various species of the shrubby California-lilac (such as *Ceanothus parryi* and *C. thyrsiflorus).* As the average rainfall decreases even more, the North Coastal Forest may be replaced by Valley and Foothill Woodland, Valley Grassland, or in some areas, Chaparral.

Because of its floristic complexity, it is difficult to make many meaningful generalizations about the North Coastal Forest; however, a few species deserve special comment. Perhaps the best-known phase of the North Coastal Forest is that segment of it dominated by coast redwood. This tree occurs in the coastal fog belt of northern California and extends into southern Oregon. Rather few other plant species grow with it. The understory vegetation is typically sparse and consists of species such as sword fern, redwood sorrel, inside-out flower *(Vancouveria parviflora),* and the slightly woody, trailing saxifrage modesty *(Whipplea modesta).* Characteristic shrubs include California or evergreen huckleberry, California rose bay, salal, and wax-myrtle *(Myrica californica).* Like various species of closed-cone pines, coast redwood had a much wider distribution across North America in the geological past than it does under the current drier climatic conditions and should be considered a species that is on its way out, in an evolutionary sense.

Ecological Characteristics of Coast Redwood

A few other tree species occur with coast redwood, although perhaps with only a modest degree of success. Obviously, areas in California with a "redwood climate" generally support a coast redwood forest. But what is it about coast redwood that allows it to be so successful in these areas, almost to the exclusion of other species of herbs, shrubs, or trees? Coast redwood casts considerable shade, and its roots pervade the ground under the trees. In addition, the area under the trees is covered with a layer of needles, branches, and other redwood debris that may be several inches deep. This combination of shade, root competition, and a deep organic layer on the soil surface probably is effective in reducing the number of species of plants that can thrive under coast redwood trees.

Study of the soils and past history of coast redwood forests indicates that these forests have been subjected to periodic burning and also to periods of heavy silting as a result of floods (such as the periodic floods that have devastated the redwood region in recent years). These two ecological factors are probably very important in eliminating the potential tree competitors of coast redwood. Coast redwood is fairly tolerant of fires, and even young plants can produce new shoots from the roots or lower trunks if the upper portions of the tree are completely destroyed. Some of the potential tree competitors of coast redwood are not fire tolerant, however, and are completely destroyed by these periodic fires. Furthermore, coast redwood can tolerate silting by floods because the species can produce new surface-feeding roots either by developing new roots from the old ones after they have been buried under silt, or by the production of completely new root systems from the trunks of the tree just below the surface of the silt deposit. In contrast, some of the potential competitors of coast redwood are intolerant of silting and die very soon after their roots have been covered by the layer of silt deposited during floods.

The potential tree competitors of coast redwood over much of its area of distribution are tan-oak, Douglas-fir, grand fir, and California bay. None of these species is very tolerant of either silting or fire. Even if individuals of these species become established in an undisturbed coast redwood forest, they are at a competitive disadvantage compared with coast redwood. For example, California bay is a relatively slow grower and rather intolerant of shade. Consequently, one rarely encounters a full-grown or fully vigorous California bay tree in a well-established coast redwood forest. Douglas-fir can compete successfully with coast redwood if both species start out simultaneously in an area as seedlings, but Douglas-fir will eventually disappear from the area because of its shorter life span and because its seedlings cannot become established in the dense shade of coast redwood. Similar explanations can be offered for other tree species that occur in the redwood region but that generally do not occur in a vigorous state in association with coast redwood. Because of the intolerance of coast redwood to prolonged drought, shallow soils, and hot climates, this species is replaced on the eastward side of its range (in many areas) by Douglas-fir, a species that tolerates these conditions rather well. Thus, the mosaic effect of local tree dominants in the North Coastal Forest can be explained by the individual ecological characteristics of the local dominants, as well as those of their potential competitors.

Coastal Sage Scrub (Map 3)

In some respects, a southern counterpart of the Northern Coastal Scrub is the Coastal Sage Scrub, also called Soft Chaparral. It is called a counterpart because the Coastal Sage Scrub occupies a narrow strip along the coast stretching along the coastward side of the South Coast Ranges (and some of the Peninsular Ranges) into Baja California, in much the same relative position occupied by Northern Coastal Scrub in the northern portion of the state. But although the general aspect of the two communities is similar, little floristic similarity exists between the Northern Coastal Scrub and the Coastal Sage Scrub. Coastal Sage Scrub occurs on rather dry, often steep, gravelly or rocky slopes below 3,000 feet. Climatically, the area occupied by this vegetation type is rather mild and has an average of 20 inches of rainfall per year or less. The "scrub" refers to the fact that the major plant species found in the community are shrubby species one to six feet tall, although a few of the component species are considerably larger than this and might be considered small trees.

The name of this vegetation type comes from the presence of *Salvia* species such as black sage *(S. mellifera)* and purple or white-leaved sage *(S. leucophylla)*. Other shrubs present are the coastal sagebrush *(Artemisia californica)*, wild buckwheat *(Eriogonum fasciculatum)*, and coyote brush *(Baccharis pilu-*

Plate 106. Coastal Sage Scrub is the southern counterpart to the Northern Coastal Scrub. This view shows mixed stands of wild buckwheat *(Eriogonum fasciculatum)*, coastal sagebrush *(Artemisia californica)*, and giant coreopsis *(Coreopsis giganteum)*, in the sunflower family, found occasionally along coastal sea bluffs in southern California.

Plate 107. Along the coast in southern California and in Baja California, a kind of maritime coastal scrub occurs in which cactus *(Opuntia* spp.) and California buckwheat *(Eriogonum fasciculatum)* are common elements along with coyote brush *(Baccharis pilularis)*.

Plate 108. Near the coast, the handsome shrub lemonadeberry *(Rhus integrifolia,* shown here*)* grows with sagebrush (*Artemisia* spp.) and buckwheat (*Eriogonum* spp.).

Plate 109. Zonation of vegetation in the Transverse Ranges.

laris, also found in Northern Coastal Scrub). Larger species are the handsome lemonadeberry *(Rhus integrifolia)* and its toxic relative western poison-oak *(Toxicodendron diversilobum)* (pls. 106–109).

Chaparral (Map 3)

Chaparral is one of the most characteristic vegetation types of California and occurs only in the California Floristic Province. Chaparral is a broad-leaved sclerophyll type of vegetation. *Sclerophyll* means "hard-leaved," in reference to the hard, stiff, thick, heavily cutinized, and generally evergreen nature of the leaves of chaparral shrubs. This type of leaf is characteristic of many xerophytic shrubs. The shrubs that dominate chaparral are generally rather short, the average being between three and six feet, although occasional individuals may reach up to 10 feet. Chaparral vegetation is dense, often impenetrable, and notably deficient in trees and herbs. Indeed, the ground underneath or among chaparral shrubs is often completely devoid of herbaceous plant species. This may be due in part to shading or to competition from roots of

Plate 110. *Chaparral* means a place of scrub oak in Spanish. Shrubs characteristically are stiff and densely branched with small, tough, waxy leaves and extensive root systems. Two-thirds of California watersheds are covered with chaparral-type vegetation, which enhances water storage and collection.

chaparral shrubs for water, although much of this phenomenon is probably also due to allelopathy, which some shrubs (e.g., chamise *[Adenostoma fasciculatum]*) in the Chaparral are known to exhibit. Chaparral species living in hot, summer-dry habitat have a compact, tight-branching form that reduces moisture loss; small, waxy leaves that grow perpendicularly to the sun; and an extensive dual root system: a deep tap-root and extensive shallow roots to quickly take advantage of moisture falling on the soil surface.

The word *chaparral* is of Spanish origin. In Spain, *chaparro* refers to a "scrub oak." The suffix *-al* means "a place of." Thus, *chaparral* is "a place of scrub oak." In California, this term came to be applied to a specific vegetation type consisting of a dense growth of evergreen, hard-leaved shrubs, although taxonomically these shrubs are mostly not oaks. Characteristic species of Chaparral are chamise or greasewood *(Adenostoma fasciculatum)*, California-holly or toyon *(Heteromeles arbutifolia)*, holly-leaf cherry *(Prunus ilicifolia)*, birch-leaf mountain-mahogany *(Cercocarpus betuloides* var. *betuloides)*, all in the rose family, and various species of manzanita (*Arctostaphylos* spp.) and California-lilac (*Ceanothus* spp.). Also present are scrub oak *(Q. berberidifolia* and *Q. dumosa)* and western poison-oak. In southern California, additional species in the Chaparral are Spanish bayonet *(Yucca whipplei)* and laurel sumac *(Malosma laurina)* and sugar bush *(R. ovata)*, both in the sumac family (pls. 110, 111).

Plate 111. Eastwood manzanita *(Arctostaphylos glandulosa)*, shown here, is one of many species of manzanita common to the chaparral community. Note the small upright angle of the leaves that reduces their exposure to the sun.

The foregoing shrub species are characteristic; however, numerous other plant species also occur in Chaparral. A tally of plants that commonly occur in the Chaparral community in California reveals that nearly 900 species of vascular plants occur in this vegetation type. About 240 of these are woody plants, most of which are shrubs; well over 300 are annual or biennial herbs; an equal number of perennial herb species is present. The largest plant families present in Chaparral are the sunflowers (Asteraceae), with over 90 species; figworts (Scrophulariaceae), with nearly 70 species; and grasses (Poaceae), legumes (Fabaceae), waterleafs (Hydrophyllaceae), mints (Lamiaceae), heathers (Ericaceae), and lilies (Liliaceae), with between 30 and 40 species of each. Thus, the list of characteristic species in any vegetation type is a gross oversimplification of what one can expect to find there. The species that have been chosen as typical, however, generally are widely distributed, common, and conspicuous in these vegetation types, and because of these traits they are listed in preference to less conspicuous species, less widely distributed ones, or ones with less of an ecological fidelity.

Chaparral occurs in areas with wet, mild winters and long, dry, hot summers, in other words, a Mediterranean climate. Average annual rainfall ranges from about 15 inches to 25 inches. However, summer rainfall accounts for less than 20 percent of the annual total. Soils occupied by Chaparral are often gravelly or sandy, are shallow, and have a low water-holding capacity. The distribution of Chaparral in California is a "spotty" one that shows no clear geographic coherence; however it dominates much of the landscape of the Sierra foothills, coast ranges, and southern mountains. A probable explanation for this is that Chaparral often occurs in an area having a climate that would lead one to expect a woodland community, but because of the local barren, rocky, nutrient-poor soil conditions, forest communities are absent and are replaced by a shrub community.

The flowering and growth behavior of chaparral shrubs

merits some comment. Some shrubs, such as some manzanitas, typically flower in midwinter (sometimes in December) or very early spring and produce vegetative growth after flowering. At the termination of the vegetative growth, flower buds are produced, which remain dormant throughout the succeeding summer and fall drought, although they burst into flower very quickly in winter. In contrast, some other species (such as chamise) produce vegetative growth in late winter or early spring and then flower in June. The flower buds of these species are produced at the termination of growth, as they are in winter-flowering species, except that there is no bud dormancy; flowering occurs immediately after development of flower buds. One result of this phenomenon is that most chaparral shrubs have a similar growing period, but flowering in the community may extend over a period of six months or longer, because various species have different flowering periods. The majority of shrubby species flower in April, however, when soil moisture conditions are optimal and the air and soil temperatures also are warm. Summer and fall are resting seasons.

Chaparral is a vegetation type in which the dominant shrub species are evergreen. It is to their advantage to retain their leaves and not expend the energy to produce a whole new set of leaves all at once as do deciduous trees. Most chaparral species exhibit a leaf drop of old leaves in early summer when temperatures increase and available water decreases. After growth and leaf drop occur, the shrubs become dormant until winter rains arrive. In this respect, at least, chaparral shrubs show an interesting adaptation to the climatic regime under which they exist, an adaptation that enables them to take advantage of the limited period of rainfall.

Fire and Chaparral

Chaparral is subject to frequent burning over much of its area of distribution, and indeed, in much of its range it is a vegetation that is maintained because of periodic fires. Many chap-

Plate 112. Following a fire, chamise (*Adenostoma fasciculatum*) crown-sprouts vigorously with a different leaf form than found in a mature plant.

arral species show an interesting ecological adaptation to repeated burning. This adaptation is known as crown-sprouting, which refers to the fact that although the above-ground portions of a shrub may be destroyed by a hot brush fire, the individual produces numerous new shoots that develop from a large burl that terminates the root system at or below the soil surface. As a result of this trait, crown-sprouting shrubs are able to reestablish themselves immediately after a fire and do not go through a successional reestablishment procedure via seedlings. However, some chaparral shrubs are not crown-sprouters, and these species are killed by hot fires and must produce seedlings in order to become reestablished. The advantage of crown-sprouting is that it eliminates the uncertainties of seedling establishment, which in arid climates may be considerable (pl. 112).

Chaparral is prone to burning because the shrubs are dense, close together, and have rather dry evergreen leaves. Once a fire gets started in chaparral, it may spread rapidly and extensively. The heat is often intense. Temperatures of 1,200 degrees F have been recorded at the surface of the soil in burning chaparral; one-and-a-half inches below the soil surface the temperature may reach well over 300 degrees F. The biotic effects of chaparral fires include heating of the soil and that the fires remove the vegetation and thus allow more light to reach the soil surface. The improved light conditions, plus the absence of root competition and the vaporization of allelopathic compounds, allow the establishment of a lush herbaceous flora the first season after chaparral fires. Although herbaceous annual plants are notably uncommon under or near chaparral shrubs, their immediate and abundant appearance after a fire indicates that their seeds are present in the ground.

Several plant species in California are only found a year or two after fires have swept through an area. These include several members of the Hydrophyllaceae—whispering bells *(Emmenanthe penduliflora* var. *penduliflora)*, Parry phacelia *(Phacelia parryi)*, large-flowered phacelia *(P. grandiflora)*, California bells *(P. minor)*, and some of the native snapdragons including *Antirrhinum cornutum, A. multiflorum,* and *A. kelloggii,* all annuals. Other species such as the fire poppy *(Papaver californicum)*, *Phacelia brachyloba,* and golden corydalis *(Corydalis aurea)* are common on burned areas, although they may also appear in areas that have been ecologically disturbed in other ways.

The fire annuals listed above persist for many years as seed in Chaparral; indeed, the viability of their seed may be 100 years or more. In areas that have not been burned for 60 years, study of the soil has revealed the presence of viable seeds of these plant species, most of which were produced by the previous generation of plants that grew on the site when it last burned. Seeds of fire annuals are obviously tolerant of the very high soil temperatures that result from chaparral fires. Also, many of these species require a high-temperature shock in order to germinate and thus have a built-in mechanism that informs the seeds that a fire has occurred. Germination and growth in some species have been shown to be triggered by the chemicals in the smoke and ash. In the fall after the fire, germination of seeds occurs after the first heavy rains; in the subsequent spring, the former Chaparral site is covered with thousands fire annual plants, the offspring of parents that occupied the site up to a century before. They are accompanied by various other annual plant species that are not necessarily typical of burned areas. Some herbaceous perennials also appear in profusion on burned lands. However, all these plants are also accompanied by seedlings of chaparral species and by the rapidly growing shoots of the crown-sprouting shrubs. As a result, within a few years chaparral shrubs have reoccupied the site and the annuals disappear—until another fire occurs (pl. 113).

Most chaparral areas in Chaparral that have been studied show a recent history of fire, and fire is clearly an important natural disturbance element and evolutionary force in all

Plate 113. Annual spring wildflowers bloom profusely in the first years following a chaparral fire.

forms of chaparral. However, some stands of chaparral may go for over 100 years and still remain dominated by the same species. Transitory forms of chaparral, succeeding to woodlands or forests are relatively uncommon in much of California because fire is frequent enough to maintain the shrubby chaparral species. Certain species of chaparral plants clearly have shorter life spans than others. These are frequently the "obligate seeders," which do not resprout following fire and must regenerate directly from seed banks stored in the soil. Many species of nonresprouting *Ceanothus,* for example, persist for relatively short periods without fire (less than 60 years). On the other hand, many species of resprouting shrub oaks *(Q. berberidifolia, Q. dumosa, Q. pacifica,* and *Q. corneliusmulleri),* manzanitas, and other species such as flowering ash *(Fraxinus dipetala),* holly-leafed cherry *(Prunus ilicifolia),* birch-leaved mountain-mahogany, and California-holly or toyon *(Heteromeles arbutifolia)* may simply grow progressively larger over time. These potentially old-aged shrubs tend to occur on more sheltered, often northerly facing slopes and may grow into a form of "woodland" with the long absence of fire. These "old growth" stands of chaparral are, like the old growth forests, becoming progressively less common, a result of higher fire frequencies due to human-initiated fires.

Valley and Foothill Woodland (Map 4)

Large areas of the valleys and eastern slopes of the North and South Coast Ranges, the valleys of interior southern California, and the western foothills of the Sierra Nevada are occupied by the Valley and Foothill Woodland vegetation type. It occurs at elevations ranging from 300 or more feet above sea level to as high as 5,000 feet in southern California. It is characterized by scattered trees with an undergrowth that may consist almost exclusively of herbaceous plants, especially grasses, and scattered low shrubs; in some areas (the phase characterized by Munz and Keck as Foothill Woodland) the trees may be rather dense, with scattered shrubs underneath

Plate 114. Scattered trees, largely oaks, found on slopes of the inner Coast Ranges and the foothills of the Sierra Nevada, characterize Valley and Foothill Woodland vegetation. Widely spaced blue oaks *(Quercus douglasii),* with grasses growing in the understory, predominate in this view.

them. Variations in appearance of this vegetation type depend to some extent upon its location as well as upon its species composition. Once away from a maritime influence, summers are hotter, longer, and drier, and winters are colder with less rainfall. Here, hilltops tend to be grassy, and Chaparral often covers south-facing slopes.

In some areas, the Valley and Foothill Woodland is dominated chiefly by oaks, such as Garry oak *(Q. garryana);* valley oak *(Q. lobata),* which grows best in deep valley soils; blue oak *(Q. douglasii),* which forms extensive, well-spaced stands on the western foothill slopes of the Sierra Nevada, Engelmann oak *(Q. engelmannii),* and live oaks such as coast live oak *(Q. agrifolia)* and interior live oak *(Q. wislizenii).* Other trees present may be foothill or gray pine *(Pinus sabiniana),* with its peculiarly forked trunks and massive cones, the attractive California buckeye *(Aesculus californica),* and the southern California walnut *(Juglans californica).* Understory plants are species that occur also in Valley Grassland or in Chaparral (pls. 114–116).

Plate 115. Valley oaks *(Quercus lobata)* grow to great sizes in the deeper soils of the valley. Sadly, they are becoming rare in California from habitat loss, heavy browsing of seedlings, and alterations in the understory.

Plate 116. This bright red catchfly *(Silene californica)* occasionally brightens the understory of Valley and Foothill Woodlands.

Valley Grassland (Map 2)

In many respects the Valley and Foothill Woodland may be considered as a vegetation type that is transitional between the true forest communities (such as North Coastal Forest or Montane Forest) of upland areas or coastal moist areas and the treeless grassland communities of the valleys represented in California by the Valley Grassland. The Valley Grassland vegetation type occupies (or occupied) most of the floor of the Central Valley. It has been greatly reduced in size in the past two centuries, because it occupied lands that have been trans-

Plate 117. Valley Grasslands were once the site of great wildflower displays in spring that stretched for miles, similar to this display of California-poppy *(Eschscholzia californica)*. Only remnants of these grasslands remain today.

formed to agricultural use. As a result, Valley Grassland occupies only a small remnant of its former area.

Originally, Valley Grassland was made up of various perennial bunch grasses such as needle grass (*Stipa* spp.), bunch or blue grass (*Poa* spp.), and three-awn (*Aristida* spp.). These grasses have completely disappeared in large areas of the Central Valley where the native grass cover has been removed and the land has been planted with cultivated crops, or where destructive sheep or cattle are pastured. Much of the Central Valley is still grassland, but even in grazed areas the cattle or sheep have exterminated the native perennial grasses. These have been replaced by introduced annual grasses such as brome grass (*Bromus* spp.), wild oats (*Avena* spp.), and fescue (*Festuca* spp.). The golden hills that characterize much of California are golden in the summertime because of the dry stems and leaves of these introduced annual grasses; it is probable that when these areas were occupied by the native perennial grasses, they were green or gray green during most of the year.

Valley Grassland occurs most extensively in the Central

Plate 118. Great displays of wildflowers occur in Bear Valley, Colusa County, every spring that are a reminder of the once extensive grasslands that stretched across the Great Valley, where wildflowers were so thick it was said an ant could walk from flower to flower for miles never touching the ground.

Valley but also is present in some of the low valleys or gentle slopes of the Coast Ranges and in some areas of the Transverse and Peninsular Ranges. It also occurs along the coast from San Luis Obispo County southward to the Mexican border. Rainfall in the Valley Grassland is variable but is generally less than 20 inches per year. This low amount of rainfall probably is responsible for the absence of trees in the Valley Grassland. Summer temperatures may be very high, and heavy frosts are common in some areas in the winter.

In spring, portions of the Valley Grassland are covered by a rich array of spectacularly colorful spring annuals. Areas that are well known to professional and amateur botanists include the low hills and valley bottoms in the Bakersfield area and the Tehachapi foothills, the Solano delta area, the Red Bluff region, and some of the interior valleys of the Coast Ranges, such as Bear Valley in Colusa County. In years with abundant

Plate 119. Vernal pools occur in many places in the valley where underlying clay hardpans allow winter rains to pond; as the water evaporates, successive species of spring wildflowers create rings of bright color. Because of their isolation in these pools, many rare and endangered species are associated with vernal pools, such as this species of goldfield *(Lasthenia fremontii).*

rainfall, hundreds or thousands of acres of Valley Grassland are occupied by masses of these showy annuals (pl. 117, 118).

Of particular interest in the Valley Grassland is the type of habitat known as a vernal pool, sometimes locally called hog wallows. These pools occupy depressions in the grassland area that fill with water during winter. As the pools begin to dry up in spring, various annual plant species begin to flower. Some pools are small and others cover vast areas of the valley floor. The result is local patches of color that may persist for relatively long periods until the pools dry up. A number of plants are restricted to these vernal pools of the Valley Grassland, including several species of meadowfoam (*Limnanthes* spp.), downingia (*Downingia* spp.), goldfields (*Lasthenia* spp.), and other colorful genera, and are among the most characteristic endemic species of the California Floristic Province. Over 200 taxa of plants are known to be largely associated with vernal pools in California (pls. 119, 120).

Plate 120. Many colorful vernal pools are small; however, some are large enough to cover many acres.

In Miocene and Pliocene times the area now occupied by the Central Valley was a large inland sea that persisted into recent times in the form of extensive lakes and marshlands that occupied the Central Valley well into this century. One consequence of this relatively recent availability of the valley floor for occupation by plants is that many of the plant species that are restricted to the Central Valley are of recent evolutionary origin: the evolution of these species was associated with the appearance of a new and ecologically distinctive land area for occupation by land plants. The surrounding upland areas have been occupied by plants for a much longer period of time than the Central Valley and support evolutionarily older plant species and vegetation types.

Riparian Woodland

Because of the greater availability of water from streams and rivers, trees along a riparian corridor stand out against a hillside of trees growing in a more mesic soil. They are usually de-

Plate 121. Riparian Woodland occurs along streams and rivers, often quite distinguishable from adjacent evergreen vegetation by the different form and color of the deciduous trees. Here, willows and cottonwood trees follow a stream course in the desert.

ciduous, lush in summer, bare in winter. Trees respond to the year-round availability of water by becoming tall and widely branched, with an abundance of leaves in summer months. Riparian woodlands typically have cascades of wild grape (*Vitis californica*) and clematis (*Clematis* spp.) hanging from long branches. The understory can become thick and impenetrable with fallen limbs, berry vines (some with massive thorns), wild rose (*Rosa* spp.), and western poison-oak. Air temperature in a riparian grove is noticeably cooler than in adjacent, more arid habitat. Sandbars often detach from the main stream of a river and are bare or covered with flood-resistant species such as willow (*Salix* spp.) or mule fat (*Baccharis salicifolia*). Riparian growth can be lush and abundant where water is abundant and less so where streams are intermittent.

Various portions of California stream- and riverbanks are occupied by trees such as bigleaf maple, black cottonwood (*Populus balsamifera* subsp. *trichocarpa*), and white alder (*Alnus rhombifolia*). At lower elevations and on the valley

Plate 122. A band of cottonwood or poplar (*Populus* spp.), leafing out in spring, forms a narrow band along a river in the southern Sierra Nevada. Where a stream disappears, Valley and Foothill Woodland community species replace the more water-dependent riparian species.

floors, watercourses are lined with California sycamore *(Platanus racemosa)*, California box elder *(Acer negundo* var. *californicum)*, and Fremont cottonwood *(Populus fremontii* subsp. *fremontii)*, along with a number of species of willows. Once out of the mountains, rivers slow down and become meandering, sluggish, and muddy as they cross the valley floor to the sea. Where river valleys are broad, the extent of riparian influence is often correspondingly broad. Majestic valley oak or tall cottonwood grow out on the floodplain by sending their roots down into the high water table. At higher elevations, where watercourses are narrow and stream banks are relatively steep, riparian vegetation may form a very narrow strip of forest that is only a few yard wide. Riparian habitat is especially important to nesting and migrating birds, insects, and amphibians. The distribution of this vegetation type has not been included on the map of woodlands, but it can be plotted easily on a map that shows the occurrence of year-round rivers and streams in the state (pls. 121–123).

Plate 123. Quaking aspen *(Populus tremuloides)* are found along streams and moist slopes from 6,000 to 10,000 feet, where their leaves turn a golden color in the fall.

Freshwater Marsh (Map 2)

Areas of the state with fairly large expanses of standing or very sluggishly moving shallow water generally have the Freshwater Marsh vegetation type. Floristically, this vegetation type is a relatively simple one whose main components are various species of cattails (*Typha* spp.), bulrush or tule (*Scirpus* spp.), and sedges (*Carex* spp.). Freshwater Marsh occurs in the Central Valley along river courses, creeks, and sloughs, or in the vicinity of lakes such as Tulare Lake; extensive marshes also occur in the Sacramento–San Joaquin delta area. Marshlands are present in some inland areas such as Sierra Valley north of Lake Tahoe and in the Modoc Plateau area east of the Sierra-Cascade axis (pls. 124, 125).

The characteristic plant species of the Freshwater Marsh are mostly monocots, one of two divisions of flowering plants, with a superficial grasslike appearance. Nearly all of the

Plate 124. Freshwater marshes occur where fairly large expanses of standing or very sluggish water occur. Cattails (*Typha* spp.), shown here, bulrushes (*Scirpus* spp.), or sedges (*Carex* spp.) usually dominate and can spread rapidly via vegetative reproduction.

Plate 125. Where water is a little deeper, waterlilies *(Nuphar lutea* subsp. *polysepala)* with bright yellow flowers can cover large stretches of open water. Species diversity is quite limited in freshwater marshes.

species are perennials that have excellent means of vegetative propagation. One immigrant cattail in a marshy area can occupy many square yards of marsh in a rather short period of time because of rapid vegetative increase. In many areas of the state, open waterways are becoming clogged by masses of a weedy species from the tropics, water hyacinth *(Eichhornia crassipes)* (pl. 126).

Plate 126. Water hyacinth *(Eichhornia crassipes)* is an invasive non-native plant that grows so successfully it clogs freshwater lakes, streams, and rivers in California.

Accounts of early nineteenth century explorers in the Central Valley indicate the great difficulty that these people had in getting their horses across the valley because of the marshlands. Thomas Coulter, an Irish physician and botanist who visited California in the 1830s, mentioned that the accounts of the large size of the lakes in the Central Valley were exaggerated; neither of the lakes, he stated, was over 100 miles long! However, the Freshwater Marsh vegetation type has become considerably more restricted in its distribution than it was in former times. Much of the decrease in marshlands in the Central Valley has been in response to the increasing aridity of the California climate, but the natural process has been overshadowed by the draining of marshes in order to increase the expanse of land available for agriculture, by withdrawing ground water for irrigation purposes, and by the diversion or retention of water by dams in the Sierra and the Coast Ranges. Until the 1900s, Tulare Lake was a large, shallow lake in the San Joaquin Valley.

CHAPTER 7

VEGETATION TYPES IN MONTANE AND TRANSMONTANE CALIFORNIA

Previous chapters were concerned with the major vegetation types that were encountered along coastal and central valley areas in northern and central California, where most of the vegetation types tend to be distributed in a pattern related to north-south mountain ranges. We now turn to vegetation types restricted to the montane areas of California, to the areas east of the Sierra Nevada crest (transmontane), and to southern California's desert areas. In southern California, the topography forms more of a mosaic pattern of numerous mountain ranges and valleys. A large proportion of the plant species in the montane forests of the mountains of southern California have a strong affinity to those found in the pine belt of the Sierra Nevada, the result of a cooler climate in southern California in the past. There is also a marked similarity of distribution patterns between the Mojave Desert and the Great Basin at lower elevations. The lower Sonoran Desert is hotter and has quite a different assemblage of species compared to the Mojave. These patterns of plant distribution have evolved over time from past geologic and climatic changes and can be further studied in Axelrod's publications listed in the references.

Montane Region (High Mountain Areas)

Montane Forest (Map 4)

After leaving the Valley and Foothill Woodland, discussed in the previous chapter, and encountering a further increase in elevation, coniferous trees begin to appear in abundance. At this point we have entered the Montane Forest vegetation type. In the Sierra Nevada, the Montane Forest begins at approximately 2,000 feet in elevation (depending on latitude and local ecological conditions). It may extend up to 8,000 feet in the southern California mountains. Coniferous Montane Forest also occurs in the North Coast Ranges and the Klamath-Siskiyou region and extends into northeastern California. Perhaps the most common and conspicuous conifer in the

Montane Forest is ponderosa pine *(Pinus ponderosa)*. Also present are incense-cedar *(Calocedrus decurrens)*, white fir *(Abies concolor)*, Douglas-fir *(Pseudotsuga menziesii* var. *menziesii)*, sugar pine *(P. lambertiana)*, and in some areas Coulter pine *(P. coulteri)*. In some portions of the Sierra Nevada, the Montane Forest is locally dominated by giant sequoia *(Sequoiadendron giganteum)*, which like its coastal cousin, is a narrow endemic with a long fossil record. The present scattered distribution of giant sequoia can be traced back to the patterns of Pleistocene glaciation several thousand years ago. This massive tree species has not been successful at reoccupying its former pre-Pleistocene range. In southern California, a component of Montane Forest is bigcone spruce *(Pseudotsuga macrocarpa)*, a close relative of Douglas-fir, but a species that is adapted to more arid conditions than Douglas-fir. A few deciduous hardwoods are associated with the coniferous trees of the Montane Forest. Also present are canyon oak *(Quercus chrysolepis)* and California black oak *(Q. kelloggii)*. At the upper, cooler, and wetter margin of the Montane Forest, Jeffrey pine *(P. jeffrei)*, red fir *(A. magnifica)*, and lodgepole pine *(P. contorta* subsp. *murrayana)* begin to appear (pls. 127, 128).

Because of the large area occupied by the Montane Forest and the diversity of ecological niches that it spans, one might expect a large number of shrubby and herbaceous plant species to occur in this vegetation type, and according to Munz's *A California Flora* (1959), approximately 1,200 herbaceous plant species occur in the Montane Forest, and somewhat over 200 shrub species occur in the understory of the Montane Forest. It is therefore difficult to give a list of representative understory species, but a few genera or species of wide distribution in the forest community can be mentioned. These include mountain misery *(Chamaebatia foliolosa)*, a low, rather attractive but malodorous member of the rose family that forms large masses under the conifers. Also present are various species of gooseberry or currant *(Ribes* spp.), blackberries *(Rubus* spp.), manzanitas *(Arctostaphylos* spp.),

Plate 127. Coniferous Montane Forests in the Sierra Nevada begin at around 2,000 feet and may extend to around 8,000 feet in the mountains of southern California. These forests are rich in the diversity of coniferous species. Yellow pine *(Pinus ponderosa)* is prominent in the lower- to midelevation forests.

and California-lilacs (*Ceanothus* spp.). Growing near streams, alders *(Alnus rhombifolia)* and at higher elevation from 5,000 to 8,000 feet a shrubby alder, *Alnus tenuifolia,* play an important role because of their nitrogen fixing ability.

One of the tree species present in the Montane Forest is sugar pine. When California was first settled by immigrants from the eastern states, sugar pines were much more common in the Sierra Nevada than they now are. This former abundance was the result of the fact that forest fires raged unchecked through many areas of the Sierra, and sugar pine was perpetuated as a result of these fires. Seedlings of this species compete successfully only in areas that have been opened up by fires (or some other ecological disturbance). With the subsequent effective fire control that has existed in much of the forested area of the Sierra, natural succession has resulted in the reduction in numbers of sugar pines, which have been replaced in the ecological succession by incense-cedar and white fir. It is probable that several of the other tree

Plate 128. At the upper, cooler, wetter margin of the forest in the Sierra Nevada, red fir *(Abies magnifica)* appears in large stands.

species in the Montane Forest are also "fire type" trees, and their numbers may also be changing as a result of the efficiency of the fire control activities of federal, state, and private agencies.

Montane Chaparral

At moderate to high elevations in the mountains, particularly in the Sierra Nevada, a coniferous forest may be interrupted by patches of Montane Chaparral. This vegetation type resembles in general aspect the Chaparral of lower elevations but is given separate recognition because the number and identity of the species of shrubs that occur in the two vegetation types are different. Although manzanitas and California-lilacs occur in both vegetation types, different species are represented in each. The regions in which Montane Chaparral occurs receive considerably higher precipitation than those occupied by Chaparral, but with few exceptions the shrubs maintain a strong xerophytic appearance, that is, small, upright, waxy leaves and tight, twiggy growth form. Snow bush *(Ceanothus cordulatus),* chinquapin *(Chrysolepis [Castanop-*

Plate 129. Montane Chaparral occurs at moderate to high elevations, particularly in the Sierra Nevada, usually where fires have destroyed trees or where soils are particularly thin. Manzanitas (*Arctostaphylos* spp.) and California-lilac (*Ceanothus* spp.) are usually represented as in the chaparral of lower elevations, although by different species.

Plate 130. *Ceanothus* spp. fills in where a recent fire has killed an area of pine forest in the Sierra Nevada. These shrubs will create shady conditions for the trees to germinate and grow back.

sis] sempervirens), and huckleberry oak *(Q. vacciniifolia)* are all commonly found in Montane Chaparral. In many areas of the mountains, Montane Chaparral is successional in nature and develops on previously forested sites after forest fires have eliminated the trees. Because of its sporadic distribution, this vegetation type is not included on the maps (pls. 129, 130).

Subalpine Forest (Map 4)

Immediately above the Montane Forest, and not sharply differentiated from it, is the Subalpine Forest vegetation type. Some of the coniferous tree species, characteristic of the upper reaches of the Montane Forest, also occur in the lower reaches of (or throughout) Subalpine Forest, with a resulting gradual transition between the two forest communities. The Subalpine Forest occurs above the Montane Forest in the Sierra Nevada and is present to a lesser extent in the Cascade Range in the Lassen Peak–Mount Shasta vicinity. The elevation at which it occurs is variable; at its lowest it occurs between 5,000 and 6,000 feet. In southern California or the desert ranges (such as the White Mountains) it may extend up to 11,000 feet. The climatic regime in Subalpine Forest is variable, although in general it is somewhat more rigorous than that of the Montane Forest. Winters are usually very cold and associated with heavy precipitation; the winter snows may provide the explanation for the conical form of subalpine conifers, which inspired the idea for the original A-frame building construction.

The Subalpine Forest is as rich in its number of coniferous dominants and its local diversity as is the Montane Forest. One dominant conifer is lodgepole pine, which has a sporadic distribution. This relatively small conifer seems to occur in areas in which the local climatic or soil conditions are rather unfavorable for the full development of other coniferous species. Other subalpine inhabitants are western white pine *(P. monticola)* and mountain hemlock *(Tsuga mertensiana)*. At timberline, one finds gnarled and windswept individuals of whitebark pine *(P. albicaulis)*. Other pine species are the closely

Plate 131. The Subalpine Forest is a transitional zone above the Montane Forest and is also rich in coniferous species. Lodgepole pine *(Pinus contorta* subsp. *murrayana)* grows where climatic or soil conditions are unfavorable for some of the larger coniferous species.

related trio consisting of limber pine *(P. flexilis)*, foxtail pine *(P. balfouriana)*, and bristlecone pine *(P. longaeva)*. Bristlecone pine occurs (in California) in the very dry White Mountains, where it receives average precipitation of about 12 inches per year; the trees are widely spaced and not especially tall. Despite its unfavorable environment, bristlecone pine has a remarkably long life span and is perhaps the longest-

Plate 132. The bristlecone pine *(Pinus longaeva)* withstands forceful winds and harsh weather near timberline in the White Mountains, yet it lives to a very old age.

Plate 133. The spiny fruit of the Sierra gooseberry *(Ribes roezlii)* is widely distributed in yellow pine *(Pinus ponderosa)* and red fir *(Abies magnifica)* forests in California mountains.

lived organism on earth. One individual shows growth rings that suggest it is 4,600 years old, an age exceeding that of the oldest giant sequoia. Even the leaves of the bristlecone pine are long lived; needle life has been estimated to be as much as 30 years (pls. 131–132).

In many areas occupied by Subalpine Forest, particularly at higher elevations, trees are widely scattered. The spaces among the trees are frequently occupied by a number of colorful herbaceous perennials and shrubs such as various wild currant (*Ribes* spp.), willow (*Salix* spp.), and huckleberry (*Vaccinium* spp.) species.

Montane Meadow

Where shallow or continuously moist soil in upper montane areas occurs, treeless meadows are encountered that are occupied by a distinctive array of perennial herbs. These meadows support the Montane Meadow vegetation type, which is characterized by a variety of perennial grasses, sedges, and rushes and a number of low, broad-leaved herbs. Plant assemblages vary with soil conditions including moisture content, acidity, organic content, and depth. Montane meadows of varying sizes are found at a broad range of elevations. Montane Meadow is usually and intermediate stage in a natural succession from a montane lake with freshwater species to a coniferous forest, thus a wide range of soil conditions is found. The tall, striking corn-lily *(Veratrum californicum* var. *californicum)* that so commonly decorates the Montane Meadow, is well named for its appearance that mimics a Kansas corn stalk. It commonly accompanies a striking and colorful wildflower display in mid- to late summer in drier meadows. In wetter meadows, such as Tuolumne Meadows, vast deposits of decaying plant material quickly surround and bury any pebbles or rocks and create a soft boggy texture underfoot. Shooting stars *(Dodecatheon hendersonii)* usually appear first at the edges of lakes as the snow melts, followed by white violets *(Viola ocellata),* blue camas lilies *(Camassia quamash),* wild iris *(Iris* spp.), orange and maroon lilies *(Lilium* spp.), purple monkshood *(Aconitum columbianum),* and an array of buttercups (*Ranunculus* spp.) and other wildflowers. Around the meadow edge and away from moist or marshy areas, western blueberry *(Vaccinium uliginosum* subsp. *occidentale)* spreads in low-growing clumps, perhaps mingling with species of willow that thrive in wet places. Because of the irregular distribution of this vegetation type, it is not included in the maps (pls. 134, 135).

Alpine Fell-field

Despite the ability of pines and other conifers to survive and even prosper under the unfavorable environmental conditions at high elevations, there is a point of elevation at which the climatic regime is too stringent for successful growth of trees of any kind. The point at which this ecological circumstance develops is called timberline and is marked by a sharp reduction in number and size of trees. Above this zone of dwarfed and stunted trees is another vegetation type that occupies very high elevations in the mountains. This is the Alpine Fell-field vegetation type, a community of low, perennial plants that occurs above 9,500 feet in the Sierra Nevada (primarily) and also in parts of the Cascade Range, the White and Sweetwater Mountains of the Great Basin, and the San

Above: Plate 134. Large Montane Meadows sometimes form as lakes fill in, eventually to become forests. From the dense vegetation, composed largely of species of sedges (*Carex* spp.) and wildflowers, which die seasonally, soil layers build up over time.

Left: Plate 135. The striking corn-lily *(Veratrum californicum)* is a common feature of montane meadows in the Sierra Nevada.

Plate 136. Alpine Fell-fields lie above timberline and mostly above 9,500 feet. Only low, densely formed perennial herbs can survive the harsh conditions here but in the short summer produce a brilliant display of color.

Bernardino and San Jacinto Mountains. Precipitation in the Alpine Fell-field occurs mostly as snow in the winter, because the elevation is above the point of maximum rainfall on the slopes of the mountains. In many respects, this vegetation type occupies an alpine desert. The growing season is less than two months long—sometimes as short as six weeks—and heavy frosts may occur during almost any night of the summer. The appearance of this vegetation type is much like that of a rock garden. The rock-strewn peaks, slopes, or open fields are frequently covered by masses of perennial herbs that form a low, dense turf. Many of the plants in these areas form small, cushionlike mats with densely packed leaves. A few grass and sedge species occur in the Alpine Fell-field, but these are accompanied by a large variety of dicots, another group of flowering plants belonging to diverse genera in several families. Many of the dwarfed inhabitants of the Alpine Fell-field (such as the crucifers or mustards [Brassicaceae], sunflowers [Asteraceae], penstemons [*Penstemon* spp.], phloxes [*Phlox* spp.], wild buckwheats [*Eriogonum* spp.], and sky pilot [*Polemonium ex-*

Plate 137. This tiny buckwheat *(Eriogonum ovalifolium* subsp. *nivale)* demonstrates a cushion form of growth that is typical for this harsh windy environment.

Plate 138. The relatively large flowers of sky pilot *(Polemonium eximium)* produce bright patches of color in late summer to attract pollinators during their short blooming period in the high mountains.

imium]) have large, brilliantly colored flowers, thus producing a mosaic of bright colors across the fell-fields in late summer. Although the climb to these fields may be difficult, the reward is great. The distribution of this vegetation type is not mapped (pls. 136–138).

Transmontane Region (Areas East of the Sierra Nevada Crest and the Deserts)

Pinyon-Juniper Woodland (Map 4)

Plate 139. Pinyon-Juniper Woodland is the first forest to occur over the crest on the dry eastern slopes of the Sierra Nevada. The name is derived from the single-leaf pinyon pine *(Pinus monophylla)* and junipers such as the California juniper *(Juniperus californica)*. Trees are widely scattered and small in this dry habitat.

The upper reaches of California mountains are occupied by a treeless vegetation type, and certain peaks are sufficiently high that they support no vascular plants at all. However, over the crest of the Sierra Nevada and down along the eastern slopes of these mountains, trees again begin to be evident. The species of trees and the localities in which they appear vary, but on the average we can expect to find Pinyon-Juniper Woodland as the first "forest" community encountered on the eastern slopes of the Sierra Nevada as we descend in elevation from the crest. Pinyon-Juniper Woodland represents a transition between forest and nonforest vegetation types in some areas, although in a less consistent way than does the Valley and Foothill Woodland in cismontane California. In some

Plate 140. Pinyon pine *(Pinus monophylla)* is one-leafed, as its name signifies, and produces a large seed, a favorite food of native animals and of humans .

areas, Pinyon-Juniper Woodland is drier than Montane Forest or Subalpine Forest, but in some localities—such as in the desert mountains—Pinyon-Juniper Woodland is bordered above and below by scrub communities of various kinds.

Pinyon-Juniper Woodland takes its name from the single-leaf pinyon pine *(P. monophylla)* and various junipers such as California juniper *(Juniperus californica)*, Utah juniper *(J. osteosperma)*, and western or Sierra juniper *(J. occidentalis)*. These trees are not very tall and occur as fairly widely scattered individuals in this vegetation type. Also present are desert scrub oak *(Q. turbinella)*, mountain-mahogany *(Cercocarpus ledifolius)*, antelope brush or bitter brush *(Purshia tridentata)*, and all species of the Sagebrush Scrub vegetation type, to be mentioned next. Pinyon-Juniper Woodland occurs in the Great Basin and in California mountain ranges from Modoc County into southern California, where it is associated with the Transverse and Peninsular Ranges and some of the desert ranges (pls. 139–141).

Sagebrush Scrub (Map 3)

A plant community that is often adjacent to Pinyon-Juniper Woodland is the Sagebrush Scrub. This community occurs in relatively deep soils along the eastern base of the Sierra-Cascade axis from Modoc County southward to the San Bernardino

Plate 141. Bitter brush *(Purshia tridentata),* in the rose family, is one of several shrubs well adapted to live in very dry habitats by having very reduced, hairy, tough leaves.

Mountains. A few small patches of it occur locally elsewhere. The average annual precipitation ranges from eight to 15 inches, and much of this falls as winter snow. Summers may be very hot and winters relatively cold. The elevations occupied by this vegetation type range from about 4,000 to 7,000 feet.

Sagebrush Scrub is characterized by the presence of various low, silvery gray shrubs that are two to six feet tall or more. The plant community is named after Basin sagebrush *(Artemisia tridentata),* a member of the sunflower family (Asteraceae), which occupies vast areas of the Great Basin. Other species of sagebrush present are the related *A. nova, A. arbuscula,* and *A. cana* subsp. *bolanderi.* Associated shrubs are rabbit brush *(Chrysothamnus* spp.), blackbush *(Coleogyne ramosissima,* Rosaceae), cotton thorn *(Tetradymia s*pp., Asteraceae) and a few other superficially similar shrub species (pls. 142–144).

Shadscale Scrub (Map 3)

Woodland (or forest) communities also are more extensive in the northern portion of the state (i.e., north of the Transverse Ranges) than in the south. Examination of patterns of distribution of the scrubland communities, however, indicates that these are better developed in southern California than in the

Plate 142. Sagebrush Scrub occurs adjacent to the Pinyon-Juniper Woodland community in hot, dry country along the eastern Sierra Nevada across into the Great Basin. It is characterized by several species of low, silvery gray shrubs.

Plate 143. Sagebrush Scrub is named after Basin sagebrush *(Artemisia tridentata)*, in the sunflower family, that extends for such great distances in eastern California it is sometimes called "the sagebrush ocean."

Plate 144. Rabbitbrush (*Chrysothamnus* spp.) grows luxuriantly beneath the cottonwood trees on fairly deep soils in the valley of the Owens River.

northern part of the state. The Shadscale Scrub vegetation type is named after one of the dominant species, shadscale *(Atriplex confertifolia)*, an erect, rigidly branched, spiny shrub with rather crowded, round leaves that resemble fish scales. (Curiously, neither Munz and Keck nor Jepson listed shadscale as the common name for this shrub, even though this name is widely used for the shrub in much of the Great Basin, and it gave its name to the vegetation type in which it occurs.) Other members of this desert vegetation type are hop sage *(Grayia spinosa)*, winter fat *(Krascheninnikovia lanata)*, spiny sagebrush *(Artemisia spinescen)*, matchweed *(Gutierrezia* spp.), burrobrush *(Hymenoclea salsola)*, blackbush *(Coelogyne ramosissima)*, and the peculiar gymnospermous shrub Mormon tea *(Ephedra* spp.) (pls. 145, 146).

Despite the fact that the characteristic shrubs of Shadscale Scrub belong to several plant families that are taxonomically unrelated, they have a strong superficial similarity. The shrubs are rather small, seldom over one-and-a-half feet tall. Generally, they are grayish, small leaved, much branched, and some-

Plate 145. Shadscale Scrub occurs in heavy, saline soils at 3,000 to 6,000 feet, often around shores of now-dry Pleistocene lakes. The plants in this community are grayish, small leafed, much branched, and sometimes spiny. The dominant plant, shadscale *(Artemisia confertifolia)*, is shallow rooted, and its growth is severely limited by water availability.

Plate 146. Mormon tea (*Ephedra* spp.) has a jointlike appearance to its leafless form. Flowers lacking petals and sepals emerge at the joints.

times spiny and produce smallish flowers. Shadscale Scrub occurs in very heavy, often alkaline (pH 8 to 10) or saline soils that are frequently underlain with a hardpan. The Shadscale Scrub vegetation type occurs on mesas and flatlands at elevations of 3,000 to 6,000 feet in various parts of the transmontane desert regions such as the Owens Valley and the Mojave Desert. It becomes more common and widespread in the eastern and northeastern portions of the California desert, often near Joshua Tree Woodland, where soils are less saline. Its center of distribution is in the Great Basin of Nevada. It is uncommon in the Colorado Desert areas, which are occupied chiefly by Creosote Bush Scrub. Rainfall in these areas is very low, averaging less than seven inches per year. Summers are dry and hot.

Perhaps the most interesting feature of this vegetation type is the peculiarity of the common names given to its component shrubs. Otherwise, it covers large monotonous areas between Creosote Bush Scrub and Joshua Tree Woodland, both of which communities are clearly aesthetically preferable to the Shadscale Scrub.

Alkali Sink Scrub (Map 3)

Another scrub community of arid regions is the Alkali Sink Scrub. This vegetation type is made up of halophytic shrubs that belong largely to the goosefoot family (Chenopodiaceae), whose members are salt tolerant. Characteristic species of the Alkali Sink Scrub are saltbush (*Atriplex* spp.), iodine bush *(Allenrolfea occidentalis),* pickleweed (*Salicornia* spp.), greasewood *(Sarcobatus vermiculatus),* and seep weed (*Suaeda* spp.). All these genera are members of the goosefoot family. Note that *Suaeda* and *Salicornia* are also present in the Coastal Salt Marsh vegetation type, which is not surprising in view of their high salt tolerance (pls. 147–149).

The Alkali Sink Scrub occupies the low-lying, poorly drained alkali flats and playas in the San Joaquin Valley (especially around Tulare Lake) and also occurs in similar habi-

Plate 147. Alkali Sink Scrub occurs in the San Joaquin Valley where an annual salt-tolerant goldfield (*Lasthenia* sp.) provides a showy display between iodine bush *(Allenrolfea occidentalis)* and other halophytic shrubs.

Plate 148. Iodine bush *(Allenrolfea occidentalis),* named for the brown stain it leaves on skin when the beadlike stems are crushed, is a widespread halophyte in the goosefoot family found in Alkali Sink Scrub in California deserts and the San Joaquin Valley.

Plate 149. Seep weed (*Suaeda* spp.) is another plant in the goosefoot family well adapted to life in a salty desert environment. It grows in salt marshes also.

tats in transmontane deserts such as those in Panamint and Death Valleys. The rainfall in such areas may be as low as two inches per year or less, but the soil is often saturated with highly saline water for much of the year because of seepage into these low areas. Summer temperatures in these desert regions may be excessively high (as they are, for example, in Death Valley). As might be expected in view of their halophytic nature, Alkali Sink Scrub shrubs characteristically have fleshy leaves and stems. Outside California, this vegetation type is especially well developed in the low areas around the Great Salt Lake in Utah.

Because these low desert areas are frequently inundated with water during the rainy season, a hard saline crust may form on the soil surface when the soil is dry. In association with this soil phenomenon, a curious symbiotic relationship has developed between local ant species and Alkali Sink Scrub plants. Ants bury seeds below the surface in the process of carrying them to their nest (or perhaps storing them) for use as food. This procedure results in the seeds being planted below the hard surface crust at a level where the salinity is lower and the moisture conditions are more favorable to germination.

Joshua Tree Woodland (Map 4)

Another desert community that is well known to many Californians is the Joshua Tree Woodland, a vegetation type that only marginally deserves the name "woodland." Joshua tree is a handsome treelike yucca *(Yucca brevifolia)*, its name describing it's the shorter leaves than are found in other species of yucca. It is one of the most characteristic species of the Mojave Desert, which is at a higher elevation than the Sonoran Desert by 2,000 to 3,000 feet and thus has more rainfall and less severe temperatures. Common associates of Joshua tree are Mojave yucca *(Y. schidigera)*, junipers, Mormon tea, cotton thorn, California buckwheat *(Eriogonum fasciculatum)*, bladder sage *(Salazaria mexicana)*, box thorn (*Lycium* spp.,), and many species of the cholla cactus (*Opuntia* spp.). Rather few

Plate 150. Joshua Tree Woodland is a woodland only because of the presence of the handsome treelike yucca *(Yucca brevifolia)* called the Joshua tree. This vegetation type is found on well-drained mesas and slopes 2,500 to 4,000 feet or higher that receive six to 14 inches of rain per year.

of the woody plant species generally considered to be members of this vegetation type are restricted to it (pls. 150–152).

Joshua Tree Woodland occupies well-drained mesas and desert slopes from Owens Valley to the Little San Bernardino Mountains and southern Nevada and extreme southwestern Utah. It occurs at moderate elevations from somewhat over 2,000 feet to about 6,000 feet. The average annual rainfall is between six and 15 inches, depending on locality. Unlike most of the lowland vegetation types in California, Joshua Tree Woodland receives occasional summer showers. The individual Joshua trees and associated junipers are rather widely spaced and are seldom over 30 feet high. Numerous shrubby plants in addition to those listed above occur among the trees, and during the spring following a wet winter the ground among the shrubs and trees is carpeted with spectacular masses of showy annuals in flower.

Plate 151. Teddy bear cholla *(Opuntia bigelovii)* is also known as jumping cholla because its vicious spines readily fasten onto passing animals and humans.

Plate 152. Spring brings spectacular wildflower displays including this desert primrose *(Oenothera deltoides)* that is common in sandy areas and is pollinated by nocturnal hawkmoths.

Creosote Bush Scrub (Map 3)

The last vegetation type to be discussed is the one that is the most widespread in the southern desert portions of California. This is the Creosote Bush Scrub (pl. 153). Creosote bush *(Larrea tridentata)* is a rather attractive, tall shrub in the caltrop family (Zygophyllaceae) and dominates much of the desert landscape below 3,500 feet from Inyo County southward. It also occurs locally in some interior cismontane valleys such as at Poso Creek, Tulare County, and localities in western Riverside County. Also present as plant associates of the creosote bush are burro-weed *(Ambrosia dumosa)* and the colorful and brittle bush *(Encelia farinosa)*, both in the sunflower family; burrobrush *(Hymenoclea salsola);* the showy, red-flowered ocotillo *(Fouquieria splendens* subsp.

Plate 153. Creosote Bush Scrub occurs on the well-drained soils of slopes, fans, and valleys below 3,500 feet in deserts of California. Large assemblages of plant species take advantage of the many different microhabitats within this vegetation type. In this view a mixture of Antelope bush *(Purshia tridentata)*, sagebrush *(Artemisia* spp.), and California buckwheat *(Eriogonum fasciculatum)* grow on a rocky sloping hillside.

splendens); and prickly pears and chollas of the cactaceous genus *Opuntia.*

Over much of the Mojave Desert, creosote bush covers the landscape in a widely spaced, even monotonous fashion. It leafs out and blooms with yellow five-petaled flowers that are quickly replaced with white, fuzzy fruits in spring, which are particularly abundant in years of good rainfall. Often, shrubs by a roadside grow to a larger size as a result of the extra moisture from road drainage. In the 1970s, Frank Vasek from the University of California, Riverside, noticed that creosote bush grew in large clumps and that each clump had numerous stems at ground level. These turned out to emanate from several root crowns that appeared to have been connected at some time in the past. Thus the original seedling matures and crown sprouts, forming a ring away from the central stem. In time, a ring of genetically identical plants grows around the original plant. After Vasek had the centers of large, old rings carbon dated, he determined an average growth rate for the species. Assuming this same growth rate through time, he estimated that a large clone measuring 35 by 26 feet (King Kong clone) was 11,700 years old, making it the oldest living plant and twice the age of the oldest known bristlecone pine.

Because of the limitations of water supply in the area occupied by the Creosote Bush Scrub, watercourses (which are dry most of the year) support a characteristic flora that takes advantage of the abundant supply of water during rainy periods of winter or summer. In more complex vegetation-type listings, botanists consider this watercourse flora as a separate vegetation type called Wash Woodland; however, here it is included with the plants in Creosote Bush Scrub. Certain desert trees and shrubs generally occur only along these water courses. These include ironwood *(Olneya tesota),* palo verde *(Cercidium floridum* subsp. *floridum),* smoke tree *(Psorothamnus spinosa),* and catclaw *(Acacia greggii),* all in the pea family; desert willow *(Chilopsis linearis* subsp. *arcuata);* chuparosa *(Justicia californica);* and desert lavender *(Hyptis emoryi).* An-

Plate 154. Ocotillo (*Fouquieria splendens* subsp. *splendens*) is a conspicuous shrub of the Creosote Bush Scrub below 2,500 feet. Its stout spiny stems grow to 20 feet, terminating in inch-long red flowers that attract hummingbirds and brighten the landscape.

other interesting tree that occurs around moist, somewhat alkaline spots in the Creosote Bush Scrub is California fan palm (*Washingtonia filifera*), which often coexists with various willows (*Salix* spp.). This species is rather uncommon in nature, although it is widely planted as an ornamental in subtropical regions (pls. 153–156).

The seeds of many Wash Woodland tree species are very hard coated and will not germinate even if left in water for more than a year. It is necessary to scratch the coat of these seeds for germination to take place; otherwise, they are impervious to water. The grinding action of sand and rocks in the flash floods of the desert performs the scarification function, and the floods provide the seedlings with abundant water to supply their requirements during the first few weeks of growth. Such floods also serve to disperse the seeds. Like many desert perennials, seedlings of Wash Woodland trees produce

Plate 155. White bear-poppy *(Arctomecon merriamii)* is a perennial herbaceous plant, now rare because of mining and damage from off-road vehicles in the desert.

Plate 156. Brittle bush *(Encelia farinosa),* in the sunflower family, is common in washes and stony slopes in Creosote Bush Scrub, where it blooms from March to May.

only two or three leaves immediately after germination and then seemingly become dormant. However, these plants are far from dormant during this time; they are devoting their chief energies to developing extensive, deep root systems that will enable them to survive long after the moisture from the flood has dissipated.

Summer temperatures in the Creosote Bush Scrub may be very high, and in many areas winter temperatures do not drop to the freezing point. The average annual rainfall in this vegetation type is very low, ranging from two to eight inches. In appearance, Creosote Bush Scrub is composed of numerous shrubs or small trees to 10 feet high or somewhat higher that are widely and symmetrically spaced. Some of these species, particularly those that occur along the desert washes, are very colorful when in flower.

Woody plants dominate the Creosote Bush Scrub community, although it also contains a rich representation of annual plant species. In addition to the annuals are many herbaceous perennials, although they are less abundant. The general aspect of the vegetation of the Creosote Bush Scrub during almost any month of the year belies its arid nature. It is usually green, and because it supports a cover of shrubs and small trees, it may give the impression that it receives more rain than it actually does.

The natural vegetation of California represents a set of vegetation types or plant communities of varied historical origins. The landscape of the state has changed dramatically over geological time, and the vegetation has reflected these physical changes. We have already pointed out that some plant communities, such as the North Coastal Forest (or at least the segment of this community dominated by coast redwood *[Sequoia sempervirens]*), have had continuity back into the geological past that extends as far as 20 million years ago when the topography was more varied and the climate cooler. However, these "old" plant communities once occupied quite different geographical ranges. Other plant communities, such as those that are adapted to the characteristic Mediterranean or desert climates of California, are of relatively recent origin and moved northward from Mexico as the climate became warmer. These communities dominate low-elevation vegetation throughout much of the state.

According to the current theory of plate tectonics, continents float on molten magma from the earth's core, forming and reforming various land masses as they move. As landmasses rise on top of or sink (subduct) under other plates, mountains are thrust up, only to be eroded by wind and water. Although the geography of the earliest landforms on the earth is highly speculative, it is thought that around 395 million years ago, in the Paleozoic epoch, North America, Greenland, and Europe were united as a single continent called Euroamerica and were separated from proto-Asia and Gondwanaland by oceans. Paleobotanists today hypothesize that the presence of a plant considered a native on more than one continent might indicate its origin was on a single landmass that broke up millions of years ago. Today the forests of eastern North America and Europe share many genera such as *Abies* (fir), *Picea* (spruce), *Pinus* (pine), and *Acer* (maple), which indicates their early origin on a single landmass, Euroamerica. The first gymnosperms, an ancient line of plants distinguished from angiosperms by having naked seeds, include conifers and cycads that appeared sometime in the Paleozoic epoch, around 350 million years ago. The dawn redwood *(Metasequoia glyptostroboides),* which survives in the wild only in China today, is known from the fossil record to have once had a range from Asia across North America.

The Oligocene, Miocene, and Pliocene along with the older Eocene and Paleocene epochs (to 65 million years ago), constitute the Tertiary period. In the Oligocene and Miocene epochs, the area occupied by California and much of the rest of the western United States was a region of rolling plains or low mountains. No major mountain system existed in California until the close of the Tertiary.

The geological timescale in table 9 will be of some help in visualizing the past history of the rich flora that now occupies the California Floristic Province.

TABLE 9. Geological Timescale

Period	Epoch	Relative Time Began
Quarternary	Recent	11,000 years ago (post-glacial)
	Pleistocene	1 million years ago
Tertiary	Pliocene	10 million years ago
	Miocene	25 million years ago
	Oligocene	40 million years ago

Arcto-Tertiary Geoflora

As a consequence of topographical uniformity in the early Tertiary, the climate of the western part of North America was much less varied than it is at present. It is not surprising, therefore, that much of North America, northern Asia, and Europe was covered by a rather uniform type of vegetation, and a rich one in terms of number of species present. In the west, this flora extended from about the latitude of San Francisco well northward into what are now arctic regions. This forest has been termed the *Arcto-Tertiary geoflora. Arcto* refers to its

Plate 157. Remnants of the Arcto-Tertiary geoflora that once extended from mid-California into the Arctic include species such as hemlock (*Tsuga* spp.), western red-cedar *(Thuja plicata),* spruce (*Picea* spp.), and deciduous trees such as maple (*Acer* spp.) and dogwood (*Cornus* spp.). Western hemlock *(Tsuga mertensiana)* today grows from California to Alaska.

northern distribution; *Tertiary* refers to the time period during which it flourished; and a *geoflora* is a major vegetation unit that has continuity in space and time. In recent years, the concept of the Arcto-Tertiary geoflora has been a subject of some dispute; nevertheless, it does help to bring home the idea that the contemporary flora of California has had a long history in time and space.

The Arcto-Tertiary geoflora contained a number of tree genera that have persisted on the Pacific coast until the modern day, including hemlock *(Tsuga),* canoe-cedar or western red-cedar *(Thuja plicata),* spruce *(Picea),* maple *(Acer),* and dogwood *(Cornus).* However, in response to climatic changes that occurred over a long period of time, other genera in this forest disappeared from the western part of the continent, although they still persist in the eastern part of the continent. These include genera as such as beech *(Fagus),* chestnut *(Castanea),* elm *(Ulmus),* sweet gum *(Liquidambar),* and some other hardwoods (pls. 157–159).

It is interesting that the remnants of the Arcto-Tertiary

Plate 158. Engelmann spruce *(Picea engelmannii)* is rare in California (the three known populations are found in the Klamath and Cascade mountains), but its distribution extends from British Columbia southward through the Rocky Mountains.

Plate 159. Bigleaf maple *(Acer macrophyllum)* is deciduous and is commonly found along streambanks and in shady canyons.

geoflora that persisted in the west are largely coniferous genera—the deciduous genera mostly disappeared from this region—whereas in the eastern portion of the continent the reverse was true—the conifers largely disappeared and the hardwoods remained. Some genera that still occur in either the eastern or the western forests of North America also survived in the Old World, although there they are now represented by different species from those present in North America. Other genera, such as the maidenhair tree *(Ginkgo)* and the tree of heaven *(Ailanthus)* disappeared completely from North America, whereas others, such as sequoia *(Sequoia)*, disappeared completely from the Old World.

Since the middle of the Miocene, three major climatic and geological changes in the area that is now the western United States have been responsible for the elimination of the old Arcto-Tertiary forest over much of the area and its replacement by other plant communities:

1. Since the Tertiary, winter rainfall has become reduced, and summer rainfall has essentially disappeared over much of California.
2. Starting in the Pliocene, the Sierra Nevada and the Cascade Range were created. The result of this major geological event was the formation of a rain shadow to the east of these mountains and the appearance of new upland areas for plant colonization, particularly on the western slopes. Furthermore, the western slopes of these mountains are now comparatively well watered with rain and snow.
3. During the Pleistocene, much of northern North America was covered with glacial ice sheets. In the west, these barely extended southward across what is now the U.S.-Canadian border, but because of the cooler climatic conditions that prevailed on the continent during this time, many of the upper reaches of the Sierra Nevada in California were covered with glaciers of various sizes. In addition, there was a general cooling trend over much of western North America.

The biological consequences of these geological and climatic features are complex. The development of a cooler climate and the action of the glaciers in mountainous areas clearly had their effect in eliminating certain species from California and in altering the distribution ranges of other species.

As an example, giant sequoia *(Sequoiadendron giganteum)* now occurs only in areas of the western slopes of the Sierra Nevada that were not devastated by the action of glaciers. The reduction in total annual rainfall to the east of the Sierra Nevada eliminated the forest climate and replaced it with a scrubland or grassland climate. The rich Arcto-Tertiary forest was rapidly eliminated from much of the Great Basin because of this climatic change. However, the relatively moderate and moist climate that remained along certain areas of the western slopes of the Sierra Nevada provided pockets in which some of the Arcto-Tertiary forest species took refuge. It was from these pockets that a recolonization of the Sierra Nevada took place following the retreat of the last Pleistocene glaciers and the subsequent warming of the climate. It was also in relatively recent times that the zonation of forest communities took place on the western slopes of these mountains. It has been suggested that the major reorganization of the Arcto-Tertiary forest in California occurred on the western slopes of the Sierra Nevada and that the forest communities that developed in this area subsequently invaded the Coast Ranges, the mountains of southern California, and the mountains of Baja California. It has even been suggested that some species of conifers now considered typical of the North Coast Ranges (such as coast redwood, Port Orford–cedar *[Cupressus lawsoniana],* and canoe-cedar) are probably fairly recent immigrants into this area from the western slopes of the Sierra Nevada, where they have subsequently become extinct (pl. 160).

Many of the modern plant communities in California contain vestiges of the Arcto-Tertiary geoflora. It seems probable that some of these communities represent local aggregations of species whose immediate ancestors occurred with the ancestors of species that are present in other remnant plant communities. In recent times there has been a segregation of the descendants of Arcto-Tertiary tree species into smaller, more homogeneous plant communities than were occupied by their

Plate 160. Because of geologic and climatic changes in California, giant sequoia *(Sequoiadendron giganteum)* now occur only in limited areas of the western slopes of the Sierra Nevada.

predeccessors. Some of these derivative communities (such as the Closed-Cone Pine Forest) are not very successful in coping with the contemporary biotic and climatic conditions of the Pacific coast and seemingly are on their way to complete disappearance as communities. Other of these communities (such as most phases of the North Coastal Forest) seem to be well adapted to current ecological conditions and are therefore successful.

Neotropical Tertiary Geoflora

At the southern edge of its range, the Arcto-Tertiary geoflora merged into the Neotropical Tertiary geoflora. This second geoflora covered the southern portion of North America, although its boundaries with the Arcto-Tertiary geoflora oscillated in response to long-term climatic changes. In the Eocene, for example, segments of the Neotropical Tertiary geoflora extended as far north as Alaska, at which time the Arcto-Tertiary geoflora must have been squeezed into a rather small area along the northern fringe of North America and northward. The Neotropical Tertiary geoflora was composed of diverse tropical or subtropical trees such as figs, avocados, cinnamon, palms, and others. This geoflora has now disappeared from most of North America, although it is represented in the region of southern Mexico southward to northern South America and is now restricted to tropical areas with high rainfall. Its disappearance from much of its former area was due to the cooler, drier climates that have prevailed over much of North America since the Eocene. Few living remnants of this rich flora are left in California, although some genera managed to survive here into the Pliocene.

The description given above of the former and present ranges of the Arcto-Tertiary and Neotropical Tertiary geofloras and their response to climatic changes suggests that a large area of the southwestern portion of North America is generally unfavorable for occupancy by the modern descendants of either one of these geofloras. Yet a rich flora now occupies this southwestern area. What is the origin of these plants?

Madro-Tertiary Geoflora

According to the late D.I. Axelrod of the Department of Botany, University of California, Davis, in the middle Miocene, the countryside south of San Francisco was occupied largely by an oak woodland flora that had migrated into this area from the Sierra Madre Occidental region in northwestern Mexico. The plants of this oak woodland were adapted to a year-round rainfall but to a warmer, somewhat drier climate than were the plants of the Arcto-Tertiary forest to the north of it. Presumably this oak woodland occupied some of the area that formerly had been occupied by the Neotropical Tertiary geoflora, which in turn had become gradually eliminated from the North American southwest because of climatic changes. It is probable that some species of this oak woodland evolved directly from subtropical precursors in the Neotropical Tertiary geoflora. This oak woodland has been termed by Axelrod the *Madro-Tertiary geoflora*, the term *Madro-* coming from the name of the Mexican mountains (Sierra Madre Occidental) that now occupy the general area from which this flora is believed to have migrated northwestward.

The Madro-Tertiary geoflora consisted largely of sclerophyllous, small, hard-leaved trees and shrubs similar to those that presently occupy many areas of California. Even as early as the middle Eocene some of the immediate ancestors of species present in Chaparral, Coastal Sage Scrub, and Valley and Foothill Woodland were present in California, although it is doubtful if these plant communities would have been recognizable at that time. During the middle Pliocene, the oak woodland dwindled and disappeared over many areas of what later became the southwestern deserts, because the rainfall in these areas became sharply reduced as the Sierra Nevada and the Peninsular Ranges were uplifted. The increasing dryness that characterizes the climatological history of the Pacific coast is one that has been developing gradually, although erratically, over perhaps as many as 100 million years. Therefore, during this time plants have been gradually adapting to these altered moisture conditions; those that did not adapt either became extinct or persist only in areas where the rainfall is sufficiently high to support them. For example, Catalina ironwood (*Lyonothamnus floribundus,* Rosaceae) was once present on the mainland of California but presumably became extinct there because of its inability to tolerate the increasingly dry climatic conditions. As a consequence, it now persists as an endemic relict species of the Channel Islands.

Likewise, some of the pine species in the Closed-Cone Pine Forest once were also more widely distributed, and these are barely persisting in isolated pockets along the cool and relatively moist Pacific coast. Evidence exists that the increasing aridity of the California climate has altered the composition of some plant communities that we consider to be characteristic of the contemporary climate. For example, Chaparral was probably once more widespread than it now is and also contained a larger number of species of shrubs than it now does. Also, areas existed where the chaparral contained some trees and also some of the thorn-scrub plants that are now found only to the south of the present range of Chaparral. Genera

Plate 161. Catalina ironwood *(Lyonothamnus floribundus)* once grew on the mainland, but conditions have become drier, and it persists today only as a relictual species on the Channel Islands off the coast of southern California.

such as acacia *(Acacia)* and ocotillo *(Fouquieria)* once were components of Chaparral, but now these occur in another plant community to the south (pl. 161).

Uplift of the mountain ranges had an important effect in creating new habitats because of the cooler climates that prevail in upland areas and because of the increased rain- or snowfall on the western slopes of the mountains. The Montane Forest and the Subalpine Forest plant communities both occupy habitats that were not present before the uplift of the mountains in the Pliocene. However, most of the genera of trees present in both of these plant communities were also present in the Miocene Arcto-Tertiary geoflora and are likely derived from these species. The plant species present in the Alpine Fell-field plant community were not derived from precursors present in the forest communities. Some of these species undoubtedly migrated into their present habitats from similar habitats far to the north. As a consequence, some species in these fell-fields are related to those presently widespread in arctic regions. A second source of derivation of these high-altitude plants is from the adjacent deserts; some of the genera of the fell-fields (such as buckwheat [*Eriogonum* spp.]) fall into this category. It is not surprising that this desert derivation has occurred, because the fell-field climate is virtually that of a desert, albeit one at a very high altitude.

Plate 162. Flannelbush (*Fremontodendron* spp.), in the tropical family Sterculiaceae, is probably a remnant representative of the Neotropical Tertiary geoflora.

The three geofloras discussed here were complexes of several distinctive plant communities, and their composition and ranges fluctuated considerably over long periods of geological time. On the average, however, the two geofloras that have made major contributions to the contemporary flora of California were very different ones, adapted to different average climatic regimes. As a consequence, the plant communities derived from these two geofloras have sorted themselves out into a fairly well marked pattern: the Arcto-Tertiary derivatives currently inhabit the mountainous areas and the northern part of the state, both of which are comparatively cool and well watered; the Madro-Tertiary derivatives occupy the cismontane and the southern portion of the state including the deserts. Although seemingly little direct heritage of the Neotropical Tertiary geoflora appears in contemporary California, it is likely that some of the California representatives of essentially tropical families may be derived from this third geoflora. These would include California bay (*Umbellularia californica,* Lauraceae), flannelbush (*Fremontodendron* spp., Sterculiaceae), and California fan palm *(Washingtonia filifera)* (pls. 162, 163).

Plate 163. The California fan palm *(Washingtonia filifera)* is a relictual species from another tropical family, Palmaceae. It is occasionally found in moist, somewhat alkaline areas in desert canyons or along desert streams.

Fossil History of Coast Redwood

The coast redwood has an interesting fossil history that was not fully understood until quite recently. Publications dealing with the fossil plants of the Northern Hemisphere have statements regarding the wide distribution of "redwoods" in the geological past. These redwoods in the fossil record are widely distributed around the Northern Hemisphere. For many years they were all referred to the genus *Sequoia,* and most of them were considered to represent very close relatives of the modern coast redwood. In the early 1940s, however, a Japanese botanist noted that the arrangement of leaves and the cone structure of some of the fossil remains were different from those of coast redwood. He named the fossils with opposite leaves and stalked cones as a new genus, *Metasequoia.* Reexamination of the fossil redwoods indicated that *Metasequoia* occurred in North America, Greenland, and Asia, although these fossils had previously been referred to *Sequoia.*

Fossil examples of *Sequoia* are known from western Europe, Greenland, portions of Asia, and also from North America.

In the mid 1940s a Chinese forester reported the occurrence of an unusual and previously unknown conifer growing in the province of Szechuan, central China. Subsequent examination of branches of this tree revealed that it was a living example of *Metasequoia!* The living specimens were named *M. glyptostroboides* (the specific name after *Glyptostrobus,* a genus of Taxodiaceae related to the redwoods). A few small groves of *M. glyptostroboides* were later located in the vicinity of the originally discovered tree. The seed that was collected and sent to the United States all originated from this tree, which had survived because it was venerated and protected by local people. Named the dawn redwood, it is now widely planted as an ornamental tree and is able to tolerate a wide variety of ecological conditions. Unlike coast redwood, dawn redwood is deciduous (like its relatives in the bald cypress genus *[Taxodium]*).

The fossil history of coast redwood goes back several million years and indicates that this species and its immediate ancestors were once scattered over much of the Northern Hemisphere. Climatic changes in the relatively recent geological past have resulted in the gradual extinction of *Sequoia* over much of its former range, with the result that *S. sempervirens* is now restricted to the outer Coast Ranges from extreme southern Oregon southward to Santa Cruz County (more or less continuously), with a few outlying groves in Monterey County. The rainfall in this coastal strip is variable, ranging from a high of over 100 inches annually in the north to a low of 35 inches in the south. However, because coast redwood is generally restricted to the coastal fog zone, transpiration during the dry summers is much reduced by the effect of the fog. In addition, as much as 10 inches of added precipitation per year has been recorded as a result of fog drip under the trees, with the result that coast redwood is able to exert a favorable influence over its immediate environment by adding to the effective precipitation.

Plate 164. The fossil redwood (*Metasequoia glyptostroboides*) today is native to China, where it grows to large sizes near streams in the remote Xiang Valley in Hubei Province.

The phase of North Coastal Forest occupied by coast redwood is esthetically very pleasing but rather monotonous botanically. Rather few plant species are associated with coast redwood; the forest floor under these gigantic trees is remarkably uniform in terms of the few herbs that grow there. One finds sword fern (*Polystichum munitum*), redwood sorrel (*Oxalis oregana*), inside-out flower (*Vancouveria parviflora*), and the slightly woody, trailing saxifrage modesty (*Whipplea modesta*). Characteristic shrubs include California or evergreen huckleberry (*Vaccinium ovatum*), California rose bay (*Rhododendron macrophyllum*), salal (*Gaultheria shallon*), and waxmyrtle (*Myrica californica*). In some areas, coast redwood coexists with California bay (*Umbellularia californica*), Douglas-fir (*Pseudotsuga menziesii* var. *menziesii*), and tan-oak (*Lithocarpus densiflorus*). However, these trees are not very successful competitors with coast redwood, for reasons that are discussed below.

The fossil history of coast redwood suggests that it has

Plate 165. This large fossil redwood grows in the Chinese village of Xiashe in the Xiang Valley and is a favorite meeting place.

grown with its present major plant associates or their ancestors for some time. Some years ago, Ralph Chaney, of the Department of Paleontology at the University of California, Berkeley, examined the fossil flora from deposits near Bridge Creek in the John Day River basin of north-central Oregon. This fossil deposit dates from the Miocene and represents an assemblage of fossil plants that grew together in that part of Oregon between 15 and 20 million years ago. The present xerophytic vegetation of the Bridge Creek area is a very different one from that present in the Miocene. Chaney identified almost 21,000 individual fossil remains from the Bridge Creek deposit. Fragments of coast redwood or its Miocene counterpart were common in these remains. Then Chaney scooped up and catalogued the plant fragments that had been deposited in recent times in the bed of a stream running through Muir Woods in Marin County, an area occupied by a modern coast redwood forest. Table 10 compares the composition of the Miocene redwood forest in Oregon and the modern coast redwood forest in Marin County.

In table 10, the column on the left gives the name of the four tree species that are most commonly encountered in the bed of the Muir Woods stream as leaf, twig, or cone fragments. The proportion of the plant remains that is made up by each

TABLE 10. Modern and Miocene Redwood Forests

MUIR WOODS	Frequency (in percent)	BRIDGE CREEK	Frequency (in percent)
Sequoia sempervirens	39	S. langsdorfii	15
Alnus rubra	27	A. carpinoides	54
Lithocarpus densiflorus	5	Quercus consimilis	9
Umbellularia californica	13	Umbellularia sp.	9
Total	84	Total	87

of them is also given. That is, 39 percent of the fragments
found in the Muir Woods stream are coast redwood twigs,
leaves, and cones. The column on the right gives the figures for
the four most common woody species encountered in the
Miocene Bridge Creek flora. The binomials given in this right-
hand column may be unfamiliar ones, but they are the names
that are given to the fossil counterparts of the species listed on
the left. That is, *S. langsdorfii* is the Bridge Creek counterpart
of *S. sempervirens; Quercus consimilis* is the counterpart of the
modern *Lithocarpus densiflora.* The figures for each of the four
species are somewhat different between the Miocene representatives and the modern Redwood Forest counterparts, although the total figures for the four species at each time period are similar (84 percent versus 87 percent). Because we are
dealing with the representation of plants that grew in two
widely separated areas at time periods that are separated by
15 or 20 million years, it is remarkable that there is so strong
a similarity between the species composition of the Miocene
redwood forest and the modern one. It would seem that coast
redwood and its woody associates have had an amazingly long
and relatively consistent association over many millions of
years. It is probable that this is also the case for a number of
other vegetation types in California. Some—such as the
Closed-Cone Pine Forest or segments of the North Coastal
Forest (as exemplified by the coast redwood forest)—are very
old and conservative vegetation types.

In less than a century, 89 years to be exact, from the year 1790 until the close of the period of the Great Surveys in 1879, the trans-Mississippi West changed from an unknown and unmapped wilderness belonging to England, France, Spain, and later Mexico, to a settled part of the United States. During these years, and certainly early in this period, when the country was unsettled and the wilderness dangerous, plant collections for both botanical and horticultural purposes were made in association with exploring expeditions, pioneer settlements, early commerce such as fur trading, and military movements.

The early history of the botanical exploration of California is intimately associated with the botanical exploration of the entire West. Many early expeditions by sea visited not only California but other areas of the Pacific coast of North America as well. Later, overland expeditions from the eastern United States aimed for California as their goal and collected plant specimens on the way. Because of this, much of the following discussion is concerned with the American West, and not with California alone.

The activities of the plant collectors were often associated with historical events. However, because it was the enthusiasm and energy of the individual plant collectors that gave them the needed impetus for carrying on against many obstacles, their accomplishments and the plants that they made known are related here with only casual mention of the historical events.

Early Explorers

Four early expeditions or voyages of discovery from Europe, usually referred to by the names of their commanders, Laperouse, Malaspina, Vancouver, and Kotzebue, set the stage for later individual collectors sent out for the purpose of bringing back to Europe some of the new and unusual plants from the Pacific coast of North America. The individual collectors including Douglas, Coulter, Hartweg, Jeffrey, and Lobb first brought to Europe many western American plants, which are still grown there. The period of their activities, the second quarter of the nineteenth century, has been called the Golden Age of Horticultural Exploration in the American West. During this period, European botanists including William Jackson Hooker (earlier of the University of Glasgow and later the first director of the Royal Botanical Gardens at Kew) and Augustin Pyrame DeCandolle (director of the herbarium and botanical garden in Geneva) worked on the scientific collections brought from North America to Europe by these early collectors.

Information brought back to Europe from the third and last voyage of Captain Cook influenced the formation of the ill-fated Laperouse expedition. It was shipwrecked and did not return, and a large collection of plants was lost with it. In August 1785, the French navy sent out a well-equipped expedition under the command of Jean Francois Galaup de Laperouse to circumnavigate the globe. There were two vessels, the *Boussole* and the *Astrolabe,* and a scientific staff of 17, which included a botanist-gardener, Collignon. In mid-September of 1786, the expedition visited the Spanish mission settlement at Monterey, California. The Spaniards were cordial and helpful, and Laperouse wrote that they reciprocated with gifts, among which were some potatoes from Chile. This probably represents the first introduction of the South American tubers to the Pacific coast of North America. Collignon made a collection of a few plants and seeds from Monterey, which he shipped to France before the expedition proceeded. Among these was seed of the rose red sand-verbena. From this seed a plant was grown at the Jardin des Plantes in Paris, which the French botanist Lamarck named *Abronia umbellata.* This was the first plant from California to be grown in the Old World, and also the first one from western North America to be described and named according to Linnean taxonomic rules. The name persists to this day.

A Spanish voyage of discovery under the command of

Alexandro Malaspina left Spain in July 1787. There were two vessels, the *Descubierta* and the *Atrevida,* and a staff of six, including two botanists, Luis Nee and Tadeo (Thaddeus) Haenke. One of its objectives was to search for an oceanic connection across northern North America. The summer of 1791 was spent along the coast of Alaska and southward looking unsuccessfully for the mythical northwest passage. They eventually reached Monterey Bay in California in September, where they were received cordially by their fellow countrymen and spent several days. While in Monterey, Haenke made a collection of plants that included mahonia *(Berberis [Mahonia] pinnata),* California-fuchsia *(Zauschneria californica),* and alkali heath *(Frankenia salina).* Haenke also first collected coast redwood *(Sequoia sempervirens)* in 1791 while in the Monterey area. From the Pacific coast the Malaspina expedition proceeded around the world and returned to Spain in 1794.

Haenke's Monterey collections were the earliest made in California and gave him the honor of being the first botanist to visit this state. Luis Nee stayed in Mexico while the expedition traveled northward along the Pacific coast in 1791. We are certain that he did not visit California, although in 1801 he published in a scientific journal in Madrid the first names and descriptions of two oaks from California, California live oak *(Quercus agrifolia)* and California valley oak *(Q. lobata).*

Two British expeditions visited the Pacific coast of North America in the late 1780s and early 1790s. The first, actually for the purpose of fur trading, was under the command of Captain Colnett on the *Prince of Wales,* and although its accomplishments in the field of natural history were small, its surgeon was Archibald Menzies. The *Prince of Wales* arrived at Nootka, in what is now Alaska, in July 1787, and there Menzies found the flowering currant *(Ribes sanguineum),* a rose *(Rosa nutkana),* and a wild raspberry *(Rubus nutkanus).*

After his return to England, Menzies was appointed by the British government to be the naturalist to accompany Captain George Vancouver on the *Discovery.* Menzies was given careful instructions by Sir Joseph Banks for the investigation of the natural history of all countries visited. In April 1792 Menzies was back on the Pacific coast, landing at Port Discovery in May, where a wild valerian growing on the beach attracted his attention. For three years the *Discovery* spent winters in the Sandwich Islands (now Hawaii), returning each spring to the Pacific coast of North America. Menzies collected about 300 species on the Pacific coast and was the first to observe many trees such as California laurel or Oregon myrtle *(Umbellularia californica)*, grand fir *(Abies grandis)*, bigleaf maple *(Acer macrophyllum)*, madrone *(Arbutus menziesii)*, Nootka cypress or Alaska-cedar *(Cupressus nootkatensis)*, California wax-myrtle *(Myrica californica)*, Sitka spruce *(Picea sitchensis)*, Douglas-fir *(Pseudotsuga menziesii* var. *menziesii)*, and California-holly or toyon *(Heteromeles arbutifolia)*.

Early in the nineteenth century the Russian government sent out a well-equipped expedition that visited the Pacific coast. Under the command of a young lieutenant in the Russian navy, Otto von Kotzebue, the vessel called the *Rurik* sailed in 1815 on a voyage of discovery that lasted three years. Among the scientific staff were the naturalist Adelbert von Chamisso (1781–1838) who was the principal scientist aboard the Rurik and who had fled France from the French Revolution, a young surgeon Johann Friedrich Eschscholtz (1793–1831) who Chamisso described as "almost reserved, but as true and noble as gold" (Geary 1979, 4), and the draftsman Louis Choris (1795–1828) (pl. 166).

In California, particularly around San Francisco, many plants were collected for the first time by Chamisso and Eschscholtz, and of all the important discoveries and contributions resulting from this expedition, none were more important than those in botany. Among the 10,000 to 12,000 plants that they collected and the 82 plants that they described, the best known is surely the California-poppy, which Chamisso named *Eschscholzia californica* in honor of his friend on the voyage. In addition, Chamisso named more than 30 new

Plate 166. The type specimen (the single plant for which a species name is given, thereafter used for comparative purposes) of the California-poppy (*Eschscholzia californica*) is located in the Herbarium in St. Petersburg, Russia. (From Parsons 1907.)

species collected in San Francisco, and in 1829–1833 he published a five-volume account of the voyage of the *Rurik* around the world (pl. 167).

Early Plant Collectors

David Douglas (1799–1834), a native of Scotland, was the first of several collectors sent out from England to the Pacific coast. Douglas was trained as a gardener, and it was at the Botanical Garden in Glasgow that he came under the influence of Dr. William Jackson Hooker. Through the recommendation of Hooker to Joseph Sabine, Honorary Secretary of the Horticultural Society of London (which in 1866 became the Royal Horticultural Society), Douglas was sent by the Society to North America. Douglas was instructed to collect living plant material to be used in the gardens of the British Isles, and dried specimens to be used by botanists, particularly Hooker who was working on a flora of North America.

Plate 167. Chamisso and Eschscholtz, while staying at the Presidio in San Francisco for a month in 1816, described the flora as "poor though offering much novelty to the botanist." (Courtesy of the Jepson Herbarium.)

Douglas left England by ship, the *William and Ann*, July 26, 1824, for the Pacific Northwest. The ship's surgeon, Dr. John Scouler (for whom the Pacific coast leather fern *[Polypodium scouleri]* was named), was already known to Douglas because the two shared common interests. Before leaving England, Douglas had become familiar with the plants collected by Menzies and later by Lewis and Clark in the region of Fort Vancouver and the Columbia River, and therefore he was somewhat prepared for the trees and other plants that he saw along the 90 miles from the mouth of the Columbia to Fort Vancouver, a Hudson's Bay trading post (on the opposite side of the river from today's Portland, Oregon). Douglas used Fort Vancouver as his base for two years and received help and courtesies from the company's officers. During this time he found the Douglas-fir and the madrone *(Arbutus menziesii),* already seen by Menzies, and a shrub that the natives called *salal (Gaultheria shallon).*

Douglas returned to England in 1827, and in 1829, again

under the auspices of the London Horticultural Society, he left for a second trip. Toward the end of 1830, he arrived in Monterey, California, where he made his headquarters for two years, collecting over 800 species in many parts of the state. Toward the end of 1833 he sailed for the Sandwich Islands where he met his death on July 13, 1834, through an unfortunate accident.

Douglas's accomplishments were so great that he overshadowed those who followed him. Among the many plants that he collected, some of which he introduced to English gardens, are several firs *(Abies grandis, A. lasiocarpa, A. nobilis, A. amabilis)*, the vine maple *(Acer circinatum)*, one of the serviceberries *(Amelanchier alnifolia)* and two that had been earlier discovered by Menzies, the Sitka spruce *(Picea sitchensis)*, and the California wax-myrtle *(Myrica californica)*.

Dr. Thomas Coulter (1793–1843), a native of Ireland, was one of the important early botanical explorers in North America, particularly in California and Mexico. He studied in Dublin and Paris and then went to Geneva, where he came under the influence of DeCandolle, to whom he later sent his botanical collections. Coulter went to Mexico in 1824 as physician to a mining company. It was from Mexico in 1828 that he sent a collection of cacti to Trinity College, in Dublin, for its botanical garden. These may represent his only horticultural introductions. In November 1831 he arrived in Monterey, where he met Douglas. The two botanists explored and collected together during the following winter and spring. Among Coulter's many discoveries, some of which were named for him, are the Coulter pine *(Pinus coulteri)*, which is remarkable for its large, heavy cones, and the matilija-poppy *(Romneya coulteri)*, a handsome, large, white-flowered poppy occasionally seen in gardens.

The Horticultural Society in London, which had sponsored Douglas, sent Karl Theodore Hartweg (1812–1871) first to Mexico and then to California. The society specifically requested Hartweg to look for the Zauschneria and the "evergreen Castanea"; the latter probably refers to the giant chinquapin *(Chrysolepis chrysophylla)* discovered in 1831 by Douglas. At Monterey, Hartweg collected the first specimen of the endemic Monterey cypress *(Cupressus macrocarpa)* at Cypress Point near Monterey, which resulted in its introduction to England, although it had first been mentioned by Laperouse and seen but not mentioned as recorded in Douglas's field notes. The coast redwood *(Sequoia sempervirens),* which had been seen earlier by Menzies and Douglas, was introduced into England by Hartweg. The canyon oak or maul oak *(Quercus chrysolepis)* and the knobcone pine *(Pinus attenuata)* were discovered by Hartweg while he was at Monterey, and the California black oak or Kellogg oak *(Q. kelloggii)* while he was near Sonoma. He found California fuchsia *(Zauschneria californica),* first collected by Haenke in 1791, as well as the giant chinquapin, and sent seeds of both to England. However, Hartweg's introductions were probably of lesser importance than his collections of dried botanical specimens, which, at least those from California, were worked on and published by George Bentham, one of the leading English botanists of the day. Bentham's enumeration of Hartweg's plants in the publication titled *Plantae Hartwegianae* (McKelvey 1991) was one of the important early publications dealing with California plants and included about 400 species, about 80 of which were new.

The widespread interest in Douglas's plant introductions to the British Isles led to the formation in 1850 of an organization in Scotland known as the Oregon Botanical Association, or simply as the Oregon Expedition, which engaged John Jeffrey in 1850 to go to western North America for three years to bring back seeds to be divided among the subscribers. Early in June 1850, Jeffrey sailed from England for Hudson Bay and, in May 1851, after crossing the continent reached southern British Columbia. He explored there and in northern Washington, and among his introductions from that area were the whitebark pine *(Pinus albicaulis)* and the mountain hemlock

(Tsuga mertensiana). The following year he went south to Washington, Oregon, and northern California, where he discovered the foxtail pine *(P. balfouriana)* and the Jeffrey pine *(P. jeffreyi).* Traveling south and east to the Sacramento Valley and the central Sierra Nevada (where he spent the summer of 1853), he arrived in San Francisco in October. He remained in San Francisco and vicinity until January 1854, then went south to San Diego and from there to Yuma, Arizona. Yuma was the last place he was heard from, and what happened to him still remains a mystery. Jeffrey collected over 400 species of plants and sent home seeds of many of them.

During the nineteenth century and the early part of the twentieth century, the leading British nursery firm was that of Messrs. Veitch of Exeter and Chelsea. It was notable for its many introductions from America and Asia that became well-known garden plants, and for having trained many fine gardeners. The firm of Veitch sent William Lobb (1809–1863) to North America as one of their collectors. From 1849 to 1853 he was on the Pacific coast where he explored and collected in California and Oregon. He arrived in San Francisco in the summer of 1849, a year and a half after the discovery of gold in California, but he had not come for gold.

During his first season of collecting, he visited the Santa Lucia Mountains where he found the Santa Lucia fir or bristlecone fir as it is sometimes called *(Abies bracteata,* synonym: *A. venusta),* which had been discovered in 1831 by Thomas Coulter. Lobb also introduced from California several other trees, the western red-cedar *(Thuja plicata),* the Douglas-fir, and the noble fir *(A. procera,* synonym: *A. nobilis),* all of which had been seen earlier by Douglas. However, the introduction that gave him his greatest fame was the giant sequoia or bigtree *(Sequoiadendron giganteum,* synonym: *Sequoia gigantea).* Lobb was not the discoverer of this tree but learned of it through Dr. Albert Kellogg at a meeting of the California Academy of Natural Sciences, and according to Sargent "immediately started for the Sierra Nevada, where he secured specimens and two living trees, which he carried to England on the first steamer leaving San Francisco" (McKelvey 1991, 922), thus heralding the exporting of one of the world's largest, oldest, and most famous trees to England, where it was described and is known today as *Wellingtonia gigantea.*

The First American Explorers

The earliest expeditions to western North America were European in origin, their results were published in Europe, and the specimens collected by their naturalists were deposited in European cities. It was not until after the Louisiana Purchase in 1803 that the first transcontinental expedition was sent out by the government of the United States. This expedition, initiated by President Thomas Jefferson in 1803 when he obtained from Congress the necessary funds, had as its primary objective the exploration of the Missouri River and related streams with a view toward identifying the most direct and practicable water communication across the continent for purposes of commerce. The expedition was well equipped with 25 men under the two leaders, Meriwether Lewis and William Clark. Both leaders had previous military experience and were expert woodsmen, but neither had had any scientific training. However, before leaving, Lewis visited Benjamin Smith Barton, a leading botanist of the day, in Philadelphia, for instructions in botany, zoology, and Indian history. The expedition left St. Louis in the spring of 1804. It traced the course of the Missouri River, crossed the Rocky Mountains to the Clearwater River in northern Idaho, and finally descended the Columbia River to the Pacific. Then, turning eastward, they reached St. Louis in September 1806, after traveling hundreds of miles through unexplored territory.

Considering the vicissitudes of travel, the expedition made noteworthy contributions in many fields. They collected both seeds and botanical specimens. Today, the Philadelphia Academy of Natural Sciences has about 200 herbarium specimens from them. Many represented new species because, except for Oregon where Menzies had been earlier, they traveled through a vast region not previously explored scientifically. Although their collections represented only a few of the plants that they saw, their journals mention for the first time many of the plants later collected by others.

After the expedition, the plant collections were sent to Philadelphia where they were studied by Frederick Pursh, who was preparing a flora—which in this usage means a treatise on the plants of a region—of North America. Bernard McMahon, a nurseryman in Philadelphia, asked President Jefferson for seeds collected on the expedition. Jefferson generously gave McMahon the whole of his own share, and from these, McMahon grew for the first time some garden plants now well known, such as the Oregon-grape *(Berberis aquifolium)* and snowberry *(Symphoricarpos rivularis),* which was introduced into England about 1817. The bitter-root *(Lewisia rediviva)* was grown by McMahon from a root removed from a dried herbarium specimen that led Pursh to write of it "This elegant plant would be a very desirable addition to the ornamental perennials, since, if once introduced, it would be easily kept and propagated" (McKelvey 1991, 82). Some plants named by Pursh that we know as ornamentals are golden currant *(Ribes aureum),* salmonberry *(Rubus spectabilis),* snow-on-the-mountain *(Euphorbia marginata),* vine maple *(Acer circinatum),* and bigleaf or Oregon maple *(Acer macrophyllum).*

Thomas Nuttall (1786–1859), born in Yorkshire, came from England to Philadelphia in 1808. There he studied botany under Benjamin Smith Barton, and later he traveled along the east coast, collecting and becoming acquainted with plants of the region. Nuttall lived in the United States for over 30 years, during which he made three journeys to the west and made extensive plant collections. His great contribution to botany, aside from his collections, was the publication of his "Genera of North American Plants" (Nuttall 1841), a classic among early North American botanical works.

Nuttall, on his first journey, accompanied the fur-trading expedition led by Wilson Price Hunt, which was sent out by John Jacob Astor and was known as the Astorian Expedition. Nuttall traveled to St. Louis to join the expedition in March of 1811 and proceeded up the Missouri River, eventually reaching the country of the Mandan Indians in North Dakota. John Bradbury (1768–1823), a Scottish naturalist and botanist who came to North America to collect seeds and natural history objects for the botanical garden in Liverpool, was also a member of this expedition. Nuttall and Bradbury were together during a part of the expedition's travels.

Nuttall returned to St. Louis late in 1811, and from there went to New Orleans from where he sailed for England just before the war of 1812. He took with him seeds, roots, and bulbs of plants, much of which went to Fraser's Nursery in London. This nursery was so successful in growing plants from Nuttall's materials that in 1813 a small catalogue was issued with the title *A Catalogue of New and Interesting Plants, Collected in Upper Louisiana, and Principally on the River Missourie, North America, For Sale at Messrs. Fraser's Nursery, Sloane Square, King's Road, Chelsea, London.* It listed 89 species, many of which were new. It is significant to note that although Nuttall is usually thought of as a scientific collector, he made horticultural collections as well.

The first maritime expedition sent out by the United States to aid commerce and navigation was the United States Exploring Expedition of 1838–1842, under the command of Captain Charles Wilkes of the U.S. Navy. It visited the Pacific coast in 1841. William Dunlop Brackenridge (1810–1893) served as naturalist and horticulturist on the expedition's staff and collected botanical specimens in the Pacific coast states. These, as part of the herbarium material from the expedition, were included in botanical parts of the expedition's reports. Probably the most remarkable flowering plant found by Brackenridge was the California pitcher plant *(Darlingtonia californica)*, collected in marshes at the headwaters of the

Sacramento River near Mount Shasta. (It is an insectivorous, or "fly catching," plant.)

Another contribution made by Brackenridge, and one often overlooked, is his living plant collection, which led to the establishment of the garden of the National Institute. The National Institute (the forerunner of the Smithsonian Institution) had been founded to take care of the materials collected by the Wilkes Expedition, and the garden established to care for Brackenridge's living plants was the first attempt to establish in the United States a national arboretum and botanical garden. It was nearly a 100 years before the establishment of the present United States National Arboretum of Washington, D.C.

Following the Lewis and Clark Expedition, it was nearly 20 years before another American overland expedition set out to explore the vast area west of the Mississippi River. Secretary of War J.C. Calhoun, in 1819–1820, sent out the Rocky Mountain Expedition under Major Stephen H. Long (1784–1864) to determine the western boundaries of the Louisiana Purchase and the adjoining Spanish territory. This expedition had a scientific staff including a botanist, a zoologist, a geologist, an artist, and a topographer. The botanist was Edwin James (1797–1861) who had studied botany under both John Torrey and Amos Eaton. James was the first botanist to collect in the central Rocky Mountains, and many of the plants he collected were new to science. He turned his collections over to Torrey, who published an account of them. One of James's discoveries was the limber pine *(P. flexilis)*, which was widespread in the mountains of western North America and James himself named and described in his account of the expedition.

Nearly 40 years after the Lewis and Clark Expedition, the U.S. government sent a second expedition west to the Pacific coast. By 1840, Americans were moving westward beyond the Mississippi River, first to the Pacific Northwest and later to California, particularly after the discovery of gold in 1848. The routes to the west were unmapped and were passed by word of mouth from those who had gone before, mostly courageous frontiersmen, trappers, and Indian guides. In order to gain information about the west, the government sent out three expeditions under John Charles Fremont (1813–1890) between 1842 and 1846. Fremont's career as an explorer began when he became a second lieutenant in the United States Topographical Corps and assisted with surveys made by the Corps in the eastern United States. This experience, which developed his zeal for exploration and his ability at map making, his meeting with Senator Thomas Hart Benton of Missouri who was an advocate of westward expansion, and his marriage to Benton's daughter all contributed to his appointment as leader of the three expeditions during the early and mid-1840s.

Fremont explored and mapped routes to the west in the short space of a few years, considering the difficulties encountered. He mapped two routes between the Great Salt Lake and California, one into the northern part and a second into the southern part of California. These routes were used by the Mormons in their westward migration to Utah in 1847, and later, by those who came to California after the discovery of gold.

Fremont was not a botanist by training, but because of his interest in the subject, he made collections, some of which were later worked on by Torrey. In the Sierra Nevada of California he discovered two of California's choicest ornamental shrubs, Fremontia or flannelbush (*Fremontodendron californicum*) and tree-anemone *(Carpenteria californica)*, and two trees, interior live oak *(Quercus wislizenii)* and incense-cedar *(Calocedrus decurrens)*. In addition he discovered two other trees, the single-needle pine *(P. monophylla)*, near Cajon Pass in southern California (San Bernardino County), and Fremont cottonwood *(Populus fremontii)*, in the foothills along Cottonwood Creek in the northern Sacramento Valley (Tehama County).

During the decade of 1850 to 1860 the U.S. government sent many survey groups to the west. Among these were the

Plate 168. John Fremont was a controversial character whose interest in plants ended when he entered California and became involved in politics and silver mining.

United States and Mexican Boundary Surveys and the Pacific Railroad Surveys. Accompanying these surveys were geologists, geographers, zoologists, and botanists, who through reports of the various surveys made valuable and often the first contributions to the knowledge of the vast unknown territory through which they had traveled.

Charles Christopher Parry (1823–1890) served with the United States and Mexican Boundary Survey from 1849 to 1852, in that segment of the survey that was in the charge of Major William H. Emory (1811–1877). While with the survey, Parry traveled between Texas and southern California, collecting plants and observing the vegetation. After 1852 he visited other parts of the west. Because of his interest in the alpine vegetation of the central Rocky Mountains, he spent many summer months in Colorado collecting plants found earlier by Edwin James. He made several trips to California where he collected plants in the chaparral, including manzanitas *(Arctostaphylos spp.)* and California-lilacs *(Ceanothus spp.)*. Among the many plants that he discovered are the Tor-

Plate 169. Charles Parry left his vast collection of 30,000 plant specimens, collected primarily on surveys over a period of 48 years, to the "botanical room" at the Academy of Natural Sciences in Davenport, Iowa.

rey pine *(Pinus torreyana)*, Parry pinyon pine *(P. quadrifolia)*, western bristlecone pine *(P. longaeva)*, California black walnut *(Juglans californica)*, Engelmann spruce *(Picea engelmannii)*, lemon lily *(Lilium parryi)*, and the Ensenada buckeye *(Aesculus parryi)* (pl. 169).

Surveys for Railroads

The Pacific Railroad Survey, along the 35th Parallel from western Texas to southern California in 1853 and 1854, was in the charge of Lieutenant Amiel Weeks Whipple. John Milton Bigelow (1804–1878) accompanied this expedition as surgeon and botanist and probably collected most of the plants of the survey. After the termination of the survey in February 1854 near Los Angeles, Bigelow traveled on his own northward to San Francisco and east to the Sierra Nevada. He wrote a botanical narrative of the route of Lieutenant Whipple's expedition and an account of the valuable and remarkable forest trees of California, both of which are published in the report of this survey. *Clematis bigelovii* and *Aster bigelovii* were discovered by Bigelow in New Mexico. His best-known discovery, however, is the jumping cholla or teddy-bear cactus *(Opuntia bigelovii)*, frequently seen on the Sonoran Desert of California, Arizona, and adjacent Mexico.

George Thurber (1821–1890), through the influence of his friend John Torrey, was appointed in 1850 to the United States and Mexican Boundary Survey and served for nearly four years as botanist, quartermaster, and commissary. Thurber, as well as Bigelow, was attached to the segment of the survey traveling with John R. Bartlett, U.S. Commissioner of the Boundary Survey. Thurber's plant collections were worked on by Asa Gray at Harvard, who published the new species in his *Plantae Novae Thurberianae* (McKelvey 1991, 911). Among these are several well-known shrubs from the southwest, including the New Mexican locust *(Robinia neomexicana),* the desert smoke-tree *(Dalea spinosa),* and the crucifixion-thorn *(Holocantha emoryi).*

The last of the government surveys, usually referred to as the Great Surveys, led by J. W. Powell, F. V. Hayden, Clarence King, and George M. Wheeler, completed their work in 1879. this was the end an era of American exploration in the west that had begun with the departure of the Lewis and Clark Expedition into an unexplored wilderness. At the close of the Great Surveys, the wilderness had been explored, mapped, and partially settled, the major geographical and geological features were at least partially known, and many of the plants had been described and their distributions recorded.

The history of botanical exploration in the west, which began with European explorers who took their collections home, was continued by Americans whose collections remained in the United States. During the middle years of the nineteenth century, the period of westward expansion when military and scientific surveys of the resources of the west were taking place, three American botanists worked on the collections made by these surveys and by individual collectors who came west. The names of these three men have already appeared on these pages: John Torrey (1796–1873) of Columbia College in New York, Asa Gray (1810–1883) of Harvard University in Cambridge, and George Engelmann (1808–1884) of St. Louis. For about half a century, these three dominated the

Plate 170. John Torrey, for whom the Torrey pine *(Pinus torreyana)* is named, named many of the plants John Fremont collected during his topographical surveys and had an important influence on Charles Parry.

Plate 171. Asa Gray was a foremost botanist at Harvard during the mid 1800s, where many plant collectors sent their specimens to be studied and named.

American botanical scene. They kept in touch with those in the field, encouraged new collectors to go out, recommended botanists and naturalists to the leaders of surveys, corresponded and collaborated with each other, and published new genera and species of plants in numerous scientific journals and reports. They themselves had little opportunity to collect, but their work at home on the collections from those in the field made the botany of the West known and laid the foundation for the more detailed work that came later (pls. 170, 171).

Botany in California Since Statehood

California entered the Union in 1850, a year after the great goldrush began. One of the most important midnineteenth century influences in the development of a knowledge of the flora of California was the California Academy of Sciences in San Francisco, founded in 1853. One of the founders of the

Academy was Albert Kellogg, a physician who had a strong interest in botany. Other natural historians associated with the Academy were H. H. Behr, author of several local floras of central California, W. G. W. Harford, G. Eisen, and Katherine Brandegee. Mrs. Brandegee was curator of botany at the Academy from 1883 to 1894, at which time she moved to San Diego. Brandegee was an avid collector, copublisher of the natural history journal *Zoe,* and an important con-

Plate 172. Alice Eastwood dominated the field of botany at the California Academy of Sciences until well into her nineties.

tributor to California botany. Brandegee was succeeded at the Academy in 1894 by Alice Eastwood, whose tenure at the institution extended to 1949. Eastwood collected widely in western North America and considerably augmented the Academy's collections of plants from California. During the fire after the earthquake of 1906, she heroically saved the type specimens at the Academy, an action that earned her a legendary reputation. Eastwood and her colleague J. T. Howell started a journal, *Leaflets of Western Botany,* in 1932. Howell eventually succeeded Eastwood, added about 40,000 collections to the Academy herbarium, published a flora of Marin County, and collaborated with other botanists in several other works dealing with the floristics of various portions of California (pl. 172).

Another institution in the San Francisco Bay area has had an even more prominent influence on the development of botany in the state. This is the University of California at Berkeley, founded in 1868. The first plant taxonomist at Berkeley was E. L. Greene, who was there from 1885 to 1895.

Plate 173. E.L. Greene, the first plant taxonomist at the University of California, Berkeley, published two floras of the Bay region.

Greene was a colorful and controversial individual often at loggerheads with Brandegee. He collected widely in the West, established two botanical journals, and described for the first time a large number of California plant species. In addition, he published two floras of the bay region, one of which is considered the first local manual for any part of California that could be called scholarly. Many subsequent taxonomists have criticized Greene for his excessive taxonomic "splitting," but nevertheless he was a careful observer of variation in flowering plants who made an immeasurable contribution to the knowledge of the flora of the state (pl. 173).

Greene was succeeded at Berkeley by W. L. Jepson, a botanist who dominated the taxonomic scene in the state for many decades and whose influence is still evident. Jepson produced his *Manual of the Flowering Plants of California,* completed in 1925, plus a flora of "western middle" California in 1911. In addition, he initiated a detailed monographic publication *A Flora of California,* parts of which first appeared in 1909 (vol. 1, part 1), whereas the last of the projected five-volume work (vol. 3, part 2) was published in 1943. The work was never completed. Jepson also founded the California Botanical Society in 1913 and served as the first editor of its continuing journal *Madrono* (pl. 174).

At Stanford University, W. R. Dudley collected large numbers of California plants, although he did not publish extensively on the flora of the state. One student of Dudley's, L. R.

Abrams, served on the Stanford faculty for nearly 40 years and published widely on the flora of the western United States. His best known work is the four-volume *Illustrated Flora of the Pacific States,* the final volume of which was produced by R. S. Ferris in 1960. Other important Stanford botanists are J. H. Thomas, who published a flora of the Santa Cruz Mountains of California in 1961, and I. L. Wiggins, who collected over much of western North America and produced a flora of the Sonoran Desert in 1964.

Plate 174. Willis L. Jepson's legacy is well preserved at the Jepson Herbarium, established at the University of California, Berkeley through the terms of his will.

In southern California, the Pomona Herbarium has been a dominant influence on the botanical studies of the state flora. One of the most prolific collectors of western American plants was M. E. Jones, who made about 100,000 plant collections before his death in 1934. Jones was a colorful, cantankerous, and opinionated individual who freely expressed himself in his *Contributions to Western Botany,* a journal he published and mostly handset himself. More recently, P. A. Munz—a faculty member at Pomona College and later director of the Rancho Santa Ana Botanic Garden at Claremont—produced a flora of southern California and the monumental *A California Flora.* This last work, produced in collaboration with D. D. Keck in 1959, and with a supplement added in 1968, served as the standard manual for identifying California plants for over three decades.

In 1993, the Jepson Herbarium at the University of California, Berkeley, published *The Jepson Manual: Higher Plants of California* (Hickman 1993) an ambitious project undertaken by Laurence Heckard, then curator of the Herbarium, and James Hickman, editor. This Jepson manual has 186 authors of generic or family treatments and currently serves as the standard reference for California's flora. In addition, a number of specialized and popular works have been issued that deal with certain areas or habitats of the state. The California Native Plant Society has published seven local floras including ones for Sonoma, Monterey, Butte, and Kern Counties. The California Academy of Sciences is preparing a revision of the Howell's *Marin Flora* (1970). H.L. Mason's (1957) *A Flora of the Marshes of California,* although in need of updating, remains a valuable illustrated work that covers aquatic or semiaquatic plants of the state. The University of California Press publishes books in its Natural History Guide Series that are too numerous to mention but are widely available as paperbacks. They have a wide coverage of various regions of the state and are illustrated, relatively simple in their language, accurate, and inexpensive. Today it is far easier to study and learn the flora of California than it was 200 or 300 years ago!

Present-day California vegetation and flora trace their history back several tens of millions of years into the early Tertiary. Humans have been in California for only a brief period of geologic time, arriving in waves over a 12,000-year span and dispersing along its coastline, along its inland waterways, and into its foothill woodlands. However, humans have been responsible for drastic and rapid alterations in the flora of California that are paralleled in magnitude only by the long-term changes that occurred slowly in response to geological and climatic shifts over past geological eras. Clearing land for agricultural purposes, building of roads and highways, and extensive development of housing and industrial sites have resulted in the destruction or alteration of major areas of California. The introduction of grazing animals such as cattle, sheep, and goats has also altered millions of acres, particularly riparian areas, and has eliminated entire native plant communities. Elimination of predators has resulted in an increasingly large population of native herbivores such as deer and rabbits. The decline of oak woodlands has resulted in part because of heavy grazing pressures. The western concept of land ownership by an individual rather than land stewardship has not worked well for plants, their diversity, or their well-being.

Climate Change

Through a host of human activities that alter the thin shell of atmosphere surrounding the earth, global atmospheric changes are occurring at unprecedented rates. These include climatic change from greenhouse warming, the depletion of a protective ozone layer in the upper atmosphere, and air pollution from industrial wastes. These kinds of change have the potential to alter significantly the present distribution of plants in California and future levels of biodiversity. Air pollution from ozone buildup damages foliage in forests and chaparral areas; acid rain in lakes and streams alters vegetation and animal life. The effects of increased ultraviolet light and climate warming on the biology of individual plant species and on worldwide weather patterns remain to be better understood.

Between 1969 and 1986, North American latitudes experienced a decrease in ozone of 4.7 percent in winter and 3 percent year-round (Jensen, Torn, and Harte 1993). The rate of global warming being predicted, a 2.5 to 10 degree F increase in global average temperature in the next 70 years, is 10 to 40 times faster than any climatic warming the earth has experienced since the last Ice Age (Field 2002). At this rate, plants will have to move north by about five miles per year or uphill at three feet every 45 days to stay in their current climate zone. This is faster than the seeds of most bush and tree species can disperse. Survival of a species will depend on its genetic diversity and its ability to adapt to altering conditions; however, at this rate of climate change, it is extremely likely that many species will not be able to adapt or have suitable space to move to and will become extinct.

Over the past 200 years, much of the California landscape has been transformed into cities, freeways, suburbs, agricultural and grazing lands, or other sorts of developed lands that are essentially devoid of natural vegetation. Approximately 30 million acres of land in California are cultivated or grazed. However, beyond this agricultural conversion of land, the California landscape has been significantly modified by the introduction and rapid spread of nonnative invasive weeds. Some weeds are relatively benign and do not affect the native flora greatly; however, a number of invasive and aggressive weeds have an extensive and negative effect on most plant communities.

Native American Usage of the Land

The changes that the Native Americans brought about in the native flora are not known well. They were, as a group, hunter-gatherers and processed wild foods, plants, and animals. Most

Plate 175. Pinyon pine *(Pinus monophylla)* that grows on the east side of the Sierra Nevada above the Great Basin desert provided food, medicine, and building materials to the Native Americans.

groups were seasonally mobile and moved from one plant community into another. They practiced soil and weed management, coppicing, limited tilling, and burning. Some of the burning practices carried on by several tribes undoubtedly had an important local effect in eradicating certain native species and encouraging others. Because acorns were a staple of their diet, they may have expanded the number of oaks directly by planting acorns and indirectly by limiting the size of the deer population.

The present distribution of the northern California walnut *(Juglans californica* var. *hindsii)* is undoubtedly partly due to the Californian's practice of carrying the edible nuts of this species from place to place. Many individual specimens or small colonies of this rather uncommon tree are located at the sites of former aboriginal campsites in the region to the north and east of San Francisco Bay, although the degree to which the present distribution of this tree has been influenced by the

Plate 176. Honey mesquite *(Prosopis glandulosa* var. *torreyana),* found in desert alluvial flats and washes, was another staple food of the Native Americans.

activities of native tribes is still a matter of contention. A single plant species, valued as a food staple, might also be hewn into a shelter, a garment, or a tool. Pinyon pine *(Pinus monophylla)* that grow on slopes of mountains near the desert provided food (pine nuts rich in fat), medicine, and building materials to Native Americans. Desert tribes ate honey mesquite *(Prosopis glandulosa* var. *torreyana)* as a staple. Pods were dried, and later, pod and seed were made into a coarse meal that contained 30 percent sugar. Native Californians also made extensive use of wild plants such as rushes *(Juncus* spp.) and sedges *(Carex* spp.) for basketry. Many of these baskets were artistic as well as functional. The decline of native cultures was closely tied to the decline of pristine vegetation types such as tule marshes, oak and pinyon woodlands, and montane meadows. Land became fragmented, fenced, grazed, and privately owned. Sadly, most of their ecological knowledge of the land has also been lost with their cultures (pls. 175, 176).

The Impact of Agriculture and Grazing

A combination of factors set the stage for a major vegetation type conversion of vast tracts of land in California to today's annual grasslands. The Spanish importation of large herds of cattle was accompanied by the importation of Mediterranean annual grasses as feed into California. These annual grasses prospered under the heavy grazing regime of the early settlers. Following the gold rush that brought a rapidly expanding population, extensive plowing for crops created prime conditions for weed seed establishment. In the 1860s, a prolonged drought greatly accelerated the weedy invasion by furthering conditions already highly favorable to annual weed seeds. Today, one can still get glimpses of pre-European conditions and native plant assemblages in places where environmental conditions are rigorous and plants have evolved special adaptations to flourish. Some of these places include northern coastal bluffs, mountaintops, forested lands, vernal pools, and salt marshes. In these specialized habitats, few weeds can establish, and native plant communities remain intact. Elsewhere, in less rigorous habitats, many of the native perennial grasses and wildflowers are still present but grow sparsely in and among the annual grasses and weeds that characterize the landscape today.

The California flora evolved for thousands of years under a complex grazing and browsing regime with mastodons, mammoths, horses, camel, and deer all present. Grazers specialize on grasses and other herbaceous plants (forbs), whereas browsers forage on forbs, woody plants, and a few grasses. Heavy grazing leads to the replacement of perennial grasses with annual grasses because the repeated removal and resprouting of stems and leaves of perennial bunch grasses from grazing weakens the plants, giving an advantage to an annual lifestyle of rapid growth followed by early seed-setting. Weakened or dying perennials no longer shade out annuals, which rapidly take over habitat space. Today, 99 percent of all

California grasslands are covered with nonnative annual grasses. Restoring native perennial grasslands is difficult because of the immense seed bank annual weeds create and the diverse set of plant forms and growth habits that block perennial seedling emergence.

Considerable controversy exists as to proper stewardship of public lands with regard to proper levels of grazing. Overgrazing eliminates perennial grasses and most wildflowers, whereas eliminating all livestock results in a dominance of nonnative annuals such as ripgut *(Bromus diandrus)* and wild oats *(Avena* spp.), a suppression of native wildflowers and grasses, and often an increased fire hazard. Limited, properly timed grazing and some controlled burning to reduce the level of litter and the vast annual grass seed bank appear to be beneficial for wildflowers and native bunchgrasses. The parameters for proper grazing levels vary from site to site and from soil type to soil type. General rules are difficult to establish, and managers often lack the information they need to get "best results" and to withstand opposition by interested groups who oppose one direction for management or another. Much research is needed along with cooperative efforts with land managers to restore perennial grasslands and the native wildflowers for which California is famous.

The Impact of Invasive Weeds

About one-quarter of the present flora of the state consists of plant species, mostly undesirable and invasive, that have been introduced into the state from elsewhere in the last 200 years. Most of these plants are considered to be weeds. Weeds possess several characteristics that enable them to survive in disturbed habitats, and indeed, a number of weed species do grow only in disturbed areas. Weeds, like cultivated crops, usually require human-controlled conditions in order to establish and survive.

The first weeds known to arrive in California have been

"fossilized" in adobe bricks. Filaree (*Erodium cicutarium*, Geraniaceae), curly dock (*Rumex crispus*, Polygonaceae), and sow thistle (*Sonchus asper*, Asteraceae) are all Old World weeds whose seeds have been found in adobe bricks of old Spanish buildings constructed before the Mission Period (1769–1824). Examination of adobe bricks made in the Mission Period indicates that an additional number of weedy species arrived and became established during that time. These include black mustard (*Brassica nigra*, Brassicaceae), wild oats (*Avena* spp., Poaceae), and wild carrot or Queen Anne's lace (*Daucus carota*, Apiaceae), all from the Old World. Interestingly, however, the extensive and rich botanical collections of such early plant explorers as David Douglas, Thomas Nuttall, and John Fremont who visited the state in the 1830s and 1840s contained only a single weed species. In view of the fact that some of these men had to carry their own collections and collecting gear on their backs, perhaps they consciously avoided collecting plants that they knew to be introduced, because they were more interested in new and unusual native species that they were continually encountering. In the early 1840s, the Russians made extensive collections in Sonoma County, working out of their settlement at Fort Ross. These collections reveal a varied assortment of introduced weeds, indicating that a number of these had been introduced long before extensive settlement of the area and suggesting that these introduced plants were present but avoided by other collectors.

After 1860, more attention was given to recording the nonnative flora of the state, with the result that in the past century the arrival of new weeds and their spread have been fairly well documented. Jepson's original *Manual of the Flowering Plants of California,* the first comprehensive flora of the state, was published in 1925 and recognized 292 exotic species. In 1959, Munz in *A California Flora* included 725 species and increased that to 874 in a 1968 revision in collaboration with D. Keck, *A California Flora and Supplement.* The new *Jepson Manual: Higher Plants of California* (Hickman 1993) recorded 1,023, and since that time another 22 exotic species have been reported in the literature, bringing the total to 1,045, approaching 25 percent of the total California flora.

Some weeds were introduced into California consciously because they had ornamental or other value. For example, European sweet alyssum *(Lobularia maritima)* and red valerian *(Centranthus ruber)* were introduced as garden plants because of their drought tolerance and attractive flowers. Both have become established locally as inhabitants of poorly kept gardens, in empty lots, and along roadsides. The leaf stalks of cardoon *(Cynara cardunculus)* have long been prized as a food item by people of Mediterranean ancestry; this attractive thistle has escaped from gardens and has become aggressively invasive on the hills east of San Francisco Bay. Perhaps this is the explanation for the presence of sweet fennel or finocchio *(Foeniculum vulgare)*, a favorite food of Italian immigrants, that is common in waste places of central and southern California. Blue gum *(Eucalyptus globulus)*, introduced from Australia as an ornamental and for possible lumber purposes, has become successfully established here. It effectively eliminates any close-by native plant communities by means of shade, leaf and bark droppings, and compounds toxic to most plants.

It is probable that the majority of weeds in California have resulted from accidental introductions of seeds rather than from intentional introductions. In former days, much of the seed of various field or garden crops planted in California originated from Old World areas and was contaminated with a number of weed seeds from those regions. Planting the seeds of imported crop or ornamental plants resulted in accidental planting of weeds as well. Weeds were also introduced into the American West as contaminants of wool imported from the British Isles, South America, or Australia. These weeds initially became established in the vicinity of woolen mills, but many of them spread rapidly from these sites. In the nineteenth and early twentieth centuries, ships visiting the west coast of North America carried ballast in the form of soil or rocks that had been put on board in various foreign ports. Ballast was emptied from the ships at dockside, and a number of unusual and interesting botanical aliens have arrived in California via these ballast dumps. A tidal wetland cord grass *(Spartina densiflora(,* arrived in Humboldt Bay in the late 1800s in this way and is now a dominant plant in Humboldt Bay tidal marshes. It is spreading in San Francisco Bay from an introduction in a 1974 marsh restoration project (pl. 177).

Plate 177. Smooth cord grass *(Spartina densiflora)* was brought into Humboldt Bay from Chile on timber ships in the 1800s. It now covers vast areas around the bay and has eliminated native marsh species and is spreading in San Francisco Bay.

The greatest damage to California lands is from invasive weed species that alter ecosystem processes such as nutrient recycling, intensity and frequency of fire, hydrological cycles, sediment deposition, and erosion. Cheat grass *(Bromus tectorum),* for example, has invaded millions of acres of the Great Basin and desert, leading to increases in fire frequency from once in 60 to 110 years to every three to five years. Native shrubs cannot recover with this frequency and are eliminated or severely reduced (pl. 178). Several species of tamarisk

Plate 178. Cheat grass *(Bromus tectorum)* has invaded millions of acres of the Great Basin and deserts of California and now endangers numerous native shrub species because the grass causes an increase in fire frequency from which the plants cannot recover.

(Tamarix spp.) have become established along watercourses, causing dramatic changes by drying up desert springs and altering groundwater supplies, increasing fire frequency, and eliminating the native flora. Although the trees were originally introduced as ornamentals or as windbreaks, they are one of the most damaging of weedy invasions. The California Natural Diversity Database (California Department of Fish and Game) reports that 181 of the state's rare plants are experiencing threats from invasive weeds (1997).

Some of the most damaging weeds in the central coastal area of California include the brooms (pea family): French broom *(Genista monspessulana)*, Spanish broom *(Spartium junceum)*, and Scotch broom *(Cytisus scoparius)*. Pampas grass *(Cortaderia jubata)* is also invading and significantly altering several plant communities along miles of Highway 1 on the central coast (pl. 179).Gorse *(Ulex europaeus)* is a relatively well behaved shrub in its native Europe but has become a very

Plate 179. Several species of broom such as this Spanish broom *(Spartium junceum)* have been imported by the nursery trade into California and have escaped to become widely invasive.

troublesome weed from central California northward into southern Oregon. Where spiny gorse shrubs invade pasturelands, hundreds of acres can made unavailable to grazing animals. Gorse also burns very easily and rapidly and as a consequence is a considerable fire hazard in areas where it has become established. In the 1930s much of the town of Bandon in southern Oregon was destroyed by a fire whose destruc-

Plate 180. Gorse *(Ulex europaea)* is an aggressively invasive nonnative species found in coastal areas and the foothills of the northern Sierra Nevada. It is spreading rapidly into pastures, particularly in coastal areas.

Plate 181. A member of the pea family, gorse *(Ulex europaea)* is spiny and difficult to control because it produces many seeds and stump sprouts.

tiveness was due to the large areas of land in and around the town that were (and still are) covered by gorse (pl. 180, 181).

A few native species have developed weedy tendencies. For example, the fall- and winter-flowering telegraph weed *(Heterotheca grandiflora)* is a native species that probably originated as an inhabitant of sandy soils in southern California. In recent years this species has spread northward into central and northern California, where it is now common along roadsides or in sandy fields. The fiddleneck genus *(Amsinckia)* also has been successful in spawning weeds along roadsides and grasslands over much of California.

Most of the weedy plant species in California, however, are not derived from native species but have been introduced from elsewhere. About 75 percent of the weeds in California are of European and western Asian origin, which is not surprising because these regions have been settled and cultivated for very long periods of time. About 10 percent of the weeds in California are of South American origin, and the remainder comprises miscellany from elsewhere in the world—Eurasia, Africa, and Australia. Members of the grass (Poaceaee) and sunflower (Asteraceae) families together are responsible for about 40 percent of the weed species in the state.

The most effective method for weed control is prevention through early detection and removal of invasions before they spread. Once weeds are established, eradication is often not achievable. Successful techniques for weed control include manual removal, mulching, flooding, or draining. Manual removal can be very effective but is labor intensive. Sometimes biological control agents (insects or bacteria) are available, but their use can be risky, as they may turn to native species and become more of a problem than a solution. Grazing and chemical controls are also employed. Many volunteer groups are involved with weed control and work with parks and park associations, homeowner groups, and plant organizations. The California Exotic Pest Plant Council, a nonprofit organization, is devoted to providing information about exotic plants, developing best methods for control, and working with both the public and public agencies to protect California's biodiversity.

Tracking Habitat Destruction and Loss of Species

Europeans have been in California less than 300 years, yet every plant community has been severely affected by their presence and activities. Ninety to 95 percent of all vernal pools are gone; 90 to 95 percent of all tidal salt marshes are gone; and 99 percent of all native grasslands are gone. About 30 plants are presumed to have become extinct in the past 100 years. Hundreds more are endangered and could become extinct in the near future. California's flora is unusually rich in annual species as opposed to perennial species, and these annuals are more susceptible to disturbance by human activities. It is also disproportionately rich in subspecies and varieties. Because subspecies and varieties typically have smaller ranges than

Plate 182. Cuesta Pass checker-bloom *(Sidalcea hickmanii* subsp. *anomala)* grows in a closed-cone coniferous forest in the Los Padres mountains on serpentine soil and is known from only three populations.

Plate 183. Chinese Camp brodiaea *(Brodiaea pallida)* grows on serpentine soils in valley and foothill grasslands and is known from only two locations, both of which have been degraded as habitat.

species, they are biologically rarer to begin with and are more vulnerable to disruption. Some rare species, such as large-flowered fiddleneck (*Amsinckia grandiflora,* Boraginaceae), Hickman's mallow (*Sidalcea hickmanii,* Malvaceae), Catalina ironwood (*Lyonothamnus floribundus,* Rosaceae), Shasta snow-wreath *(Neviusia cliftonii),* and pale or Chinese Canys brodiaea (*Brodiaea pallida,* Liliaceae), have been rare since they were first brought to the attention of biologists and are rare for natural rather than human-made causes. However, the vast majority of species that are rare, endangered, and threatened are in decline because of human activities (pls. 182, 183).

In the late 1960s the late G. Ledyard Stebbins of the University of California, Davis, began collecting names and locations of rare plants in California. In 1974, the relatively young

California Native Plant Society (CNPS) published his list in *An Inventory of Rare and Endangered Vascular Plants of California* (York 1974). CNPS began to track levels of endangerment and distribution of the rare plants in California. Over the intervening years, the CNPS Rare Plant Program has developed a statewide monitoring program of rare and endangered plants, with cooperation by the California Department of Fish and Game. Six updated editions of the rare plant inventory have been published. Although the tabulating methods changed in the first three inventories, it is nonetheless clear that the percentage of rare and endangered plants and plants of limited distribution has increased alarmingly over the past 27 years, from 22 percent of the native flora in 1974 to 33 percent in 2001.

Interestingly, the number of presumed extinct species has decreased. Many more botanists are out looking for these species, and several have been found. In 1980, a small population of the Sonoma spineflower *(Chorizanthe valida),* once collected in Sonoma and Marin Counties and thought to be extinct, was rediscovered on the Point Reyes Peninsula by members of the Marin chapter of CNPS. In 2001 botanist Glen Clifton of Shasta snow-wreath fame discovered another species of spineflower along the road in Point Reyes, Scott's

Plate 184. Showy Indian clover *(Trifolium amoenum)* had been last collected in 1969 and was thought to be extinct, but in 1993 it was rediscovered by Dr. Peter Conners in a grazed meadow in Sonoma County that is now protected.

Valley spineflower *(Chorizanthe robusta)*, that until then had been known from only three occurrences in Santa Cruz County. In 1988 the Humboldt milk vetch *(Astragalus agnicidus)* was discovered on a ranch in Humboldt County by field survey volunteers and botanists from the Department of Fish and Game who have organized searches. In 1993 a single plant of showy Indian clover *(Trifolium amoenum)*, last collected in 1969 and thought to be extinct, was found in a grazed meadow in Sonoma County by Dr. Peter Conners from the Bodega Marine Laboratory. The very small population is now fully protected. These isolated finds, although interesting and exciting for the botanical community, should not obscure the bleak picture presented in table 11, which shows that the number of

TABLE 11. Numerical Comparison of Rare and Endangered Plants in California

CNPS List	1974	1980	1984	1988	1994	2001
1A. Presumed extinct		44	34	39	34	29
Very rare and rare and endangered	704	656				
Rare and not endangered	554	446				
1B. Rare and endangered in California and elsewhere			604	675	857	1,021
Rare and endangered in California but not elsewhere		237	198	177	272	417
Need more information			114	149	47	52
Plants of limited distribution	135		449	508	532	554
TOTAL	1,393	1,383	1,399	1,548	1,742	2,073

Total Native Flora for California is approximately 6300 in 2001.

Source: Tibor 2001.

rare and endangered species has increased steadily from 1,393 in 1974 to 2,073 in 2001 (pl. 184).

Habitat Restoration

Habitat restoration is a relatively new science and remains a controversial one. Duck clubs have manipulated wetlands to obtain better duck habitat for many decades, but restoring the functions of a wetland is a relatively new endeavor. Until the late 1960s a generally accepted truth was that "once wetlands are gone, they are gone forever." In the late 1960s and early 1970s, this "truth" was reexamined, and various restoration and enhancement projects have been underway since. Once tidal waters are restored to former baylands, we have learned that tidal salt marshes will reestablish at suitable elevations. With several decades of experience, however, the subject remains controversial. A common shortcoming of restoration projects has been the inability to re-create all the known functions of a natural marsh. Most restoration projects serve as mitigations for development projects, and many restoration attempts are sited in disturbed or marginally appropriate locations. Many suffer from poor design or contradictory goals, such as for joint use as flood control projects and as natural habitat. Too often, inadequate or no monitoring exists to better understand the results. Over the years the science of wetland restoration has made progress, and it has become apparent that restoration of a tidal marsh takes far longer than once thought and requires greater patience from the public and public agencies.

Restoration and creation of riparian forests is one of the most difficult types of habitat restoration as it must occur next to a stream or along a river in a floodplain, locations that naturally are subject to rapidly changing conditions of erosion or sedimentation. Because of development, gravel mining, or extensive deforestation in their watersheds, most streams in Cal-

Plate 185. Large deciduous trees such as these western sycamores *(Platanus racemosa)* once lined most streams and waterways in California. Restoring them is a challenge.

ifornia are eroding along their banks and cutting down below their historic floodplains. Other streams have been channelized, altering the stream hydrology and reducing options for restoration. In nature, riparian species are adapted to flood events, and many streamside plants require clean sand to become established, places where trees have been uprooted in past storm events. Significant restoration efforts for riparian forests will require watershed-scale planning and the cooperation of flood control districts to reduce rapid runoff and erosion (pl. 185).

Re-creating vernal pools presents quite a different challenge in habitat restoration. Vernal pools are seasonal wetlands formed in shallow basins that are underlain by heavy clay soils that retain seasonal rainfall. Pools fill with winter rains and completely dry out in summer. Vernal pools are known by various names; in the San Joaquin Valley they are called hog wallows because of their appearance in the landscape. Pool basins fill with sufficient water to prevent upland plants from invading, and summer desiccation prevents aquatic and wetland plants from establishing. As opposed to tidal salt marshes or riparian forests, where most of the species are common and/or adapted to habitat disturbance, the unique conditions found in vernal pools have resulted in an abundance of rare plant species that have evolved over centuries, isolated in individual pools. This isolation has led to the development of many species unique to individual pools. Purposeful re-creation of vernal pools began in the 1980s to serve as mitigation for extensive pool destruction. In general, re-creation failures have resulted from insufficient soil and hydrology analyses and a lack of understanding of the biology of rare species, particularly their pollination requirements. The re-creation of vernal pools remains a controversial subject today because it usually results in a general loss of biodiversity. Such levels of uncertainty argue strongly for maximum efforts to preserve the natural landscape.

Saving Biodiversity: A Call for Action

California's riches are, in large part, its biological diversity. Biodiversity is defined as the full range of variety and variability within and among all living organisms (plants and animals), and the ecological complexes in which they occur. It encompasses ecosystem or community diversity, species diversity, and genetic diversity. This great diversity developed because of California's complex geology, its current and past climates, and its varied topography. The key question for today's and tomorrow's leaders is, with so much conversion of land for agricultural, industrial, and residential use, can we save California's biodiversity? Can we save some of what is left, all of what is left, or none of it?

As climate varies from year to year, so plant populations also vary from year to year. Some annual species may not appear at all in drought years, only to be abundant when suitable rainfall and temperature patterns arrive. Within wild populations, a wide variety of genetic combinations exist that allow species to accommodate to climate changes. As it warms, some species retreat through successive generations to higher elevations, but they need space to make these accommodations and will fail if their habitat is too fragmented.

It has only been within the past 20 years that plant protection was defined in legal terms, and even today plants are not often included in federal administrative orders. Since the early 1900s, plants were protected by the creation of national parks and national forests, but these protections protect the landscape and are not species specific. Some additional protection came with the National Environmental Protection Act of 1970 and the California Environmental Quality Act of 1970 that require the preparation of full disclosure documents for project impacts. The first federal protection for plant species came when Richard Nixon signed the federal Endangered Species Act in 1973. It extends protections to plants and establishes a category for threatened species before they become endangered. This act has been instrumental in protecting habitat and slowing the population decline of hundreds of species of plants. Further plant protection stems from three other laws: the 1977 Native Plant Protection Act, the 1984 California Endangered Species Act, and the 1991 Natural Communities Conservation Planning Act. These laws promote rare species protection through prohibition, disclosure, and planning. They all affect private lands in California where strong legal privilege for private land ownership exists. Although the endangered species laws have been powerful tools, especially for protecting specific plant populations, the long-range outlook for plants is poor unless planning tools protect them for the long run. Only by using regional approaches that avoid patchwork habitat and destructive water diversions will we maintain our present level of biodiversity.

The California Department of Fish and Game is the lead state agency for the protection of species, both plants and animals. This agency, however, is one that was formed to regulate hunting and fishing, so its mission is somewhat ambivalent and the resource conservation staff underfunded. It does, however, have a central role in identifying, protecting, and managing rare plants and natural plant communities in California, and as part of this program, it maintains the California Natural Diversity Database. California's tradition of citizen activism has played a key role in the development of laws protective of native species of plants and animals. Continuing public support for the protection of species is essential. The nonprofit California Native Plant Society's inventory of rare, endangered, and threatened plants serves as a guide for the public as well as public agencies and private landowners to carry out protections for plants. The Nature Conservancy has played an important role in preserving important habitat and species. Over the years, they have made a transition in their protection strategy from buying and managing lands they have identified as important examples of unique or representative habitat ("the best of the rest") and acquiring scarce and endangered populations of plants and animals ("the last of the least"), to focusing on large, landscape-size projects with cooperative public partners. They felt time was running out, and their protective efforts needed to be faster and larger.

In 1991, southern California was on the verge of becoming the greatest battleground in the nation over endangered species. Conservationists had petitioned the U.S. Fish and Wildlife Service to add the California gnatcatcher, which depends on coastal sage scrub habitat for survival, to the federal endangered species list. Much of the prime real estate in southern California is also in coastal sage scrub. A state program supported by the federal government, Natural Community Conservation Planning (NCCP), was adopted by the legislature. It creates a framework for regional protection and management of wildlife habitat, while allowing development to proceed in certain areas. The NCCP planning process provides a welcome tool because it elevates plants to the same status as animals and covers listed as well as unlisted plants. The standard under the NCCP program is to provide conservation

Plate 186. Each decade has fewer and fewer of these magnificent displays of wildflowers across California because of habitat degradation and destruction that accompany rapidly expanding population pressures.

management of all covered species, as well as a recovery plan for the plan area. The first conservation NCCP plan was adopted by Orange County in 1996, creating a 38,000-acre Orange County Nature Reserve. Other approved plans are in San Diego County where already 200 plant and animal species are rare, endangered or threatened, and 98 percent of the vernal pools, 95 percent of perennial grasslands, 90 percent of freshwater marshes, and 90 percent of coastal maritime chaparral are already gone. A 44,000-acre San Diego National Wildlife Refuge is planned, most of which is on private lands at present. The biggest challenge is keeping a flow of money available to fund acquisition of lands in plan areas, provide proper management of these lands, and set up monitoring programs to understand the status of plants and animals on the lands. How much real plant protection accrues from this NCCP process remains to be seen as development interests can often act faster than public agencies; but it is a welcome tool if used effectively.

To maintain what remains of California's biodiversity, a most desirable action would be to mandate the protection of the state's biodiversity as state policy. National policy is to have no net loss of wetlands, for example. Unfortunately, the steps to achieve this are in conflict with the development and resource-consumptive industries, and this goal is not likely to be accomplished in the near future. Still, other smaller steps would be beneficial. California has no law protecting its natural habitats. Existing laws protect species but not habitats. Streams, wetlands, vernal pools, coastal dunes, and old-growth forests all are disappearing or being degraded. A law requiring specific conservation goals for natural habitats to be included in general plans statewide would require local planning jurisdictions through the planning process to slow down the fragmentation and degradation that is occurring today.

Because of the strength of laws protecting rare and endangered species, state and local agencies and jurisdictions are working more cooperatively in multiagency and multijurisdictional regional planning efforts toward Habitat Conservation Plans. The California Resources Agency is developing a program, the California Continuing Resources Investment Strategy Program that will maintain comprehensive map information and refined databases of land and species resources. This will assist landowners, public agencies, and the interested public in more effective habitat conservation, as well as more sensitive development. The secret to success, as will all conservation and landscape-scale planning efforts, requires experience and greater scientific information and analysis to be successful.

Greater commitment of funding for scientific work and enforcement of existing laws would better protect biodiversity. Better funding would allow more acquisition of special lands in fee or for conservation easements, and better management of parks for the protection of biodiversity. A statewide system of preserves using ecosystem approaches, such as maintaining corridors between habitat patches and encompassing whole watersheds, would maximize conservation benefits for preserving biodiversity.

Through extensive educational programs currently offered in many schools and through nonprofit organizations, both public awareness and biological literacy are increasing. It will be the commitment of the public that will decide the level of biodiversity retained in California into the future. The public needs to demand the election of conservation-minded politicians who support and enact protective laws and establish effective government resource agencies whose missions are to protect living resources. They also need to support the work of nonprofit land trusts to set aside important lands. The challenge to overcome the influence of money and political power is great, but the future of our biodiversity is at stake.

GLOSSARY

Allelopathy   The production and release of chemical compounds by a plant that are toxic to other plants (and in some instances are toxic also to seedlings of the same species), resulting in suppression of growth.

Annual (plant)   A plant that completes its life cycle in one growing season.

Anther   The sac at the top of the stamen that produces pollen.

Biodiversity   The full range of variety and variability within and among all living organisms (plants and animals), and the ecological complexes in which they occur.

Bract   Any modified leaf associated with a flower or flowers. Bracts may be green, like leaves, or colored, like petals.

Calyx   The outer whorl of a flower consisting of sepals; the collective term for sepals.

Chaparral   A broad-leaved sclerophyll type of vegetation.

Climax (vegetation)   The final, self-perpetuating vegetation type that occurs in an area under stable ecological conditions.

Coniferous (shrub or tree)   A shrub or tree with needlelike or scalelike leaves that bears its seeds in cones. Conifers do not produce true flowers.

Deciduous (tree)   A tree that loses its leaves seasonally, usually in fall.

Dicot   A flowering plant that has its flower parts in fours or fives, vascular bundles of the stem arranged in a ringlike pattern, and two seed leaves, or cotyledons.

Ecotype   A locally adapted, genetically distinct race within a species. An ecotype can be seasonal, climatic, or edaphic (soil).

Elaiosome   A food-body appendage on a seed that induces an ant to carry seeds to its nest where the seed may in time germinate.

Endemic (plant species)   A plant species that is restricted to a specific locality or habitat.

Floret   A single flower and its immediately subtending bracts.

Floristic province   A geographic unit that reflects the wide variations in natural landscapes and assists botanists in predicting where a given plant might be found.

Geoflora   A major vegetation unit that has continuity in space and time.

Granitic (soil)   A type of usually acid soil that forms from accumulations of crumbling rock material containing little organic matter.

Halophyte   A plant that can tolerate salt in the soil.

Herbaceous (plant)   A plant that is nonwoody.

Herbivory   Plant tissue damage from animal consumption.

Limestone (soil)   A type of usually alkaline soil derived from limestone rocks (an accumulation of the shells of once-living organisms, formed under the sea).

Mesic (soil)   Soil that is moist.

Monocot   A flowering plant that has its flower parts arranged in threes, scattered vascular bundles, and one seed leaf.

Neoendemic (plant species)   A new plant species frequently found on geologically youthful habitats that has not had time to expand its range to its climatic and geological limits.

Ovary   The bottom saclike part of the pistil, which contains the future seeds or ovules. Ovaries ripen into various kinds of fruits as the seeds inside mature.

Paleoendemic (plant species)   An old plant species that was at one time more widely distributed but has retreated to its current range in response to dramatic climatic changes.

Perennial (plant)   A plant whose life cycle extends over more than one growing season.

Perianth   The collective term for both sepals and petals.

Phreatophyte   A perennial plant that has an extensive and deep root system that enable it to tap underground sources of water.

Pistil   The central, female part of a typical flower. The pistil consists of an ovary, a style, and a stigma.

Pollen   The fine, often yellow powder produced by the stamens.

Pollination   The transfer of pollen to female flower parts.

Riparian (plant)   A plant or plant community that occurs next to a stream or along a river in a floodplain.

Rhizome   An underground, more or less horizontal stem.

Samara   A single-seeded fruit dispersed by an attached wing.

Saprophyte   A plant, such as a fungus, that obtains much of its nutritional requirements from decomposing organic material, such as dead leaves or wood.

Sclerophyll (forest)   Trees and shrubs with tough leaves adapted to relatively dry climates.

Serpentine (soil)   A type of soil that has a very low calcium content and correspondingly high magnesium content, a high nickel and chromium content, and a low nutrient content. Serpentine soils have a very high proportion of endemic plant species restricted to them.

Stamen   The male part of a typical flower, consisting of a stalk (filament) and a sac (anther) and producing pollen.

Stigma   The tip of a flower's pistil, often sticky or fuzzy, where pollen is deposited during the process of pollination.

Style   A stalk between the ovary and stigma of the pistil.

Succession   The change in vegetation that may occur on a given site over a period of time.

Vascular plant   A plant that has a well-developed vascular system to transport water, dissolved minerals, and other substances throughout the plant body.

Vernal pool   Seasonal wetlands formed in shallow basins that are underlain by heavy clay soils that retain seasonal rainfall.

Xerophyte   Plants such as cacti and members of other families that are able to economize on water by either storing it for long periods of time or obtaining it from the soil even when it is present in very low amounts.

SUPPLEMENTAL READING

For local or regional floras, contact the California Native Plant Society, Sacramento, California.

Bakker, Elna S. 1971. *An island called California.* Berkeley: University of California Press.

Barbour, M.G., B. Pavlik, F. Drysdale, and S. Lindstrom. 1993. *California's changing landscapes: Diversity and conservation of California vegetation.* Sacramento: California Native Plant Society Press.

Bossard, C.C., J.M. Randall, and M.C. Hoshovsky, eds. 2000. *Invasive plants of California's wildlands.* Berkeley: University of California Press.

Evarts, J., and M. Popper, eds. 2001. *Coast redwood: A natural and cultural history.* Los Olivos, Calif.: Cachuma Press.

Faber, P.M., ed. 1997. *California's wild gardens: A living legend.* Sacramento: California Native Plant Society Press.

Hickman, J.C., ed. 1993. *The Jepson manual: Higher plants of California.* Berkeley: University of California Press.

Kruckeberg, A.R. 1984. *California serpentines: Flora, vegetation, geology, soils, and management problems.* Berkeley: University of California Press.

Pavlik, B.M., P.C. Muick, S. Johnson, and M. Popper. 1991. *Oaks of California.* Los Olivos, Calif.: Cachuma Press.

Sawyer, J.O., and T. Keeler-Wolf. 1995. *A manual of California vegetation.* Sacramento: California Native Plant Society Press.

Schoenherr, A.A. 1992. *A natural history of California.* Berkeley: University of California Press.

REFERENCES

Some titles are out of print but have been included for historic reasons.

Abrams, LeRoy. [1923, 1944, 1951] 1960. *Illustrated flora of the Pacific states,* 4 vols. Reprint, Stanford, Calif.: Stanford University Press.

Allan, Mea. 1977. *Darwin and his flowers: The key to natural selection.* New York: Taplinger Publishing.

Armstrong, Margaret. 1915. *Field book of western wild flowers.* New York: G. P. Putnam's Sons.

Arnberger, Leslie P., and Jeanne R. Janish. 1968. *Flowers of the southwest mountains.* Globe, Ariz.: Southwestern Monuments Association.

Axelrod, D. I. 1958. *Evolution of the Madro-Tertiary geoflora. Botanical Review* 24:433–509.

Axelrod, D. I. 1967. *Evolution of the California closed cone pine forest.* In *Proceedings of the symposium on the biology of the California islands,* edited by R. N. Philbrick. Santa Barbara, Calif.: Santa Barbara Botanic Garden.

Baerg, Harry J. 1955. *How to know the western trees.* Dubuque, Iowa: Wm. C. Brown Co.

Baker, Richard St. B. 1960. *The redwoods.* Healdsburg, Calif.: Naturegraph Co.

Bakker, Elna S. 1971. *An island called California.* Berkeley: University of California Press.

Balls, Edward K. 1962. *Early uses of California plants.* Natural History Guide Series no. 10. Berkeley: University of California Press.

Barbour, M. G., and J. Major. 1977. *Terrestrial vegetation of California.* New York: John Wiley.

Barbour, M.G., B. Pavlik, F. Drysdale, and S. Lindstrom. 1993. *California's changing landscapes: Diversity and conservation of California vegetation.* Sacramento: California Native Plant Society Press.

Barth, F.C. 1991. *Insects and flowers: The biology of a partnership.* Princeton, N.J.: Princeton University Press.

Bell, C.R. 1967. *Plant variation and classification.* Belmont, Mass.: Wadsworth Publishing.

Benson, Lyman. 1969. *The native cacti of California.* Stanford, Calif.: Stanford University Press.

Benson, Lyman, and Robert A. Darrow. 1954. *The trees and shrubs of the southwestern deserts.* Albuquerque: University of New Mexico; Tucson: University of Arizona. Semipopular or semi-technical manual for identification of trees and shrubs of the deserts of southwestern United States.

Berry, James B. 1924. *Western forest trees.* New York: Dover Publications.

Billings, W.D. 1970. *Plants, man, and the ecosystem.* Belmont, Mass.: Wadsworth Publishing.

Bossard, C.C., J.M. Randall, and M.C. Hoshovsky, eds. 2000. *Invasive plants of California's wildlands.* Berkeley: University of California Press.

Boughey, A.S. 1968. *A checklist of Orange County flowering plants.* Irvine: Museum of Systematic Biology, University of California.

Bowerman, Mary L. 1944. *The flowering plants and ferns of Mount Diablo.* Berkeley, Calif.: Gillick Press

Bowers, Nathan A. 1965. *Cone-bearing trees of the Pacific coast.* Palo Alto, Calif.: Pacific Books.

Brockman, C. Frank. 1947. *Broad-leaved trees of Yosemite National Park.* Yosemite, Calif.: Yosemite Natural History Association.

Cain, S.A. 1944. *Foundations of plant geography.* New York: Harper & Bros.

Campbell, D.H., and I.L. Wiggins. 1947. *Origins of the flora of California. Stanford University Publications in Biological Science* 10:3–20.

Chapman, V.J. 1960. *Salt marshes and salt deserts of the world.* New York: Interscience Publishers.

Cheatham, N.D. and J.R. Haller. 1975. *An annotated list of California habitat types.* Unpublished report on file at California Natural Diversity Database, Department of Fish and Game, Sacramento.

Clausen, Jens, D.D. Keck, and W.M. Hiesey. 1940. *Experimental studies on the nature of species: I, Effect of varied environments on western North American plants.* Publication 5201. Washington, D.C.: Carnegie Institution of Washington.

Clements, Edith S. 1959. *Flowers of coast and sierra.* New York: Hafner Co.

Clements, F. E. 1936. *The origins of the desert climax and climate.* In *Essays in geobotany in honor of W.A. Setchell,* edited by T.H. Goodspeed. Berkeley: University of California Press.

Cole, James E. 1939. *Cone-bearing trees of Yosemite.* Yosemite, Calif.: Yosemite Natural History Association.

Collins, Barbara J. 1972. *Key to coastal and chaparral flowering plants of southern California.* Northridge: California State University Foundation.

Cook, Lawrence F. 1961. *The giant sequoias of California.* Washington, D.C.: U.S. Government Printing Office.

Cooke, William B. 1940. *Flora of Mount Shasta.* American Midland Naturalist, vol. 23. Notre Dame, Ind.: The Notre Dame University Press

Cooke, William B. 1941. *Flora of Mount Shasta.* First supplement, American Midland Naturalist, vol. 26. Notre Dame, Ind.: The Notre Dame University Press.

Cooke, William B. 1949. *Flora of Mount Shasta.* Second supplement, American Midland Naturalist, vol. 41. Notre Dame, Ind.: The Notre Dame University Press.

Cooper, W.S. 1922. *The broad-sclerophyll vegetation of California.* Publication 319. Washington, D.C.: Carnegie Institution of Washington.

Cooper, W.S. 1967. *Coastal dunes of California.* Memoir 104. Denver, Colo.: Geological Society of America.

Crampton, Beecher. 1974. *Grasses in California.* Natural History Guide Series no. 33. Berkeley: University of California Press.

Critchfield, W.B. 1971. *Profiles of California vegetation.* Forest Service Research paper PSW-76. Berkeley, Calif.: U.S. Department of Agriculture.

Dafni, A. 1992. *Pollination ecology: A practical approach.* London: Oxford University Press.

Dale, R.F. 1959. *Climates of the states: California.* Washington, D.C.: U.S. Bureau of Commerce Weather Bureau.

Dawson, E. Yale. 1966a. *Seashore plants of northern California.* Natural History Guide Series no. 19. Berkeley: University of California Press

Dawson, E. Yale. 1966b. *The cacti of California.* Natural History Guide Series no. 18. Berkeley: University of California Press.

Dodge, Natt N., and Jeanne R. Janish. 1969. *Flowers of the southwest deserts.* Globe, Ariz.: Southwestern Monuments Association.

Dowden, A. O. T. 1963. *Look at a flower.* New York: Thomas Y. Crowell Co.

Durrenberger, Robert W. 1968. *Patterns on the land.* Palo Alto, Calif.: National Press Books. Geographical, historical, and political maps of California.

Edwards, S. W. 1992. *Observations on the prehistory and ecology of grazing in California. Fremontia* 20(1):3–11.

Engbeck, Joseph H. Jr. 1973. *The enduring giants.* San Francisco: Save-the-Redwoods League.

Evarts, J., and M. Popper, eds. 2001. *Coast redwood: A natural and cultural history.* Los Olivos, Calif.: Cachuma Press.

Faber, P. M., ed. 1997. *California's wild gardens: A living legend.* Sacramento: California Native Plant Society Press.

Farb, Peter. 1959. *Living earth.* New York: Harper and Row.

Ferguson, C. W. 1968. Bristlecone pine: Science and esthetics. *Science* 159:839–846.

Ferris, Roxana S. 1962. *Death Valley wildflowers.* Death Valley, Calif.: Death Valley Natural History Association.

Ferris, Roxana S. 1968. *Native shrubs of the San Francisco Bay region.* Natural History Guide Series no. 24. Berkeley: University of California Press.

Ferris, Roxana S. 1970. *Flowers of the Point Reyes National Seashore.* Berkeley: University of California Press.

Fiedler, Peggy. L. 2001. Rarity in vascular plants. In *2001 inventory of rare and endangered plants of California,* edited by David P. Tibor. 6th ed. Sacramento: California Native Plant Society Press.

Fiedler, Peggy L., and Jeremy J. Ahouse. 1992. Hierarchies of cause: Toward an understanding of rarity in vascular plant species. In *Conservation biology: The theory and practice of nature conservation, preservation, and management,* edited by Peggy L. Fiedler and Subodh K. Jain. New York: Chapman and Hall.

Field, Chris. 2002. Global change and California ecosystems. Lecture presented by the California Botanical Society, April 18, 2002, University of California, Berkeley.

Fultz, Francis M. 1923. *The elfin forest.* Los Angeles: Times-Mirror Press. Classic work on the chaparral.

Gankin, Roman, and J. Major. 1964. *Arctostaphylos myrtifolia,* its biology and relationship to the problem of endemism. *Ecology* 45:792–808.

Geary, Ida. 1979. Chamisso, Eschscholtz, and plants of the Presidio. *Fremontia* 6(4):3–9.

Gillett, George W., John Thomas Howell, and Hans Leschke. 1995. *A flora of Lassen Volcanic National Park, California,* revised by V.H. Oswald, D.W. Showers, and M.A. Showers. Sacramento: California Native Plant Society Press.

Gordon, H. 2002. *Revised descriptions of the CALVEG vegetation cover types in California.* Unpublished administrative report, U.S. Forest Service Remote Sensing Lab, Sacramento, Calif.

Griffin, James R., and William B. Critchfield. 1973. *The distribution of forest trees in California.* Forest Service Research paper PSW-82. Berkeley, Calif.: U.S. Department of Agriculture.

Grillos, S.J. 1966. *Ferns and fern allies of California.* Natural History Guide Series no. 16. Berkeley: University of California Press.

Grossman, D.H., D. Faber-Langendoen, A.S. Weakley, M. Anderson, P. Bourgeron, R. Crawford, K. Gooding, S. Landaal, K. Metzler, K. Patterson, M. Pyne, M. Reid, and L. Sneddon. 1998. *International classification of ecological communities: Terrestrial vegetation of the United States.* Vol. 1 of *The National Vegetation Classification Standard.* Arlington, Va.: The Nature Conservancy.

Hall, Harvey M., and Carlotta C. Hall. 1912. *A Yosemite flora.* San Francisco: Paul Elder & Co.

Hamilton, Jason G. 1997. Changing perceptions of pre-European grasslands in California. *Madrono* 44(4):311–333.

Harrington, H.D., and L.W. Durrell. 1957. *How to identify plants.* Chicago: Swallow Press.

Hickman, J.C., ed. 1993. *The Jepson manual: Higher plants of California.* Berkeley: University of California Press.

Hinde, H.P. 1954. The vertical distribution of salt marsh phanerogams in relation to tide levels. *Ecological Monographs* 24:209–225.

Holland, R.F. 1986. Preliminary descriptions of the terrestrial natural communities of California. Unpublished report on file at California Natural Diversity Database, Department of Fish and Game, Sacramento.

Hood, Mary, and Bill Hood. 1969. *Yosemite wildflowers and their stories.* Yosemite, Calif.: Flying Spur Press.

Hoover, Robert F. 1970. *The vascular plants of San Luis Obispo County, California.* Berkeley: University of California Press.

Howell, John T. 1957. The California flora and its province. *Leaflets of Western Botany* 8:133–138.

Howell, John T. 1970. *Marin flora.* Berkeley: University of California Press.

Howell, John T., Peter H. Raven, and Peter Rubtzoff. 1958. A flora of San Francisco, California. *Wasmann Journal of Biology* 16(1):1–157.

Howitt, Beatrice F., and John T. Howell. 1964. The vascular plants of Monterey County, California. *Wasmann Journal of Biology* 22(1):1–184.

Jaeger, E. C. 1978. *Source book of biological names and terms,* 3rd ed. Springfield, Ill.: Charles C. Thomas.

Jaeger, E. C., and A. C. Smith. 1966. *Introduction to the natural history of southern California.* Natural History Guide Series no. 13. Berkeley: University of California Press.

Jaeger, Edmund C. 1968. *Desert wild flowers.* Stanford, Calif.: Stanford University Press.

Jensen, D.B., M.S. Torn, and J. Harte. 1993. *In our own hands: A strategy for conserving California's biological diversity.* Berkeley: University of California Press.

Jepson, Willis L. 1909–1922. *A flora of California,* vol. 1. Berkeley: Associated Students Store.

Jepson, Willis L. 1910. *The silva of California.* Berkeley: University of California Press.

Jepson, Willis L. 1923. *The trees of California.* Berkeley: Associated Students Store.

Jepson, Willis L. 1923–1925. *A manual of the flowering plants of California.* Berkeley: University of California Press.

Jepson, Willis L. 1935a. *A high school flora for California.* Berkeley: Associated Students Store.

Jepson, Willis L. 1935b. *Trees, shrubs and flowers of the redwood region.* San Francisco: Save-the-Redwoods League.

Jepson, Willis L. 1936. *A flora of California,* vol. 2. Berkeley: Associated Students Store.

Jepson, Willis L. 1939. *A flora of California,* vol. 3, part 1. Berkeley: Associated Students Store.

Jepson, Willis L. 1943. *A flora of California,* vol. 3, part 2. San Francisco: California School Book Depository.

Keeler-Wolf, T., D. Elam, K. Lewis, and S. Flint. 1998. *California ver-*

nal pool assessment preliminary report. Unpublished document available at the California Department of Fish and Game Wildlife and Habitat Data Analysis Branch Web site: http://maphost.dfg.ca.gov/wetlands/.

Keeler-Wolf, T., C. Roye, and K. Lewis. 1997. The definition and distribution of Central California sycamore alluvial woodland. Unpublished administrative report to the Department of Water Resources, on file at the California Natural Diversity Database, Department of Fish and Game, Sacramento.

Kirk, D. 1970. *Wild edible plants of the western United States.* Healdsburg, Calif.: Naturegraph Publishers.

Kruckeberg, A. R. 1954. Plant species in relation to serpentine soils. *Ecology* 35:267–274.

Kruckeberg, A. R. 1984. *California serpentines: flora, vegetation, geology, soils and management problems.* Berkeley: University of California Press.

Legg, K. 1970. *Lake Tahoe wildflowers, and of the central Sierras.* Healdsburg, Calif.: Naturegraph Publishers.

Lenz, Lee W. 1956. *Native plants for California gardens.* Claremont, Calif.: Rancho Santa Ana Botanic Garden.

Lindsay, George. 1963. *Cacti of San Diego County.* San Diego, Calif.: Society of Natural History.

Lloyd, Robert, and Richard S. Mitchell. 1973. *Plants of the White Mountains, California and Nevada.* Berkeley: University of California Press.

Mason, H. L. 1949. Evidence for the genetic submergence of *Pinus remorata.* In *Genetics, paleontology, and evolution,* edited by G. L. Jepsen. Princeton, N.J.: Princeton University Press.

Mason, H. L. 1955. Do we want sugar pine? *Sierra Club Bulletin* 40:40–44.

Mason, H. L. 1957. *A flora of the marshes of California.* Berkeley: University of California Press.

Mason, Herbert L. 1946a. The edaphic factor in narrow endemism: I. The nature of environmental influences. *Madroño* 8:209–226.

Mason, Herbert L. 1946b. The edaphic factor in narrow endemism: II. The geographic occurrence of plants of highly restricted patterns of distribution. *Madroño* 8:241–257.

McClintock, Elizabeth. 1967a. Early plant explorers in the West, part 1. *California Horticultural Society Journal* 28(1):114–121.

McClintock, Elizabeth. 1967b. Early plant explorers in the West, part 2. *California Horticultural Society Journal* 28(2):152–160.

McClintock, Elizabeth, and Walter Knight, with Neil Fahy. 1968. *A flora of the San Bruno Mountains, San Mateo County, California.* San Francisco: California Academy of Sciences.

McKelvey, Susan Delano. 1991. *Botanical exploration of the trans-Mississippi West (1790–1850).* Corvallis: Oregon State University Press.

McMillan, C. 1956. The edaphic restriction of Cupressus and Pinus in the coast ranges of central California. *Ecological Monographs* 26:177–212.

McMinn, Howard E. 1939. *An illustrated manual of California shrubs.* Berkeley: University of California Press.

McMinn, Howard E., and Evelyn Maino. 1937. *An illustrated manual of Pacific Coast trees.* Berkeley: University of California Press.

McPherson, J.K., and C.H. Muller. 1969. Allelopathic effects of Adenostoma fasciculatum, "Chamise", in the California chaparral. *Ecological Monographs* 39:177–198.

Merriam, C.H. 1898. *Life zones and crop zones of the United States.* U.S. Department of Agriculture Biological Survey Bulletin 10.

Metcalf, Woodbridge. 1959. *Native trees of the San Francisco Bay region.* Natural History Guide Series no. 4. Berkeley: University of California Press..

Meyer, K., and W. Laudenslayer. 1988. *A guide to the wildlife habitats of California.* Sacramento, Calif.: Resources Agency.

Moe, Maynard L. 1995. A key to vascular plant species of Kern County, California. In *A key to vascular plant species of Kern Count, California, and a flora of Kern County, California.* Sacramento: California Native Plant Society Press.

Muller, Katherine K. 1958. *Wildflowers of the Santa Barbara region.* Santa Barbara, Calif.: Santa Barbara Botanic Garden.

Munz, P.A. 1959. *A California flora.* Berkeley: University of California Press.

Munz, P.A. 1962. *California desert wildflowers.* Berkeley: University of California Press.

Munz, P.A., and D.D. Keck. 1949. California plant communities. *El Aliso* 2:87–105; 199–202.

Munz, Philip A. 1961. *California spring wildflowers.* Berkeley: University of California Press.

Munz, Philip A. 1963. *California mountain wildflowers.* Berkeley: University of California Press.

Munz, Philip A. 1964. *Shore wildflowers of California, Oregon, and Washington.* Berkeley: University of California Press.

Munz, Philip A., in collaboration with David D. Keck. 1968. *A California flora and supplement.* Berkeley: University of California Press.

Munz, Philip A. 1974. *A flora of southern California.* Berkeley: University of California Press.

Niehaus, Theodore. 1974. *Sierra wildflowers: Mount Lassen to Kern County.* Natural History Guide Series no. 32. Berkeley: University of California Press.

Noldeke, A.M., and J.T. Howell. 1960. Endemism and the California flora. *Leaflets of Western Botany* 9:124–127.

Nuttall, Thomas. 1841. Genera of North American plants. *Transactions of American Philosophers.* 7:283–453.

Oakeshott, G. 1971. *California's changing landscape.* New York: McGraw-Hill.

Oosting, H.J., and W.D. Billings. 1943. The red fir forest of the Sierra Nevada. *Ecological Monographs* 13:259–274.

Ornduff, Robert. 1974. *An introduction to California plant life.* Berkeley: University of California Press.

Parsons, Mary E. 1907. *The wildflowers of California: Their names, haunts, and habits.* San Francisco: Cunningham, Curtis, and Welch.

Pavlik, B.M., P.C. Muick, S. Johnson, and M. Popper. 1991. *Oaks of California.* Los Olivos, Calif.: Cachuma Press.

Peattie, Donald C. 1953. *A natural history of western trees.* Boston: Houghton Mifflin.

Peñalosa, Javier. 1963. A flora of the Tiburon peninsula, Marin County, California. *Wasmann Journal of Biology* 21(1):1–77.

Peterson, P. Victor. 1966. *Native trees of southern California.* Natural History Guide Series no. 14. Berkeley: University of California Press.

Peterson, P. Victor, and P. Victor Peterson Jr. 1974. *Native trees of the Sierra Nevada.* Natural History Guide Series no. 36. Berkeley: University of California Press.

Philbrick, R.N. 1972. Plants of Santa Barbara Island. *Madroño* 21(5[part2]):329–393.

Proctor, M., and P. Yeo. 1972. *The pollination of flowers.* New York: Taplinger Publishing.

Purer, E.A. 1942. Plant ecology of the coastal salt marshlands of San Diego, California. *Ecological Monographs* 12:81–111.

Raven, P.H., and D.I. Axelrod. 1995. *Origin and relationship of the California flora.* Sacramento: California Native Plant Society Press.

Raven, Peter H. 1963. A flora of San Clemente Island, California. *Aliso* 5(3):289–347.

Raven, Peter H. 1966. *Native shrubs of southern California.* Natural History Guide Series no. 15. Berkeley: University of California Press.

Reid, T., and T. Peterson. 1994. Laws for rare plant conservation. *Fremontia* 22(1):20–27.

Rickett, H.W. 1970. *Wild flowers of the United States.* Vol. 4, *The southwestern states.* New York: McGraw-Hill.

Rickett, H.W. 1971. *Wild flowers of the United States.* Vol. 5. *The northwestern states.* New York: McGraw-Hill.

Robbins, Wilfred W., Margaret K. Bellue, and Walter S. Ball. 1951. *Weeds of California.* Sacramento: State of California.

Rodin, Robert J. 1960. *Ferns of the Sierra.* Yosemite, Calif.: Yosemite Natural History Association.

Rubtzoff, Peter. 1953. A phytogeographical analysis of the Pitkin Marsh (Sonoma County). *Wasmann Journal of Biology* 11(2):129–219.

Sauer, J.D. 1988. *Plant migration: The dynamics of geographic patterning in seed plant species.* Berkeley: University of California Press.

Sawyer, J.O., and T. Keeler-Wolf. 1995. *A manual of California vegetation.* Sacramento: California Native Plant Society Press.

Schoenherr, A.A. 1992. *A natural history of California.* Berkeley: University of California Press.

Sharsmith, Helen K. 1945. Flora of the Mount Hamilton Range of California. American Midland Naturalist, vol. 34. Notre Dame, Ind.: The Notre Dame University Press.

Sharsmith, Helen K. 1965. *Spring wildflowers of the San Francisco Bay region.* Natural History Guide Series no. 11. Berkeley: University of California Press.

Skinner, M.W., and B.M. Pavlik. 1994. *Inventory of rare and endangered vascular plants.* 5th ed. Sacramento: California Native Plant Society Press.

Smith, A.C. 1959. *Introduction to the natural history of the San Francisco Bay region.* Natural History Guide Series no. 1. Berkeley: University of California Press.

Smith, Gladys L. 1962. *Flowers of Lassen.* Mineral, Calif.: Loomis Museum Association.

Smith, Gladys L. 1963. *Flowers and ferns of Muir Woods.* Mill Valley, Calif.: Muir Woods Natural History Association.

Soule, M.E., ed. 1986. *Conservation biology: The science of scarcity and diversity.* Sunderland, Mass.: Sinauer Associates.

St. Andre, G., H.A. Mooney, and R.O. Wright. 1965. The pinyon woodland zone in the White Mountains of California. *American Midland Naturalist* 73:225–239.

Stebbins, G.L., and J. Major. 1965. Endemism and speciation in the California flora. *Ecological Monographs* 35:1–35.

Stearns, W.T. 1983. *Botanical Latin,* 3rd ed. London: David & Charles.

Stevenson, R.E., and K.O. Emory. 1958. *Marshlands at Newport Bay, California.* Allan Hancock Foundation Occasional Paper No. 20.

Stine, S. 1996. Climate: 1650–1850. In *Sierra Nevada Ecosystem Project: final report to Congress,* edited by D. Erman. Vol. 2, *Assessments and scientific basis for management options.* Davis: University of California Centers for Water and Wildland Resources.

Storer, T.I., and R.L. Usinger. 1963. *Sierra Nevada natural history.* Berkeley: University of California Press.

Sudworth, George B. 1967. *Forest trees of the Pacific slope.* New York: Dover Publications.

Sweeney, J.R. 1956. Responses of vegetation to fire. *University of California Publications in Botany* 28:143–250.

Taylor, D. 1993. Shasta snow-wreath in California: A new genus in California. *Fremontia* 22(3):3–7.

Thomas, John H. 1961. *Flora of the Santa Cruz Mountains of California.* Stanford, Calif.: Stanford University Press.

Thomas, John H., and Dennis R. Parnell. 1974. *Native shrubs of the Sierra Nevada.* Natural History Guide Series no. 34. Berkeley: University of California Press.

Thorne, Robert F. 1967. A flora of Santa Catalina Island, California. *Aliso* 6(3):1–77.

Thurston, Carl. 1936. *Wildflowers of southern California.* Pasadena: Esto Publishing.

Tibor, David P., ed. 2001. *Inventory of rare and endangered plants of California.* 6th ed. Sacramento: California Native Plant Society Press.

True, Gordon H. 1973. *The ferns and seed plants of Nevada County, California.* San Francisco: California Academy of Sciences.

Twisselmann, Ernest C. 1956. A flora of the Temblor Range. *Wasmann Journal of Biology* 14:161–300.

Twisselmann, Ernest C. A flora of Kern County, California. In *A key to vascular plant species of Kern County, California, and a flora of Kern County, California.* Sacramento: California Native Plant Society Press.

Watts, Tom. 1963. *California tree finder.* Berkeley: Nature Study Guild.

Weiss, M.R. 1995. Floral color change: a widespread functional convergence. *American Journal of Botany* 87(2):167–185.

Went, F.W. 1955. The ecology of desert plants. *Scientific American,* April.

Williams, J.C., and H.C. Monroe. 1969. *The natural history of the San Francisco Bay area.* Berkeley: McCutchan Publishing.

Witham, Helen V. 1972. *Ferns of San Diego County.* San Diego, Calif.: Natural History Museum.

Wright, R.D., and H.A. Mooney. 1965. Substrate-oriented distribution of bristlecone pine in the White Mountains of California. *American Midland Naturalist* 73:257–284.

York, R. 1974. An inventory of rare and endangered vascular plants of California. Sacramento: California Native Plant Society Press.

ART CREDITS AND ADDITIONAL CAPTIONS

Photographs credited to the California Academy of Sciences Collection are also credited to their individual photographers.

Figures

PETER GAEDE 1, 2, 3, 4, 5, 6

BILL NELSON 7

Maps

BILL NELSON 2, 3, 4

PAULA NELSON 1

Plates

VIRGINIA BATES 50, 73, 75, 109

CALIFORNIA ACADEMY OF SCIENCES 1, 17, 21, 38, 39, 57, 65, 76, 104, 135, 138, 140, 141, 143, 146, 154, 158, 159, 160, 162, 176

PHYLLIS FABER 47, 55, 67, 77, 93, 95, 96, 97, 109, 148, 149, 164, 165, 177

WILLIAM T. FOLLETTE 3, 4, 5, 7, 8, 9, 10, 11, 12, 13, 14, 15, 20, 24, 25, 26, 42, 49, 58, 62, 68, 71, 83, 86, 99, 101, 102, 132, 133, 106, 150, 155, 157, 161, 178, 180, 181, 182

JOHN GAME 30, 31, 32, 35, 47, 55, 94, 95

SAXON HOLT 4, 33, 84, 113, 120, 185, 186

TODD KEELER-WOLF 18, 36, 51, 72, 78, 81, 82, 98, 107, 110, 134, 136, 142, 153

TOM OBERBAUER 5, 34

JO-ANN ORDANO 144

ROBERT ORNDUFF 2, 6, 16, 19, 23, 27, 29, 37, 40, 41, 43, 44, 45, 46, 48, 53, 54, 64, 66, 74, 79, 80, 85, 87, 88, 90, 100, 108, 112, 114, 116, 117, 118, 119, 121, 122, 124, 125, 126, 127, 128, 129, 130, 131, 137, 139, 147, 151, 152, 163, 175, 179, 183, 184

ROBERT ORNDUFF, PRIVATE COLLECTION 166, 167, 168, 169, 170, 171, 172, 173

BRUCE PAVLIK 28

ED ROSS 56, 61

SCIENTIFIC PHOTO LAB, UC BERKELEY 174

DOREEN SMITH 22, 111, 113

MARTHA WEISS 59

Additional Captions

PAGES II-III San Jacinto Mountains, by John Game.

PAGE VI Elkhorn Slough, by Saxon Holt.

PAGES 2–3 Point Reyes National Seashore, by Saxon Holt.

PAGES 40–41 Bush lupine and cow parsnip, by Jo-Ann Ordano.

PAGES 68–69 Oak savannah, by Saxon Holt.

PAGES 96–97 Boggs Lake, by Saxon Holt.

PAGES 110–111 Carrigo Plain, by John Game.

PAGES 198–199 Sawtooth Ridge, Trinity Alps, by John Game.

PAGES 228–229 White Mountains, by John Game.

PAGES 246–247 Mineral King, Tulare County, by Saxon Holt.

PAGES 270–271 Owens Valley, by Jo-Ann Ordano.

INDEX OF PLANT NAMES

GENERAL INDEX

Boldface page numbers indicate main discussions of specific vegetation types.

Series Design:	Barbara Jellow
Design Enhancements:	Beth Hansen
Design Development:	Jane Tenenbaum
Composition:	Impressions Book and Journal Services, Inc.
Cartographers:	Bill Nelson and Paula Nelson
Text:	9.5/12 Minion
Display:	ITC Franklin Gothic Book and Demi
Printer and Binder:	Everbest Printing Company